The Sciences Po Series in International Relations
and Political Economy

Series Editor
Alain Dieckhoff
Center for International Studies (CERI)
Sciences Po - CNRS
Paris, France

Advisory Editor
Miriam Perier
Center for International Studies (CERI)
Sciences Po - CNRS
Paris, France

The Science Po Series in International Relations and Political Economy consists of works emanating from the foremost French researchers from Sciences Po, Paris. Sciences Po was founded in 1872 and is today one of the most prestigious universities for teaching and research in social sciences in France, recognized worldwide. This series focuses on the transformations of the international arena, in a world where the state, though its sovereignty is questioned, reinvents itself. The series explores the effects on international relations and the world economy of regionalization, globalization, and transnational flows at large. This evolution in world affairs sustains a variety of networks from the ideological to the criminal or terrorist. Besides the geopolitical transformations of the globalized planet, the new political economy of the world has a decided impact on its destiny as well, and this series hopes to uncover what that is.

More information about this series at
http://www.palgrave.com/gp/series/14411

Thierry Balzacq · Frédéric Charillon ·
Frédéric Ramel
Editors

Global Diplomacy

An Introduction to Theory and Practice

Translated by William Snow

palgrave
macmillan

Editors
Thierry Balzacq
Sciences Po
Paris, France

Frédéric Charillon
University of Clermont Auvergne
Clermont-Ferrand, France

Frédéric Ramel
Sciences Po
Paris, France

Translated by
William Snow
Paris, France

The Sciences Po Series in International Relations and Political Economy
ISBN 978-3-030-28788-7   ISBN 978-3-030-28786-3 (eBook)
https://doi.org/10.1007/978-3-030-28786-3

This book has been translated from the French by William Snow, except for Chapters 1, 6 and 18, that have been written in English by their authors.
Translation from the French language edition: *Manuel de diplomatie* by Thierry Balzacq, Frédéric Charillon, and Frédéric Ramel, © Presses de Sciences Po 2018. All Rights Reserved.
© The Editor(s) (if applicable) and The Author(s), under exclusive license to Springer Nature Switzerland AG 2020, corrected publication 2020
This work is subject to copyright. All rights are solely and exclusively licensed by the Publisher, whether the whole or part of the material is concerned, specifically the rights of translation, reprinting, reuse of illustrations, recitation, broadcasting, reproduction on microfilms or in any other physical way, and transmission or information storage and retrieval, electronic adaptation, computer software, or by similar or dissimilar methodology now known or hereafter developed.
The use of general descriptive names, registered names, trademarks, service marks, etc. in this publication does not imply, even in the absence of a specific statement, that such names are exempt from the relevant protective laws and regulations and therefore free for general use.
The publisher, the authors and the editors are safe to assume that the advice and information in this book are believed to be true and accurate at the date of publication. Neither the publisher nor the authors or the editors give a warranty, expressed or implied, with respect to the material contained herein or for any errors or omissions that may have been made. The publisher remains neutral with regard to jurisdictional claims in published maps and institutional affiliations.

Cover image: © MirageC/Moment/Getty Images

This Palgrave Macmillan imprint is published by the registered company Springer Nature Switzerland AG
The registered company address is: Gewerbestrasse 11, 6330 Cham, Switzerland

The original version of the book was revised: Copyright page text has been updated. The correction to the book is available at https://doi.org/10.1007/978-3-030-28786-3_23

Contents

1 Introduction: History and Theories of Diplomacy 1
Thierry Balzacq, Frédéric Charillon and Frédéric Ramel

Part I Places and Vectors of Diplomacy
in the Twentieth Century

2 Bilateral Relations 19
Alice Pannier

3 Multilateral Diplomacy 35
Franck Petiteville and Delphine Placidi-Frot

4 Paradiplomacy 49
Stéphane Paquin

5 Club and Group Diplomacy 63
Christian Lechervy

6 Communication and Diplomacy: Change and Continuity 79
Brian Hocking

7	From Negotiation to Mediation Valérie Rosoux	97
8	Rituals and Diplomacy Thierry Balzacq	111

Part II The Actors

9	States and Their Foreign Services Christian Lequesne	125
10	Intergovernmental Organizations Cédric Groulier and Simon Tordjman	139
11	Supranational Diplomats Stephanie C. Hofmann and Olivier Schmitt	155
12	Sub-State Diplomacies: Regions, Parliaments, and Local Authorities Benjamin Puybareau and Renaud Takam Talom	167
13	Diplomacy by Non-State Actors Auriane Guilbaud	183
14	Individuals and Diplomacy Pierre Grosser	195

Part III Sectors

15	Economic and Corporate Diplomacy Laurence Badel	211
16	Cultural Diplomacy Marie-Christine Kessler	227

17	Environmental Diplomacy Amandine Orsini	239
18	Humanitarian Diplomacy Elise Rousseau and Achille Sommo Pende	253
19	Defense Diplomacy Frédéric Charillon, Thierry Balzacq and Frédéric Ramel	267
20	Entertainment Diplomacy Maud Quessard	279
21	International Expertise and the Diplomacy of Influence Nicolas Tenzer	297
22	Conclusion: Drowning Diplomats Frédéric Ramel, Thierry Balzacq and Frédéric Charillon	307

Correction to: Global Diplomacy — C1
Thierry Balzacq, Frédéric Charillon and Frédéric Ramel

References — 315

Index — 341

Notes on Contributors

Laurence Badel is Professor of Contemporary History and Director of the Centre d'Histoire des Relations Internationales (Center for the Study of the History of International Relations) at Université Paris I Panthéon Sorbonne, France.

Thierry Balzacq is Professor of Political Science at Sciences Po, Paris, France, and a Researcher at the Centre for International Studies (CERI Sciences Po). He is currently preparing *The Oxford Handbook of Grand Strategy* (co-edited with Ronald Krebs). His most recent book is *Comparative Grand Strategy: A Framework and Cases* (Oxford: Oxford University Press, 2019), co-edited with Peter Dombrowski and Simon Reich.

Frédéric Charillon is Professor of Political Science at Université Clermont Auvergne (UCA) and coordinator for international studies at ENA (French National School of Administration). His research themes include foreign policy analysis, defense studies, and French diplomacy. Recent publications include *Diplomatie française. Outils et acteurs depuis 1980*, with M. Vaïsse (ed.) (Odile Jacob, 2018), *Les Etats-Unis dans le monde*, with Célia Belin (eds.) (CNRS, 2016), and "Public Policy and Foreign Policy Analysis," in Cameron G. Thies, *The Oxford Encyclopedia of Foreign Policy Analysis* (OUP, 2018).

Pierre Grosser teaches International History and World Politics at Sciences Po Paris, France. He was Head of Studies of the Diplomatic Institute of the French Foreign Ministry (2001–2009). His most recent book is *L'Histoire du monde se fait en Asie* (*How Asia Made XXth Century International History*) (Odile Jacob, 2017).

Cédric Groulier is a Lecturer in Public Law (Ph.D., 2006, *Permissive Norms and Public Law*). He worked at the University of Paris Est (2008–2016) and was appointed at Sciences Po Toulouse (France) in 2016. He teaches European Law and Administrative Law (master's degree). His main research fields are normativity, hard and soft law, and better regulation policies. Recent publications include "La 'gouvernance réglementaire' de l'OCDE : vers une globalisation légistique ?" *Revue de Droit Public* 2015(3).

Auriane Guilbaud is an Associate Professor of Political Science at the University Paris 8 and a member of the research center Cresppa-LabToP (Paris Center for Sociological and Political Research), France. Her research interests include the role of non-state actors in international relations, global health governance, and a sociological approach to the study of international organizations.

Brian Hocking is Emeritus Professor of International Relations at Loughborough University, UK, and Senior Visiting Research Fellow at the Clingnedael Institute in The Hague, The Netherlands.

Stephanie C. Hofmann is Professor in the Department of International Relations and Political Science, Graduate Institute of International and Development Studies. Her research revolves around international security, international organizations, and global order. Her work has appeared with Cambridge University Press and *European Journal of International Relations, Journal of Common Market Studies, Journal of Conflict Resolution, Journal of European Public Policy, Journal of Peace Research, Perspectives on Politics*, and *West European Politics*.

Marie-Christine Kessler is Emeritus Research Director at the French National Center for Scientific Research (CERSA, CNRS/University Paris 2). She is a political scientist, author of several books on the administrative elites and their relationship with politics. After a five-year stay at the French Ministry of Foreign Affairs (direction des Relations culturelles), she worked on the theme of decision-making in the field of diplomacy. She is the author of *Les ambassadeurs* (Presses de Science Po, 2012).

Christian Lechervy is Ambassador of France to Myanmar since October 2018, was Permanent Secretary for the Pacific affairs and Ambassador to the Pacific Community (SPC, 2014–2018). Personal advisor for Strategic Affairs and Asia-Pacific to the President of the French Republic (2012–2014), he was previously Deputy Director of the Policy Planning Division at the Ministry of Foreign Affairs, Ambassador to Turkmenistan (2006–2009), and advisor for international affairs to the Minister of Defense (1997–2002).

Christian Lequesne is Professor of Political Science at Sciences Po, Paris. He was formerly director of the Center for International Studies (CERI Sciences Po) and Sciences Po-LSE Alliance Professor at the London School of Economics. He has two fields of research: the politics of the European Union and the sociology of diplomatic practices. His latest book *Ethnographie du Quai d'Orsay. Les pratiques des diplomatiques français* (CNRS Editions, 2017) analyzes the practices of French diplomats based on fieldwork.

Amandine Orsini is Professor of International Relations at CResPo—Université Saint-Louis—Brussels. A specialist of global environmental politics and international institutions, she has published, among others, *Essential Concepts of Global Environmental Governance* (Routledge, 2014) and *Global Environmental Politics: Understanding the Governance of the Earth* (Oxford University Press, 2019).

Alice Pannier is an Assistant Professor of International Relations and European Studies at the Paul H. Nitze School of Advanced International Studies (SAIS) at Johns Hopkins University, Washington, DC. Her research focuses on French and British defense and foreign policies, European security and defense cooperation, and transatlantic relations.

Stéphane Paquin is Tenured Professor at the École nationale d'administration publique (ENAP) in Canada. He has written or co-written 20 books including *Theories of International Political Economy* (Toronto, Oxford University Press, 2015) and many more books and articles about paradiplomacy and the international relations of non-central governments. He has also published in several journals including *International Journal*, *International Negotiation*, *The Hague Journal of Diplomacy*, *Nationalism & Ethnic Politics*, *Canadian Journal of Political Science*, *Revue canadienne d'administration publique*, *Revue internationale de politique comparée* and *Études internationales*.

Achille Sommo Pende is a Researcher at the Tocqueville Chair in Security Policy, University of Namur, Belgium. He conducts research on the inclusion of women in peacebuilding processes, with a focus on the integration of the UN Security Council's agenda for "women, peace and security" in Rwanda and DRC. He also examines the transformations of public policies in a fragile state due to an international gender norm.

Franck Petiteville is Professor of International Relations at the School of Political Studies, University of Grenoble Alpes (France). His publications relate to multilateralism and international organizations.

Delphine Placidi-Frot is Full Professor of Political Science at the Faculté Jean-Monnet, Université Paris-Sud (Université Paris-Saclay). Her research focuses on international organizations and negotiations as well as French and Russian foreign policies. Recent publications include *Espace mondial. L'Atlas* (coord. Marie-Françoise Durand, Presses de Sciences Po, 2018) and *Négociations internationales* (co-ed. Franck Petiteville, Presses de Sciences Po, 2013).

Benjamin Puybareau is a Ph.D. candidate in Political Science (at Sciences Po & the University of Namur) with a focus on international relations. His research agenda in security studies includes particular interests in state secrecy and intelligence cooperation.

Maud Quessard is a Senior Research Fellow at the Institute for Strategic Research at the Military School, Paris. She is also a lecturer on North American civilization, a graduate from Sciences Po, and an American foreign policy specialist, and she taught until 2017 at the University of Poitiers and at Sciences Po Paris. Her research focuses on public diplomacy, American soft power, and information warfare. She was a Visiting Fellow in the History Department at Harvard University in 2015. She is the author of *Stratégies d'influence des États-Unis: information, propagande et diplomatie publique depuis la guerre froide* (Presses Universitaires de Rennes, 2019). She recently published with David Haglund, "How the West Was One: France, America, and the 'Huntingtonian Reversal'," *Orbis Journal of World Affairs*, 2018, 62(4).

Frédéric Ramel is Professor of Political Science at Sciences Po, Paris, France, and a Researcher at CERI Sciences Po. After a postdoc at Raoul Dandurand Chair, University of Quebec in Montreal, he joined Jean Moulin-Lyon 3 University as Lecturer. Further in his career, as tenured professor, he taught at the Jean Monnet Faculty, Paris Sud 11 University.

Cofounder of the Institute for Strategic Research of the Military Academy (IRSEM), of which he was the scientific director between 2009 and 2012, Ramel focuses on diplomacy and strategy but also arts and esthetics in IR. Recent publications include *International Relations, Music and Diplomacy* (co-edited with CécilePrévost-Thomas, Palgrave Macmillan, 2018).

Valérie Rosoux is a Senior Research Fellow at the Belgian National Fund for Scientific Research (FNRS) and a member of the Belgian Royal Academy. She teaches *International Negotiation* and *Transitional Justice* at the UCLouvain. She is an External Scientific Fellow at the Max Planck Institute Luxembourg since 2017. In 2010–2011, she was a Senior Fellow at the United States Institute of Peace (Washington). She has a *Licence* in Philosophy and a Ph.D. in International Relations.

Elise Rousseau is a Research Fellow at the Belgian National Fund for Scientific Research (F.R.S.-FNRS) and a Ph.D. candidate in Political Science at the University of Namur. Under the supervision of Prof Thierry Balzacq, she conducts research on blame games in international arenas and questions how the attribution of moral responsibility influences diplomatic actions. More particularly, she investigates the "blood diamond" blame and diplomatic practices in the Kimberley Process.

Olivier Schmitt is an Associate Professor at the Center for War Studies, University of Southern Denmark. His work focuses on transatlantic security, multinational security cooperation, and military change. He currently directs the research project "Transforming Armed Forces in the 21st Century" supported by the Carlsberg Foundation and the Danish Research Council. His recent publications include *Allies That Count, Junior Partners in Coalition Warfare* (Georgetown University Press, 2018) and *Raymond Aron and International Relations* (Routledge, 2018).

Renaud Takam Talom is a career diplomat and Ph.D. student at Tocqueville Chair in security policies at the University of Namur, Belgium.

Nicolas Tenzer, senior civil servant, is Guest Professor at Sciences Po (Paris School of International affairs) and former Head of Department of the French Strategic Planning Office. He is the author of 22 books on political theory, science of government and international issues, and the author of three official reports to the government, including one on international expertise and strategy of influence.

Simon Tordjman is Associate Professor at Sciences Po Toulouse (France) and Research Associate with *Laboratoire des Sciences Sociales du Politique*. His areas of research focus on the transformation of multilateralism and international democratization policies, especially in the post-Soviet area. His latest publications include "Ambiguity as a Condition of Possibility: The European Endowment for Democracy and Democracy Promotion in the Caucasus," *Studies of Transition States and Societies*, 9(1), 2017.

Acronyms

ACD	Asia Cooperation Dialogue
ADMM	ASEAN Defence Ministers' Meeting
AEBF	Asia-Europe Business Forum
AEYLS	Asia-Europe Young Leaders Symposium
AFII	French Agency for International Investment
AIIB	Asian Infrastructure Investment Bank
AIVP	Worldwide Network of Port Cities
ALBA	Bolivarian Alliance for the Peoples of Our America
AMDIE	Moroccan Investment and Trade Agency
ANC	African National Congress
ANSA	Armed Non-State Actors
ANZUS	Australia, New Zealand, United States Security Treaty
AOSIS	Alliance of Small Island States
APEC	Asia-Pacific Economic Cooperation
APF	Parliamentary Assembly of La Francophonie
ARF	ASEAN Regional Forum
ASEAN	Association of Southeast Asian Nations
ASEM	Asia-Europe Meeting
AWEX	Walloon Exports and Foreign Investments Agency
BIE	Brussels Invest & Export
BRICS	Brazil, Russia, India, China and South Africa
BTI	British Trade International
CALRE	Conference of European Regional Legislative Assemblies
CANCC	Coalition of Atoll Nations on Climate Change
CBSS	Council of the Baltic Sea States
CCF	Congress for Cultural Freedom

CCTV	China Central Television
CDB	Convention on Biological Diversity
CELAC	Community of Latin American and Caribbean States
CENTCOM	United States Central Command
CETA	Comprehensive Economic and Trade Agreement
CFAC	Conference of Central American Armed Forces
CFS	Committee on World Food Security
CHEM	Centre for Advanced Military Studies
CHINCOM	Coordinating Committee for Multilateral Export Controls
CIA	Central Intelligence Agency
CJEU	Court of Justice of the European Union
COCOM	Coordinating Committee for Multilateral Export Controls
COP	Conference of the Parties (United Nations Framework Convention on Climate Change)
COREPER	Committee of Permanent Representatives in the European Union
CPD	Center on Public Diplomacy
CPI	Committee on Public Information
CPLP	Community of Portuguese Language Countries
CROP	Council of Regional Organizations in the Pacific
CSIS	Center for Strategic and International Studies
CTI	Coral Triangle Initiative
DAAD	German Academic Exchange Service (Deutscher Akademischer Austauschdienst)
DC	Developing Country
DCAF	Democratic Control of Armed Forces
DCMD	Directorate of Military Cooperation and Defence
DFAIT	Department of Foreign Affairs and International Trade
DFATD	Department of Foreign Affairs, Trade and Development
DFID	(British) Department for International Development
DGRIS	(French) Directorate General for International Relations and Strategy
EABC	European-American Business Council
EAS	East Asia Summit
ECOSOC	United Nations Economic and Social Council
ECOWAS	Economic Community of West African States
EEAS	European External Action Service
EEC	European Economic Community
ENA	National School of Administration (École nationale d'administration)
EU	European Union
FARC	Revolutionary Armed Forces of Colombia

FCO	Foreign and Commonwealth Office
FDI	Foreign Direct Investment
FEALAC	Forum of East Asia-Latin America Cooperation
FGYO	Franco-German Youth Office
FIPIC	Forum for India-Pacific Islands Cooperation
FIT	Flanders Investment & Trade
FLNKS	Kanak and Socialist National Liberation Front
FOCAC	Forum on China-Africa Cooperation
FOSS	Forum of Small States
GATT	General Agreement on Tariffs and Trade
GCCA	Global Climate Change Alliance
GHG	Greenhouse Gas
GIZ	German Corporation for International Cooperation (Gesellschaft für Internationale Zusammenarbeit)
GMO	Genetically Modified Organism
GMS	Greater Mekong Subregion
GTAI	Germany Trade and Invest
HBO	Home Box Office
IAEA	International Atomic Energy Agency
IAFAS	India–Africa Forum Summit
IBSA	India, Brazil, South Africa Dialogue Forum
ICAO	International Civil Aviation Organization
ICJ	International Court of Justice
ICRC	International Committee of the Red Cross
ICRI	International Coral Reef Initiative
ICT	Information and Communication Technologies
IGO	Intergovernmental Organization
IHL	International Humanitarian Law
IISS	International Institute for Strategic Studies
ILO	International Labour Organization
IMF	International Monetary Fund
IMG	Informational Media Guarantee
ISDS	Investor-State Dispute Settlement
KFW	Credit Institute for Reconstruction (Kreditanstalt für Wiederaufbau)
LN	League of Nations
MAE	(French) Ministry of Foreign Affairs (Ministère des Affaires Étrangères)
MATIS	Moroccan Agency for Trade, Investment and Services
MCC	Millennium Challenge Corporation
MDG	Millennium Development Goals
Mercosur	South American Regional Economic Organization

MGC	Mekong-Ganga Cooperation
MGM	Metro-Goldwyn-Mayer
MIF	Micronesian Islands Forum
MSF	Doctors Without Borders (Médecins sans frontières)
MSG	Melanesian Spearhead Group
NAFTA	North American Free Trade Agreement
NAI	New African Initiative
NATO	North Atlantic Treaty Organization
NED	National Endowment for Democracy
NEPAD	New Partnership for Africa's Development
NGO	Non-Governmental Organization
OBOR	One Belt, One Road Initiative
OCHA	United Nations Office for the Coordination of Humanitarian Affairs
OECD	Organization for Economic Cooperation and Development
OIF	The Francophonie
OMC	Open Method of Coordination
OPEC	Organization of Petroleum Exporting Countries
OSCE	Organization for Security and Co-operation in Europe
OSS	Office of Strategic Services
OWI	Office of War Information
PALM	Pacific Island Leaders Meeting
PISA	Programme for International Student Assessment
PLG	Polynesian Leaders Group
PLO	Palestine Liberation Organization
PSVI	Prevention of Sexual Violence Initiative
R2P	Responsibility to Protect
RCEP	Asian Regional Comprehensive Economic Partnership
SACU	Southern African Custom Union
SIDS	Small Island Developing States
SOM	Meetings of Senior Officials (Réunion des fonctionnaires de haut niveau)
SSR	Security Sector Reform
SWPD	Southwest Pacific Dialogue
TABC	Transatlantic Business Council
TABD	Transatlantic Business Dialogue
TEU	Treaty on European Union
TICAD	Tokyo International Conference on African Development
TPP	Trans Pacific Partnership
TRIPS	Agreement on Trade-Related Aspects of Intellectual Property Rights
TTIP	Transatlantic Trade and Investment Partnership

UCLG	United Cities and Local Governments
UFM	Union for the Mediterranean
UKTI	UK Trade and Investment
UN	United Nations Organization
UNDP	United Nations Development Programme
UNEP	United Nations Environment Programme
UNESCO	United Nations Educational, Scientific and Cultural Organization
UNFCCC	United Nations Framework Convention on Climate Change
UNHCR	Office of the United Nations High Commissioner for Refugees
UNICEF	United Nations Children's Fund
UNODC	United Nations Office on Drugs and Crime
URSS	Union of Soviet Socialist Republics
USAID	United States Agency for International Development
USIA	United States Information Agency
USIS	United States Information Services
USPACOM	United States Pacific Command
WFP	World Food Programme
WHO	World Health Organization
WIPO	World Intellectual Property Organization
WTO	World Trade Organization

LIST OF FIGURES

Fig. 3.1   UN Multilateral Diplomacy Personnel in New York (*The United States, Russia, China, Germany, Japan [37 for France]; *Source* United Nations [Protocol and Liaison Service], Permanent Missions to the United Nations, New York [NY], United Nations, 306, June 2016, ST/PLS/SER.A/306)   41

Fig. 3.2   UN Multilateral Diplomacy Personnel in Geneva (*United States, Russia, China, Japan; *Source* UN Office in Geneva, *Missions permanentes auprès des Nations unies à Genève*, Geneva, 115, 2017, ST/GENEVA/SER.A/115 available at www.unog.ch/bluebook [visited April 16, 2018])   42

Fig. 3.3   UN Multilateral Diplomacy Personnel in Vienna (*United States, Russia, Austria; *Source* United Nations Office in Vienna, Permanent Missions to the United Nations [Vienna], Information Services for member states, Bluebook www.unodc.org [visited May 4, 2017])   42

LIST OF TABLES

Table 4.1   Typology of various political regimes in relation
            to the autonomy of non-central governments   55
Table 18.1 The main instruments of international human rights
            and international humanitarian law   255

CHAPTER 1

Introduction: History and Theories of Diplomacy

Thierry Balzacq, Frédéric Charillon and Frédéric Ramel

What is diplomacy? The term covers considerable territory, but the key element is that it deals with international relations, broadly understood. In the *Encyclopédie Larousse*, for example, there are at least three meanings attached to the word "diplomacy." First, diplomacy refers to the "action and (the) manner of representing one's country to a foreign nation and in international negotiations." Second, diplomacy is concerned with the "external policy of a country, of a government." Finally, diplomacy is the

---

1. Balzacq (✉) · F. Ramel
Sciences Po, Paris, France
e-mail: thierry.balzacq@sciencespo.fr

F. Ramel
e-mail: frederic.ramel@sciencespo.fr

F. Charillon
University of Clermont Auvergne, Clermont-Ferrand, France

© The Author(s) 2020
T. Balzacq et al. (eds.), *Global Diplomacy*,
The Sciences Po Series in International Relations and Political Economy, https://doi.org/10.1007/978-3-030-28786-3_1

"branch of political science which concerns international relations." Therefore, it refers to at least three distinct realities: It is, simultaneously, a particular activity, a sector of state intervention, and a subspecialty of political science. Yet, within public service, the word may also serve to designate the *career* devoted to representing a country or the *group of individuals* who fulfill this undertaking.

Be that as it may, the ordinary use of the term remains unaccounted for. In general, the term "diplomacy" is often employed metaphorically, to refer to the tact and skill considered to define diplomatic action. Here, the term applies to all behavior or attitudes which correspond to this way of conducting oneself. Nonetheless, we will see below that the etymology of the concept reveals an entirely different story.

This textbook aims to define the particular field of diplomacy, starting with an examination of its nature and its functions. Thus, we will attach a contextual importance to different usages of the term, with content varying from one chapter to another. Accordingly, the objective of this introduction is to further clarify the concept of "diplomacy," notably through explaining its connection to foreign policy.

This introduction proceeds in three parts. First, it traces the historical evolution of practices defined as "diplomatic," taking issue with conventional accounts that single out Greece as the starting point. Our interpretation breaks with the most common approach in the literature (Berridge 2015), while reflecting the latest work done on the historical archives of diplomacy. In the second section, we explore debates about the theorization of diplomacy. Finally, the introduction proposes a fresh examination of the concept of diplomacy, to further explain both its nature and content. We hope such a counterintuitive approach will encourage new engagement with both the theory and practice of diplomacy today.

The Diplomatic Phenomenon in History

When texts on diplomacy seek to explain how it has evolved, they often begin with an omission: The norms, institutions, and instruments of diplomacy (protocol, notes and treaties, etc.) existed well before the Greek or Florentine periods that laid claim to them. Indeed, for almost two thousand years, that is between approximately 2500 and 609 B.C.,[1] the Middle

---

[1] The period broadly covers a major part of the history of Mesopotamia, in particular, that which encompasses the period of the city-states of Lower Mesopotamia up until the fall of

East experienced exchanges similar in form to what is currently understood as diplomacy. Consequently, recent research on the history of diplomacy argues for a recognition of the diversity of its origins, in fact, of its decentering (Sharlach 2005). Cohen (2001), for example, suggests that there is a "grand tradition" in diplomacy that runs from the Mesopotamian period to the Roman epoch, through ancient Greece. In support of this thesis, Cohen stresses that from one historical perspective to another—with more or less significant variations—one may detect a series of ideas, norms, practices, and roles structuring the relationships between sometimes sovereign political entities, which still characterize diplomatic interactions today (Weinfeld 1993). In this reorientation of the history of diplomacy, classical and modern forms (still referred to as European by some) are preceded by a Middle Eastern touch, which in many respects renews the interpretation previously made of the other two forms. What follows will explain exactly how this occurs.

Diplomacy in the ancient Middle East is associated with a collection of norms, instruments, and institutions settled over time, thanks, in particular, to the practices of various successive dynasties in what now constitutes the territory of Iraq. Some documents dating from 2500 B.C. refer to the existence of kings' envoys or messengers. Here, there is often mention of cuneiform diplomacy, insofar as the medium of communication is writing of this type developed in lower Mesopotamia, between 3400 and 3200 B.C. Besides a shared system of royal envoys, a language (Sumerian) and writing, cuneiform diplomacy includes an entire complex network of relations between kings linked by fraternity, the obligations of reciprocity, an embryonic form of protocol, the bases of an ethical system of negotiation, the exchange of gifts, and the rudiments of a bureaucracy responsible for processing and attributing assignments to envoys, of managing correspondence and of archiving documents (Cohen 2017, 22). Nonetheless, during this period, there was no diplomatic immunity, as such. However, envoys were protected against any form of attack on their person.

We owe our knowledge of many diplomatic practices from the ancient Middle East to clay tablets discovered at various sites. Two collections constitute the core of the material. The first, the Royal Archives of Mari (1700–1670 B.C.), was brought to light in Syria. In these tablets, the

---

the Assyrian Empire in 609 B.C. For more details, please see Grandpierre (2010) and Roux (1995), among others.

norms, instruments, and organizations responsible for diplomacy are developed. For example, envoys are henceforth differentiated as a function of their rank. Some are mere messengers, while others can negotiate and sign treaties in the name of their sovereign, which is, in fact, the current equivalent of plenipotentiary ambassadors. The latter are recognized in the texts as representatives of kings and, thus, receive the honors due to the sovereigns whose agents they are. Some of these new diplomats reside in a foreign location for many years. It seems that this period also saw the emergence of "letters of accreditation" and what came to be known—much later—as "diplomatic passports."

The Amarna Archives, discovered in Egypt, provide additional clues.[2] The cornerstone of the system of Amarna is the emissary, endowed with exceptional diplomatic talents. In the name of their sovereigns, emissaries negotiated various types of agreements, marriages, and commercial treaties. At the same time, the archives confirm the interweaving of ritual and diplomacy, reciprocity as a basic principle of interactions between kingdoms, the significant role of protocol in the conduct of diplomatic affairs, and the crucial place of the exchange of gifts in both the construction and consolidation of diplomatic ties.

Classical diplomacy brings us back to the legacy of ancient Greece[3] as much as to that of the Roman Republic (509–27 B.C.) and the Roman Empire (27 B.C.–641 A.D., corresponding to the fall of the Roman Empire of the East). The extraordinary interconnection of the two worlds, as the works of Paul Veyne (2005) have demonstrated, should not overshadow the singular identity of the diplomatic processes of each space. Greek diplomacy of the time was, in some ways, essentially turned inward since its main preoccupation was to regulate interactions among city-states. There, diplomacy was not considered an important domain for government action. Decisions concerning the relationships with other entities were taken in public. Moreover, contrary to the Mesopotamian period, diplomacy in classical Greece was especially distinguished by minimal, in fact, nonexistent, protocol. The diplomats sent to Athens were not protected, and it was not uncommon for them to be executed.

---

[2] The age of El Amarna is often associated with the period from 1460 to 1220 B.C.

[3] In particular, the classical (the end of the fifth to the fourth century B.C.) and the Hellenistic periods (fourth to the first century B.C.).

That being said, ancient Greece, especially during the Hellenistic period, contributed to the development or reinforcement of certain diplomatic institutions. For example, in the seventh century B.C., Sparta invented the multilateral alliance mechanism as a security guarantee and to preserve the common peace. The diplomatic phenomenon is distinguished by two other institutions of this period. On the one hand, there is the recourse to arbitration as a means of settling differences. On the other hand, there is the reliance upon the *proxenos*, a citizen of the state in which he resides, responsible for protecting the interests of citizens of the state whose representative he is. However, the *proxenos* remains loyal to the state to which he belongs and not to the one whose interests he has agreed to defend. Finally, it seems that the title of *proxenos* was often inherited (Gerolymatos 1986).

Despite its rudimentary practices, diplomacy in ancient Greece provided some elements that inspired the Roman model, notably the usage of arbitration in the resolution of conflicts. Yet the Roman Republic and the Roman Empire are rarely associated with diplomacy. Their military prowess attracts more attention. Thus, Harold Nicolson (1950, 14) claims that the Romans developed no notable diplomatic methods, due to their tendency to prefer military coercion to the detriment of negotiation on the basis of principles of reciprocity. However, such a position does not stand up to scrutiny. If Rome became an empire, it owed this to its diplomatic skill, as much as to its military genius. Brian Campbell (2001) effectively demonstrates that, in its conquest of Italy, Rome, which until that point had been merely one small city-state among others in Latium, sometimes employed war, sometimes negotiation, to expand its network of allies. And, he asks, how can one explain the unshakeable loyalty of numerous allies of Rome during Hannibal's invasion (218–203 B.C.), if it was not due to the Roman Republic's power of persuasion and seduction?

Diplomacy in the Republic or the Empire was, first and foremost, a matter of personal contacts. Its formalization remained fragile (Eilers 2009). Nevertheless, we can observe that the signing of treaties, such as the declaration of war, followed a rigorously defined ritual, overseen by the college of fetials (the college of priests of ancient Rome). This ritual served the purpose of ensuring that acts were accomplished in accordance with religious requirements. In this sense, diplomacy in ancient Rome fell under the authority and protection of the gods (Saulnier 1980). The envoys of the Roman state, responsible to the Senate, had a limited right of initiative in their transactions with foreign entities. The Senate could, in effect, unravel everything which had been discussed or even finalized with foreign states.

The principal functions of Roman diplomacy recorded in the literature are: the establishment of peace; the sharing of the spoils of war; the signing of treaties; the resolution of commercial differences; and the regulation of commerce. Such a variety of exchanges required the use of a common language. Yet, there was no established diplomatic language, even if Greek and, to a certain extent, Latin, were commonly used in diplomacy. Consequently, in most interactions with foreigners, the Roman authorities relied upon interpreters.

Modern diplomacy is a direct product of the Italian Renaissance (Fletcher 2015). Yet we now know that the Italian Renaissance did not invent diplomacy. Nonetheless, it did introduce a number of innovations, regarding its actors on the one hand, and with respect to the conduct of diplomacy on the other hand.

First, regarding its actors, modern diplomacy did not break radically with the past, but prolonged and stabilized the advances of the medieval period. The figure of the ambassador (*ambactiare*—"to go on a mission"), for example, appears in the thirteenth century in Italy, but it carries within it the traces of two other types of envoys already mandated by different political entities to communicate with each other: that of the nuncio (*nuncius*) and that of the *procurator*. The nuncio acts as a "living letter" (Queller 1984, 201), in that he recites the content of the message, orally confided by the sender, to the recipient. He cannot stray from the strictly defined terms of the mandate which he receives. Acting at the behest of another, the nuncio is an envoy with absolutely no margin of maneuver. The distance between the entities engaged in interaction made the task of the nuncios very demanding, since all new information liable to alter the original mandate had to be confirmed by the authority he/she represented. As a result, this necessitated quite frequent trips back and forth and a considerable loss of time, especially in situations requiring a rapid decision. From the Middle Ages, therefore, a new form of representative emerged. These were the procurators.

Contrary to the nuncio, the procurator enjoyed the right of initiative. Not only could he negotiate the terms of an agreement with a foreign sovereign, but he was also entitled to conclude such an accord in the name of the sovereign who appointed him. The procurator's field of activity extended to private matters. For example, Frédéric II's counselor, Peter della Vigna, represented the emperor at his wedding to Isabella of England in 1235. Therefore, it was with Peter della Vigna, and not with Frédéric II, that Isabella exchanged vows.

As for the use of the title of ambassador, it is difficult to define, at least at the outset. Indeed, any person responsible for a public mission for peaceful purposes was called "ambassador" (Maulde La Clavière 1892–1893). Thus, even ordinary citizens could have their ambassadors vis-à-vis other citizens. For our purposes, however, the most important aspect concerns the circumstances surrounding the emergence of the figure of resident ambassador, between the midpoint of the Middle Ages and the fifteenth century. The frequency and density of exchanges, on the one hand, and the duration of missions, on the other hand, convinced sovereigns that foreign residence was the most effective, and surely the most economical way to allow the ambassador to conduct his mission. In addition, being resident allowed the ambassador to withdraw from permanent attention and, thus, from analysis of absolutely everything he did, which was often the case for ad hoc envoys. The principal responsibilities bestowed upon the ambassador during this period involved the collection and transmission of information to his sovereign and the function of ceremonial representation, for example on the occasion of a wedding, birth, or death. It is worth noting, however, that the Venetian ambassador did not always have the right of initiative. Indeed, he was often summoned to note the terms of the discussion and the intentions of the other party and to transmit them to Venice. He could take no decision on his own without prior formal approval from Venice. In other words, it seems that in practice, and depending on the circumstances, the resident ambassador sometimes resembled a nuncio and at other times a procurator.

In terms of material organization, modern diplomacy has favored the spread of new institutions and novel practices. Among the notable advances of this period, we may highlight four. *First*, while until the sixteenth century it was enough to swear to a treaty for said pledge to be recognized as valid, from the seventeenth century on, formal ratification (signature and affixing a seal to the document) became the norm. Second, we observe a generalization of credentials (i.e., of a document signed by the recognized sovereign who bestows it on the new ambassador so that he may transmit it to the head of state or government of the host country).[4] Third, the organization of great "multilateral" conferences became a favored mechanism for resolving the most urgent international problems (e.g., the Congress of Cateau-Cambresis in 1559, the Congress of Westphalia 1643–1648, the Congress of Vienna in 1815, the Congress of Paris in 1856, and the Congress of Berlin in 1878). Finally, chancelleries capable of conducting diplomatic relations in a continuous fashion arose, and the system of immunities became accepted.

During this period, France, which had become one of the dominant European powers, contributed to professionalizing diplomatic practices, to such an extent that one could speak of a French diplomatic system, alongside an Italian system inherited from Venice. In 1626, Cardinal Armand de Richelieu established a Minister of Foreign Affairs to attempt to articulate the different policies of the kingdom with respect to foreign powers. Subsequently, French became the *lingua franca* of diplomatic exchanges. The culmination of this codification of practices was the Convention of Vienna on diplomatic relations, signed August 18, 1961.[5]

Theoretical Reflections on Diplomacy

Long considered a nebulous field devoid of content, regarding foreign policy in particular, the study of diplomacy has suffered from limited theoretical awareness (Sharp 1999). This insufficient theorization has also been due to the anti-theoretical attitude of a major segment of one of the intended target audiences for diplomatic studies: the diplomats themselves. Yet, in both cases, at its heart, it seems that the problem stems from a lack of agreement over the meaning and functions of theory. In our view, theory must enable one to analyze and sometimes describe with further information, or to explain what diplomacy entails and how it operates, both in the long-term and on a daily basis. Theory can also give rise to a more reflexive ambition on the part of diplomats, through spurring them to question their own practices, in comparing them to those of others, in space and time.

---

[4] The acceptance of the credentials allowing an ambassador to exercise his functions in the host country. If one considers the etymology of the term "credentials" (from the Latin *credentia*—"confidence" or "belief"), it may be noted furthermore that the objective of the credentials is to allow the ambassador to "gain credence" in the host country, that is, to be believed and treated as a person worthy of confidence.

[5] Complemented by the Convention of Vienna on consular relations in 1963.

While modesty, charm, and tact must characterize the diplomat (Nicolson 1950, 126), the ability to take a critical look back at his or her words and deeds should also be a required characteristic. Theory is an instrument, perhaps the most effective, which can foster this. In more disciplinary terms, the theorization of diplomacy may serve to better explain the relationships between diplomatic studies and the other branches of knowledge in international relations, particularly foreign policy and also, to a certain extent, defense and the economy.

In the literature, the current debates stem from a shared difficulty: the dramatic increase in the number of activities and actors characterized or judged to be "diplomatic" raises questions about boundaries or what is typical of the phenomenon. The debate is not new but, since the 1980s, has tended to structure the choices made by some concerning the center of gravity of theorization in diplomatic studies. For example, one group, in which we find Nicolson and Berridge, situates diplomacy in the arena of interstate security relationships. In this sense, diplomacy is essentially, perhaps exclusively, concerned with high politics. The other group takes the opposite stance, postulating that diplomacy is much more extensive than the advocates of a high politics approach would have us believe. It covers not only questions of security, but also, at a minimum, commercial and cultural issues (see Langhorne 2004; Lee and Hudson 2004; Hocking 1999). And, for that reason, the number of actors involved is much greater than those who fall within the framework of traditional diplomacy dominated by official state diplomats.

Diplomatic activity has skyrocketed, and the number of actors associated with it has also been consistently growing (Kerr and Wiseman 2017, 1–18). Yet this does not resolve the question of diplomatic theory. Certainly, we may examine the role of these new actors and the manner in which they transform or fail to transform the field or the perception of diplomatic activity. Similarly, as in the third part of this book, we may painstakingly analyze the different sectors of diplomacy (economic, humanitarian, etc.). Yet the question of what constitutes diplomacy remains open.

To unpack the precise nature of diplomatic activity, which could serve to bolster theorization, a number of authors have offered suggestions, of varying degrees of relevance. Some propose to further draw out what constitutes the main activity of the diplomat. Research, for the most part, focuses on two functions: representation and negotiation. For example, echoing Richelieu, who defined diplomacy as permanent negotiation, William Zartman (2008) considers that negotiation is at the heart of the diplomat's endeavor. In this sense, studying diplomacy amounts to studying the mechanisms of negotiation (Schelling 1966; Petiteville and Placidi-Frot 2013; Rosoux 2013, 795–821). In reality, the function of negotiation stems from a broader activity, namely that of communication. Indeed, when not seeking to find common ground among the parties, diplomats are working to prevent disagreements from turning into conflicts, or avoiding such disagreements at an earlier stage. When not undermined by propaganda, one of the tasks assigned to public diplomacy is precisely to improve relations between actors in the international system by creating conditions conducive to communicating everyone's intentions. For Paul Sharp (1999), in addition to communication, we should add representation to understand what distinguishes diplomacy from other practices in the international system, since the diplomat acts and speaks in the name of a sovereign, whose interests and identity he/she represents. In this context, diplomacy is a tool for adjustment, since actors with different interests and identities come to construct a mutual understanding through it—one could say intersubjectively. Thus, "diplomacy is characterized by alienation," the managing of otherness (Der Derian 1987, 96. Compare with Constantinou 1996).

Meanwhile, other scholars have attempted to grasp the daily routine of the diplomat and its supposed or real effects on the structuring of the world order. For example, Geoffrey Wiseman (2015), Vincent Pouliot, and Jérémie Cornut (2015) suggest that we focus on the practices of actors in order to better trace how their activities allow us to understand certain contours of the international system.

In sum, the theorization of diplomacy oscillates between the quest for its essence and the study of micropractices, sometimes with a view to further generalization and sometimes to grasp the here and now, through a dense description, along the lines of Geertz, of what the diplomat does (Barber 2016; Lequesne 2017; Neumann 2012). However, none of these theoretical initiatives has yet led to a real characterization of what distinguishes diplomacy from other activities. Indeed, negotiating, communicating, and representing are functions that one currently encounters in other sectors of activity, both public and private. Thus, diplomacy finds itself confronted with the same risk as strategic studies several decades ago. Unfortunately, we are familiar with the outcome: a dilution and a loss of consistency in the concept of strategy, which became an empty signifier.

THE CONCEPT OF "DIPLOMACY"

How do we escape this impasse? Perhaps through referring to the etymology of the concept of "diplomacy" (Leira 2016, 28–38).[6] Up until this point, indeed, we have used this term in a transparent manner, transposing some practices to a term which did not exist in its current usage. We are not alone in employing this artifice. A great deal of extant research proceeds in this way, but the fault lies in being satisfied with it. And this is widespread. In this case, engaging in reflection on the distinctive contours of diplomacy could prove to be perilous.

The term "diplomacy" is of Greek origin, and its meaning is twofold. On the one hand, as a verb—*diploo*, it comes back to a double folding, and on the other hand, as a noun—*diploma*, throughout the Middle Ages, it designated official documents folded in a particular way which conferred on their bearer certain rights and privileges. During the Renaissance, *diplomas* were associated with papal acts. In particular, a *diploma* is a letter of papal nomination. These letters were written by a cleric who was called a *diplomatarius*. From the end of the seventeenth century, the methods necessary to verify the authenticity of these documents are brought under the term *diplomatica*. Moreover, it is in this sense that the word appeared for the first time in the *Dictionnaire de l'Académie française* in 1762.

During the same period, concomitantly, we witness an extension of the term *diploma*. Not only does it continue to refer to documents attributing privileges to certain individuals, but, through a series of associations cumbersome to disentangle, the term *diploma* also progressively comes to designate the collection of official documents and treaties concluded between various sovereigns. Thus, because this falls within the context of treaties between sovereign entities, the adjective derived from *diploma*, diplomatic, becomes associated with the activities of envoys of one sovereign in another sovereign's court (Leira 2016). This explains the link between diplomatic activity, on the one hand, and peace, war, and alliances, on the other hand.

An evolution, technically similar to that of the term *diploma*, occurred around the notion of the diplomatic corps. While in the seventeenth century the diplomatic corps was analogous to the people's body of law, from

---

[6]See also Satow (1922).

the middle of the eighteenth century it began to designate all of the ministers accredited in another court (Leira 2016, 31). Finally, the term "diplomacy" made its way into the 1798 edition of the *Dictionnaire de l'Académie française* and signified the "Science of the relationships, of interests between powers." In *Webster's Dictionary* of 1817, diplomacy is perceived in a broader sense since, henceforth, it covers "the customs and rule of public ministries, the forms of negotiation; and the corps of ambassadors and envoys." By and large, this is the definition of diplomacy as it has come down to us. Overall, besides the conceptual variations characterized by the upheavals in etymology, we can stress that diplomacy falls into a distinct field of practice: that of war, peace, and alliances. In other words, this is the political domain. In that respect, everything that one could term new forms of "diplomacy" (humanitarian, cultural, or others) above all serves these original goals of diplomacy.

Yet what of its relationship to foreign policy? Certain institutional ambiguities offer little relief to those who would like to differentiate them. In the International Studies Association (ISA), there is, indeed, a specific section dedicated to the analysis of foreign policy, which is linked to the journal *Foreign Policy Analysis*. In addition, there is a section on diplomatic studies. This decoupling is surprising when we know how difficult it is to get an autonomous section recognized in the ISA. In reality, in our view, diplomacy and foreign policy evolve at distinct but complementary levels. Foreign policy is situated at a meta-level. It formulates objectives which diplomacy pursues. Certainly, diplomacy is based on means and instruments. Yet it is also about the form that interactions take. A poor ambassador can derail years of serene relations. Thus, diplomacy concerns instruments and practices through which not only states, but also actors support, coordinate, and achieve their identities, interests, and values.

ABOUT THIS BOOK'S RATIONALE AND CONTENTS

Diplomatic studies have recently witnessed a strong resurgence of interest, at both the academic and practical levels. The broadening of the diplomatic scene to include societal actors but also emerging powers cannot be the only explanatory factor. Other parameters must be taken into consideration. For example, consider how the following changes call into question the traditional perimeters and operation of diplomacy: the diversification of ranges of action in an environment characterized by concerns about image and reputation (*branding*); diplomacy's resonance with antiterrorism mechanisms; the pressure of budgetary constraints on public policies (compelling a redefinition of the conditions for diplomatic action); the rise of information and communication technologies associated with the sophistication of means of digital navigation; taking into account emotions and affect in order to make diplomatic activity more intelligible; the development of intergovernmental organizations, especially regional ones, which bring about the creation of new diplomatic spaces, including those of inter-organizational and inter-regional cooperation.

All sectors of diplomatic intervention (from trade and security to finance, culture, and the environment) are influenced by these reconfigurations. While the Anglophone market has seen the publication of a number of influential offerings, culminating in the *Oxford Handbook of Modern Diplomacy* (2013), the Francophone market remains fragmented in terms of what is available. Thus, to our knowledge, this volume constitutes the first French textbook on diplomacy.

The question of the adaptation of diplomatic tools (classic or modern) permeates the entire work. While the diplomatic dimension in international relations is broached in a number of works, it is not the specific focus. Instead, existing works consider the profession of diplomat and, more rarely, the sociology of this occupation (Report to the Ministry, by Loriol, Piotet, and Delfolie, published by Hermann in 2013). Others touch on a particular aspect of diplomacy, for example negotiation (Petiteville and Placidi-Frot 2013). Nonetheless, most reference texts give considerable attention to diplomacy. In the *Traité de relations internationales* (Balzacq and Ramel 2013), for example, a number of facets of diplomacy are examined (diplomatic history, conflict analysis, international negotiation, public diplomacy, foreign policy, etc.). Be that as it may, whether they are more open, like the *Handbooks and Treaties*, or concentrated on a single theme, these texts often presuppose a working knowledge of international relations.

This book on diplomacy has a more precise goal, and all the chapters have an identical approach, presenting an *Introduction* to the study and practice of diplomacy. In simple terms, it provides an initial contact with diplomacy. Whether in English or French, most textbooks on diplomacy target advanced undergraduate and postgraduate students. On this count, Kerr and Wiseman's book is a notable example (Kerr and Wiseman 2017). The present textbook has a more defined audience. It is particularly suitable for undergraduate university studies, but does not require any basic training in political science or international relations. It does, however, assume a healthy dose of intellectual curiosity and some general culture.

The textbook is divided into three sections. The first explores both the environments at the heart of which diplomacy is conceived and developed, and its various possible configurations, from bilateralism to multilateralism, including possible intermediate nuances (club and group diplomacy, paradiplomacy, etc.). In addition, it examines the various methods of supporting diplomacy, there too from the most classic (negotiation, rituals, and protocols) to the latest information and communication technologies. The second section concentrates more on the actors participating in diplomacy. It therefore covers not only state actors, but also sub- and supra-state actors. It confirms the way in which the twofold pressure of sub-national entities and of international and non-governmental organizations has radically transformed the task of state diplomats. Yet it substantiates this analysis with some original data. Here, for example, the role of legislatures is key to the extent that it raises the question of a fair balance between, on the one hand, discretion (or secrecy)—one of the traditional attributes of diplomacy—and, on the other hand, transparency, a requirement for certain new actors on the international stage. Finally, the third section examines various diplomatic sectors. The objective is not to compile an inventory of all possible incarnations of the diplomatic phenomenon. Instead, it is a matter of testing the hypothesis that diplomacy changes in nature in different sectors. Thus, in total, seven sectors are analyzed: the economy, culture, the environment, defense, the humanitarian field, entertainment, and expertise. In the conclusion, we discuss some difficulties facing contemporary diplomacy. The textbook suggests different ways to successfully overcome those challenges.

References

Balzacq, Thierry, Ramel, Frédéric (eds.), *Traité de relations internationales*, Paris, Presses de Sciences Po, 2013.

Barber, Brian, *What Diplomats Do: The Life and Work of Diplomats*, Lanham (MD), Rowman & Littlefield, 2016.

Berridge, Geoffrey R., *Diplomacy: Theory and Practice*, New York (NY), Palgrave Macmillan, 2015.

Campbell, Brian, "Diplomacy in the Roman World (c. 400 BC–AD 235)," *Diplomacy and Statecraft*, 12 (1), 2001: 1–22.

Cheyre, Juan Emilio, "Defence Diplomacy," in Andrew F. Cooper, Jorge Heine, Ramesh Thakur (eds.), *The Oxford Handbook of Modern Diplomacy*, Oxford, Oxford University Press, 2013.
Cohen, Raymond, "The Great Tradition: The Spread of Diplomacy in the Ancien World," *Diplomacy and Statecraft*, 1 (1), 2001: 23–38.
———, "Diplomacy Through the Ages," in Pauline Kerr, Geoffrey Wiseman (eds.), *Diplomacy in a Globalizing World: Theories and Practices*, New York (NY), Oxford University Press, 2017, pp. 21–36.
Constantinou, Costas M., *On the Way to Diplomacy*, Minneapolis (MN), University of Minnesota Press, 1996.
Der Derian, James, "Mediating Estrangement: A Theory of Diplomacy," *Review of International Studies*, 13 (2), 1987: 91–110.
Eilers, Claude, *Diplomats and Diplomacy in the Roman World*, Leiden and Boston, Brill, 2009.
Fletcher, Catherine, *Diplomacy in Renaissance Rome: The Rise of the Resident Ambassador*, Cambridge, Cambridge University Press, 2015.
Gerolymatos, Andre, *Espionage and Treason: A Study of the Proxeny in Political and Military Intelligence Gathering in Classical Greece*, Amsterdam, Brill, 1986.
Grandpierre, Véronique, *Histoire de la Mésopotamie*, Paris, Gallimard, 2010.
Hocking, Brian, *Foreign Ministries: Change and Adaptation*, New York (NY), Palgrave Macmillan, 1999.
Kerr, Pauline, Wiseman, Geoffrey, "Introduction," in Pauline Kerr, Geoffrey Wiseman (eds.), *Diplomacy in a Globalizing World: Theories and Practices*, New York (NY), Oxford University Press, 2017, pp. 1–18.
Langhorne, Richard, "The Regulation of Diplomatic Practice: The Beginnings to the Vienna Convention on Diplomatic Practice (1961)," in Christer Jönsson, Richard Langhorne (eds.), *Diplomacy, vol. II, History of Diplomacy*, London, Sage, 2004, pp. 315–333.
Lee, Donna, Hudson, David, "The Old and New Significance of Political Economy in Diplomacy," *Review of International Studies*, 30 (3), 2004: 343–360.
Leira, Halvard, "A Conceptual History of Diplomacy," in Costas M. Constantinou, Pauline Kerr, Paul Sharp (eds.), *The Sage Handbook of Diplomacy*, London, Sage, 2016, pp. 28–38.
Lequesne, Christian, *Ethnographie du Quai d'Orsay. Les pratiques des diplomates français*, Paris, CNRS Éditions, 2017.
Loriol, Françoise, Piotet, Marc, Delfolie, David, *Splendeurs et misères du travail des diplomates*, Paris, Hermann, 2013.
Maulde la Clavière, M., *La Diplomatie au temps de Machiavel*, 3 vols., Paris, Ernest Leroux, 1892–1893.
Neumann, Iver B., *At Home with the Diplomats: Inside a European Foreign Ministry*, Ithaca (NY), Cornell University Press, 2012.
Nicolson, Harold, *Diplomacy*, London, Thornton Butterworth, 1950.

Petiteville, Franck, Placidi-Frot, Delphine (eds.), *Négociations internationales*, Paris, Presses de Sciences Po, 2013.
Pouliot, Vincent, Cornut, Jérémie, "Practice Theory and the Study of Diplomacy: A Research Agenda," *Cooperation and Conflict*, 50 (3), 2015: 297–315.
Queller, Donald E., *Dictionary of the Middle Ages*, New York (NY), Scribner, 1984.
Rosoux, Valérie, "Négociation internationale," in Thierry Balzacq, Frédéric Ramel (eds.), *Traité de relations internationales*, Paris, Presses de Sciences Po, 2013, pp. 795–821.
Roux, Georges, *La Mésopotamie*, Paris, Seuil, 1995.
Saulnier, Christine, "Le rôle des prêtres fétiaux et l'application du ius fetiale à Rome," *Revue historique du droit français et étranger*, 58 (2), 1980: 171–199.
Schelling, Thomas C., *Arms and Influence*, New Haven (CT), Yale University Press, 1966.
Satow, Ernest M., *A Guide to Diplomatic Practice*, London, Longmans, Green & Co, 1922.
Sharlach, T. M., "Diplomacy and the Rituals of Politics at the Ur III Court," *Journal of Cuneiform Politics*, 57, 2005: 17–29.
Sharp, Paul, *Diplomatic Theory of International Relations*, Cambridge, Cambridge University Press, 1999.
Veyne, Paul, *L'Empire gréco-romain*, Paris, Seuil, 2005.
Weinfeld, Moshe, "Covenant Making in Anatolia and Mesopotamia," *Journal of the Ancient Near Eastern Society of Columbia University*, 22, 1993, pp. 135–139.
Wiseman, Geoffrey, "Diplomatic Practices at the United Nations," *Cooperation and Conflict*, 50 (3), 2015: 316–333.
Zartman, William I., *Negotiation and Conflict Management: Essays in Theory and Practice*, London, Routledge, 2008.

PART I

Places and Vectors of Diplomacy in the Twentieth Century

CHAPTER 2

Bilateral Relations

Alice Pannier

Bilateral relations are the founding element of international relations, or, as Thomas Gomart has suggested, "the basic form of the diplomatic game" (Gomart 2002, 65). The centrality of bilateral relations can be seen on the historical, strategic, and numerical levels. First, on a historical level, the use of diplomatic relations between states through official missions began in the seventeenth century among European monarchies, the equivalent of what may be called "traditional diplomacy" or "old diplomacy." The Congress of Westphalia in 1648 recognized equal status among all sovereign nations, whose mutual recognition was conducted through receiving foreign consular agents. This mainly European bilateral diplomacy, widespread until the First World War, was characterized by the central role played by embassies, a high degree of secrecy in negotiations, and bonds created through intermarriage among major ruling families that went hand in hand with political alliances. Colonial empires and decolonization subsequently led to the development of a profusion of other types of bilateral relations between Europe and the rest of the world.

A. Pannier (✉)
Johns Hopkins University, Washington, DC, USA

© The Author(s) 2020
T. Balzacq et al. (eds.), *Global Diplomacy*,
The Sciences Po Series in International Relations and Political Economy, https://doi.org/10.1007/978-3-030-28786-3_2

The central role of bilateral relations in diplomacy can then be explored through their strategic role in promoting national interests and structuring international negotiations. Through foreign affairs ministries, embassies, and consulates, bilateral diplomacy indeed remains the best tool for pursuing a state's interests, whether through trade and investments, by promoting a country's image and culture, or in communicating with the diaspora. Furthermore, bilateral relations are an important phase of engaging in international negotiations, as mutual interests are first developed on a bilateral level in order to build coalitions and more effectively highlight those interests in multilateral negotiations. Bilateral relationships tend to be favored when actors perceive them as a tactical advantage. Thus, bilateral relations are often undertaken as a strategic interaction, a power struggle where the actors are driven by their own interests rather than by a desire to be inclusive. The challenge in bilateral relations is then to succeed in pursuing those interests through cooperation, without undermining one's sovereignty and freedom of action (Devin 2013, 93-94).

Due to the central role they have played historically and strategically, bilateral relations are also at the heart of international relations from a numerical standpoint. Although multilateral relations have become increasingly diverse and intense since the second half of the twentieth century, particularly as of the 1990s, and have been the focus of growing attention from scholars of international relations, bilateral relations remain to this day the favored platform for agreements reached internationally. From 1990 to 1999, the United Nations (UN) recorded the signing of over 5000 bilateral treaties, covering the fields of economics and finance, politics and the military, etc. Today, trade agreements such as the Comprehensive Economic and Trade Agreement (CETA) and the Transatlantic Trade and Investment Partnership (TTIP), the United Kingdom's planned exit from the European Union, and increasingly fragile major military alliances appear to confirm the trend identified by Newman, Thakur, and Timan in 2006 of a "crisis" of multilateralism and a relative reinforcement of bilateralism within the international system (Newman et al. 2006).

This chapter begins by exploring how bilateral relations are conducted, presenting the role of the various actors, official or otherwise, that take part in them. It then examines the ties between the bilateral and multilateral levels in current international relations. Finally, it takes a look at the "qualification" of bilateral relations and shows why a typology is hard to establish due to the complex and changing nature characteristic of bilateral relations.

Conducting Bilateral Relations

Diplomatic missions and international treaties provide the institutional foundations for bilateral relations. States have "diplomatic relations" when they enjoy continuous unhindered communications. Maintaining such diplomatic relations is based on agreements between states. Beyond this mere ability to communicate, bilateral relations are mainly structured around relations between heads of state and/or government, embassies, private stakeholders, and relations between civil societies.

Relations Between Heads of State and Government

Official visits are an integral part of bilateral relations, for Ministers of Foreign Affairs and possibly technical ministries such as Defense and Finance. State visits involve the head of state and constitute the highest level of diplomatic contact between two countries. They entail a range of ceremonies and usually last more than one day. Below state visits are official visits (or working visits), which may involve the head of state (monarch, president, etc.) or of government (prime minister, chancellor, etc.). Bilateral summits also involve heads of state or government and are held on a regular basis on a schedule set up by the various partners. European countries hold bilateral summits (annual or biennial) in particular to engage in pre-negotiations before EU summits. In addition to neighboring countries and/or allies, there are many types of bilateral partnerships that lead to high-level summit meetings, including global partnerships, strategic partnerships, and security dialogues.

Summits and visits perform various functions. For instance, they may send a diplomatic signal about the importance of a certain bilateral relationship, consolidate it, move matters forward that cannot be dealt with by embassies, and sign declarations and/or binding agreements (intergovernmental treaties or accords on trade, technical cooperation, etc.).

Due to the role these meetings play in shaping bilateral relations—more than in other forms of international relations—the identity and role of heads of state and government are highlighted, as well as the quality of their interpersonal relationships. The latter are seen as directly affecting the tenor of bilateral relations and potential progress in cooperation and settling disputes. This is especially true in studying relations among democratic regimes. Through the perspective of diplomatic history, one may examine their relationships via the declarations, gestures, and symbols that occur in bilateral meetings. Diplomatic archives, when available, can provide access to preparatory notes before visits, and correspondence. Memoirs written by heads of state and government at the end of their term of office are another major source of information in grasping the nature of relationships between heads of state and/or government.

The Role of Embassies

While the identity of heads of state and government is an important factor in marking major developments in bilateral relations (either stepping forward or backward), its daily routine business—and the preparation of these "key events"—is the result of work done by diplomats and embassies. To carry out that work, embassies are divided into different departments by activity sectors. These departments are under the supervision of the Ministry of Foreign Affairs or so-called technical ministries (environment, transportation, education and research, defense, health, justice, culture, etc.). The role of these departments is to implement policies decided on a national level. However, special relationships in specific fields of public policy proceeding from technical exchanges may also lead to new avenues of cooperation between countries.

Historically, the economy and trade were the first spheres of action for embassies. Starting in the sixteenth century, the consul's mission—in addition to protecting his country's citizens abroad—was to "provide information about anything that could facilitate or hinder trade" with his country of residence (Kessler 2012, 341). In the late nineteenth century, the economic aspect was assigned to ambassadors. They then became responsible for negotiating bilateral treaties, rapidly increasing in the areas of trade and economics, in particular concerning the colonies. There were diverse sectors involving business interests: exports, infrastructures, transportation, and communications. As Kessler explains, relations in France between political and economic interests were not without problems in their exchanges with former colonies: During the 1960s, the French Presidency's networks, created around De Gaulle's adviser and former tradesman Jacques Foccart, were characterized by interpersonal ties and the pursuit of mutual interests between French representatives (diplomats), African dictator presidents, and French businessmen from companies like Elf and Total, leading to some "slip-ups" by French embassies. The 1970s saw the emergence of liberalized economies domestically and, on the international level, the establishment of international regimes regulating trade that restricted the scope of action of states. The only economic agreements they could still negotiate bilaterally were with political regimes that had no market economy or were very fragile. Furthermore, multinational companies today undertake their own "diplomacy," which often escapes national political control (cf. infra). Bilateral relations between states via their embassies have therefore become less central in economic spheres.

The embassies' second main sphere of action involves political and military cooperation and secret services. In addition to economic exchanges, information gathering (about a local political or security situation, for instance) has always been one of the main missions of embassies. But the Internet and 24-hour news channels now supply a great deal of the information that embassies once provided to the state they represented. This function of diplomatic missions has not become obsolete however. Agents from intelligence services are operative in all embassies, whether identified as such or acting incognito as undercover "cultural advisors" or "humanitarian attachés" for example. Moreover, while information may be more easily available nowadays, there is also greater cooperation among states, and the role of military missions in particular is to promote international cooperation on security and defense issues. Depending on the depth of the relationship, a military or defense attaché may come with a team composed of representatives from each army as well as from agencies in charge of weapons acquisitions.

Finally, embassies play an important role in cultural relations and promotion, and in interuniversity cooperation. This may involve setting up national institutes offering access to cultural activities, language courses, and educational grants. Initiatives in this area are usually undertaken with actors from civil society (cf. infra).

Other Political Actors: Parliaments and Parties

Bilateral diplomatic channels traditionally have three main functions: representing, informing, negotiating and cooperating. Apart from official representation, embassies today no longer have a monopoly on these activities. In addition to diplomats, actors in bilateral relations include other political actors such as parliaments and political parties (particularly since the creation of the European Union), actors from the private sector (corporations) and civil society.

Among political actors, parliaments and political parties maintain bilateral relations with allied countries, neighbors, and/or members of the same international organizations. For example, there are parliamentary "friendship groups" with nearly all countries in the world, provided they have a parliament. The aim of these inter-parliamentary groups is to create ties with other parliamentarians, as well as to contribute to national influence and wherever possible to impact policies carried out by other states. In addition to friendship groups, there are inter-parliamentary working groups with more specific purposes, such as the Parliamentary Working Group on Defense Cooperation between the United Kingdom and France. Special national commissions (for instance, "Finance," "Social Welfare," or "Defense") go on fact-finding missions to their equivalents abroad. Thus, parliamentarians on the national level are also allied with diplomats in defending their country's interests through initiatives lobbying their counterparts, with a view to impacting political decisions in the partner country (Rozental and Buenrosto 2013).

Lastly, political parties maintain bilateral relations and partnerships, in particular within the European Union and European Parliament, but not exclusively. It is customary for the major French political parties to attend American political conventions.[1] Furthermore, political parties may maintain relations with foreign governments.[2]

Corporations

Although relationships between ministries and political actors provide the structure and framework for bilateral relations, a study of official actors should not obscure the host of transnational ties underlying relations between two states. It is important to examine these ties between societies, through actors from the private sector. Corporations may have commercial interests in a country because they export goods and services and/or have branches there. As we saw earlier, in the case of nationalized companies, that interest may be the same as the state's "interests," notably in the weapons and energy sectors. Contracts may be cancelled and economic sanctions could block exports to a state with which political relations are conflictual. In 2015, France cancelled a contract for the sale of two Mistral

---

[1] Pascal Drouhaud, "L'UMP et les relations internationales," *Revue internationale et stratégique*, 55 (3), 2004: 11–18.

[2] Nicolas Lebourg, "Les dimensions internationales du Front national," *Pouvoirs*, 57 (2), 2016: 105–113, for example, examined the underpinnings of the relationship between the French far-right party Front National and the Russian regime of Vladimir Putin.

helicopter carriers to Russia in order to comply with European sanctions following the Russian intervention in Ukraine in 2013.

Outside these special cases, companies have become more independent in all sectors, and even small and mid-sized companies have begun to make their products abroad or export them, giving them increasing influence in bilateral relations all over the world. States may support firms through their chambers of commerce, which provide appraisals, resources, and networks for companies eager to export. Official visits may also afford a chance to facilitate access to foreign markets, notably through pooled delegations of corporate CEOs. Firms may also be required to lobby foreign governments and parliaments to obtain contracts or exert their influence to pass favorable legislation (regulations, standards). This might come in the form of marketing and communications initiatives, support for think tanks and foundations, developing coalitions with actors in the target state (political actors, firms, experts), and maintaining interpersonal networks, etc.

Civil Society

Diasporas may play an important, specific role in relations between two states. These are generally focused on energizing members to support policies in the country of immigration that are favorable toward one's country of origin through lobbying. Diasporas may therefore use the same means of pressure employed by other non-state actors to influence bilateral relations (advocacy, fundraising, networking). This is the case in the United States, where multiculturalist policies accord diasporas greater influence than in other countries. The role of diasporas involves not only Israel, although it is given greater media coverage,[3] but also other countries such as India. New Delhi has used the presence of two million Indians in the United States to gain support for economic investments in India, and more generally to lobby for American policies favorable to India, such as lifting economic sanctions imposed after India's nuclear tests in 1998.[4]

In addition to diasporas, ethnic groups and religious and linguistic communities may maintain relations with cross-border regions. Such relations,

---

[3] John Mearsheimer and Stephen Walt, "The Israel Lobby", in *The London Review of Books* (Vol. 28, No. 6, March 23, 2006).

[4] Ingrid Therwath, « La diaspora indienne aux Etats-Unis comme acteur international », in Christophe Jaffrelot (dir.), *New Delhi et le monde*, Paris, Autrement, 2008.

often in a postcolonial context (Latin America, Africa, Asia), may be complicated by the existence of distinct states experiencing negative political relations, or even where the territorial status quo is contested (e.g., the Kashmir region, disputed by India and Pakistan; or relations between Russia and Ukraine).

At the other end of the spectrum, ties between populations may be promoted by political or economic actors and civil society. Cultural, academic, economic, and social cooperation may go through official bilateral initiatives and the establishment of semi-public organizations, or private and nonprofit initiatives supported by governments and/or embassies. In the case of France and Germany for example, there is a Franco-German Youth Office (FGYO) created by the Élysée Treaty in 1963 to organize youth exchanges and town twinning. This kind of transnational initiative, known as "parapublic," must contribute to building ties between societies (Krotz and Schild 2012). That said, the effects of such programs are hard to prove. Jean-Jacques Roche considers the programs' effects to be limited, after observing a low level of "friendly feelings" between French and German citizens of an age to profit from these bilateral programs. Repeated exchanges between two countries are in fact often a privilege of internationalized elites, as attested by bilateral exchange networks for "future leaders."[5] Young leader programs exist between many countries with the aim of connecting actors from the worlds of business, academics, and civil service.

Thus, bilateral relations are the result of interactions among multiple actors, from the state or otherwise, who cover a variety of public policy spheres. When studying a bilateral relationship, "one must avoid at all costs limiting it only to diplomatic exchanges," as Thomas Gomart has advocated, drawing from Jean-Baptiste Duroselle: "Commercial and financial relations, the two people's images of one another, intellectual exchanges in the broad sense and, finally, migration issues must all be taken into account" (Gomart 2002, 66). Furthermore, powerful interactions exist between official representatives, other political actors, actors from the private sector and civil societies. There are often interconnections among these actors, who

---

[5] Jean-Jacques Roche, "The French-German Couple: Elites' Affairs or Peoples' Friendship?" in Brigitte Vassort-Rousset (ed.), *Building Sustainable International Couples in International Relations. A Strategy Towards Peaceful Cooperation*, 111–124. London, Palgrave Macmillan, 2014.

may create a network or coalition around a particular topic in order to support their interests and ideas on an international level or, conversely, come into conflict.

Bilateral Relations and the Multilateral Context

Bilateral relations cannot be explored without considering how they fit into the multilateral framework of contemporary international relations, whether in negotiations within international organizations or in regional matters. Indeed, as Richard Neustadt has observed, "reality is not bilateral" (Neustadt 1970, 5). Some deem that multilateralization on a global scale and Europeanization on a regional scale have made bilateral relations and negotiations superfluous. However, others have shown that such levels of international action are based on a multiplicity of bilateral diplomatic relations, and the need to coordinate policies increases their importance. In fact, all multilateral negotiations (e.g., at the UN and the World Trade Organization WTO) require pre-negotiations and coalition-building on a bilateral level. Thus, bilateral relations "are still necessary [...] as an indispensable condition in a multilateral world" (Gomart 2002, 66).

In turn, multilateralism has spread throughout the activities of foreign affairs ministries (there is a Globalization Department in the French Ministry of Foreign Affairs), outside of geographical departments (the "Middle East" or "Oceania" for example) which have maintained chiefly bilateral activities. In Europe, policy integration in all sectors has also increased direct bilateral links between technical departments. Thus, bilateral relations usually fall within a multilateral context, whether regional or sectorial.

Depending on the issue, certain bilateral relations may have more weight than others. The Franco-German relationship, seen as a fundamental one for the building of Europe, has influenced the development of European institutions and is embedded in that institutional network. In strategic matters, the Franco-British "couple" is the one that "counts" at the UN, as the two partners are behind many of the proposals for resolutions in the Security Council, and their votes are in sync 80% of the time. Other bilateral relations may be called upon ad hoc, to handle specific matters where interests are aligned.

Bilateral partnerships may therefore affect negotiations at the multilateral level, and in return, strong bilateral relations tend to influence national strategies and stances in multilateral arenas. On the one hand, a bilateral relationship deemed highly important (cf infra, "special relationships") may, in any given multilateral negotiation, lead a government to take a position that seems not to be in line with "national interests," with the aim of preserving that bilateral relationship. Conversely, conflictual bilateral relations may have the effect of blocking multilateral relations: the abysmal relations between Greece and Turkey regarding the island of Cyprus continue to put to the test the cohesion of the North Atlantic Treaty Organization (NATO) and the partnership between the European Union and Turkey.

Lastly, multilateral issues may lead to divergences and be harmful to bilateral relations. The Brexit negotiations begun in early 2017 clearly illustrate the persistent centrality of bilateral relations in Europe and represent new difficulties in conducting those relationships in a changing international context in the grip of tough negotiations. Thus, multilateral institutions generate specific constraints and opportunities for conducting bilateral relations.

Qualifying Bilateral Relations

As we saw in the previous section, certain bilateral relations "count" more than others. There is a range of potential relations based on the institutional elements common to all bilateral relations, from "friendships" and "special relationships" to "enmity" and other conflictual relations, and including a myriad of possible degrees of proximity. It is not enough to talk about "bilateral relations" as such; they must be qualified and defined. In fact, bilateral relations may be relevant at a general or sectorial level; they may be symmetrical or asymmetrical, involve dependence or interdependence, be institutionalized or not, consensual or debated, new or old, founded on shared interests and/or values, and may experience phases, changes, and regressions in all of these aspects, which is not an exhaustive list. It is the role of diplomacy to determine when, where, and how bilateral relations become more important.

Privileged Bilateral Relations

According to Helen Wallace, bilateral relations between governments may come in at least three distinct forms (Wallace in Morgan and Bray 1986, 136–155). At the first level, two governments engage in a dialogue merely because there are transactions between their two countries that directly or indirectly involve the governments. On a second level, two states may be "condemned" to consult and cooperate because transactions between the two countries are so high in volume and complexity that their governments are obliged to show explicit consideration in their bilateral relations. It may be due to geographical proximity, to the volume of goods and services exchanged, to the number of individuals living in one or other of the countries, or to both belonging to an international organization. Finally, on a third level, the concept of a "special relationship" may be used in reference to relationships deemed privileged by the governments.

Based on cultural proximity and/or a shared history, privileged relationships—"couples" or "special relationships"—are the most successful and lasting ones in the international system. They are identifiable when these qualifiers are used by successive governments, the media, and the population. This generally means that preserving the relationship is deemed a part of "national interest," not merely involving economic or security interests that are cyclical. "Special relationships" tend to be institutionalized with regular summits, frequent official visits, daily work, and staff exchanges between administrations, all regulated by intergovernmental agreements, treaties, and protocols. Theoretically, such relationships suppose general alignment on political, diplomatic and economic issues, on core values providing a strong and sustainable shared foundation, enabling them to exert influence together in negotiations or crisis management on a multinational level. Such relationships are also characterized by a high level of resilience despite crises they may go through, as well as political changeovers.

The most well-known example is the relationship between Great Britain and the United States, the strengthening of which resulted in their shared management of the Second World War. Today, the "special" nature of that relationship is based on extremely close ties in the military and international security: armed forces, secret services, arms industry, and nuclear deterrence. The Franco-German "couple" is another example of a "special relationship," but one whose substance is chiefly economic and political, and with different origins from the transatlantic relationship, involving on the contrary growing closer in order to promote reconciliation after the war.

"Particular relationships" may also exist between former colonial powers and their ex-colonies. Furthermore, on a less demanding level than "special relationships," there are "friendships" that may be (semi-)institutionalized by treaties or partnerships enabling greater cooperation in certain sectors. However, these "friendships" do not presume a level of mutual consultation or symbolism as is the case with "couples" and "special relationships."

Conflictual Bilateral Relations

Like cooperative relations, conflictual bilateral relations come in varying degrees. We can distinguish between enmity and rivalry to start. In the most heightened cases, conflict tends to be an integral part of the relationship's conception, not only because of the political, economic, and territorial issues behind the conflict, but also due to a certain representation of the "other" among elites and the population. The conflict is kept alive by reproducing an image of the other as an "enemy" and as inherently constituting an existential threat.[6] It is based on rhetoric that highlights differences in interest, culture, ideology, and/or identity seen as irreconcilable. Bilateralism, combined with this construction of the other as enemy, can lead to the "rise to extremes" conceptualized by Carl von Clausewitz, potentially resulting in "absolute war." One historic example is the war between the Greeks and Persians in the fifth century B.C., the confrontation between the Axis and Allied powers during the Second World War, and the relations between the USSR and the United States during the early years of the Cold War. A "rival" may be distinguished from an "enemy" in that it permits coexistence, but with the desire to constrain the other's behavior or profits. Also, in cases less extreme than military confrontations, noncooperative bilateral relations may be based on economic competition, such as is the case currently between China and India.[7]

Between neighboring countries, conflictual bilateral relations may also be marked by territorial separations in the form of walls and/or demilitarized zones (e.g., between Israel and the Palestinian Territories, the Republic of Cyprus and Northern Cyprus, or South Korea and North Korea). That said, barriers may also exist between states that are not in conflict but have not found an alternative, either collectively or individually, for managing the flow of people and illegal goods between them, for example between the United States and Mexico, India and Bangladesh, or Morocco and the Spanish enclaves Ceuta and Melilla. One of the problems with this kind of border management is that walls reduce incentives for cooperation and

---

[6]Carl Schmitt, *The Concept of the Political*, Chicago, University of Chicago Press, 1996 [1932].

[7]Yves-Heng Lim, "Enduring Divorce: Multi-layered Causes of the China-India Rivalry", in Brigitte Vassort-Rousset (ed.), *Building Sustainable International Couples in International Relations...*, op.cit., 167–189.

obstruct seriously dealing with the source of the problems, only further alienating neighbors and leading to greater security risks and threats.

Situations of conflict tend to persist where cooperation is considered fragile; however, all bilateral relations are subject to change. Conflict resolution between two states often occurs through a mediator: an international organization, individual mediator, or third country. Nevertheless, here too it is direct relations between societies that usually enable them to achieve reconciliation and thereby transform bilateral relations. Thus, if bilateralism tends to be reduced de facto to binary conceptions—to a spectrum opposing friend and enemy, partner and adversary, ally and rival, oneself and "the other"—by leaving behind that kind of binary conception in talking about conflictual bilateral relations, one may take into account the malleability of bilateral relations and how they evolve.

The Limits of Qualification

While it is necessary to characterize bilateral relations for the sake of accuracy, the limits of such qualifications must be stressed, given their great diversity. Most interstate relations are not as clearly characterized as those described in binary terms. Indeed, as was pointed out earlier, bilateral relations are fluid: As long as there is a relationship, conflict and cooperation may coexist, and there is a potential for change. The semblance of eternity evoked by the terms "friend" and "enemy" in fact conceal a far more events-based reality.

In a short-term perspective, bilateral relations experience fluctuations depending on events, heads of state and government, and context. International crises are occasions for temporary divisions that may be highly intense but do not necessarily reflect the routine everyday tenor of a fertile bilateral relationship, as evidenced by the Franco-American diplomatic crisis in 2003 over the invasion of Iraq. The tenor of bilateral relations also depends on the sector, given that relations between two states imply the coexistence of areas of conflict and of cooperation.

In the long-term perspective, I have highlighted the issues involved in transforming a conflictual relationship into a peaceful one. France and Germany, for example, went from a mutual conception as enemies to an effort at reconciliation, ultimately leading to one of the deepest bilateral relations in the contemporary international system.

A change in bilateral relations may occur in the opposite direction. Even when shaped by diplomatic representations and exchanges between actors from the private sector and civil society, relations may come to an abrupt halt in a major crisis, generally linked to an interstate conflict or civil war, prompting the breaking off of diplomatic relations. This is a radical decision resulting in one of the two countries not maintaining a diplomatic mission on the other's territory. Breaking off relations is the highest degree of diplomatic crisis, and in wartime situations, states may withdraw or reduce their diplomatic mission without breaking off relations.

* * *

Despite the development of multilateral cooperation since the second half of the twentieth century, bilateral relations remain at the core of diplomacy. There has even been a certain "return to the bilateral" in the contemporary era. This is illustrated, for example, by American President Donald Trump's questioning of the multilateral order, or the United Kingdom's decision to leave the European Union. These phenomena have put negotiations and bilateral relations at the heart of international relations and research agendas, meriting further study.

Nevertheless, as has been shown in this chapter, studying bilateral relations is not as simple as it appears. We must distinguish the form, content, and dynamics of all bilateral relations, given their great variety, while refraining from attempting stringent qualifications. Bilateral relations are indeed remarkably fluid and evolving. Finally, even in studying a particular case, one should refer to bilateral relations in the plural—"Franco-German relations"—in order to grasp what constitutes a whole set of sectors and actors, situations of cooperation and conflict, differentiated and on several levels.

References

Devin, Guillaume, "Paroles de diplomates: comment les négociations multilatérales changent la diplomatie," in Franck Petiteville, Delphine Placidi-Frot (eds.), *Négociations internationales*, Paris, Presses de Sciences Po, 2013, pp. 77–104.

Gomart, Thomas, "La relation bilatérale: un genre de l'histoire des relations internationales," *Matériaux pour l'histoire de notre temps*, 65–66, 2002: 65–68.

Hocking, Brian, Spence, David, (eds.), *Foreign Ministries in the European Union: Integrating Diplomats*, New York (NY), Palgrave Macmillan, 2002.

Kessler, Marie-Christine, *Les Ambassadeurs*, Paris, Presses de Sciences Po, 2012.

Krotz, Ulrich, Schild, Joachim, *Shaping Europe: France, Germany and Embedded Bilateralism from the Elysee Treaty to Twenty-First Century Politics*, Oxford, Oxford University Press, 2012.

Morgan, Roger, Bray, Caroline (eds.), *Partners and Rivals in Western Europe: Britain, France and Germany*, Aldershot, Gower Publishing Company, 1986.

Neustadt, Richard, *Alliance Politics*, New York, Columbia University Press, 1970.

Newman, Edward, Thakur, Ramesh, Timan, John (eds.), *Multilateralism Under Challenge? Power, International Order and Structural Change*, Tokyo, United Nations University Press, 2006.

Rozental, Andrés, Buenrosto, Alicia, "Bilateral Diplomacy," in Andrew F. Cooper, Jorge Heine, Ramesh Thakur (eds.), *The Oxford Handbook of Modern Diplomacy*, Oxford, Oxford University Press, 2013, pp. 229–246.

Vassort-Rousset, Brigitte, (ed.), *Building Sustainable International Couples in International Relations: A Strategy Towards Peaceful Cooperation*, London, Palgrave Macmillan, 2014.

CHAPTER 3

Multilateral Diplomacy

Franck Petiteville and Delphine Placidi-Frot

Nearly as old as state diplomacy, multilateral diplomacy today deals with the full range of international issues: war and peace, human rights, trade, the environment, etc. Strictly speaking, multilateral diplomacy involves relations between at least three states. In practice, it often brings together dozens of states (represented by their diplomats and delegations) and a growing number of non-state actors. Multilateral diplomacy was long conducted in the form of ad hoc conferences. Since the creation of the League of Nations (LN), then of the United Nations (UN), it has also frequently been conducted through international organizations. Multifaceted and ever evolving, it has often been neglected in international relations studies despite its long history and omnipresence on the international scene.

F. Petiteville (✉)
University of Grenoble Alpes, Grenoble, France
e-mail: franck.petiteville@sciencespo-grenoble.fr

D. Placidi-Frot
University Paris-Saclay, Saint-Aubin, France
e-mail: delphine.placidi-frot@u-psud.fr

© The Author(s) 2020
T. Balzacq et al. (eds.), *Global Diplomacy*,
The Sciences Po Series in International Relations and Political
Economy, https://doi.org/10.1007/978-3-030-28786-3_3

The Historicity of Multilateral Diplomacy

Modern residential diplomacy began to develop in Europe when states opened embassies and created the first ministries of foreign affairs by the sixteenth century. From the beginning, this nascent state diplomacy was faced with a highly multilateral task when the Thirty Years War (1616–1648), which had sparked a major confrontation between powers that devastated continental Europe, was settled. 194 delegations representing political entities of all sizes, from free cities in the Holy Roman Empire up to major European monarchies, negotiated the Treaty of Westphalia (1648). In the seventeenth and eighteenth centuries, dynastic quarrels and lust for territory (notably in Louis XIV's France) continued to trigger constant wars. Diplomacy was frequently called upon to incorporate the territorial consequences of these wars in treaties. This diplomatic practice was undertaken at vast congresses. 80 delegations took part in the Congress of Utrecht (1712–1713), for example, to settle the War of the Spanish Succession.

A century later, the Congress of Vienna (1814–1815) brought together more than 200 heads of diplomatic missions from all over Europe, putting an end to the Napoleonic Wars. The congress redrew the map of Europe (France, in particular, was scaled back to its 1789 borders) and established solidarity among European monarchies around the dynastic principle that had been so ill-treated during the French Revolution and the Napoleonic Empire. However, the multilateral diplomacy at work at the Congress of Vienna was largely driven by the four major powers that defeated Napoleon (Britain, Prussia, Austria-Hungary, Russia). The spirit of the Congress of Vienna was prolonged by the "Concert of Europe"— an alliance among the four powers to which France was invited during the (Bourbon) Restoration—leading to regular meetings, in particular at the ambassadorial level. The Concert of Europe crumbled during the second half of the nineteenth century with new wars in Europe (Crimea in 1854–1855, the Wars of Italian Unification in 1870, the Franco-Prussian War in 1870) and collapsed permanently when antagonistic alliances were formed (Triple Alliance against Triple Entente) leading to the First World War. Meanwhile European diplomacy began opening up to the rest of the world through peace conferences in The Hague (1899 and 1907), the second involving 44 out of 57 sovereign states at the time.

Multilateral diplomacy was reestablished at the end of the First World War when the Treaty of Versailles was negotiated in 1919, with 70 delegates representing 27 states participating. But here too the negotiations were driven by the winning powers (Britain, France, Italy, the United States), while the defeated countries (that were to pay a very heavy price, especially Germany) were excluded. Multilateral diplomacy at Versailles was a return to power politics, despite the new principles of "moral diplomacy" displayed by President Wilson.

Yet the Treaty of Versailles led to the creation of the LN, the first collective security organization in history, with 60 member states in the early 1930s. Weakened from the beginning by the withdrawal of the United States (the Treaty of Versailles not being ratified by the Senate), the LN gradually revealed the inability of European democracies to thwart power grabs by authoritarian and totalitarian states during the 1930s. However, the LN was a critical point in the institutionalizing of multilateral diplomacy. While conference diplomacy from Westphalia to Versailles was conducted ad hoc, member states were now negotiating within the arena of the LN (Assemblies, Councils) and sending resident diplomats to LN headquarters in Geneva. Multilateral diplomacy was often referred to as "parliamentary," or institutionalized, in accordance with rules decreed by the Covenant of the LN, in particular equality of member states and the rule regarding unanimous decision-making.

The end of the Second World War reinforced the institutionalizing of multilateral diplomacy with the creation of the UN, the World Bank and the International Monetary Fund (IMF). However, the negotiations overseeing the birth of these organizations were as hegemonic as ever. Indeed the UN Charter, signed by representatives of fifty states at the conclusion of the San Francisco Conference in June 1945, was largely drawn up by the United States during the war ("Declaration by United Nations" required its signing by the states at war against the Axis powers in January 1942), then amended during close negotiations with the UK, Russia and China at Dumbarton Oaks (1944).

The history of multilateral diplomacy from 1815 to 1945 thus reveals two essential features. On the one hand, the negotiations focused on key issues of war and peace, and on the other hand, they remained largely driven by the major powers. What changed in the twentieth century, however, was that multilateral diplomacy began to globalize outside Europe while becoming institutionalized, mainly by playing out within the arena of large international organizations. Nevertheless, the Cold War put an end to the expansion of multilateral diplomacy, at the UN in particular. This was already reflected in the 1950s by the polarization of the UN General Assembly between states affiliated with the "Western camp" and vassals of the Socialist bloc. The UN Security Council (increasing from 11 to 15 members in the 1960s) immediately ceased to be the collegial body for world conflict resolution stipulated in its charter and became an arena of East-West confrontation. Vetoes, by the Soviets in particular (120 between 1946 and 1989) and by the Americans (63 during the same period), were employed regularly by one or the other power to reject UN engagement in conflicts where they were involved. To be sure, throughout the Cold War, the East and West succeeded in collaborating on a few exercises in multilateral diplomacy (in negotiating the Nuclear Non-Proliferation Treaty in 1968 and on the Helsinki Accords in 1975 within the framework of the conference on security and cooperation in Europe). Yet during the Cold War as a whole, world diplomacy was largely obstructed. At the same time, decolonization, the emergence of states from the Third World and from the Non-Aligned Movement added a North-South division within multilateral diplomacy following the Bandung Conference (Indonesia, 1955), then the creation of the G77 in 1964 in Geneva, which began to mobilize at the UN General Assembly during the 1970s in favor of establishing a "new international economic order."

Thus, multilateral diplomacy did not reassert itself at the UN until the end of the Cold War. The Security Council in particular succeeded in rekindling collegial practices on major security issues by reacting vigorously to Iraq's annexation of Koweit in 1990 (with sanctions and legitimizing the use of force by the United States and its allies in early 1991) and increasing UN involvement in peacekeeping operations in the early 1990s (the tragic failures in ex-Yugoslavia and Rwanda notwithstanding). The Security Council was now adopting around 80 resolutions per year, but deadlocks resurfaced whenever the major powers disagreed (when the Bush administration unilaterally invaded Iraq in 2003, for instance, or in the Syrian conflict when Putin's Russia exercised its veto twelve times between March 2011 and April 2018 to protect Bachar Al-Assad's regime from any critical resolutions).

Yet, the international organizations created in 1944–1945 have remained the foundation of contemporary multilateral diplomacy. The number of UN member states has nearly quadrupled from 1945 (51) to today (193). The World Bank and IMF have almost as many (188). For over seventy years, the UN has succeeded in surviving decades of the Cold War, conflicts and crises without being rendered powerless and avoiding the fate of the LN. The UN General Assembly has initiated a great many important international treaties (particularly regarding human rights), while adopting some 300 resolutions per year laying out major directions in multilateral diplomacy on all key issues of international politics.

Moreover, since the end of the Cold War, multilateral diplomacy has become increasingly visible in major world conferences on non-strategic issues, including the environment, the economy, development aid, and human rights. The Rio conference on the environment and development, held by the UN in 1992, led to the adoption of the framework convention on climate change, with 178 states represented. During the same period, over 120 states took part in negotiations in the Uruguay Round of the General Agreement on Tariffs and Trade (GATT), a vast exercise in multilateral trade diplomacy, leading to the creation of the World Trade Organization (WTO, currently 164 member states). 189 countries participated in the (fourth) world conference on women in Beijing in 1995.

Today, that global diplomacy configuration is widespread. In 2000, the 189 UN member states adopted the Millennium Development Goals (MDGs); in Paris in December 2015, the 195 states supporting the UN convention on climate change negotiated a global climate agreement. The COP 21 personifies the transformations in multilateral diplomacy, as an exercise in global diplomacy no longer focused on classic high politics issues, despite being widely seen as such, and involving a host of non-state actors (international organizations, scientific networks, NGOs, corporations, and major cities) where negotiations and key issues are staged in global media campaigns.

Adaptation of States' Diplomatic Operations to Multilateralism

The rise of multilateral diplomacy led states to gradually develop administrative and human resources devoted to international organizations, although with some reluctance. It was not until the creation of the LN and the International Labour Organization (ILO) in 1919 that diplomatic chancelleries made adjustments and bureaucratic innovations to adapt to a multiparty, permanent and increasingly institutionalized form of representation and negotiations.

Ministries of foreign affairs began by setting up services devoted to international organizations. Their evolution—for both terminology and organization charts—illustrates how puzzled some chancelleries were about these novel diplomatic practices. Whether they were called "conference services," "international organizations directorate," or "department of global governance," whether they reported to the "political affairs department" or to that of "globalization," or whether they were directly assigned to the minister, these different services were designed to enable member states to coordinate and attune foreign policy developed by the executive branch with the international organizations involved (in highly centralized political systems) and to cooperate with legislative bodies (in parliamentary systems). These administrative structures were also designed to interact with other ministries considered more technical (Justice, Education, Health, Defense, etc.) and even to manage certain national administrative functions (interministerial coordination procedures, independent agencies, local and regional authorities, etc.).

Secondly, member states established representation or permanent missions at international organizations (the multilateral equivalent of bilateral embassies) in order to carry out the traditional diplomatic functions of representation, information, and above all negotiation. Certain states (such as France, the UK, Germany, Italy and the Soviet Union) had not deemed it necessary to establish a permanent mission at LN headquarters in Geneva in-between the wars, settling for sending delegations to Council meetings and Assembly sessions. But those diplomatic posts soon proved to be critical elements of multilateral diplomacy.

Indeed, they were at the forefront of the decision-making process in international organizations since permanent representatives have seats on its supreme executive bodies (UN Security Council, the European Union's Committee of Permanent Representatives—Coreper, NATO's North Atlantic Council, etc.).

Permanent missions have also played a central role in the diplomacy of many states with insufficient diplomatic resources to cover the entire world, thus focusing their efforts on multilateral hubs such as New York (headquarters for the UN and the UNDP[1]), Washington (World Bank, IMF), Geneva (UN office, ICRC, UNHCR, ILO, WTO, WHO[2]), Vienna

---

[1] United Nations Development Programme.

[2] United Nations Organization, International Committee of the Red Cross, UN High Commissioner for Refugees, International Labor Organization, World Trade Organization, World Health Organization.

(IAEA,[3] UN office, UNODC, OPEC, OSCE[4]), Brussels (NATO, European Union), Paris (OECD, IOF, Unesco[5]), and The Hague (International Court of Justice, International Criminal Court, Europol).

Nearly all states are now involved in multilateral diplomacy, at both the global and the regional levels. Yet glaring differences in resources have persisted between those with the administrative and human means to ensure a continuous, recognized presence within the various multilateral institutions they belong to, and those who must make drastic trade-offs by selecting the arenas, conferences, and meetings they must and/or wish to participate in, and the issues they must give priority to. While the most well-established missions—which can have dozens and even hundreds of diplomats—resemble miniature ministries of foreign affairs, the smallest rely on the involvement of a handful of diplomats (see Figs. 3.1, 3.2, and 3.3, infra).

To address these differences in resources, certain multilateral organizations have set up informal coordination structures among small countries in order to create a consensus within the group before its consideration by the General Assembly Plenary and/or the Executive Committee. While all member states have now complied with the permanent mission

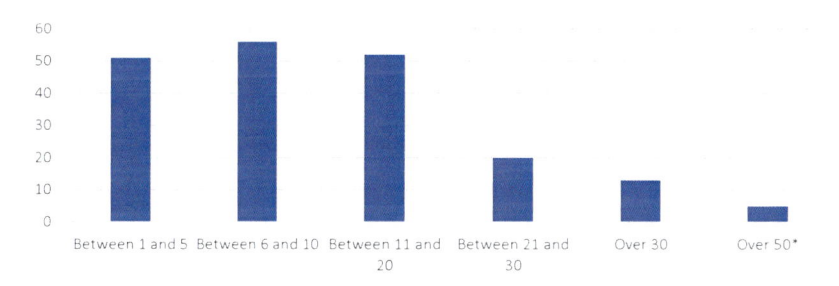

Fig. 3.1 UN Multilateral Diplomacy Personnel in New York (*The United States, Russia, China, Germany, Japan [37 for France]; *Source* United Nations [Protocol and Liaison Service], Permanent Missions to the United Nations, New York [NY], United Nations, 306, June 2016, ST/PLS/SER.A/306)

---

[3]International Atomic Energy Agency

[4]UN Office on Drugs and Crime, Organization of Petroleum Exporting Countries, Organization for Security and Cooperation in Europe.

[5]Organization for Economic Cooperation and Development, International Organization of La Francophonie, United Nations Educational, Scientific and Cultural Organization.

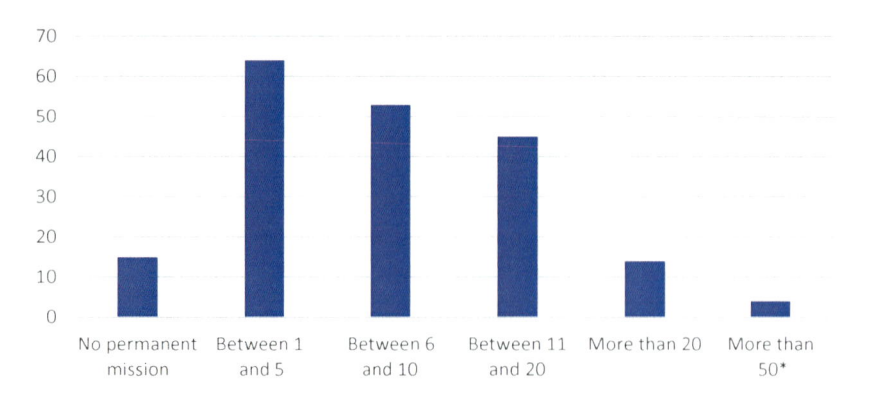

Fig. 3.2 UN Multilateral Diplomacy Personnel in Geneva (*United States, Russia, China, Japan; *Source* UN Office in Geneva, *Missions permanentes auprès des Nations unies à Genève*, Geneva, 115, 2017, ST/GENEVA/SER.A/115 available at www.unog.ch/bluebook [visited April 16, 2018])

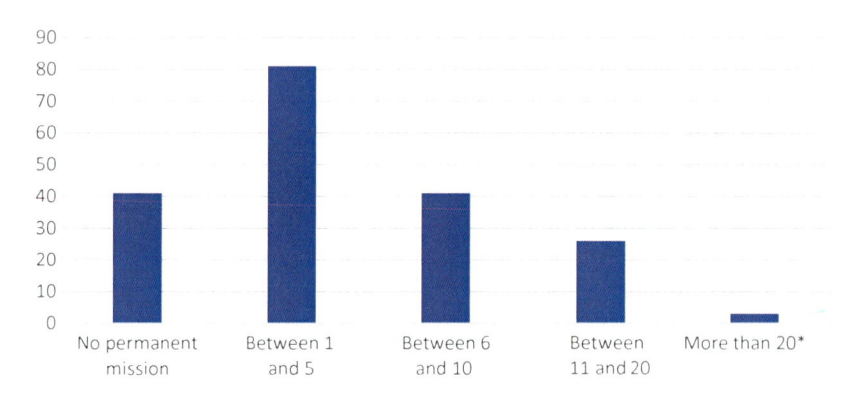

Fig. 3.3 UN Multilateral Diplomacy Personnel in Vienna (*United States, Russia, Austria; *Source* United Nations Office in Vienna, Permanent Missions to the United Nations [Vienna], Information Services for member states, Bluebook www.unodc.org [visited May 4, 2017])

format, they have also revived the old practice of itinerant ambassadors (ad hoc or at large), now entrusted with thematic mandates (women's rights, religious freedom, fighting climate change, counter-terrorism, war crimes, etc.).

Thirdly, states have also had to attend to the rise of international civil service, a corollary of that of international organizations. The first administrative unions set up in the second half of the nineteenth-century employed national civil servants assigned by the appropriate technical ministries of the main member states. With the creation of the LN in 1919, international organizations adopted an international civil service that was neutral, impartial, and independent from member states and acted in the organization's interests (see the oath of loyalty established by the LN in 1932 or article 100 of the UN Charter). Whether regional or global in composition, international organizations all use equitable geographical distribution criteria that are based on member states' financial contributions and are designed to ensure the diversity and representative nature of international administrations.

The highest postings in international civil service are coveted, involving tacit transactions by states eager to place their citizens in strategic positions, convinced that they will be better informed about goings-on within the organization, that their interests will be better defended and that they will wield more influence. Thus, the IMF has always been run by Europeans since its creation in 1944, whereas management of the World Bank is systematically reserved for Americans. The main foreign affairs ministries have alternately created structures designed to optimize their citizens' candidacy within international civil service and to facilitate career tracking (e.g., the *Mission des fonctionnaires international* created in 1995 by the French Ministry of Foreign Affairs). In addition, the institutionalization of gender quotas (genderization or gender mainstreaming) since the 1990s has contributed to the feminization of diplomatic personnel from countries often a long way from gender parity.

Increasing numbers of non-state actors (NGOs, firms, interest groups, lobbies, etc.) are contributing to multilateral diplomacy among States by directly or indirectly participating in official delegations, international negotiations, meetings before or after preparing international texts, and by organizing summits parallel to major international conferences (see Chapter 13 by Auriane Guilbaud, "Diplomacy by Non-State Actors"). Moreover, the increasing technicization of multilateral negotiations requires the participation of state or non-state experts in all phases of the process alongside diplomats and at times in their place. Their designation takes various forms, linking them more or less to states, depending on whether they were appointed by them or chosen in a private capacity (see

Chapter 10 by Cédric Groulier and Simon Tordjman, "Intergovernmental Organizations").

The Omnipresence of Multilateral Negotiations in International Relations

Multilateral diplomacy is based on a negotiating practice akin to the process of "managing complexity" (Zartman 2012). For this reason, multilateral negotiations are often long. It took eight years of negotiations to conclude the GATT Uruguay Round (1994), and eight years to reach a post-Kyoto climate agreement (2015), nine years to negotiate the UN convention on the law of the sea (1982), and seventeen years to draw up the Chemical Weapons Convention (1993). Certain negotiations get bogged down. The Doha Development Round, started in 2001 and meant to be concluded in 2005, still has not led to any general agreements after fifteen years of negotiations at the WTO. Negotiations may also fail spectacularly, such as the Copenhagen climate conference in 2009 or the WTO conference in Seattle in 1999.

A common explanation for the complexity of multilateral negotiations consists in highlighting the number of states involved. A process like climate negotiations, where 195 states try to reach an agreement on regulating global warming, is obviously complex. It is interesting to note that, since its origins, multilateral diplomacy has mobilized a great many actors. The issue of their numbers is thus not in itself a disqualifying factor in concluding a multilateral agreement. Another explanation often advanced about the sometimes inextricable nature of multilateral negotiations is their "sensitivity," multidimensionality, and technicity. At the WTO, for example, member states negotiate dozens of tariff, regulatory, and financial issues impacting all economic sectors (agriculture, industry, services, etc.). However, one could argue that past negotiations on the consequences of major wars dealt with issues (territorial ones notably) no less sensitive than current multilateral negotiations.

What makes contemporary multilateral diplomacy more complex is above all its spirit and rules, which have changed with regard to past situations where a few victorious powers imposed a peace accord on all the other states present. In fact, the unique feature of multilateralism developed after 1945 is that, while continuing to maintain special rights for the major powers (permanent membership and veto rights on the Security Council for the five victorious powers in 1945), it conveys basic standards such as equal rights among sovereign states (established by article 2 of the UN Charter), inclusivity of international organizations, reciprocity, collegiality of decision-making, and a spirit of compromise.

Consequently, the use of coercive power and hegemony is less accepted today. In multilateral negotiations, all states are heedful of their rights being respected, starting with states from the South and "smaller states" that are the majority on the international stage (105 out of 193 UN member states have less than 10 million inhabitants). A vital illustration of this new "ethos" in multilateral diplomacy is the frequent recourse to consensus in approving final agreements, a practice that treats the sovereignty of each country with consideration, legitimizing collective decisions in an irrefutable manner, and often entails a truly "collective accomplishment" in negotiations (Pouliot 2017, 120).

Consensus is a required practice for the UN climate negotiations, for WTO negotiations, in the European Union (even if it also uses a qualified majority), as well as in NATO decision-making. Multilateral negotiations are very likely to be complex and difficult when many states strive to reach a multidimensional agreement by consensus.

To account for that complexity, the literature on international negotiations has produced many model calculations inspired by game theories. These theories distinguish between "distributive" negotiations (where negotiators have a fixed amount of profits to share) and "integrative" negotiations (where, on the contrary, they provide the means to increase the potential for collective profits). These theories also highlight the advantages of sequential negotiating strategies: breaking down multisectoral negotiations into sectorial negotiations, developing compromises sector by sector, and then bargaining between those sectorial compromises to reach a package deal corresponding to the "focal point" of the negotiations where the various parties' preferences are combined (Schelling 1986).

Sociological studies of multilateral diplomacy are full of less rationalizing lessons. The salient feature is that multilateral negotiations are relational configurations in which "one agrees to gain less to gain together" and that, against this background, uncertainty is a great constraint on actors' strategies: "Inaction is unwise and action perilous, such that a defensive posture often seems the most appropriate" (Devin 2013, 87).

Secondly, formal equality among states in negotiations seems to be combined with the inevitable asymmetry among major powers and smaller states. Provided that the major powers driving negotiations agree on a common strategy, which is not always the case (witness the divisions at the WTO between the United States, Europe, India, Brazil, and China), the major powers usually provide the impetus in negotiations. However, that role is played less through coercion and pressure than through the use of soft leadership mindful of the interests of others (in particular of the smaller states), capable of convincing the greatest number of the potential for collective profit and of elaborating collective compromises acceptable to all. In this kind of process, developing shared perceptions of solutions to be adopted is often more important than the game of mutual concessions (Winham 1977).

Thirdly, few multilateral negotiations manage to avoid coalition building. These coalitions are sometimes longstanding at the UN (the G77 now includes over 130 states from the South) and multiply during certain negotiations such as the WTO (eight alliances and seventeen coalitions identified in recent years), and climate negotiations ("alliance of small island states," "Bolivarian alliance," etc.). In principle, coalition building among likeminded states, which come together through an affinity of interests or due to regional proximity, is a logical and potentially positive phenomenon. In fact, since coalitions have the effect of homogenizing their members' preferences, the emergence of coalitions can facilitate global negotiations, which then become transactions between major coalitions. The European Union works as a constructive coalition when speaking with one voice in trade or climate negotiations, following a process of internal harmonization among member states. But some coalitions may be defensive or obstructionist, acting as veto players (e.g., the G20 within the WTO created in 2003 in reaction to American and European proposals on agriculture), and many other coalitions are "monothematic" interest groups that have little to offer in global negotiations (groups of countries created around the export of the same product in the WTO, for example). It is thus difficult to say if the phenomenon of coalition-building facilitates the outcome of multilateral negotiations.

Lastly, international organizations improve the efficiency of multilateral negotiations in several respects: by providing an institutional framework for them, by requiring equal rights for all states meeting and negotiating, by decreeing a set of explicit decision-making rules for their use, and by drawing on instruments of international law (agreements, resolutions, treaties) to ensure the respect of the commitments agreed to by the states. The institutionalist theory of international organizations (Keohane 1989) has copiously documented this added value in international organizations. The drawback, however, since with the law the devil is in the details, is that the legal formalization of negotiated agreements adds more complexity to the task of multilateral diplomats.

* * *

As soon as modern states established diplomatic relations, they were confronted on a regular basis with situations of collective peace to be rebuilt via multilateral diplomacy, as illustrated by the founding episode of the Treaty of Westphalia in 1648. Over the next three centuries, states pursued multilateral diplomacy at regular intervals (at major peace conferences), while transforming the practice by globalizing dialogue beyond Europe, institutionalizing it via international organizations, and opening it up increasingly to non-military issues and non-state actors. At the same time, this centrality of multilateral diplomacy forced states to turn their diplomatic operations into permanent modes of representation within international organizations and into negotiating frameworks and procedures that were both vast and codified. Finally, in multilateral diplomacy, states learned about the complexity of negotiations in large numbers that bring together diverse issues and actors. Although momentarily undermined by the Trump administration's disengagement from the UN and major multilateral initiatives from the Obama era (Paris climate accord, Iran nuclear agreement in 2015), multilateral diplomacy has a bright future ahead of it. In the context of increasingly advanced globalization, neither isolationist nations nor world governance—highly abstract for now—are capable of taking up the great challenges of global interdependence in its place.

References

Devin, Guillaume, "Paroles de diplomates: comment les négociations multilatérales changent la diplomatie," in Franck Petiteville, Delphine Placidi-Frot (eds.), *Négociations internationales*, Paris, Presses de Sciences Po, 2013, pp. 77–104.
Keohane, Robert, *International Institutions and State Power*, Boulder (CO), Westview, 1989.
Pouliot, Vincent, *L'Ordre hiérarchique international*, Paris, Presses de Sciences Po, 2017.
Schelling, Thomas C., *Stratégie du conflit*, Paris, Presses universitaires de France, 1986.
Winham, Gilbert, "Negotiation as a Management Process," *World Politics*, 30 (1), 1977: 86–113.
Zartman, William I., "La multilatéralité internationale: essai de modélisation," *Négociations*, 17 (1), 2012: 37–50.

CHAPTER 4

Paradiplomacy

Stéphane Paquin

The neologism "paradiplomacy" appeared in scientific literature in the 1980s, during a revival in the study of federalism and comparative politics. It was basically used to describe the international activities of Canadian provinces and American states in the context of globalization and an increase in cross-border relations in North America (Paquin 2004).

The concept's inventor, Panayotis Soldatos, defined paradiplomacy as "a direct continuation, and to varying degrees, from sub-state government, foreign activities" (Soldatos 1990, 34). Ivo D. Duchacek also espoused the concept, finding it superior to his idea of microdiplomacy, to which a pejorative meaning could be attributed. For Duchacek, adding "para" before "diplomacy" adequately expressed what was involved, namely a sub-state's international policies that could be parallel, coordinated, or complementary to the central government's, but could also conflict with the country's international policies and politics (Duchacek 1990, 32).

S. Paquin (✉)
École nationale d'administration publique (ENAP), Montréal, Canada
e-mail: Stephane.paquin@enap.ca

© The Author(s) 2020
T. Balzacq et al. (eds.), *Global Diplomacy*,
The Sciences Po Series in International Relations and Political Economy, https://doi.org/10.1007/978-3-030-28786-3_4

Although the concept of paradiplomacy tends to be the most widely used, it nonetheless remains contested by several authors. Some prefer to use the expression "regional sub-state diplomacy" (Criekemans 2011) while others favor multi-track diplomacy or "multi-level diplomacy" (Hocking 1993). In France, the expression "decentralized cooperation" is sometimes used.

This article is divided into four parts. In the first part, I present the debate around the concept of paradiplomacy. In the second section, I address the issue of the phenomenon's magnitude in the world. In the third part, I examine how foreign policy skills are formed and shared, and in the last section, I strive to describe what kinds of international actors represent non-central governments in world politics.

THE CONCEPT OF PARADIPLOMACY

According to Brian Hocking, the concept of paradiplomacy was created to reinforce the distinction between the central government and sub-national governments, thereby increasing aspects of conflict between the two levels of government. For Hocking, however, that approach is incorrect. It would be preferable to situate sub-national or non-central governments in their "diplomatic complex environment" (Hocking 1993).

In Hocking's view, diplomacy cannot be seen as a segmented process between actors within the same state structure. Diplomacy must be perceived as a system intermingling actors from different levels of government and ministries. Actors change according to issues, interests, and their ability to operate in a multi-tiered political environment. Hocking's rejection of the concept of paradiplomacy is based on "imperatives of cooperation" that exist between central governments and federated states. Thus, rather than talking about paradiplomacy, it would be preferable to refer to it as "catalytic diplomacy" or "multi-level diplomacy" (Hocking 1993). A similar argument is put forward by authors interested in multilevel governance, notably in the context of the European Union. The concept strives to describe the role of Europe's regions in the process of European construction (Hooghe and Marks 2001).

These concepts are interesting and useful in particular contexts, but they remain limited as they tend to underestimate the autonomy of regions, non-central governments, or federated states in pursuing their own international policies. Bavaria, for instance, is not active solely in Europe. It is deeply involved in activities within the conference of heads of government in partner regions. This group includes seven regions of sub-state governments (Bavaria, the Western Cape, Georgia, Upper Austria, Quebec, São Paulo, and Shandong) on four continents; they represent around 180 million inhabitants with a total gross domestic product of 2000 billion euros and are working toward economic and sustainable development. The conference of heads of government also strives to create a network that will enable them to deal with the international challenges regions are facing on the international level.

The concept of paradiplomacy should also be distinguished from that of "protodiplomacy" and of "identity paradiplomacy" (Paquin 2002, 2005). Protodiplomacy refers to international strategies designed to promote diplomatic recognition as a way of preparing the establishment of a sovereign country. It is by definition a transitional phase. The concept could define the Catalan government's strategy in 2017 or that of the government of Quebec before the 1995 referendum on sovereignty-partnership.

The concept of identity paradiplomacy occurs on another level. It represents the international policies of a nation without a sovereign state, such as Quebec, Scotland, Flanders, Wallonia, or Catalonia, when the governments of those nations are not seeking independence (Paquin 2002, 2005; Paquin et al. 2015). Thus, one of the fundamental goals of these nations is to work internationally to further the strengthening or building of their nation within a multinational country. The identity entrepreneurs' objectives are to promote exports, attract investments, seek resources they lack domestically, and try to gain recognition as a nation in the global arena, a crucial process in any attempt at nation-building. This situation tends to be highly conflictual if the central government is hostile to the "other nation's" identity-based demands, such as with Catalonia and the Basque region in Spain or with Quebec in Canada.

The concept of identity paradiplomacy is useful in explaining why the Quebec government, for instance, has adopted different international policies from other Canadian provinces. There is a strong identity-driven element in the Quebec government's international policies. The government's goal, whether run by federalists or sovereignists, is to reinforce the French language, to support the development of Francophonie, as well as to gain recognition from foreign governments that it forms the "nation" of Quebec. The Quebec government's bilateral relations with the French government are greater than those between Canada and France and perhaps between Canada and Great Britain. Former Prime Minister of Quebec Jean

Charest met French President Nicolas Sarkozy more often than any other head of state, with the exception of the German Chancellor Angela Merkel.

Furthermore, a distinction should be made between "networks of government representatives" and paradiplomacy. According to Anne-Marie Slaughter, networks of government representatives are governmental or paragovernmental actors who exchange information and coordinate their activities in order to manage shared problems on a global scale (Slaughter 2004, 2). Among these actors are financial regulators, police investigators, judges, legislators, and central bank directors, for example. These international governmental networks are a key feature of the current world order according to Slaughter and are increasingly concerned with areas of jurisdiction on all levels of governments. When the Canadian and American police forces coordinate their activities to prevent terrorist attacks, for instance, it involves networks of government representatives rather than bilateral paradiplomacy.

In the case of paradiplomacy, an actor—for example, a ministry—is formally mandated by a federated state or sub-state government to defend the state's interests and promote them in the international arena. The ministry represents the government as a whole and speaks on its behalf. For example, the empowering legislation for the Quebec government's Ministry of International Relations and la Francophonie entrusts the ministry with the task of establishing and maintaining relations with foreign governments as well as with international organizations. The ministry must safeguard Quebec's interests in international negotiations and oversee the negotiations and implementation of "agreements" and international treaties. It attends to the implementation of Quebec's international policies and handles its 32 representation abroad.

Magnitude of the Phenomenon

A marginal phenomenon in the 1960s and 1970s, paradiplomacy was not only in evidence in North American federated states. It also developed in Europe and elsewhere around the world and even became widespread within unitary states or ones with decentralized or devolved governments such as France, Great Britain, and Spain. It was also increasingly present at the municipal level, notably in global cities like London, New York, Paris, and Shanghai.

Nowadays, the paradiplomatic phenomenon is large, intensive, extensive, and permanent despite the sizeable decline after the 2008 crisis.

The actors of paradiplomacy, protodiplomacy, and identity paradiplomacy have a considerable degree of autonomy, numerous resources, and increasing influence in international politics (Paquin 2004; Aldecoa and Keating 1999; Tavares 2016).

Quebec already had offices in Paris and London in the nineteenth century, despite the fact that very few cases of federated states have been identified as active in the international arena before the 1960s. Since then, things have evolved quickly, to the point where the phenomenon has become quite ordinary. In the United States, for instance, only four states had foreign offices in 1980, compared to 42 with 245 representatives in around 30 countries in 2008. Due to the recession, that number went down to 212 in 2015. In comparison, the American federal government has 267 embassies and consulates around the world (Fry 2017). Germany's Länder have created around 130 political representations around the world since the 1970s, including over twenty in the United States. In Spain, Catalonia has 4 delegations (France, Belgium, Great Britain, Germany) as well as 34 trade bureaus, 4 cultural and linguistic representatives, 9 overseas development offices, 10 tourism centers, and 5 cultural industries representatives. In 2019, the Quebec government had 32 political representations in 18 countries, including the Quebec General Delegation in Paris whose status is akin to that of an embassy. Flanders has had 100 economic offices since 2004 although its activities mainly concern export and investment issues. Wallonie-Brussels international is the institution with the greatest number of trade offices per capita in the world. The phenomenon is also present in more centralized countries. In France, for instance, the Rhône-Alpes region and its partner Entreprise Rhône-Alpes International have several economic representations abroad. The same phenomenon can be observed in Japan, India, Australia, Austria, Switzerland, Brazil, and several other countries (Paquin 2004; Aldecoa and Keating 1999; Criekemans 2011).

The international policies of federated states are an important phenomenon involving all international spheres of action, including economic and trade policies, promoting exports, attracting foreign investments and decision-making centers, science and technology, energy, the environment, education, immigration, and the movement of people, bilateral and multilateral relations, international development, and human rights, which are the major paradiplomatic issues. Paradiplomatic actors are also taking an increasing interest in non-traditional security issues such as terrorism, respecting human rights, cybersecurity, pandemics, and public health (Paquin 2004; Lequesne and Paquin 2017).

Some examples of non-central governments participating in various international arenas are: the creation by the governments of California, Quebec, and Ontario of the second largest international carbon market in the world after the European Union; the presence of Australian states in the Australian government's delegation at a UN conference on development and the environment; the presence of representatives from Texas at meetings of OPEC member countries, whereas the United States is not a member of the organization; Jordi Pujol's one-on-one discussions with all the G7 heads of state (with the exception of Canada) while he was President of Catalonia; and the Mexican state of San Luis Potosí's activities to facilitate money transfers sent by immigrants in the United States (Lequesne and Paquin 2017).

Regarding security issues, one may observe: Baden-Württemberg's participation in peacekeeping missions in Bangladesh, Russia, Bosnia-Herzegovina, Burundi, and Tanzania; the sanctions imposed by the state of Maryland against South Africa in 1985, or the 1996 Massachusetts Burma Law, since invalidated by the US Supreme Court, forbidding public contracts for companies working in Myanmar (Burma); the pressure exerted on the state of Victoria, Australia, to cancel contracts with French companies to protest against the nuclear tests carried out by France in the South Pacific in 1995; national guard officers from American states participating in international military exchange programs, etc. (Paquin 2004).

Constitutions and Non-Central Governments

Non-central governments hold asymmetrical powers in matters of international politics, which has a considerable effect on their ability to act. That asymmetry exists between countries as well as between regions within them. As a rule, the more decentralized a country, the more non-central governments have constitutional responsibilities that increase their ability to act in the international arena. The more expertise a non-central government has, the more financial resources and a large civil service (Paquin 2004; Michelmann 2009; Criekemans 2011).

In unitary states like Denmark or Israel, non-central governments have very little autonomy. In unitary states with a more decentralized structure like France, or in devolved states like the UK, or quasi-federal ones like Spain, non-central governments have more autonomy, despite the central state's powers remaining dominant (Table 4.1).

Table 4.1 Typology of various political regimes in relation to the autonomy of non-central governments

Unitary States	Decentralized and Devolved States	Federal States
Denmark	France	Belgium
Finland	Netherlands	Canada
Greece	Portugal	Germany
Ireland	Great Britain	United States
Sweden	Spain	Australia
Israel	Italy	India

Source Author

In federal countries, sovereignty is constitutionally divided between a central government and federated states, such as with Australian and American states, German Länder, Canadian provinces, and Belgium's regions and communities. To be designated a federal government, a central government cannot unilaterally modify the constitution to its advantage. In such countries, federated states hold a very high number of responsibilities. In Canada, provinces are responsible for issues of health, education, work, culture, and municipal policies. They are also partly responsible for issues relating to economic development, environmental protection, and even justice.

India and Malaysia have constitutions that explicitly assign exclusive competence in international relations to the central state. But in several other federal countries, such as Canada, Australia, and Belgium, many specialists have highlighted the difficulty for central governments to negotiate and implement international agreements when the latter involve areas of federal jurisdiction (Twomey 2009). In Australia and Canada, the courts have ruled that the central government could negotiate agreements on all subjects, including those pertaining to federal jurisdiction in domestic law, but did not have the power to force states to implement them, which can create major problems with regard to respecting those countries' international commitments. Other constitutions, including those of Australia, Germany, Switzerland, and Belgium, grant explicit powers to regional governments in matters of international relations. The Swiss, German, and Belgian constitutions even grant states the power to sign actual treaties by virtue of international law (Michelmann 2009, 6–7).

The Belgian constitution goes even further. Since 1993, Belgium has been a federation that allows states to become true international actors. The division of powers in matters of international relations follows the division of jurisdiction by virtue of the constitutional principle: *in foro interno, in foro externo*, which can be translated as an international extension of domestic jurisdiction. According to that constitution, there are three kinds of treaties in Belgium: (1) treaties within federal jurisdiction; (2) treaties within the individual states' authority; and (3) combined treaties involving two levels of government that require cooperation between the two in being negotiated and implemented. Furthermore, there is no hierarchy between levels of government, meaning that in reality a Belgian ambassador is not superior in rank to a Flemish diplomat (Paquin 2010).

What Kind of International Actors?

What kind of international actors are non-central governments? Their status is halfway between that of a sovereign country and a non-governmental organization (NGO). Their status is ambiguous due to being both sovereignty-bound and sovereignty-free, as James Rosenau has stated (1990).

Since non-central governments are sovereignty-free, they are not recognized actors in international law. Apart from certain exceptions provided for in the domestic laws of countries such as Belgium, these governments cannot formally sign real international treaties as defined by international law. Nor can they have real embassies or consulates.

That said, their status as sovereignty-free actors, thus not formally recognized by international law, does not take away their entire ability to act. Their means of action are more on the level of NGOs. Indeed, non-central governments send fact-finding and outreach missions abroad, take part in trade fairs and certain international forums such as the Davos World Economic Forum, and finance public relations campaigns to increase exports and attract investments. The Canadian province of Alberta was very active in Brussels during negotiations on the EU-Canada Comprehensive Economic and Trade Agreement in order to make sure that oil from tar sands would not be subject to sanctions by the European Union. Alberta was also highly active in Washington to pressure American officials to approve the Keystone XL pipeline project.

It is also easier for non-central governments to adopt idealistic international positions, and they have greater latitude to take a strong stance on delicate topics. For example, they can more easily condemn the non-respect of human rights. Countries, on the other hand, must take a more nuanced tone and a more diplomatic approach in order to take into account a number of political and economic factors. Sub-state governments can also defend their interests in foreign courts. The government of Ontario brought the issue of acid rain directly to American judges, as did British Columbia on the subject of the "salmon war" pitting Canada against the United States.

Non-central governments are also sovereignty-bound actors, in that they have partial sovereignty over their territory. Several non-central governments have a minister in charge of international relations and a corresponding ministry. Furthermore, the range of tools available to federated states for international action is nearly as great as for sovereign countries, with the exception of the use of military force. Indeed, several non-central governments have organized official visits with other regional leaders or those from sovereign countries, such as the alternating visits of the prime ministers of France and Quebec. They have representation or "mini-embassies" abroad, establish bilateral and multilateral relations with sovereign countries and other federated states, create institutions for regional or transregional cooperation, and can sign international agreements. In this regard, the government of Quebec has signed 751 of them, including 385 still in effect. Over 80% of these agreements have been signed with sovereign countries. In certain cases, such as the Belgian federated states, it involves actual international treaties (Paquin 2010).

Their localization within a sovereign state gives federated states access to decision-makers from the central government, including actors in the country's foreign policy. Sharing sovereignty with a central government gives non-central governments a reason to establish an international presence and develop their means of influence. Thus, contrary to NGOs and multinationals, for instance, the government of a federated state may enjoy special access to international diplomatic networks if the central government agrees, and may take part in international negotiations within their country's delegation (Paquin 2004; Lequesne and Paquin 2017).

The phenomenon is growing. Since the end of the Second World War, there has been an increase in multilateralism and international negotiations. While in the late nineteenth century only one or two conferences or congresses involving official representatives were documented, today there are around 9000. The register of UN treaties provides access to about 250,000 treaties.[1] Multilateralism and international negotiations have therefore become an indissociable component of globalization (Paquin 2013).

Parallel to the above, there has been a substantial increase in federal governments around the world. Within the European Union, for example, only two countries had federal governments after the Second World War whereas today 19 of the 27 countries in the EU have experienced a significant increase in regional governments and several have real federal governments. The Forum of Federations estimates that 40% of the world's population live in federal countries (Lequesne and Paquin 2017).

The consequence of these two phenomena has been that all fields of government activity, even in federated states and municipalities, may enter into the jurisdiction of at least one intergovernmental organization and often of several (Paquin 2010; Lequesne and Paquin 2017). Thus, in the framework of international organizations and thematic conferences, topics are addressed regarding the environment, free trade, procurement contracts, education, public health, cultural diversity, corporate subsidies, treatment of investors, the removal of non-tariff barriers, agriculture, services, etc. In this context, federated states are increasingly aware that their political power or sovereignty—in other words, their ability to develop and implement policies—is the subject of negotiations within multilateral international forums.

Since international negotiations are having a growing effect on federated states' sovereignty, the latter have become crucial actors in negotiations. In the negotiations on climate change, for instance, the UN formally recognized the importance of such actors. According to the UN Development Programme: "[...] most investments to reduce GHG (Greenhouse gas) emissions and adapt to climate change – 50 to 80 percent for reductions and up to 100 percent for adaptation – must take place at the sub-national level".[2] Furthermore, at the 16th Conference of the Parties, UN Framework Convention on Climate Change in Cancún in December 2010, the importance of the role of non-central governments was stipulated in article 7 of the Cancún Agreements. During his speech to the delegates, the Canadian representative, John Baird, explicitly recognized the role of Canadian

---

[1] From the following website: https://treaties.un.org/Pages/Overview.aspx?path=overview/overview/page1_en.xml (visited June 19, 2018).

[2] Sabban Michèle, "Réchauffement climatique: les régions veulent avancer," *Le Monde*, December 29, 2009.

provinces, notably Quebec, on the issue of climate change (Chaloux et al. 2015).

In terms of trade negotiations, the same trend can be observed. The provinces played a greater role during Canada's trade negotiations with the European Union, the largest since the Canada-US Free Trade Agreement in the late 1990s. The European Union demanded that the Canadian government include the provinces in its delegation, with the aim of starting negotiations for a "new generation" free trade agreement. The main reason being that the issue of public procurement contracts in Canadian provinces and cities was of special interest to the European Union in the negotiations.

In that context, the European Union deemed that, for the negotiations to succeed, they had to include representatives from the provinces at the negotiating table, since the latter are not required to implement agreements signed by the federal government in their areas of jurisdiction (Paquin 2013).

There are many precedents in which representatives have taken part in meetings of international institutions—the European Union, the United Nations, the World Trade Organization, the World Health Organization and Unesco, or again at the Conference of the Parties, UN Framework Convention on Climate Change—both within a country's delegation, and at times outside it, as with Quebec, New Brunswick, and the Wallonie-Brussels federation regarding la Francophonie.

When central governments block non-central governments' access to international negotiations, the latter may try to influence the negotiations by going on-site. To make its voice heard, the government of Quebec sent several representatives to the conference of the parties on climate change despite the objection of Stephen Harper's climate-skeptic government. Another strategy consists in joining networks of non-central governments and creating an accredited NGO at the negotiations, which is entrusted with the mandate of defending the interests of those actors at the negotiations. This was the case for the NGO Network of Regional Governments for Sustainable Development, which represents the regions' interests in climate change negotiations.

* * *

The paradiplomatic phenomenon, although not generally spectacular, certainly represents an important change in the study of foreign policy and international politics. It is an extensive, intensive, and permanent phenomenon. The international interests of sub-national governments are highly varied and substantial. These governments have considerable leeway and resources in their international initiatives, despite the asymmetry. In short, the phenomenon can no longer be ignored, even in centralized countries such as France or Sweden.

Although paradiplomacy has progressed a great deal in the last thirty years, and case studies are increasingly numerous, there are still several blind spots. There are few studies on paradiplomacy and security issues analyzed in the broad sense, for example. Moreover, few studies exist on non-central governments and international negotiations, in particular on negotiations and the implementation of international treaties.

References

Aldecoa, Francisco, Keating, Michael (eds.), *Paradiplomacy in Action: The Foreign Relations of Subnational Governments*, London, Frank Cass Publishers, 1999.

Chaloux, Annie, Paquin, Stéphane, Séguin, Hugo, "Federalism and Climate Change Negotiations: The Role of Québec," *International Negotiations*, 15 (1), 2015: 291–318.

Criekemans, David (ed.), *Regional Sub-State Diplomacy Today*, Leiden and Boston, Brill, 2011.

Duchacek, Ivo D., "Perforated Sovereignties: Towards a Typology of New Actors in International Relations," in Hans J. Michelmann, Panayotis Soldatos (eds.), *Federalism and International Relations: The Role of Subnational Units*, Oxford, Oxford University Press, 1990, pp. 1–33.

Fry, Earl H., "The Role of US State Governments in International Relations and International Negotiations (1980–2016)," *International Negotiation*, 22 (1), 2017.

Hocking, Brian, *Localizing Foreign Policy: Non-Central Governments and Multi-layered Diplomacy*, New York (NY), Palgrave Macmillan, 1993.

Hooghe, Liesbet, Marks, Gary, *Multi-level Governance and European Integration*, Lanham (MD), Rowman & Littlefield, 2001.

Lequesne, Christian, Paquin, Stéphane (eds.), "Federalism and International Negotiation," *International Negotiation* (Special Issue), 2 (22), 2017.

Michelmann, Hans (ed.), *Foreign Relations in Federal Countries*, Montreal, McGill University Press, 2009.

Paquin, Stéphane, "Paradiplomatie identitaire en Catalogne et les relations Barcelone-Madrid," *Études internationales*, XXXIII (1), 2002: 57–98.

———, *Paradiplomatie et relations internationales. Théorie des stratégies internationales des régions face la mondialisation*, Brussels, PIE/Peter Lang, 2004.

———, "La paradiplomatie identitaire: le Québec, la Flandre et la Catalogne en relations internationales," *Politique et sociétés*, 23 (3), 2005: 176–194.

———, "Federalism and Compliance with International Agreements: Belgium and Canada Compared," *The Hague Journal of Diplomacy*, 5, 2010: 173–197.

———, "Federalism and the Governance of International Trade Negotiations in Canada. Comparing CUSFTA with CETA," *International Journal*, 68 (4), 2013: 545–552.

Paquin, Stéphane, Kravagna, Marine, Reuchamps, Min, "Paradiplomacy and International Treaty Making: Quebec and Wallonia Compared," in Min Reuchamps (ed.), *Minority Nations in Multinational Federations: A Comparative Study of Quebec and Wallonia*, London, Routledge, 2015, pp. 160–180.

Rosenau, James, *Turbulence in World Politics: A Theory of Change and Continuity*, Princeton (NJ), Princeton University Press, 1990.

Slaughter, Anne-Marie, *A New World Order*, Princeton (NJ), Princeton University Press, 2004.

Soldatos, Panayotis, "An Explanatory Framework for the Study of Federated States as Foreign-Policy Actors," in Hans J. Michelmann, Panayotis Soldatos (eds.), *Federalism and International Relations: The Role of Subnational Units*, Oxford, Oxford Press, 1990, pp. 34–38.

Tavares, Rodrigo, *Paradiplomacy: Cities and States as Global Players*, Oxford, Oxford University Press, 2016.

Twomey, Anne, "Commonwealth of Australia," in Hans Michelmann (ed.), *Foreign Relations in Federal Countries*, Montréal, McGill University Press, 2009.

CHAPTER 5

Club and Group Diplomacy

Christian Lechervy

The United Nations Organization recognizes 197 states. However, within that assembly, in other words the G197, discussion and partnership groups have been built over time. They have been structured around geographical, thematic, functional or more ideological foundations. These restricted groups striving to orient decisions effectively have led to the establishment of specialized subregional institutions in the international arena as well as more informal focus and advocacy groups.

SOME REASONS FOR WORKING IN SMALLER INFORMAL GROUPS

Small-sized intergovernmental gatherings may have a large number of members. This is true for the G77, launched in 1964. The coalition, conceived to promote the economic and political interests of developing countries, now has 132 members. Defining goals, shared positions and synergistic modes of action in such a diverse community is not always easy.

C. Lechervy (✉)
French Embassy, Yangon, Myanmar
e-mail: christian.lechervy@diplomatie.gouv.fr

© The Author(s) 2020
T. Balzacq et al. (eds.), *Global Diplomacy*,
The Sciences Po Series in International Relations and Political Economy, https://doi.org/10.1007/978-3-030-28786-3_5

In the interest of efficiency, states are inclined to complement their participation in macro-organizations with a modus operandi that draws on a smaller number of actors. Thus in 1971, within the G77, it was decided to set up a G24 so that developing countries could be better heard at the International Monetary Fund (IMF). Establishing diplomatic tools that bring together a small number of countries does not in the least signify limited ambitions, as attested since 2005 by the G4 connecting Germany, Brazil, India, and Japan, with the aim of enabling each of them to achieve permanent member status on the UN Security Council. While interstate groupings may have one goal to reach, they can be multi-functional.

Establishing informal discussion groups to support global or subregional governance is above all a diplomatic working method, not an end in itself. It strives to reinforce relationships of trust among states, and even more among heads of state and government, as well as ministers and senior government officials. It is an intergovernmental means to wield political influence in international arenas and a choice negotiating tool for finding a way out of the most complex crises.

While states regularly use methods of engagement combining formal and informal procedures, they may expand beyond the political-administrative world strictly speaking. Advocacy groups incorporating statesmen and stateswomen, intellectuals and businessmen on a regular basis have positioned themselves in the international arena to change public opinion, reorient diplomacy conducted within international organizations and in the framework of bilateral relations. They have played a critical role in defining new international legal standards and contributed to conflict resolution.

Sustainable Praxis

Over the decades, ad hoc formats have multiplied, and circles initiated have tended to last, while their mandates have become broader and the number of associated countries increased. Known as associations, circles, clubs, coalitions, councils, forums, groups, meetings or summits of leaders, informal political cooperation mechanisms have been created and used by small developing states and emerging powers, as well as by major established powers. They have all employed them, making multilateral diplomatic maneuvering particularly complex, and at times difficult to decipher. The same subject could be broached simultaneously in several forums, while all may not be transparent about their conclusions or synergies among actors.

The creation of ad hoc discussion groups does not require bringing together heads of state and government, legally formalizing them and identifying the praxis at every hierarchical level, from ministers to senior officials. In every region of the world and in all international bodies, diplomats feel the need to gather in small groups and have informal discussions to carry out their mission in the most effective manner possible. That desire can be felt even in the most eminent international forum: the UN Security Council. Its five permanents members decided to form an unusual subset: the P5 (5 permanents), with informal meetings and its own operating rules.

At the end of the Cold War, China, the United States, France, Russia, and the United Kingdom became accustomed to meeting at their delegation headquarters to work more closely together. This involved outlining solutions to problems connected to peace and security, or more selfishly to defend their interests as—especially nuclear—powers. This diplomatic work on a smaller scale in New York required the adoption of unwritten working rules (e.g., rotating presidency every three months, ambassadorial-level meetings at the delegations' request). These mechanisms have facilitated the convergence of views on major international affairs in the utmost confidentiality. They are initiated case by case, giving a great deal of latitude to heads of diplomatic missions and to the quality of interpersonal relations.

In 2006, the P5 format—with the addition of Germany—was chosen by capitals seeking a lasting solution to the Iranian military's nuclear designs. The P5 + 1, also called E3 + 3, gave the European states (Germany, France, the United Kingdom) and senior European Union representatives for foreign policy and shared security an eminent international position. It is true that Europeans have long worked in small groups, within the framework of the UN and other international bodies, and on their own continent. The Franco-German couple has been the engine of European construction since the Élysée Treaty (1963). For over fifty years it has had no bilateral substitute, nor on a broader community scale. To be sure, there have been eurozone summits with 19 members since 2012, and mini-summits for three (Germany, France, Italy—2016—or four with Spain—2017), but broader political consultations have never developed a purpose or work pattern in the long term, with two exceptions.

One example is the Weimar Triangle, at first the preferred arena for supporting German-Polish reconciliation inspired by the Franco-German experience, then to endorse and prepare Poland's membership in the European Union (EU). Starting in 1991, that ad hoc format fulfilled historical expectations linked to German reunification. However, the Triangle changed profoundly after Warsaw joined the EU in 2004, with the primary aim of establishing close cooperation among the governments of the three countries on European issues. And yet it was not a new triumvirate on Europe, even if some east of the Oder-Neisse line hoped for or feared it.

In anticipation of joining the Union, Hungary, Poland, and Czechoslovakia formed the Visegrad Triangle in 1991. Having become the V4 after the partition between the Czech Republic and Slovakia, this informal political entity gained sufficient recognition to hold its own Weimar-Visegrad Summit in Warsaw on March 2013, a first in European defense. Contrary to other European endeavors at dialogue, these informal mechanisms for triangular and quadrangular consultation have not generated permanent administrative mechanisms with a secretariat and corresponding budget since their creation (cf. Council of the Baltic Sea States—CBSS, 1992–, Union for the Mediterranean—UFM, 2008). The club logic has been sufficient in itself. It remains to be seen if that fragmentation of political cooperation weakens or strengthens European institutions and the Union's positions in wider forums.

Meeting Informally to Reflect and Act with Complete Confidentiality

Working habits have been developed between trusted partners among Western states. Informal exchanges between senior officials from the four major powers in Western Europe in the Quint group (the Big Four: Germany, France, Italy, the United Kingdom, and the United States) have become common. Due to European construction, this configuration has led increasingly to including a senior representative for foreign affairs and security policy, or one of his/her collaborators, a practice that strives to avoid broadening the platforms involved to the 28 EU member states. This laudable practical concern is nonetheless discriminatory. Neither have collective security arenas avoided a form of governance that is restricted, and non-explicit in their founding rules. At the North Atlantic Treaty Organization (NATO), informal exchanges in Quad format (quadrilateral defence coordination group) between the United States, France, the United Kingdom, and Germany have been commonplace since the Berlin crisis in 1959. These discussions carry a great deal of weight at key moments in the life of international organizations. They may be particularly hard for non-members as they define compromises that tend to preempt decisions by legitimate decision-making bodies. Furthermore, under the same denomination, narrower formats can have diverse geographical significations. Thus, in the Pacific, the Quad format refers to the reinforced cooperation between Australia, the United States, France, and New Zealand, but also between Australia, the United States, India, and Japan regarding the Indo-Pacific area.

Defense areas have been conducive to working in narrower groups, notably because classified information is exchanged there. This is the case for cooperation in the intelligence field (e.g., the Five Eyes alliance linking intelligence communities in the United States, Australia, the United Kingdom, Canada, and New Zealand since the Second World War), in the fight against terrorism (G5 Sahel, 2014) and in monitoring exports of sensitive equipment to block the spread of technological advances to certain categories of third countries (cf. during the Cold War, monitoring of Warsaw Pact countries was conducted through COCOM, the Coordinating Committee for Multilateral Export Controls—after the fall of the Berlin Wall it was replaced in 1996 by the Wassenaar Arrangement; the Nuclear Suppliers Group—1974). These clubs are founded on strategic trust and highly confidential information sharing. They may nonetheless vary according to circumstances and political vagaries.

The dissolution of the Warsaw Pact showed that political-military alliances are by no means long-lasting. Crises have suddenly appeared in the most long-lived Western institutions, creating lasting damage to such cooperation. This was the case from 1986 to 2012 between the United States and New Zealand within the Australia, New Zealand, United States Security Treaty (ANZUS) after Auckland blocked weapons systems carrying nuclear or nuclear-powered arms into New Zealand's territorial waters.

While recourse to small trusted groups helps in developing and carrying out diplomatic initiatives, international crises may also be resolved through such arrangements. The nucleus may be limited to a few state actors in a privileged position who decide to combine their efforts. Discussions are held in a one-track format between professional diplomats and/or officially mandated persons. France and Indonesia focused their resources in this way from 1987 to 1991 to reach an end to the third Indochinese War. Stakeholders in mediation may be more numerous and more directly involved. Since June 2014, the configuration of the negotiating group seeking a solution to the clashes in Eastern Ukraine has hinged on the so-called Normandie arrangement, as Germany, France, Russia, and Ukraine began their discussions at the Château de Bénouville in conjunction with the 70th anniversary of D-Day on June 6. In this paradigm, Iran, Russia, and Turkey sponsored the Astana talks on Syria in 2017, but the state "hosting" the negotiating process may have a minor role compared to the guarantor powers for the agreement who are covertly conducting proxy wars. In any event, the issue remains the involvement of sub-state actors, and even rebels, in negotiations. That is why it may be decided to be under the auspices of several international organizations. This was the choice opted for in international discussions on security and stability in Transcaucasia, conducted in Geneva since 2006 under the supervision of the UN, the Organization for Security and Cooperation in Europe (OSCE) and the European Union. Another possible procedure is to organize peace talks around a prestigious, trustworthy mediator who is totally foreign to the crisis (cf. the former Finnish Prime Minister Martii Ahtisaari on Aceh—2005). This so-called one track and a half diplomacy has led some to believe that private conflict resolution centers (e.g., the Carter Center, the Community of Sant'Egidio) could play an increasing role in future, and even stand in for traditional diplomacy.

As crises become protracted, although negotiating groups may not alter their intergovernmental composition, they still must adapt to evolutions in leadership in the countries that constitute them. This is particularly true when brokering drags on, such as in the case of the Minsk Group. Since 1992, American, French, and Russian diplomats co-chairing the group have succeeded one another, depending on changes in administrations. Meanwhile, tensions in Nagorno-Karabakh have remained high between Armenia and Azerbaijan. The mediation group may be mandated by and report to an international organization, as is the case here with the OSCE. The quality of diplomatic reports to the supervising body is crucial. Working in small groups is often frustrating for third-party states, who feel not only that they should be more closely involved in the talks, but also that they have political grounds for joining the small group since their interests are at stake.

The Small Group as an Expression of Power

Obstructing groups, especially within international organizations, contributes to the prestige and influence of the states constituting them, to the detriment of all others. This is why self-mandated ad hoc groups emerge. In the case of armed conflicts, in order to act and try to achieve their goals, they must benefit from the good offices—and even support—of the stakeholders, as in the six-party talks following North Korea's decision to withdraw from the Non-Proliferation Treaty. Although Pyongyang and Seoul sit at the same table, the talks engaged since 2003 by North Korea, China, Russia, South Korea, Japan, and the United States are still redolent of the block mind-set prescribed during the Cold War. A final agreement was always so far away that successive phases of negotiations only involved second-tier diplomats. Yet holding a summit confronting heads of state and protagonists in the conflict is not a guarantee of success, as attested by the meeting between Armenian President Serge Sargsian and Azerbaijan President Ilham Aliyev in Bern in December 2015. Only a small number of states take that risk, due to the uncertain prospects for success of mediations and the complexity of the peace process.

Due to its international status, France has been the repository and mediator for numerous peace negotiations that have brought into play its diplomats and their savoir-faire, as well as venues that are both prestigious and liable to be out of the public eye. Since the mid-1960s, Paris has helped find solutions for American involvement in Vietnam (1969–1973), defining the terms for the end of the Third Indochina War (Fère-en-Tardenois—1987–, Saint-Germain-en-Laye—1988–, La Celle-Saint-Cloud—1989), outlining a lasting solution for Kosovo (1999) with the contact group (the United States, Germany, France, Italy, the United Kingdom, and Russia), and launched talks on Afghanistan's political and institutional future through the so-called Chantilly Process (2011–2012). They were all secret negotiations which ended twice—in 1973 and 1991—in a series of peace agreements.

Negotiating clubs composed solely of members representing states are not the only appropriate means for outlining lasting solutions to conflicts. "Citizens' diplomacy" has emerged. The Roman Catholic community of San'Egidio has even made it their specialty. The agreement ending the civil war in Mozambique in October 1992 was their most resounding success. Failing lasting solutions, private actors focus on organizing closed conferences where states may present their views. Exercises in transparency aiming at deconfliction have been established so that no one misunderstands their opponents' intentions. The London think tank International Institute for Strategic Studies (IISS) attempts it publicly every year in Singapore (Shangri-la Dialogue), Bahrain (Manama Dialogue), and Colombia (Cartagena Dialogue), bringing together the main actors in defense, armed forces, intelligence, and experts in planetary strategic affairs.

These meetings closely associating officials and experts, often government financed, have brought to light this informal, so-called second track diplomacy where influential figures can express themselves more freely about current issues and meet year after year.

Informally, they contribute to conflict-prevention and post-crisis management. Talks are not the same as negotiations. They are not a substitute for face-to-face meetings between governments and their diplomats; but they provide a testing ground for new ideas, a place to get to know one another and even to build consensus. In order to maintain a certain confidentiality at the dialogues in these clubs, they meet according to rules established by Chatham House, headquarters of the British Royal Institute of International Affairs, where participants in meetings are free to use the data gathered. However, they must not mention the identity or affiliation of the persons behind the information obtained, or reveal the identity of the other participants.

Discussion clubs on international affairs are nothing new. They deal not only with matters of defense, even if the Cold War did fuel many of the debates. These discussions by invitation only, bringing together a limited number of eminent figures from diplomacy, academia, business, and the media, have often aroused suspicions about the occult governance of world affairs. The Bilderberg Circle (1954), the Club of Rome (1968), the Trilateral Commission (1973), blending public and private actors in favor of globalized free-market exchange, are typical examples. Another object of public anger was the Tricontinental (1966) which tried to bring together and be the spokesperson for anti-imperialist forces and 82 delegations of decolonized countries, Afro-Asian liberation movements, and Latin American guerilla groups.

Informal discussion groups have proliferated since the end of the Cold War. They are the result of alliances between think tanks, as attested by the Daimler Forum's semi-annual meetings on global affairs connecting the Brookings Institution (Washington), the Centre for European Reform (London) and the Stiftung Wissenschaft und Politik (Berlin). Exchanges are not always conducted behind closed doors. Furthermore, public forums are no less influential, as proven by the success of the Munich Security Conferences (1963), the World Economic Forums at Davos (1971), the Brussels Forums (2005), and the World Policy Conferences (2008).

Although Westerners initiated this kind of international exchange, they do not have a monopoly on it. The People's Republic of China created the Boao Forum for Asia (2001) in view of its becoming a crucial venue for wielding influence. Russia has strived to do likewise with the Saint-Petersburg International Economic Forum (1997) and the Valdai Discussion Club (2004), with the distinctive feature since its creation of aiming to discuss the Federation's development and Russia's role in the world. These costly recurring forums and their complex and prestigious invitations have required the support of private sponsors and even the help of special organizers. Even so, diplomacy has not been privatized.

Adaptable Partnerships

These clubs never had a numerus clausus when created, even if their members agreed on certain criteria for admission. The group that brought together the world's main economic actors was the epitome of this, seeing its numbers increase and contract.

The Group of Seven, more commonly known by its acronym G7, started out as the informal G5 in 1974. Established following spiraling oil prices, its representatives—from the United States, Germany, France, the United Kingdom, and Japan—met in Washington. The Library Group became the G6 in 1975 adding Italy, then the G7 in 1977 when the European Union joined in. Lastly, it was named the G8 in 1997 when Russia became a formal member of the club. Since 1994, the Federation had been on the fringes, translated in diplomatic language by the name G7 + 1 or P8 (Policy 8). In 2014, the seven founding members refused not only to hold the G8 summit in Sochi, but also chose to meet once again without Russia, bringing back a de facto G7. An adaptation that was easy to bring about since the G7 was authorized without any legally binding text, had no budget nor any administrative structure in its own right. While history explains its scope, it could not be legitimate for all actors in the international arena, a fortiori in organizing global political and economic governance. For this reason the question of substituting a broader, more "representative" format was raised on a regular basis.

In 1989, a quickly assembled G15 of seventeen countries met to counterbalance the G8 and demand a fairer economic order. The succession of financial crises in the 1990s led to a concrete outcome to this question with the creation of the G20 (1999). However, even though the group of nineteen countries plus the European Union represent 85% of world trade, two-thirds of the world's population and over 90% of gross world product, other ad hoc formats were evoked, notably to make the G7/G8 a G12 by adding Brazil, China, India, and Nigeria without changing its mode of organization and continuing to rely on a loosely structured system with an annually rotating presidency.

With regard to the UN's G197, because the larger states were inclined to substitute smaller groups to organize world economic and even political affairs, and to take their own concerns for those of the whole planet, Singapore took the initiative in 2009 of forming a global governance group (3G). It was a way to give thirty countries not associated with the G20 a chance to be heard as a collective on issues they deem vital. With this same paradigm, a few years earlier Singapore developed the Forum of Small States (FOSS, 1992) to use the influence of its 107 UN members.

In a world where all states speak to each other, enjoy formal diplomatic relations, meet in a multiplicity of arenas, no state wants to be excluded on principle from global governance and its decisive moments. Everyone speaks to everyone else. This has given rise to multiple clubs within global organizations and alongside them. It has also led to a stratification of circles, including the least formal. In addition to full members, there are now partners in dialogues, associates, candidate members, and observers. This hierarchical inventiveness has broadened the legitimacy of structures of exchange and their international aura.

Over the years, leaders' clubs have proliferated, as have leaders' retreats without collaborators. This is the rule for summits involving heads of state and government at the Asia-Pacific Economic Cooperation (APEC) founded in 1989, and for the Asia-Europe Meeting (ASEM) held every two years since 1996. The seemingly relaxed style of these diplomatic moments with no witnesses, and often vague agendas, nevertheless involves precise preparatory work for meetings of ministers, notably of foreign affairs, themselves preceded by meetings of senior officials (SOM), as attested by the successive communiqués published at the end of the process and after difficult negotiations.

An exclusive mind-set has also emerged among subregional leaders, particularly in discussing development policies. In the Pacific, this has occurred through the Pacific Islands Forum (PIF, 1971). At times the intention has been to refuse to recognize a regional identity for certain states—for example, Australia and New Zealand in the framework of the Pacific Island Development Forum (PIDF, 2013)—or to validate cultural areas such as in Micronesia, Polynesia (Micronesia Islands Forum—MIF, 2017—and Polynesian Leaders Group, PLG, 2011) and Melanesia, although the Spearhead Group (MSG, 1988) set up a secretariat in Port-Vila and established a founding charter. In all three cases, representatives of UN member states converse, define cooperative actions and join together to express themselves with heads of the executive body for non-sovereign local governments (Chuuk, Kosrae, Pohnpei, Yap, Guam, Northern Marianas, New Caledonia, French Polynesia, Wallis, and Futuna Islands) or with political groups (e.g., the FLNKS, the Caledonian pro-independence party, is also an observer member of the Non-Aligned Movement). Sub-national-state chief executives have been all the more closely associated due to the informality of key moments at these forums. Mechanisms for multiple political consultations have also been developed along with these grassroots policies. In Southeast Asia, several more restricted clubs have emerged alongside ASEAN regionalism. Every three years since 2002, Burmese, Cambodian, Chinese, Laotian, Thai, and Vietnamese leaders from the Mekong region (GMS) meet to discuss agriculture, energy, urban development, trade facilitation, tourism, and transportation. Groups may combine heads of state and government on a macro-regional scale (e.g., East Asia Summit—EAS, 2005), be established according to a biregional framework (Asia Cooperation Dialogue—ACD, 2002), or limit themselves to regular exchanges among foreign affairs ministers (e.g., Mekong-Ganga Cooperation—MGC, 2000–, Forum for East Asian-Latin America Cooperation—Fealac, 1999).

Geographical multivectorialization of dialogues among leaders has become a more notably visible phenomenon among emerging powers (e.g., South Africa, Brazil, China, India, Japan, Turkey). Major emerging powers have set up regular meetings in the "1 + X" format, like the Association of Southeast Asian Nations (ASEAN) which initiated the ASEAN + 1 and Asean + 3 dialogues with China, Korea, and Japan.

In 2010, Brazil held the first summit with countries from the Economic Community of West African States. India held summits with African leaders (IAFAS, 2008) as well as with Pacific Island nations (FIPIC, 2014). Japan did the same with Africa (TICAD, 1993), Oceania (PALM, 1997), and Central Asia (2004). To its meetings in Africa (Forum on China-Africa Cooperation—Focac), China added Oceania (2014), Latin America (China-Community of Latin America and Caribbean States Forum—Celac—CCF, 2014), and Central and Eastern European countries ("16 + 1," 2012). Its "Belt and Road Initiative" (BRI, 2017) brought together leaders from 57 countries in Beijing to strengthen ties around this huge Chinese infrastructure development project for a "New silk road" on land and sea launched in 2013 by President Xi Jinping. The feeling of belonging to this new club was reinforced by including countries in the projects with the aim of connecting China to Europe, the Middle East, and Africa, but also its main financial instrument: the Asian Infrastructure Investment Bank (AIIB).

The multivectorialization of diplomatic exchanges is all the more useful in that dialogues among "major powers" (cf. the three-way China, Korea, Japan summit) are hard to organize and rarely productive. While political obstacles can be stumbling blocks to interstate dialogue, leaders' busy schedules pose even more burdensome constraints. Some meetings are therefore held back-to-back with broader forums. This was the case for the Southwest Pacific Dialogue (SWPD, 2002). Australia, Indonesia, New Zealand, Papua-New-Guinea, the Philippines, and East Timor are also now holding parallel meetings during the UN General Assembly and the ASEAN Regional Forum (ARF).

Creating Informal Groups for Greater Influence

Spheres of influence promoted by a state for its strategic interests must still espouse a narrative explaining that they were constituted in the political, economic, and social interests of all members. This is not strictly speaking a new challenge. All former colonial powers have had to deal with it in order to maintain privileged arenas of exchange and cooperation with territories once subjects but now independent. "France-Africa" summits since 1973 are in keeping with this narrative—all the more so since being renamed "Africa-France" summits in 2010. The same was true for the triennial "France-Oceania" summits started by President Jacques Chirac in 2003.

Spain, in establishing the Ibero-American summits of heads of state and government (1991), and Portugal, with its Community of Portuguese Language Countries (CPLP, 1996), have copied this same approach. Groups of leaders not only have a shared language and history, but are also striving to define themselves as a community of values in interest groups and joint ventures, especially economic ones. Groups have experienced successive enlargements to include new members, feeling more or less obliged to use adaptable selection criteria. Thus, Senegal (2008), Georgia, Japan, and Turkey (2014), then Hungary, Slovakia, the Czech Republic, and Uruguay (2016) became CPLP observer countries.

Due to their political dynamics, "linguistic" clubs have continued to grow, offering assembled states the chance to belong simultaneously to several groups. Most Portuguese-speaking countries in Africa are members of the Organisation international de la francophonie (OIF). The Republic of Mauritius, a model of successful multiple integration, is a member of the Commonwealth (1968), the OIF (1970), and the CPLP (2006). This organizational entryism shows how badly states want to broaden their partnerships, reaching the widest possible audience, for which they are willing to play on multiple identities. However, that willingness must be reciprocal. Thus, in any ad hoc arrangement, each one strives to have its share of international visibility.

For the Turkic Council, created in 2009 between Azerbaijan, Kazakhstan, Kirghizstan, and Turkey, the decision was made to set up its administrative center in Istanbul, its parliamentary assembly in Baku and its language academy in Astana. Through this geographically splintered system, each state could be symbolically rewarded and the intergovernmental organization created shown to be particularly respectful of the principles of the UN Charter, and perhaps associated in that respect with UN and global governance bodies.

A state's influence is built up over time. It is important therefore that leaders of the executive should know each other both today and in the future. Meetings, symposiums, and programs connected to transatlantic forums or regional clubs have been created to bring together promising young leaders (e.g., the annual meeting of AEYLS[1]—1997) and even transposed for target political populations such as women leaders (Global French-speaking Businesswomen Forum with the OIF, International Women's Forum—1982) and parliamentarians (the program at the Assemblée parlementaire de la francophonie on behalf of young French-speaking parliamentarians—2015—or the Commonwealth's annual program for young 18–29-year-old officials from the English-speaking institution's nine regions). Alumni networks are a complement to regular meetings. They strive to extend political contacts initiated, to expand the feeling of belonging to a select club and to give the actors chosen greater familiarity with international relations. These networking initiatives are also conducted through private actors close to official institutions. Historical gambles include the French American Foundation choosing for its exchange programs future French Presidents François Hollande and Emmanuel Macron, and their American counterpart Bill Clinton. The Ministry of Foreign Affairs contributes materially and financially to this

---

[1] Asia-Europe Young Leaders Symposium.

networking. To that end, the Quai d'Orsay created a program for future personalities in 1989. After twenty-five years of existence it has brought over 1700 people to France from 133 countries. It was an individualized political investment, an expression of soft power and of building a policy of elitist influence. France, the United States, Japan, and Hong Kong have created such tools and strive to maintain personalized relations to elucidate their country's evolution and international positions.

Creating advocacy groups is a way to promote exchanges, special ties with a host country, and more importantly to gain the upper hand and exert collective influence over other states or groups of states. Trade negotiations are particularly suited to such confrontations, at the risk of uniting countries for the occasion that are of different sizes and linked to several continents.

The Cairns Group (1986), a coalition composed of nineteen highly productive low-cost agriculture exporting countries, took on American and European trade barriers. However, through its maneuvering, it clashed with the Group of Ten generally made up of countries that are highly populated but rather small in size (South Korea, Israel, Japan, Switzerland), and with the G33 including poor countries seeking special treatment to protect their national production (Mongolia, Mozambique, Peru). The clustering of international relations was furthered by economic and trade issues, but could have been triggered by private actors.

In 2005, economists from the American investment bank Goldman Sachs invented the expression BRIC designating Brazil, Russia, India, and China as emerging markets. While the concept became a political reality at the first leaders' summit in 2009, then an expanding club when South Africa joined (BRICS, 2011), many other aggregation patterns of future economic powers remained statistical categories, or purely intellectual constructions (N11) that never materialized, even informally—BRIK (+ Korea), BRIMC (+ Mexico)—for want of the shared political will or any reason to act together. Nonetheless, since 2011 the creation of the BRICS group has shifted the dynamics in meetings of heads of state and government at the IBSA Dialogue Forum (India, Brazil, South Africa—2003) that wanted to be at the center of South-South cooperation and to be in a position to galvanize cooperation between Africa, South America, and Asia.

Building informal groups around one or more charismatic leaders may lead to occasional or ephemeral contacts among disparate states. The experience of the Bolivarian Alliance for the Peoples of Our America (ALBA, 2005) has shown that frameworks for protesting against globalization and its free-exchange areas have struggled to get organized despite finding a sympathetic ear here and there. The most lasting successes in informal arenas have been the result of defense or of promoting well-understood interests. They have given rise to informal processes for interagency consultation (Council of Regional Organizations in the Pacific—CROP, 1988) in order to keep political groups and institutions for technical cooperation from doing the same work. They have engendered instruments of global power (the Gold Pool from 1961 to 1968) and a proliferation of defense forums with the same vital interests.

The fight against global warming has resulted in a host of platforms with that purpose, as attested by the Alliance of Small Island States (AOSIS, 1990), Small Island Developing States (SIDS, 1992)—the two categories do not totally overlap—, or again the Coalition of Atoll Nations on Climate Change (CANCC, 2014), not to mention groups with a scope that is highly geographical (Coral Triangle Initiative—CTI, 2007), thematic (International Coral Reef Initiative—ICRI, 1994), or with a cooperative viewpoint (Global Alliance Against Climate Change—AMCC, 2007). The proliferation of forums for formal and informal dialogue has generated a lot of hard work before major international meetings. And it has enabled a certain specialization of arenas of exchange, spreading them to other continents, working "as a family" within like-minded groups with similar views and interests.

* * *

In future, new clubs and arenas for exchange will emerge because there is an infinite combination of circles of cooperation. Moreover, it is impossible to "disinvent" those already formed, to not resurrect others if necessary for tactical reasons and not think of forging new political combinations that are more or less sustainable and close. All countries fall into this case and prove to be inventive because their influence and the success of their diplomatic maneuvers depend on it. Circles of power are likely to be reduced to binary combinations, such as the emergence of a Sino-American G2 evoked by some forecasters, and to mechanisms with changing numerical values over time and in an enlarged "G197 X" combination.

CHAPTER 6

Communication and Diplomacy: Change and Continuity

Brian Hocking

The proposition that communication constitutes a defining feature of diplomacy (Jönsson and Martin 2003)—or as several analysts have suggested a particular modality of *institutionalised* or *regulated* communication (Constantinou 1996, 25; Pigman 2010; Bjola and Kornprobst 2018)—is well understood. It is not surprising, therefore, that changes in patterns of communication have been used as metaphors for the condition of diplomacy at specific periods. Terms such as "secret," "open" diplomacy, "public" diplomacy, "summit" diplomacy, and "track two" diplomacy each relate to modes of diplomatic communication and reflect developments in how, why, and where such communication occurs. In the era of digitalization, the "Web 2.0" metaphor is similarly applied to discussions of contemporary diplomacy. Hence, Van Langenhove employs it to describe the transformation from "closed" to "open" multilateralism, including the expanded range of stakeholders in diverse networks required to deal with increasingly multifaceted policy agendas (Van Langenhove 2010).

B. Hocking (✉)
Loughborough University, Loughborough, UK

© The Author(s) 2020
T. Balzacq et al. (eds.), *Global Diplomacy*,
The Sciences Po Series in International Relations and Political Economy, https://doi.org/10.1007/978-3-030-28786-3_6

But the identification of "new" forms of diplomacy has a long and often confused history. Labels such as "public" and "digital" diplomacy signal complex changes in which developments in communication technologies are just a part. Public diplomacy itself is adapting to changes in global and domestic environments as the direction of communication embraces both domestic and foreign publics (Pamment 2012; Huijgh 2016; Melissen 2018; Nye 2019; Bjola et al. 2019). Similarly, the utilization of social media both as a tool of diplomacy and a determinant of the broader diplomatic environment poses interpretative challenges as general dimensions of change in domestic and international policy environments sit alongside evolving communications technologies (Hocking and Melissen 2015). These complexities are underscored in an international environment in which disinformation strategies have assumed increasing importance (Nisbet and Kamenchuk 2019).

With this in mind, this chapter argues, firstly, that the "digitalisation" of diplomacy is one facet of broader developments in the global policy environment that condition the forms and role of diplomacy as a mode of communication. Appreciating the implications of digital technologies in this area requires us to understand the meanings concealed beneath the term digital diplomacy. Second, the discussion seeks to identify how these are influencing both diplomatic processes and the structures through which these processes are conducted. Here, it is argued that the realities underpinning the impact of digital technologies involve a mix of "online" and "offline" processes. Blending the two and deciding when and where digital resources are appropriate is one of the major challenges confronting practitioners of diplomacy in the twenty-first century. Finally, the discussion turns to the impact of digitalization on one of the key institutions of diplomacy: the ministry of foreign affairs (MFA) and the role of the professional diplomat.

Diplomacy in a Complex World

"Still alive in the room"—the words tweeted by François Zemeray, French ambassador to Denmark, as he was rushed out of a Copenhagen café where a terrorist attack was taking place in February 2015. For some, this symbolized a fundamental change in the character of diplomacy. Thus, a report in the *Wall Street Journal* concluded "Diplomacy is not dead, but new messaging tools like Twitter are threatening to upend a tradition of carefully worded statecraft and protocol" a view apparently shared by

Michael McFaul, a former US ambassador to Russia: "Diplomacy shouldn't be secret and Twitter helps us diplomats spread our message" (Kantchev 2015). Similarly Burson-Marsteller, the global public relations and communications firm promoting "Twiplomacy," share this view: "the time for niceties is over" suggests its annual report on the use of Twitter. However, the French embassy's guarded response to the Copenhagen incident, declining to comment on it and refusing requests to interview the ambassador, indicated that traditional patterns of diplomatic behavior based on cautious communication sit uneasily with those of openness and transparency associated with the digital age.

Such incidents and the responses to them demonstrate how, as with earlier transformations in communication technologies, the development of the Internet and the rise of social media platforms have been viewed by some as another instance of the "end of diplomacy" while for others it is becoming a key dimension of the contemporary diplomatic environment. For former Secretary of State John Kerry, "There's no such thing anymore as effective diplomacy that doesn't put a sophisticated use of technology at the center of all we're doing… The term digital diplomacy is redundant— it's just diplomacy period" (Kerry 2013).

Making sense of what is a rapidly changing and increasingly complex policy environment requires us to step back and relate the changes implicit in the attitudes cited above to the broader context in which they are occurring. As in earlier periods—for example that which saw the introduction of the electric telegraph in the nineteenth century—the implications of changes in communications technologies are hotly debated. Interpretations of the 2011 Arab Spring reflect differing views on the significance of the Internet between what have been termed "cyber-utopians"—promoting the view that social revolutions are the product of the digital revolution— and "cyber-realists." The latter, while not denying the importance of digital tools, argue that social change is the product of human agency, much of it occurring in offline environments.

From the perspective of diplomacy, the point here is that it is adapting to fundamental changes in society at various interrelated levels. Alongside the enhanced linkages between issues, actors and policy arenas that are central features of the diplomatic environment is the growth of transnational and transgovernmental networks transcending established geographical and issue boundaries. These are accompanied by the compression of time and space and the impact that this has on the ways in which people view their place in local and global environments. Here, the growth of populist nationalism as represented by the Trump Administration in the United States but evident in many locations worldwide adds to the challenges of interpreting and practicing diplomacy in the rapidly changing environment of the twenty-first century.

One result of these developments is a more complex communications environment which is reshaping diplomacy and the forms and structures through which it is required to operate. This reshaping has several key aspects:

- The *range, forms and direction* of diplomatic communication. The growing complexity of global agendas, the linkages between issues such as trade and the environment combines with the systemic features of international and domestic environments to make patterns of diplomatic communication more diverse, less structured, and hierarchical. Consequently, there is a growing emphasis on identifying stakeholders and creating and managing networks in which they can interact to achieve policy outcomes.
- The *objectives* of diplomatic communication. Increasingly, the ability to set rules has become a core feature of world politics. As van Ham writes: "the vast majority of rules, standards, and regulations that cover international society's *acquis communautaire* are set through non-hierarchical means of policy-making involving such postmodern processes as best practices, benchmarking, and naming-and-shaming" (van Ham 2010). Shaping agendas highlights the importance of knowledge and persuading other actors and agencies to adopt a government's preferred strategies by means of thought leadership. This is an increasingly important feature of diplomatic action which determines targets and methods of communication and is reflected in the growing preoccupation with soft power.
- *The nature of public and private domains.* Twenty-first-century diplomacy is confronting challenges clustered around traditional demands for secrecy—or confidentiality—set against the requirements of working in more open policy environments. Achieving preferred outcomes involves influencing attitudes among foreign and domestic publics by means of often loosely defined public diplomacy strategies. Establishing the boundaries between openness and confidentiality (challenged by a more open information environment and the WikiLeaks and Edward Snowden revelations) is a major issue for diplomatic actors at all levels.

Underpinning these changes in diplomatic communication is a shift away from diplomacy defined predominantly in traditional state-centered, hierarchical forms and principles toward what are variously termed "multistakeholder" or "network" models. Clearly, the modalities—including digital technologies—through which diplomacy is conducted are significant but are not of themselves the determinants of these broader patterns of change: the contexts in which communications and information technologies evolve have to be understood. As illustrated by the referendum on EU membership in Britain and the fraught European and domestic political negotiations that have followed in its wake together with the 2016 US presidential elections, the emergence of populism and "post-fact" politics is facilitated by, but not solely the product of, social media.

The changing character of diplomacy briefly summarized above reflects the limitations of governments in managing increasingly complex global agendas. While multi-governmental institutions remain key resources in the management of global issues, the more diverse membership and non-hierarchical qualities of public policy networks promote collaboration and learning and speed up the acquisition and processing of knowledge. Furthermore, decentralized networks face fewer transactional costs and barriers than centralized decision-making processes and are able to direct relevant information speedily to where it will have greatest effect.

The key differences between these and more traditional, state-centered forms of diplomacy lie in patterns of participation and communication. Hierarchical communication flows are replaced by multidirectional flows that are not always aimed directly at policy elites although the ultimate goal will often be to influence elite attitudes and policy choices. The challenge lies in identifying key nodes in policy arenas together with potential interlocutors located within them with a view to building relationships related to policy objectives. The significance of digital technologies is that they overlay and reinforce these trends in diplomacy. While Fergus Hanson, following the US State Department, helpfully defines the key focus of what he terms "eDiplomacy" as: "the use of the Internet and new information and communications technologies to help carry out diplomatic objectives" (Hanson 2012), digital diplomacy contains a number of elements which it is necessary to identify in making sense of complex developments.

Analyzing Digital Diplomacy

The first—and broadest—element relates to the changing foreign policy environment within which diplomacy functions. Partly, this reflects changing agendas and the ability to influence them as noted above. This phenomenon is accompanied, however, by the growing speed of events (how fast they develop) together with their velocity (speed *and* direction) and the implications of these for policy-makers (Seib 2012). This trend has long been part of globalization arguments but is reinforced by more fragmented flows of communications as new technologies—particularly mobile forms such as the smartphone—empower individuals and groups to shape rapidly unfolding events. The capacity of governments to deploy digital resources is a critical component of the digital environment as is their ability to control them through state intervention in access to the Internet and social media. Taken together, this perspective on digital diplomacy suggests diminishing control over events and agendas, the need to develop new skills and structures and adapting those already in use.

Related to changing foreign policy agendas, a second facet of the digital diplomacy environment focuses on cyber agendas. Here, such issues as cyber governance and Internet freedom have become key issues in global negotiations. Additionally, cybersecurity issues have become highly significant for all diplomatic actors, not least diplomats and foreign ministries. This is illustrated by reports in early 2011 that China had penetrated the UK Foreign and Commonwealth Office's internal communications systems and that a pirate Internet site replicating the official French Ministry of Foreign Affairs Web site was circulating bogus "official" announcements. Similarly, in 2015 the Danish Foreign Ministry was cyber-attacked through the installation (believed to have been supported by a government in the Middle East) of a remotely operated malicious program into a computer at a Danish embassy. Claims of Russian "interference" in the US presidential elections have only served to enhance growing concerns with cybersecurity.

A third dimension of the digital diplomacy debate focuses on the use of the Internet and related digital technologies for knowledge management. As with government generally, this recognizes the importance of using and managing data efficiently in an age of "big data" but has a particular significance for foreign ministries pressured to manage scarce resources more effectively. During the 1990s, the term "virtual diplomacy" came into common usage reflecting the growing demands placed on diplomatic services in the post-Cold War environment. Part of this changed environment (enhanced by the resource constraints created by the post-2007 global economic crisis) strengthened the quest for more cost-effective modes of diplomatic representation. One aspect of these changes is the development of secure e-mail. This not only strengthened the arguments of those questioning the relationship between headquarters and diplomatic posts—as two parts of the integral MFA network—it also began to alter traditional work procedures within the organization as a whole.

The fourth element in the digitalization debate relates to the usage of digital technologies to enhance the performance of the public service, improve service delivery, and reinforce participation in the shaping of policy. On one side, this reflects earlier debates on the "democratisation" of diplomacy which coincides with the growth of public diplomacy in the 1990s onward. On another level, the issue is one of utilizing new modes of communication to manage networks and to perform service functions more effectively, as in consular and crisis management (Melissen and Fernández 2011). This dimension of digital diplomacy recognizes the need to move beyond top-down or one-way information distribution models to interactive modes of communication facilitated by the use of social media platforms.

These four aspects of digital diplomacy are not discrete categories but are related features of an increasingly complex policy milieu transcending domestic and international policy environments. Consequently, we are confronted with varying possibilities regarding the condition of diplomacy in the twenty-first century: gradual change and adaptation within existing frameworks and principles versus a situation where diplomacy assumes fundamentally different forms challenging accepted notions of what diplomacy is—or should be.

In their book *The New Digital Age*, Eric Schmidt, Chairman of Google, and Jared Cohen, one of the architects of the "new statecraft" in Hillary Clinton's State Department tend toward the more radical position, arguing that the revolution in communications technologies means that governments will have to develop two general orientations—and two foreign policies—the online and the offline (Schmidt and Cohen 2013). However, the real challenge of digitalization for diplomacy is likely to be somewhat different. Rather than separate categories, the real test will be integrating these two dimensions of foreign policy. This requirement reinforces a growing *hybridity* in diplomacy as older, more traditional forms mingle with and are transformed by new forces whether these flow from changing societal pressures and/or rapid changes in communications technologies.

Hybridity is also reflected in the media environment. Preoccupation with new modalities of communication favors perceptions of the dominance of the new. However, the evolution of communications technologies rarely involves the supplanting of one form by another. Hence, the mass media of the twentieth century—both print and electronic—have not disappeared but have responded in various ways to digital technologies. The growing popularity and influence of talk radio shows in the United States is characterized by their interaction with social media, particularly Facebook and Twitter. The consequence is rapidly evolving "hybrid" media environments in which the relationship between the traditional print and electronic media are changing and the roles of "producer" and "consumer" of news and comment are redefined. This mix of hybrid diplomacy and a hybrid communications environment enhances the challenges confronting diplomats as the twenty-first century develops.

Diplomatic Processes in the Digital Age

There are two interconnected perspectives to discussions of diplomatic change and adaptation in the digital diplomacy debate: diplomatic *processes*, geared toward the functions of diplomacy, and diplomatic *structures*, such as foreign ministries at the national level and the range of multilateral organizations at regional and global levels. Analyzing the implications of changing modes of diplomatic for both aspects of diplomacy requires us to differentiate between issue areas and modes of diplomacy.

Rather than one overarching model of diplomatic interaction, several patterns co-exist. These range from diplomatic encounters marked by high levels of official input from government and/or intergovernmental organizations, through "shared" diplomatic arenas involving a range of state and non-state actors to situations where government input is low and processes less like traditional intergovernmental forms of diplomacy. Different models of diplomacy coalesce around different policy agendas involving varying actors and arenas—and, indeed, distinct communications characteristics. Consequently, developing a toolkit of digital resources is one challenge: Knowing how and where to employ them is quite another. This requires the ability to develop holistic strategies, construct, and manage diverse diplomatic spaces, persuade others outside one's own organization to work toward the accomplishment of shared goals, and to maximize knowledge capacity in producing relevant policy concepts, proposals and data capable of generating consensus for action.

Not only do these requirements vary between different policy areas but also in different phases in the diplomatic cycle. In this context, we can distinguish between three phases: agenda setting, negotiation, and implementation (Hochstetler 2013). In each of these, the patterns of diplomacy are varied and the impact and role of digitalization likely to be different. One proposition—following the assumption that the "opening up" of diplomacy is most developed at the first and third stages is that digitalization is likely to be less significant during the negotiation phase. Two points should be made here: first, that negotiations are increasingly dominated by the significance of implementation and its more complex forms; second that it depends on the context. Thus, negotiations that touch most directly on societies and group interests (such as environmental and human rights issues) are less likely to be conducted in what a former British foreign minister referred to as "the secret garden of diplomacy."

Taking the first and third of these diplomatic phases—agenda setting and implementation—the more general erosion of the separation of domestic and international policy arenas has hugely politicized diplomacy thereby opening up the possibilities for participation for civil society and even individual citizens to affect the processes of diplomacy. Digital tools have not created this situation but offer significant resources to those groups engaged in policy advocacy and a greater voice in the implementation—or non-implementation—of international agreements. This can be seen particularly clearly in trade diplomacy such as the negotiation of the Transatlantic Trade and Investment Partnership (TTIP).

The negotiations between the EU and the United States to create the world's largest free trade area quickly ran into significant opposition over one of its key features, the Investor-state dispute settlement provision (ISDS). Claims that this would conflict with governments' freedom to pursue policies in domestic domains such as health care, education, and environmental protection together with the secrecy surrounding the tribunals adjudicating on disputes between business and government generated considerable opposition to TTIP. NGOs such as Public Citizen tracked US multinationals' use of ISDS clauses in other trade agreements and developed a powerful alliance which through skilled use of digital and print media has been successful in generating public opposition to the agreement. In contrast, the EU, failed to develop an effective communications response through the most appropriate parts of the EU policy machine. Similarly, the negotiations on the Anti-Counterfeiting Trade Agreement confronted vociferous opposition over its potential impact on Internet freedom and what was seen as the closed nature of the negotiations. An EU Commission's vice-president recognized the failure of the EU to listen to the growing voices of opposition and to engage with them through social media: "We saw how our absence in the world of social media on this particular topic caused us a lot of troubles. I think this is a lesson for all of us that we have to be much more active and in a much more communicative mood when it comes to such sensitive topics in the future."[1]

If TTIP and ACTA provide examples where some diplomats have failed to grasp the significance of digitalization for diplomatic processes, the Prevention of Sexual Violence Initiative (PSVI) indicates their potential both in the agenda setting and negotiation processes. Concern with the use of rape as a tactic in warfare and terrorism has generated considerable concern but little action. In 2012 the then British Foreign Secretary, William Hague, alongside UNHCR special envoy Angelina Jolie, launched the PSVI, placing it on the 2013 G8 agenda, followed by a declaration adopted by the UN General Assembly and the 2014 Global Summit. Digital tools were key to the UK Foreign and Commonwealth Office's (FCO) PSVI campaign. Apart from awareness raising and acting as an information hub for the campaign, the FCO's digital team aimed to build a community of supporters and advocates through dedicated social media channels. According to the FCO's digital team, The End Sexual Violence in Conflict Facebook page attracted 10,000 followers worldwide with content reaching an estimated audience of 247,000 providing rolling updates for the NGOs, experts, and charities attending the summit as well as explaining and discussing the PSVI. The @end_svc Twitter channel generated some 9000 followers and was mentioned 47,000 times between March and June, reaching an audience of millions (Daniels and Childs 2014). Additionally, the aims of the Initiative were furthered through #DiploHack, a process whereby the skills and knowledge of diplomats and other stakeholders are combined in tackling issues. Both of these examples illustrate the potential of digital tools and the costs of failing to develop effective strategies for utilizing them.

Moving to the traditional foreign policy agenda, the experience of the Iran nuclear talks offers a different perspective on diplomacy in the digital age (Duncombe 2017). The pattern of the Lausanne phase of the P5+1 negotiations in March 2015 was marked by the usual practice of deadlines

---

[1] Quoted in Kurbalija, J. 'How Institutions Can Effectively Use Social Media?' Diplo blog 23 March 2012. http://www.diplomacy.edu/blog/how-institutions-can-effectively-use-social-media.

regularly missed, imminent departures, and last-minute "breakthroughs." The 600+ journalists accredited to the talks had limited access to the hotel where the negotiations were held. Digital technology made an appearance in the shape of secure videoconferencing between President Obama and the US negotiators.

Surprisingly, a key role was performed by a very traditional mode of communications technology: the mobile whiteboard. Under-secretary Wendy Sherman hit on the idea of the whiteboard as a means of illustrating what she called the "Rubik's cube" of complexity comprising the negotiations. The whiteboard was wheeled around the negotiating rooms as she and John Kerry met Iranian Foreign Minister Zarif and his team. This had an advantage for the Iranians as it avoided paper documents which had to be taken back to Tehran. But it also showed its dangers when a US negotiator inadvertently used a permanent marker to write down classified calculations.

While tweeting was a feature of the talks, a major role for social media was in "selling" the outcome of the negotiations to domestic audiences. The 2013 talks were also marked by Foreign Minister Zarif's embrace of social networks and the creation of a new Web site, Nuclearenergy.ir, aimed at explaining the history and motives of Iran's nuclear program. Zarif used social media platforms extensively on his return to Tehran—both to defend the deal at home and to "frame" it from an Iranian perspective for an international audience. As one observer noted: "Twitter diplomacy has helped President Rouhani maintain public support, bolstering his leadership image abroad. The contrast to his predecessor could not be starker" (Kabir 2013).

DIGITALIZATION: DIPLOMATIC STRUCTURES AND ROLES

Alongside their role in diplomatic processes, digital technologies are impacting on diplomatic institutions in the global, regional, and national arenas. Analyzing each of these is beyond the scope of this discussion and so we will focus on the implications of digitalization at the national level, particularly for the ministry of foreign affairs (MFA) and networks of diplomatic representation.

The problems of foreign policy management in a digital age reflect those confronting government as a whole. An accepted mantra of contemporary diplomacy is that it is increasingly a "whole of government" activity—or "full cast" diplomacy in the words of a former Japanese foreign minister. Managing an increasingly complex international policy environment thus emphasizes the linkages between the components of government, many of which would not be regarded as engaged in diplomacy as traditionally conceived. The result is that governments are reliant on more than the foreign ministry whose role is changing in the context of a broader "national diplomatic system" made of diverse bureaucratic actors (Hocking 2018).

One issue for the MFA therefore, as a subsystem within this broader national diplomatic system, is its relationship with other components of government and the impact that new communications technologies have on them (Manor 2016). Historically, the primary resource of the MFA has been its place as a dominant node in information networks that span international and domestic policy arenas. Here, digitalization is a two-edged sword. Claims that MFAs may have the role of information "gatekeeper" can no longer be taken seriously. At the same time, digitalization in the shape of access to big data, crowdsourcing ideas and the development of knowledge management tools can strengthen the MFA's significance. Furthermore, the current explosion of information and disinformation potentially enhances the value of the MFA's nodality in terms of its analytical capacity—that is using the skills of diplomacy to interpret data. In this light, it is not surprising that knowledge management was the earliest manifestation of digitalization in the US State Department (Hanson 2012, 30–38).

A key characteristic of the MFA as an integral diplomatic network is the distribution of roles between the "hub" of the system at home and its "peripheries" in the form of overseas diplomatic missions. This comprises one of the features of MFA's knowledge "nodality": It gathers and transmits information, and processes and employs it for goal attainment. Digitalization touches on this in two ways: (a) It can provide an added resource for both levels of the system; (b) it can help to change the relationships between the two parts of the subsystem and their roles within it. Digital technologies have had an impact on both dimensions. Significantly, they have also strengthened the linkage between them. The adoption of secure e-mail systems in the 1990s, for example, has been seen as providing an opportunity to redistribute policy-making functions from the center to the periphery, and to change established hierarchical patterns of information distribution. Consequently, the flow of information can become less a "hub and spoke" and more a network-like system in which the relationships between center and peripheries are becoming closer and more complex.

Associated with this are the organizational resources available to MFAs in an era of growing scarcity. Again, this is not new. The concept of "virtual" diplomacy in the 1990s was bound up with the call for expanded representation, resulting in greater demands on post-Cold War era diplomatic networks. Technology provided part of the answer as MFAs experimented with new means of establishing presence in more economical forms than the traditional embassy. Later developments in ICT have more profound implications as the purpose and forms of representation in maintaining diplomatic presence are questioned.

In the world of digital diplomacy, information flows within national diplomatic systems and between MFAs become more complex. Embassies embed themselves through social media in networks linking embassies, their own MFAs and other parts of their government, as well as host MFAs. In the context of the "social network" of embassies in Israel, it has been argued that this is surprisingly limited with only eleven of the eighty-two embassies accredited to Israel with active Twitter accounts and a presence on Facebook. Nevertheless, it demonstrates the possibilities of social media in reinforcing the significance of diplomatic networks as knowledge nodes. Not only do embassies follow their own MFAs, they can create a social network of foreign embassies in a host country and follow its MFA:

> If the ministry is followed by other embassies it is able to effectively disseminate foreign policy messages to other countries. Moreover, if it follows foreign embassies' digital diplomacy channels, the local MFA can gather information regarding foreign policy initiatives of other countries. In the case of Israel, the Israeli MFA is located at the very heart of the local diplomatic social network... (Manor 2014)

There is however no one-size-fits all for communications strategies. An analysis of the deployment of social media by foreign diplomats based in London reveals that the character of media strategies is not technologically determined. Rather, they reflect the environment in which such media are used and the role of diplomats as agents in their local settings. Facebook, Twitter, and other digital tools may well be useful but outcomes are dependent on contexts and the behavior of diplomats as social agents (Archetti 2012).

Roles and Skills

Undoubtedly, digital technologies and social media platforms are transforming the ways in which diplomats perform their roles. The use of WhatsApp—described in one report as "tailor-made for modern diplomacy"—is a case in point (Borger et al. 2016). Regarded as a convenient, fast, and (relatively) secure means of communicating, particularly in multilateral diplomatic settings such as the EU and UN, WhatsApp is increasingly seen as an essential component of the modern diplomatic armory. At the same time, there is a potential downside to digital technologies. The use of videoconferencing has raised questions regarding trust in negotiations and research on the use of smartphones for texting during meetings suggests that multitasking negotiators are regarded as less professional and trustworthy (Krishnan et al. 2014).

Not surprisingly, the ways in which social media is used by individual diplomats vary significantly. Former US ambassador to Russia, Michael McFaul, is a case in point. McFaul (a Stanford academic) was rated among the "Twitterati 100" for 2013, using social media to engage in a "Twitter war" with the Russian MFA and to engage with the Russian public on both US foreign policy and his personal life. This appears to have changed somewhat following McFaul's' resignation and his replacement by a career diplomat, John Tefft. Unlike McFaul, Tefft had no personal Twitter or Facebook accounts, the embassy being represented on these social media platforms by standard organization accounts on Twitter and the US Embassy Moscow page on Facebook.

Part of the issue here is defining what is appropriate diplomatic behavior. Former US Ambassador to the UN, Samantha Power, an enthusiastic user of social media in the pursuit of humanitarian agendas, was accused of confusing her role as articulator of US policy in key areas such as the Syrian crisis with that of social media campaigner. By contrast, Gérard Araud, French Ambassador to Washington DC between 2014 and 2019, was praised for his skillful use of social media in gaining access to the US Administration based on a clear understanding and pursuit of French foreign policy objectives. At the same time, such active communications strategies pose problems. A fundamental one, highlighted by the growing emphasis on public diplomacy, relates to the principle that diplomats should not "interfere" in the domestic politics of their host states. Long before the gradual utilization of social media by diplomats, this principle looked increasingly untenable but the use of platforms such as Twitter (not least by President Trump) challenges one of the more traditional role perceptions applying to the diplomatic profession.

Digitalization and the broader developments of which it is part pose even deeper issues relating to perceptions and definitions of diplomatic roles and, indeed, the relative importance of the professional diplomat in a changing world. According to Tom Fletcher, former British ambassador to Lebanon and keen advocate of digital diplomacy, the use of new communications technologies has to be seen in the broader context of the place of diplomats within and outside government:

> Look, power is moving from these hierarchies, and jobs like mine are in a hierarchy…power is moving out to those networks…I can feel power draining through my fingers as an ambassador. I am working in a job where I represent governments and governments are becoming weaker compared to other sources of power, and within government diplomats are becoming weaker compared to other bits of government. (Fletcher 2016, 200)

Whether or not this image of declining significance of the diplomatic role is accepted, long before the appearance of "twiplomacy," role change had become a regular feature in descriptions of diplomats' activities. Thus, the image of the diplomat as entrepreneur/coordinator developing and managing complex patterns of relationships became a familiar one. This reflects changed communications and representation rationale for diplomats: Rather than gatekeepers guarding impermeable information environments, they assume an active role as "boundary spanners" in increasingly complex policy environments involving a growing diversity of actors (Hocking 2005). Terms such as "guerrilla diplomacy" (Copeland 2009) and "naked diplomacy" (Fletcher 2016) build on these ideas by identifying patterns of role adaptation in which the use of digital technologies is a key element.

Conclusion

If communication constitutes a defining feature of diplomacy, the characteristics of the contemporary communications environment present a blend of challenges and opportunities to those engaged in increasingly diffuse diplomatic processes. From simply accepting the significance of public diplomacy two decades ago, today the definition of publics and the directions and modes of influence in an era of disinformation and "fake news" are increasingly fragmented. Similarly, the rise of digital technologies poses challenges to both the practice of diplomacy and to analysts seeking to understand them. In part, this is because communications technologies are not usually in themselves the sole generators of change. Rather they interact with developments in the environment in which they exist. Thus, twenty-first-century diplomacy reflects the evolving character of the international system, patterns of global governance, and national communities and their systems of government in an age of growing populism. Seeking to equate what are complex forces with the rise of new technologies, however significant, is always likely to result in misleading conclusions. One of the most common questions directed toward the rise of digital diplomacy is whether it fundamentally alters the character of diplomatic process and the structures on which such processes rest. The answers to this are unclear. Some of the tasks of diplomacy—such as in meeting the demands imposed by the growing number of global crises—are aided by digital technologies. But even the most ardent adherents of social media within the diplomatic community argue that the fundamental goals of diplomacy remain and that the need for offline, face-to-face communication remains an essential component of negotiation. Rather than the triumph of online communications technologies over traditional offline modalities, the real challenge for practitioners of diplomacy is blending offline and online strategies in the ongoing quest to manage evermore demanding policy environments.

References

Archetti, Cristina, "The Impact of New Media on Diplomatic Practice: An Evolutionary Model of Change," *Hague Journal of Diplomacy*, 7 (2), 2012: 181–206.

Bjola, Corneliu, Jiang, Lu, "Social Media and Public Diplomacy: A Comparative Analysis of the Digital Diplomatic Strategies of the EU, US and Japan in China," in Corneliu Bjola, Marcus Holmes (eds.), *Digital Diplomacy: Theory and Practice*, London, Routledge, 2015.

Bjola, Corneliu, Holmes, Marcus, (eds.), *Digital Diplomacy: Theory and Practice*, London, Routledge, 2015.

Bjola, Corneliu, Kornprobst, Markus, *Understanding International Diplomacy: Theory, Practice and Ethics*, 2nd edn., London, Routledge, 2018.

Bjola, Corneliu, Cassidy, J., Manor, I., "Public Diplomacy in the Digital Age," *Hague Journal of Diplomacy*, 14 (1–2), 2019: 83–101.

Borger, Julian, Rankin, Jennifer, Lyons, Kate, "The Rise and Rise of International Diplomacy by WhatsApp," *The Guardian*, 4 November 2016, www.theguardian.com/technology/2016/nov/04/why-do-diplomats-use-this-alienwhatsapp-emoji-for-vladimir-putin, accessed 13 June 2018.

Constantinou, Costas M., *On the Way to Diplomacy*, Minneapolis (MN), University of Minnesota Press, 1996.

Copeland, Daryl, *Guerrilla Diplomacy: Rethinking International Relations*, Boulder (CO), Lynne Rienner, 2009.

Daniels, Alison, Childs, Rosie, "A Digital Campaign Like No Other: Supporting the Preventing Sexual Violence in Conflict Initiative," *Foreign and Commonwealth Office*, 2014.

Duncombe, Constance, "Twitter and Transformative Diplomacy: Social Media and Iran–US Relations," *International Affairs*, 93 (3), 2017: 545–562.

Fletcher, Tom, *Naked Diplomacy: Power and Statecraft in the Digital Age*, London, William Collins, 2016.

Gilboa, Eytan, "Digital Diplomacy," in Costas Constantinou, Pauline Kerr, Paul Sharp (eds.), *The SAGE Handbook of Diplomacy*, London, Sage, 2016.

Hanson, Fergus, "Baked in and Wired. eDiplomacy@State," in *Foreign Policy Paper Series*, Washington (DC), Brookings Institution, 2012, p. 30.

Hochstetler, Kathryn, "Civil Society," in Andrew F. Cooper, Jorge Heine, Ramesh Thakur (eds.), *The Oxford Handbook of Modern Diplomacy*, Oxford, Oxford University Press, 2013, pp. 176–191.

Hocking, Brian, "Gatekeepers and Boundary Spanners: Thinking About Foreign Ministries in the European Union," in Brian Hocking, David Spence (eds.), *Foreign Ministries in the European Union: Integrating Diplomats*, New York (NY), Palgrave Macmillan, 2005, pp. 1–17.

Hocking, Brian, "The Ministry of Foreign Affairs and the National Diplomatic System," in Pauline Kerr, Geoffrey Wiseman, *Diplomacy in a Globalizing World: Theories and Practices*, 2nd edn., New York, Oxford University Press, 2018, pp. 129–150.

Hocking, Brian, Melissen, Jan, *Diplomacy in the Digital Age*, The Hague, Clingendael Institute, 2015.

Hocking, Brian, Melissen, Jan, Riordan, Shaun, Sharp, Paul, "Integrative Diplomacy for the 21st Century," *China International Strategy Review*, 2013: 53–88.

Huijgh, Ellen, "Public Diplomacy," in Costas Constantinou, Pauline Kerr, Paul Sharp (eds.), *The SAGE Handbook of Diplomacy*, London, Sage, 2016.

Jönsson, Christer, Martin, Hall, "Communication: An Essential Aspect of Diplomacy," *International Perspectives*, 4 (2), 2003: 195–210.

Kabir, Arafat, "Twiplomacy and the Iran Nuclear Deal," *The Diplomat*, 11 December 2013.

Kantchev, Georgi, "Diplomats on Twitter: The Good, the Bad and the Ugly," *Wall Street Journal*, 24 February 2015.

Kerry, John, "Digital Diplomacy. Adapting Our Diplomatic Engagement," *DipNote*, 6 May 2013.

Krishnan, Aparna, Kurtzberg, Terri, Naquin, Charles, "The Curse of the Smartphone: Electronic Multitasking in Negotiations," *Negotiation Journal*, 30 (2), 2014: 191–208.

Kurbalija, Jovan, "The impact of the Internet on Diplomacy," in Pauline Kerr, Geoffrey Wiseman (eds.), *Diplomacy in a Globalizing World: Theories and Practice*, 2nd edn., New York, Oxford University Press, 2018, pp. 151–169.

Manor, Ilan, "The Social Network of Foreign Embassies in Israel," *Exploring Digital Diplomacy*, 30 July 2014.

Manor, Ilan, "Are We There Yet: Have MFAs Realized the Potential of Digital Diplomacy?" *Brill Research Perspectives in Diplomacy and Foreign Policy*, 1 (2), 2016: 1–110.

Melissen, Jan, "Public diplomacy," in Pauline Kerr, Geoffrey Wiseman (eds.), *Diplomacy in a Globalizing World: Theories and Practices*, 2nd edn., New York, Oxford University Press, 2018, pp. 199–218.

Melissen, Jan, Mar Fernández, Ana (eds.), *Consular Affairs and Diplomacy*, Leiden, Brill Nijhoff, 2011.

Nisbet, Erik C., Kamenchuk, Olga, "The Psychology of State-Sponsored Disinformation Campaigns and Implications for Public Diplomacy," *The Hague Journal of Diplomacy*, 14 (1–2), 2019: 65–82.

Nye, Joseph, "Soft Power and Public Diplomacy Revisited," *Hague Journal of Diplomacy*, 14 (1–2), 2019: 7–20.

Pamment, James, *New Public Diplomacy in the 21st Century: A Comparative Study of Policy and Practice*, New York, Routledge, 2012.

Pigman, Geoffrey Allen, *Contemporary Diplomacy: Representation and Communication in a Globalized World*, Cambridge, Polity Press, 2010.

Schmidt, Eric, Cohen, Jared, *The New Digital Age: Reshaping the Future of People, Nations and Business*, London, John Murray, 2013.

Seib, Philip, *Real-Time Diplomacy: Politics and Power in the Social Media Era*, New York (NY), Palgrave Macmillan, 2012.

van Ham, Peter, *Social Power in International Politics*, London, Routledge, 2010.

Van Langenhove, Luk, "The Transformation of Multilateralism: Mode 1.0 to Mode 2.0," *Global Policy*, 1 (3), 2010: 263–270.

CHAPTER 7

From Negotiation to Mediation

Valérie Rosoux

"Is it not striking [...] that what separates men should generally be so minute, while the common ground on which they could come together is vast? We have far more reasons to get along than to quarrel." This reflection is from a former diplomat who wrote the novel *Saint-Germain ou la négociation*, awarded the Prix Goncourt in 1958 (Walder 1992, 69). The story unfolded in 1570 against a backdrop of negotiations between French Catholics and Protestants. It happened long ago, but the keenly described processes have remained remarkably topical. All the basic elements are still in effect: the use of secrecy, divergence of interests bordering on incompatibility, managing emotions, power struggles, personal chemistry, ruses and strategies, juggling between cooperation and confrontation.

Others have evolved. Forums where diplomats strive to broker deals are no longer the hushed halls of centuries past. Negotiations carried out in

V. Rosoux (✉)
Belgian National Fund for Scientific Research (FNRS), UCLouvain,
Louvain-la-Neuve, Belgium
e-mail: valerie.rosoux@uclouvain.be

© The Author(s) 2020
T. Balzacq et al. (eds.), *Global Diplomacy*,
The Sciences Po Series in International Relations and Political
Economy, https://doi.org/10.1007/978-3-030-28786-3_7

multilateral frameworks have increased and accelerated due to the proliferation of international organizations and processes for regional integration. The interlocutors' profiles have also changed noticeably. Far from exchanges among diplomatic dynasties generally tied to the aristocracy, interactions are now pluricultural and multilevel. Experts, practitioners, and other representatives of civil society meet around the negotiating table (whether non-governmental organizations, private groups, religious representatives, or associations of war victims). A third significant change—in addition to the plurality of venues and profiles—is the increasing use of third parties in crafting agreements. Mediation is certainly not new. Diplomats were already referring to it in the early seventeenth century. But it has gradually become more widespread with conflict resolution. Professionalized now, diplomatic mediation strives to de-escalate crises, hostage-taking, and more generally all armed conflicts, whether international or intercommunity.

The increase in multilateral negotiations, along with the growing intervention of non-official actors and mediators, in no way diminishes the crucial role of more traditional negotiations conducted by high-level diplomats. This chapter attempts to shed light on their scope and limits, focusing on three major questions. The first is knowing whether one should negotiate. The second is to specify when to negotiate. The third recalls how to negotiate.

Should One Negotiate?

Historians and ethnologists agree that all human societies are characterized by negotiation. Internationalists point out that the concepts of negotiation and diplomacy have been closely associated since the sixteenth century. In 1842, Garnier-Pagès' *Dictionnaire politique* indicated that "negotiations encompass nearly the whole field of diplomacy." The *Dictionnaire diplomatique*, published in the inter-war years, explains that "negotiation is the raison d'être not just for the diplomatic actor as head of mission, but for all diplomacy." Since then, the two terms have been systematically associated. In 2008, in a 125-page report entitled "Diplomacy, a profession and an art," the term "negotiation" was referred to 176 times, confirming Richelieu's maxim: "Negotiate, always negotiate." Whether in matters of defense or security, trade or the environment, culture or humanitarian aid, diplomats negotiate. To be sure, this is not all they do. They represent, inform, and protect their citizens. But negotiating remains one of the main diplomatic functions despite the diversity of these tasks.

Regarding a definition of the term, it designates a process through which two or more parties interact, with or without a mediator, for the purpose of reaching a position that is acceptable in light of their differences. This definition highlights four key elements in all negotiations (Dupont 2006). The first concerns its relational aspect. Negotiating inevitably involves interaction among actors and, as such, more or less formal communication. The second element deals with divergences inherent in all negotiations. They may involve events, objectives, methods, or values. Whether real or perceived, they prove to be crucial in progressing from duel to duo. The third element is a reminder that the parties are connected by a certain degree of interdependence: None can reach a satisfactory result without the others. Finally, the solution sought must be mutually acceptable even if the agreement is inequitable or even totally unbalanced. If the parties turn to a mediator, whether or not the agreement is mutually satisfying depends mainly on the level of trust each one has with the third party (Bercovitch 2014).

Within the spectrum of diplomatic activity, negotiation is different from a simple exchange of views or from coercive diplomacy through which one party tries to impose its preferences unilaterally (Thuderoz 2015). The international system's anarchic nature is the usual explanation for its importance. Negotiating is one of the only ways to promote the coexistence of sovereign societies in the absence of a true higher authority with a monopoly on the legitimate use of violence or of a legal framework that could be a reference for all states. It enables diplomats to effectively defend their national interests without triggering a situation of permanent warfare. Despite this advantage, the process is not appropriate in all cases. Can everything be negotiated? Furthermore, can one negotiate with everyone?

The first point in question involves the object of negotiations. Certain realities are non-negotiable a priori. Beliefs, values, and identities are not the result of compromise. They are by nature non-divisible and unlikely to be modified by any dealings. Similarly, notions of justice and truth do not seem open to bargaining, at least in principle.

It is therefore not rare for parties to immediately affirm the non-negotiable nature of certain positions in the framework of negotiations that are predominantly conflictual rather than cooperative. In the context of peace talks on Syria, for example, the removal of Syrian President Bachar Al Assad was long qualified as non-negotiable by representatives of the

Syrian opposition. However, the length of the conflict, the intervention of foreign powers such as Russia and Iran, and leadership changes in third parties (whether in the United States or France) seem to have shifted the inviolability of this red line. In the Middle East, issues regarding the right of return and holy places have also prompted positions presented as non-negotiable. Yet the deadlocks created by these problems do not mean there is no imaginable solution. Value conflicts certainly prove more intense and harder to settle than interest conflicts. But one should never rule out a priori that experienced negotiators and/or mediators might succeed in turning value conflicts (religious or identity-based ones, for instance) into interest conflicts.

That being the case, it seems problematic to present certain subjects as inherently non-negotiable. Certain realities—although presented and perceived as such for decades—may over time be subject to transactions, depending on the different actors' circumstances and objectives. In short, a position's non-negotiability only emerges when negotiations have failed.

The second issue does not involve the object of discussions, but the kind of actors one is dealing with. It arises when one of the parties refuses to sit down at the negotiating table with another party presented as illegitimate. The argument is often heard that one does not negotiate with a dictator, a figure inevitably associated with Adolf Hitler. Thus, at every armed intervention, states eager to attempt or prolong negotiations are associated with the spirit of "Munich." The discussions preceding the intervention of American and British forces in Iraq in the spring of 2003 are further evidence of this. Saddam Hussein is not the only head of state compared to Adolf Hitler. The accusation of a "new Munich" was ascribed at the start of the Algerian War, the Vietnam War, the wars that devastated the former Yugoslavia, and the Franco-British intervention in Libya in 2011. Moreover, it is thrown around on a regular basis in public discussions in Israel. Former Israeli Prime Minister Ariel Sharon explicitly told Western democracies: "Do not repeat the dreadful mistake of 1938, when enlightened European democracies decided to sacrifice Czechoslovakia for a 'convenient temporary solution'." He then stressed: "Do not try to appease the Arabs at our expense—this is unacceptable to us. Israel will not be Czechoslovakia" (press conference held on October 4, 2001). These examples are reminders of the possible consequences of a diplomacy of appeasement toward an insatiable dictator—whether the argument arises from a true cognitive prism or from more strategic stigmatization.

Diplomats deal with the same dilemma regarding "terrorists." Chancelleries remind them: Negotiating with terrorists is out of the question. Yet the issue crops up systematically in cases of hostage-taking, on the rise in the past fifteen years. Their objection is well known. Negotiating with terrorists would only encourage them to reoffend. But that objection does not allow for a non-deadly outcome for the hostages whose fate is at stake. As a result, most states become caught up in a game of incompatible demands: not giving in to a form of murderous blackmail on the one hand and on the other hand ensuring the protection of its citizens. In order to save face and save their countrymen, most states do not rule out the idea of conducting highly discreet negotiations with the help of their secret services and expert mediators. One of the main criteria in judging the appropriateness of this approach lies in the distinction between "absolute" and "contingent" terrorists. The former have no interest in negotiating while the latter are acting precisely with the aim of doing so. There is no clear boundary between these categories, but the distinction provides a path for reflecting on ways liable to transform certain hostage-takers in order to avoid the fatal blow of an ultimatum (Faure and Zartman 2010).

The debate over the timeliness of negotiating thus remains open. For many diplomats, the ultimate question is probably not about knowing whether one should negotiate with dictators and terrorists, but rather when and how. In dealing with these questions, the challenge is to balance ethics and pragmatism while remaining aware of how precarious an equilibrium it is. That balancing is a reminder of how the very credibility of a negotiation implies that the use of force not be ruled out in principle. The link between negotiation and armed confrontation is complex. In most cases, the use of force is followed sooner or later by a resumption of negotiations. The point behind the use of force then is not to dispense the actors from tough negotiations that cost time and energy. It is rather to postpone the process in the hope of promoting a more favorable balance of power.

WHEN SHOULD ONE NEGOTIATE?

The time variable proves to be decisive in understanding the results of a negotiation. That variable may be enumerated in two ways. The first involves the notion of timing, while the second focuses on the length of negotiations.

Is there a right time for engaging in negotiations? Should diplomats be sensitive to a form of "momentum," or *kairos*, to borrow a concept from

Ancient Greece? Researchers and practitioners agree on the fact that a conflict has little chance of being resolved until it has reached a certain degree of maturity. From that perspective, a double condition seems necessary to undertake fruitful negotiations or mediations. First, each party must understand that it is in an extremely costly stalemate and that it has no chance of prevailing through an escalation of force. Second, each party must see the negotiations as a possible way out in order to reach a satisfactory agreement.

These two conditions were met during the Oslo Process leading to the signing of an accord in 1993 symbolized by the historic handshake between Yasser Arafat and Yitzhak Rabin. No less than fourteen secret meetings were held in Norway over the seven months preceding the agreement between the Israeli government and the Palestine Liberation Organization (PLO). Throughout those meetings, the perception of the gradually untenable cost of the conflict and a certain optimism about the possible success of the negotiations enabled the parties to finalize the general principles that were the basis for establishing an autonomous Palestinian administration.

The same conditions characterize the negotiations that led to the dismantling of apartheid in South Africa. Between 1991 and 1993, the National Party in power and the African National Congress (ANC) began the final phase of negotiations after assessing the stalemate in their country, beset by violent domestic tension and increasingly pronounced international pressure. Beyond that shared perception, the head of government Frederik de Klerk and Nelson Mandela saw the negotiations as the only way liable to avoid a bloodbath. That double condition (perception of a stalemate and optimism about a positive outcome) was a turning point that led to a new South African Constitution being drafted and, in 1994, to the first elections by universal suffrage in South African history.

This example is a reminder of the importance of third parties in the maturation process, allowing a negotiated agreement to be concluded. Whether they are mediators, allied powers, or international organizations, third parties may exercise decisive pressure to hasten an awareness by the parties involved. This pressure is, however, not a sufficient condition to guarantee the success of negotiations. As attested by many stalled processes, a third-party intervention in an unripe conflict risks being counterproductive (Zartman 2015). On the whole, the mediator must not intervene too soon, nor too late, so as not to disturb the ripening process. In short, there is no cookie-cutter approach dispensing the parties from subtle and often delicate discernment.

The mediator's role can be explored in a differentiated manner according to the specific context of each case. His goal is to go beyond obstacles, deadlocks, and stalemates thwarting the negotiations. That role varies from case to case, ranging from strict neutrality to blatant pressure. Far from being systematically impartial, the mediator may act as a "communicator," an "enunciator," even as a "manipulator" (Touval and Zartman 1985). In the first case, the mediator strives to promote communication and restore trust among the parties. In the second, he does not settle for doing his best to deliver messages; he suggests the most creative possible formulas for reaching an agreement. In the third case, the mediator goes to the point of modifying the balance of power involved by intervening in the negotiations (by granting financial aid, for instance). These different forms of intervention may be illustrated by the role played by the American administration in the Camp David or Dayton peace processes.

The temporal variable helps to highlight another aspect tied to the length of negotiations. Once a process has been launched, when should it be stopped? The question proves to be fundamental, notably in the framework of peace talks. Indeed, societies ravaged by war must be observed over the long term. Countless examples have shown this: After a war, one does not count in years but in generations. As a metaphor, the geography of the German city of Koblenz is a particularly good illustration of the length of the processes envisaged. It is indeed striking to see the color of the water at the confluence of the Rhine and Moselle Rivers. Far from blending immediately, the rivers keep their own color for quite a while. Then, downstream, long beyond their confluence, the waters gradually mix to the point of being undifferentiated. Like those currents, communities affected by past violence cannot come together hastily. Negotiating processes designed to "put it all behind" after a violent period may be put in perspective through this kind of observation.

Envisaging the negotiating process in the long term affords a considerably wider perspective. There is a broad consensus around the expression "post-conflict" within international relations. Practitioners and researchers use it to distinguish between what pertains to conflict prevention, resolution, and transformation. But it may be helpful to examine this. How can we "demobilize minds"? When is one in fact in post-conflict? Based on what criteria? These questions are an inducement to consider the time frames for each actor involved in transforming relations between former enemies. The main protagonists at the negotiating table are often distinguished by their respective interests. Shouldn't they also be differentiated according to their specific time frames? Peace-keeping professionals have different time frames than new elites. Descendants of victims and legislators do not have the same timing. Donor countries are on another time scale than survivors.

Mediation's long-term implications can be explored through that diversity. Whether undertaken by a diplomatic team or by a private organization such as the Carter or Ford Foundation, or the Community of Sant'Egidio, mediation is generally aimed at reaching an agreement among protagonists. Could it not also promote the effective implementation of such agreements and, ultimately, a profusion of platforms supporting the coexistence and rapprochement of the parties? That expanded perspective leads to a consideration of the third and final question shaping this study. Beyond remarks on the legitimacy of the actors involved, and the most appropriate timing for starting negotiations, one must still agree on the main variables through which the results of negotiations can be explained.

How to Negotiate?

The rules of certain interstate conflicts provide spectacular examples of diplomatic success. These include, among others, the negotiations conducted by the United States and the USSR during the Cuban Missile Crisis in 1962, by Israel and Egypt in the 1970s, and by China and the United States in the same period. More recently, certain peace treaties have also ended civil wars. This was the case in Mozambique after an agreement was signed in 2014 by the opposition party, Renamo, and the Frelimo-led government. Similarly, a peace agreement signed in 2016 by the Colombian government and the Revolutionary Armed Forces of Colombia (FARC) was a crucial step in the conflict that had ravaged Colombia for fifty years. Conversely, the stalled peace processes in the Middle East, Libya, Syria, and Africa's Great Lakes region prove day after day the vicissitudes and probably also the limits of negotiating and mediating processes.

Many writers have explored the underlying factors behind the success or failure of negotiations. As early as 1716, François de Callières was studying negotiations. His book *De la manière de négocier avec les souverains* follows in the tradition of Machiavelli's *The Prince* in the advice it gives readers. But rather than reducing negotiations to preparing for war, he describes them also as a harbinger of peace. Since then, many handbooks have followed in succession. These works stress in particular the importance of preparation and the formal aspects of negotiation. Questions of status, choice of a particular language, setting calendars, mandates, and agendas often condition the results of a process. There are many examples of this, from the Congress of Vienna to the Camp David accords.

Most of these books present negotiating techniques, tactics, and strategies, referring above all to standards of rhetoric, argumentation, and persuasive processes. Alongside the manuals for good negotiators, many articles and books present different approaches for grasping the mechanisms of negotiation. Five of them deserve special note. The structural approach mainly focuses on the notion of power. The behavioral approach highlights the actors' attitudes and psychology. The strategic approach was drawn from game theory. The procedural approach identifies the various phases of negotiation. Lastly, the cultural approach emphasizes historical and cultural factors. Rather than evaluating these perspectives by praising some and criticizing others, it seems appropriate here to note their most salient features. Far from being incompatible, they often prove complementary in understanding the specific dynamics in each case.

According to the structural approach, all negotiations can be seen as bargaining involving manifestations of power. From this perspective, the results of international negotiations flow directly from asymmetries of power. For most authors, these results only confirm the initial distribution of power among the parties, the most powerful being in a position to orient the process. However, that opinion should be qualified by stressing the relative nature of power. Beyond the actual power of each protagonist, often measured in figures (based on strategic, economic, and demographic elements), isn't it also—and perhaps above all—a matter of considering power as perceived by the parties? Along the same lines, it is worth taking a serious look at the mechanisms enabling the parties deemed in principle the weakest to modify the initial balance of power. Consider in particular the intervention of third parties favorable to them (allied states), support provided by NGOs and the media, often liable to influence the global arena. Thus, negotiations cannot be reduced to a strict balancing of each party's material resources. To be sure, power remains one of the most fundamental variables in the diplomatic game, yet the least powerful are still not systematically at the mercy of the strongest.

The behavioral approach specifies that the results of negotiations do not merely reflect a balance of power, but also depend on the attitude, motivation, and personality of the actors. Most diplomats see negotiation as an art that cannot be taught. They consider it as an art of observation, analysis, and persuasion in which personal experience proves essential (Plantey 2002). It is a difficult art, based on realism and patience, as well as unfailing creativity and flexibility. In short, a set of talents for clarifying one's position and pinpointing the other's, dialoguing to find areas of agreement, balancing concessions to protect the relationship. The reasoning is the same with regard to mediators who should be particularly attentive, humble and tenacious, optimistic and pragmatic.

As with the preceding approach, certain nuances can be salutary. The traits of the ideal negotiator and mediator are inspiring. Even so, can one conclude that it would be vain to continue learning? Research carried out on the psychological and cognitive aspects of negotiating is not limited to the qualities of negotiators born gifted. It shows the importance of perceptions, signals communicated, the quality of the information, and messages exchanged. It seems therefore crucial to detect misunderstandings and cognitive biases behind the toughest deadlocks, whether from a lack of empathy, overconfidence (characterized by the certainty that one is right and adopting the best strategies), or one-upmanship (behind irrational risk-taking). By learning these skills, one may go beyond the rigid dichotomy between those with the qualities needed to negotiate "well" and those without them.

In addition to power and personality, the success or failure of negotiations may be elucidated by taking into account strategies chosen by the parties and their possible mediators. In this approach, the results of the negotiations are directly linked to the offers and demands made by the parties in order to obtain concessions. Game theory, economic theory (for studying comparative costs), and social psychology (analyzing cooperative and competitive behavior) are mobilized for this purpose. Based on the actors' rationality, this school asks fundamental questions about their choices, the conditions affecting those choices, and the level of trust between parties. One illustration is the study of the prisoner's dilemma that led to the development of a theory of cooperation based on a form of "conditional trust" (tit for tat). From this perspective, the most compelling long-term strategy is to start by cooperating and in the next phase to respond in the same way as the other party (Axelrod 1997).

The strategic approach cannot predict the actors' behavior, however, nor the outcome of their interactions. The negotiations themselves are based on calculations and perceptions that make their progress and conclusion unpredictable. This observation reflects the delicate balance between notions of rationality and predictability. The fact that the parties strive to act rationally and that in retrospect the results of their negotiations also seem rational does not mean the results can be calculated in advance. Historians have evoked this over and over: In considering decisions taken by actors, it is key to keep in mind their context, made of ambiguity and risks rather than certainties and foregone conclusions.

A fourth approach calls attention not to the resources of each party involved, the actors' behavior or respective strategies, but rather to the negotiating process itself. Based on the division of negotiations into successive phases, it distinguishes the initial contact from the phases of information, argumentation, and adjusting positions, and finally, of shaping the agreement. The value of this distinction is to pinpoint the functions, tools, and qualities required in each phase. However, in the field, the negotiating process rarely progresses in a linear or ideally ordered manner. Characterized by much going back and forth, it is neither irreversible nor systematically articulated in clearly identifiable phases.

Such irregularities explain why some authors prefer to highlight three main stages rather than five. From that standpoint, the first major stage is the pre-negotiation phase when conditions can be met for furthering discussions. Whether by setting up a communication channel or by gathering the information needed to make a diagnosis, those conditions draw on demands considered high priority by each party and those most likely to be so for the other party. Once the diagnosis has been made, the parties generally enter the second major stage designed to develop a jointly agreeable formula that will serve as a referent for an agreement. Long discussions then strive to determine the terms of the exchange. Does it involve negotiating resources for money, live prisoners for dead bodies, and territories for a secure withdrawal? All these formulas are imaginable. Thus, the importance of agreeing on the type of exchange that is most capable of satisfying all parties at the table. The third and final phase deals with the details of the transaction. It is the moment for fine-tuning positions, calibrating concessions, and specifying the terms of the exchange leading to the agreement's finalization. The care taken in each of these phases determines to a great extent whether or not the agreement reached will be implemented (Zartman 1977).

Finally, one last approach underscores the importance of cultural variables in the framework of all international negotiations. It reflects on the role of language, value systems, codes, or rituals. Beyond the issue of national stereotypes, often decisive during the phases of preparation and initial contact, it involves taking a serious look at the social practices, patterns of authority, and events perceived in the collective memory of each group as significant precedents. The boundary between the behavioral and cultural approaches is not always easy to draw. It seems crucial nonetheless to identify the cultural layers that condition many positions. Although we cannot predict the progress of negotiations through those elements alone, they may represent major obstacles in the areas of communication, perceptions, and emotions. In this regard, both personal and cultural empathy are among the key qualities that make a diplomat a seasoned negotiator.

* * *

In concluding this reflection, a fundamental question remains open: What is a "successful" negotiation for a diplomat? Does it mean going beyond the winner/loser dichotomy? Knowing that negotiations are not systematically based on honesty and good faith, how can you spot the signs of success? Does that kind of discernment depend on an agreement being balanced, on the public's enthusiasm, or on the increased trust between parties? This last aspect proves particularly decisive in the framework of peace accords. All the cases analyzed show that merely obtaining an agreement is not enough to bridge the gaps that have torn a community apart. A peace process cannot be sustained without concomitant steps to gradually connect all levels of a society. While official representatives may see negotiations as the most promising path given the alternatives, they must still get their decision across to the people.

Internal deals thus piggyback on diplomatic negotiations, filled with their own bargaining, power struggles, and alliances. The momentum of the rapprochement often depends on these concomitant processes. Thus, it is critical to conceive official negotiations as being positioned before and/or after collaborations between non-state actors from political, economic, social, religious, and academic circles. Such non-official meetings may prove crucial before formal procedures have begun, as they could induce representatives from each party to sit together at the negotiating table. These exchanges can also turn out to be useful after an agreement has been reached and are apt to further the practical application of measures resulting from the agreement, contributing to the gradual learning of a shared language. That perspective is like a zigzag connecting diplomatic and societal approaches, thereby enhancing the art of "finely tuned diplomacy" evoked in *Saint-Germain ou la négociation*. By going beyond institutional circles, diplomats give sociological substance to negotiations. That substance may prove to be decisive in coming to terms with reality and moving forward. It is a risky exercise and often discouraging—but always compelling. Although it can be dizzying, it is no doubt worth remembering that, in the end, "it is all about reaching a compromise. A matter of imagination" (Walder 1992, 27).

References

Axelrod, Robert, *The Complexity of Cooperation*, Princeton (NJ), Princeton University Press, 1997.
Bercovitch, Jacob, *Theory and Practice of International Mediation: Selected Essays*, London, Routledge, 2014.
Dupont, Christophe, *La Négociation post-moderne. Bilan des connaissances, acquis et lacunes, perspectives*, Paris, Publibook, 2006.
Faure, Guy Olivier, Zartman, William I., *Negotiating with Terrorists: Strategy, Tactics and Politics*, London, Routledge, 2010.
Plantey Alain, *La Négociation internationale au XXIe siècle*, Paris, CNRS, 2002.
Touval, Saadia, Zartman, I. William (eds.), *International Mediation in Theory and Practice*, Boulder, CO, Westview Press, 1985.
Thuderoz, Christian, *Petit traité du compromis. L'art des concessions*, Paris, Presses universitaires de France, 2015.
Walder, Francis, *Saint-Germain ou la négociation*, Paris, Gallimard, 1992.
Zartman, I. William, "Negotiation as a Joint Decision Making Process," *Journal of Conflict Resolution*, 21 (4), 1977: 619–638.
Zartman, I. William, *Preventing Deadly Conflict*, Cambridge, Polity Press, 2015.

CHAPTER 8

Rituals and Diplomacy

Thierry Balzacq

Whatever the activity and however profanely instrumental, it can afford many opportunities for minor ceremonies as long as other persons are present. Through these observances, guided by ceremonial obligations and expectations, a constant flow of indulgences is spread through society, with others who are present constantly reminding the individual that he must keep himself together as a well-demeaned person and affirm the sacred quality of these others. The gestures which we sometimes call empty are perhaps in fact the fullest things of all. (Goffman 1967, p. 90)

The diplomatic arena is studded with "interaction rituals" (Goffman 1974). And yet, manuals and handbooks of diplomacy almost never include a chapter on them. The Oxford Handbook of Modern Diplomacy, for example, overlooks the issue, even though the effectiveness of certain basic aspects of diplomacy such as representation, protocol, international summits, and negotiation is often based on rituals more or less skillfully managed and wisely used.

T. Balzacq (✉)
Sciences Po, Paris, France
e-mail: thierry.balzacq@sciencespo.fr

The track record is no different for diplomatic history. Considering the abundance of data, one might expect to find a large volume of work on diplomatic ceremonies during the Renaissance or the modern era, which in many respects are the background common to many contemporary diplomatic practices. In this regard, William Roosen (1980) underlines the ambivalence that the study of rituals is hostage to. On the one hand, some historians think it futile to study rituals; on the other hand, those who take an interest in them devote little attention to discussing their meaning. They would rather give a meticulous description of the ceremonies identified and described than an analysis of their possible meaning. As a result, the signs that shape ceremonies are connected to other signs, but without knowing how or why.

In recent years, however, some historians grouped under the "new diplomatic history" label have become increasingly interested in the ritualistic and ceremonial components of diplomacy. But the work has been heavily influenced by a culturalist perspective to the extent that the intention of new diplomatic history—especially in Germany—is primarily about bringing to light the symbolic aspects of diplomatic communication (Stollberg-Rilinger et al. 2008; Stollberg-Rilinger 2000). In fact, the communicational aspect of rituals is key, but as we will see later, on the one hand, the relationship between ritual and communication is less direct than it seems and, on the other hand, ritual cannot be reduced to its communicative function. Indeed, ritual may perform several roles. Thus, it frequently plays a part in building the identity of the actors involved (Elias 1974).

Before evoking the functions of ritual, the meaning of the term must be examined briefly. That is the focus of the first part of this chapter. Diplomatic protocol, a distinct ritual, and probably the most common, will then be analyzed. After that, I will focus in particular on a widespread but little studied form of diplomatic performance: the handshake. To begin dispelling the doubts often surrounding the effectiveness of rituals, I will use findings from the most recent research in neuroscience to substantiate the impact of handshaking, a promising window on the consequences of the other diplomatic rituals evoked in this chapter. Finally, I will look at some of the methodological consequences of studying diplomatic rituals.

What Is a Ritual?

In the human and social sciences, we know this type of question to be challenging. This is due in part to an author's preferences in highlighting a particular aspect of the phenomenon; it may also be in part because the phenomenon cannot be easily grasped through one sole prism; lastly, the difficulty may be compounded by its involving several disciplines. Regarding rituals, the first two reasons can be seen as the most relevant. Along with sociology, anthropology is the discipline that has given ritual its intellectual grounding. Other disciplines, including political science and history, took it on much later without developing a specific perspective, which is not to say theirs is not original. Mainly, however, they have more often adopted, then slightly modified, existing definitions. Definitions about rituals have different points of reference, but there is a dividing line separating two families: on the one hand, those following Émile Durkheim (1912) who define a ritual as an important feature of the sacred and, on the other hand, definitions that detach ritual from all references to the sacred.

Max Gluckman is a good illustration of this first approach. Indeed, he considers ritual to be "a stylized ceremonial in which persons related in various ways to the central actors, as well as these themselves, perform prescribed actions according to their secular roles; and that it is believed by the participants that these prescribed actions express and amend social relationships so as to secure general blessing, purification, protection, and prosperity [...]" (Gluckman 1966, 24).

Conceptual clarifications that stay clear of any religious references are the second possible entry into the world of rituals. Some are extensive, others are extremely sparing. Stanley Tambiah gives a broad definition. For him, "Ritual is a culturally constructed system of symbolic communication. It is constituted of patterned and ordered sequences of words and acts, often expressed in the multiple media, whose content and arrangement are characterized in varying degree by formality (conventionally), stereotypy (rigidity), condensation (fusion), and redundancy (repetition)" (Tambiah 1979, 119). Roy Rappaport, who developed one of the most powerful and concise approaches to ritual, has drawn from this definition in many respects. But he specifies that those taking part in a ritual are not the absolute authors of the sequences of words and acts repeated. In his approach, ritual thus becomes "*the performance of more or less invariant sequences of formal acts and utterances not entirely encoded by the performers*" (Emphasis in the original. Rappaport 1999, 24).

Rappaport's definition has many advantages, two of which seem most salient. The first is that it is formal, not substantive. Rappaport does not attempt to list all the ingredients of a ritual, but focuses on its essential features, on the invariants of what is known as "ritual." Here, the reference to the sacred is no longer a fundamental aspect of ritual. In other words, an analytical focus makes it possible to break free from the context and from the debate between the religious and non-religious approaches to ritual. Second, Rappaport proposes a non-functionalist conception of ritual. Indeed, his definition has no trace of a reference to the supposed functions of ritual because, for Rappaport, that undertaking does not sufficiently take into account the fact that there are several kinds of rituals, with fluid functions. In that case, a definition concerned with the multiple functions of rituals could never list them all. At best, it risks offering a host of features gleaned from all rituals (an impossible task) or, at worst, confining itself to the specificities of each ritual, instead of highlighting through different rituals what they have in common that distinguishes them from other phenomena. Furthermore, Rappaport doesn't claim that formality, invariance, and performance are exclusive features of ritual. What he maintains is that these elements are expressed in a distinctive way in rituals. That is what ultimately allows us to identify what the phenomenon known as "ritual" is, across a broad range of cases.

Although a proper definition of ritual—i.e., one that concentrates on its form rather than its variable content—must avoid listing its functions, it is crucial to take them into account when exploring a family of rituals, especially diplomatic ones. One must therefore work empirically, starting from a particular ritual. Diplomatic protocol provides such a field of investigation, from which we can specify the functions of a ritual and better clarify how they work.

Protocol, a Medium for and Expression of the Diplomatic Order

Two kinds of protocols can be roughly identified: One, official protocol, regulates interactions between authorities in the same country; the other, diplomatic protocol, designates the set of standards, conventions, and practices governing contacts and interactions between authorities in different countries. However, the fact that protocol regulates interactions says little about the latter's content. Likewise, protocol components may vary from one country to another, but the protocol's "internal necessity" (Geertz 1986, 178)—i.e., shaping the diplomatic order (Deloye et al. 1999)—remains unchanging. In short, a protocol is a way of thinking about and building the order underlying relations between states.

The development of modern diplomatic protocol goes back to the end of the seventeenth and first half of the eighteenth centuries, a barometer of international relations for some (Roosen 1980) and diplomatic weapon for others (Burke 1999). Among the precursors are two texts attesting to that evolution: *L'Ambassadeur* (1680–1681) by Abraham de Wicquefort and *De la manière de négocier avec les souverains* (1716) dashed off by François de Callières, the former secretary of Louis XIV. The two books indeed focus on negotiation and the role of an ambassador. But the striking thing is that audiences, civilities, and ceremonies are elevated as the "most essential part of an embassy" (Wicquefort 1680–1681, 416).

One of the crucial protocol issues that had to be settled by the Congress of Vienna (1815) was that of precedence. The purpose of precedence was first to establish a hierarchical order among the parties involved. Thus, it is not surprising that, before being formalized in Vienna, the issue of precedence had given rise to disagreements among European nations eager to assert their authority over each other, in particular during the Middle Ages and the modern era.

A memorable example is that of an altercation in London in 1661. As the Swedish Ambassador was presenting his credentials to the court of King Charles II, the carriages of the Spanish and French ambassadors collided. The crash occurred when each delegation tried to get ahead of the other, in other words to have precedence. A furious Louis XIV demanded an apology from the Spanish court and promised to force Philippe IV "to give precedence to [his] ambassadors in every court in Europe" (Loménie 1919, 102). According to Peter Burke, the incident had been ritualized by France to prepare for a change in the diplomatic balance in Europe. In fact, the War of Devolution between France and Spain broke out in 1667. Furthermore, for Burke (1999, 177–178), Louis XIV was an important figure in the reconstruction of official and diplomatic rituals in the modern era. He points out, for example, that the ambassadors' staircase at Versailles was the backdrop for carefully orchestrated rituals designed not only to receive representatives of foreign sovereigns with the honors due to their rank, but also to project France's power. In other words, protocol was the "domain of ritual signs of dominance" (Geertz 1986, 157).

Although the "dominance" aspect is less significant in contemporary diplomatic practices, protocol still conveys a hierarchical structuring of relations between diplomats and remains an effective tool in the structured expression of the content of relations between countries. As Serres has noted, "foreign agents represent something greater than themselves. The honors they receive are intended for the legal entity they are the expression of. It has not been sufficiently noted that protocol knows neither victorious nor defeated peoples, and that it compels mutual respect even between enemy nations, without paying heed to the balance of power [...]" (Serres 1992, 33). Thus, protocol codifies prerogatives, privileges, and immunity. Moreover, it provides a normative framework for diplomatic ceremonies that promotes peaceful interaction. In Tambiah's words (1979, 117), ritual "brings temporary perfection to an imperfect world."

In *Mais que font donc ces diplomates entre deux cocktails?*, Chambon describes a major event involving protocol in diplomatic relations between states: the presenting of credentials (cf. the introduction on this concept). This is what he says:

> Several days later, the ambassador is invited to present his credentials to the head of state for which he has been accredited. On that day, the chief of protocol, wearing a morning coat or uniform, goes to his embassy and solemnly calls on him and his main collaborators, then takes them to the palace of the head of state in large black cars used for such ceremonies, preceded by an escort of motorcycles with sirens blaring [...]. After the national anthem has been played the ambassador steps forward, presents his credentials to the head of state and gives his ceremonial speech, in which he evokes the "traditional bonds of friendship" uniting the two countries, highlighting his desire during his mission, 'to see them grow closer and further develop.' The head of state responds courteously [...]. After the traditional glass of champagne, the head of state and the ambassador engage in casual conversation in which each one tries to make out the other's true intentions [...]. (Chambon 1983, 95)

The ritual of presenting credentials is instructive in several ways. Nuances may be added from one capital to another, but it can be a delicate moment for the ambassador, especially when relations between the two countries have deteriorated. Moreover, credentials may be rejected to express disapproval of policies, decisions, or behavior. Thus, in 1987, President François Mitterrand refused the credentials of the new South African ambassador to protest the incarceration of Pierre-André Albertini, a French aid worker. The accreditation of the South African ambassador to France was granted only after Albertini was freed. More recently, the Vatican did not assent to the nomination of Laurent Stefanini as French ambassador to the Holy See. Appointed in 2015, Stefanini waited about a year for his accreditation, which was never granted. France finally decided to appoint him as ambassador to UNESCO and put forward Philippe Zeller (to Pope Francis), who was quickly accepted and given an audience, putting an end to the long-standing opposition between Paris and the Vatican.

Diplomatic rituals are mainly embodied in ceremonies (dinners, gift-giving, signing treaties, invitations to military parades, etc.), so many occasions for diplomatic performances. At official meals, for example, individuals are placed around the table based on their rank and role. Distance and proximity are used in assigning their places (Haroche 1999, 217). Similarly, the review of the troops from the Queen of England's carriage signals a desire to communicate a level of esteem, as well as physical and emotional proximity which not all heads of state are granted on an official visit.

The Handshake

The handshake is one of the most common gestures in the diplomatic ecosystem. Some have marked the history of international relations, becoming iconic. Examples include: the one between Raul Castro and Barack Obama (2013); the handshake between Yasser Arafat and Yitzhak Rabin sealing the Oslo Accords (1993); and the one between Mikhail Gorbachev and Ronald Reagan (1988). But what could be seen in principle as an ordinary act of everyday life in fact follows a precise code. There are highly detailed rules about the "ideal" handshake; it should be brief but not evasive, nor too long, which would be tantamount to taking the other person's hand hostage; it must convey force without being domineering, be warm but not invasive (Post 1940, 23). Handshakes are both a ritual of transition and of access, in Goffman's sense (Goffman 1974, 80). Indeed, a handshake signals the beginning or end of an interaction or diplomatic situation. Those shaking hands acknowledge one another and thereby "confirm that they consider one another to be civil individuals, paying quiet tribute to the person's sacred nature" (Keck 2012–2013, 486).

The handshake is a coordinated action—a movement toward the other that awaits a response, without which the situation becomes embarrassing. With an outstretched hand, one gives a part of oneself; in that sense, it is a form of "full performance" (Mauss [1923–1924] 2007). The outstretched hand, while inviting, requires an obligatory response. Thus, the absence of a handshake in a situation that ordinarily calls for one may prompt comments about the quality of relations. This was the case with Donald Trump's refusal to give the traditional handshake to the press during Angela Merkel's visit in March 2017. In side-stepping that ritual, the two leaders immediately fueled much speculation. In truth, a handshake probably would not have dispelled the speculation about sour relations between the two leaders, but it may have helped redirect attention to other topics and provided a different way of framing the visit. Thus, the analysis of a handshake, or its absence, addresses the situation as a whole. By breaking down the situation, the handshake becomes a distinct performance that requires special attention. The reason is that a handshake is an essential, constitutive unit of the meaning attributed to the situation in which it occurs (Schiffrin 1998, 201).

One might object on the grounds that handshakes are less central here than they appear. But our reading is confirmed by recent studies in the neurosciences. The work of Sanda Dolcos (2012) on the interpersonal and emotional effects of handshakes proves that shaking an interlocutor's hand does indeed have a decisive impact on social interactions, both before and after. Before the interaction, a handshake tends to improve the impression one has of the person and to reduce the negative effects of bad impressions. Likewise, a well-executed handshake is a good way of galvanizing those involved and mitigating the potential negative effects from malfunctions in interactions. Afterward, says the study by Dolcos et al., a handshake establishes one of the conditions for future interactions that are different than if the protagonists had not shaken hands at the previous meeting. In short, a handshake helps create a framework for predictable interactions, without which mutual trust is unimaginable. The mechanism underlying these effects of handshaking is located in the nucleus accumbens, a neuronal network in the basal forebrain, deeply involved in laughter, dependence and addiction, and in the reward system. Greater activity of the nucleus accumbens can be seen in an individual shaking hands than in one avoiding doing so, or using other means of opening or closing an interactional sequence. In simple terms, handshaking is thought to have a positive effect on those doing it. All the channels and consequences of handshaking, often treated off-handedly, have yet to be enumerated.

In conclusion, a handshake may be accompanied by markers of proximity such as kissing, hugging, using a familiar personal pronoun or first name. Similarly, during meetings, heads of state often take their guests onto the front steps or, again depending on the degree of proximity being communicated, to the foot of the stairs (if applicable). In front of the cameras, these markers create a more theatrical scene than a handshake.

It is clear therefore that diplomatic rituals involve real dramatization—a more or less spectacular performance. This is probably what has convinced some authors to see ritual as synonymous with theater. Thus, Wicquefort (1680–1681, 10) compares an ambassador to an actor "playing a major role, exposed before the audience in a theater." But the link between theater and ritual is not without its differences. Despite the fact that many etymological studies have pointed out the ties of filiation between ritual, on the one hand, and tragedy and dramaturgy, on the other hand (Harrison 1913), ritual has kept some distinct traits. Two essential differences stand out. The first is that ritual does not depend on an audience (which is not to say that an audience may not form around it), whereas the presence of an audience is a fundamental feature of the theater. In a word, ritual is organized around participants, who may take on different roles during the process.

The second difference concerns the deontic consequences of an act, or what it allows, prescribes, or forbids. The participants in a ritual are required to behave as the ritual stipulates, beyond the moment when it occurs. Theater does not impose the same degree of involvement on actors, and still less on audiences. By the very fact of taking part in a ritual, one agrees to be equal to what has been prescribed. In other words, the relationship to what is encoded in the process determines the respective limits of ritual and theater.

In short, ritual involves agents in a situation of co-presence. Thus, their bodies and movements must adapt to one another, in particular to make it easier to modulate interactions. In addition, the co-presence induced by ritual promotes the creation of a shared framework of attention that filters potential interference. In a certain sense, due to the framework they have built, the participants in a ritual are obliged to maintain the conditions underpinning the regular course of the interaction in progress. As a result, one of the challenges for the participants in a ritual consists in preserving situational coherence, or a shared definition of the situation, which "allows the shared reality to be indeed real for [them]" (Collins 2005, 24).

Finally, diplomatic rituals, in particular official dinners, state visits, and the signing of treaties, take shape in two stages: detailed preparation (in the wings), hidden from public view, sometimes without the participants in the ritual who are to play (onstage) the interactions prepared for them (Goffman 1974). In the framework of an official visit, for instance, the head of protocol makes sketches situating the guests, consults his foreign counterpart, asks about the number of members of the delegation, their official rank, etc. What occurs on the prescribed day is the culmination of a process that sometimes takes months (or more) of preparation backstage. In a word, ritual cannot be improvised, and the participants are in a paradoxical situation as both creators and non-creators of the gestures, movements, and words they use.

Methodological Repercussions: The Importance of the Situation

This chapter, in an introductory textbook on diplomacy, can only provide an outline of rituals, of both their content and form. By taking a closer look at diplomatic protocol, I have identified the elements indicated in the conceptual discussion. Ideally, the degree of granularity demanded by a study of rituals calls for a rigorous ethnographic study: thick description, interviews, and at times the use of sound data. But everything ultimately depends on a particular epistemological attitude, on a relationship to the object of knowledge. In fact, the study of rituals requires renewed attention to interactions in situation. This involves seeing how the actors negotiate the diplomatic order in which they are the protagonists, from one situation to another. This last section is therefore devoted to the major stakes in the epistemological orientation that Goffman and Certeau have so well illustrated in numerous works (Goffman 1959, 1969; Certeau 1980): the situation.

What is a situation and how can examining it change our way of analyzing rituals? A situation largely involves both social sources and conditions of action. It is an emerging property, in that its existence is not anterior to the actors' interactions, but materializes through the very fact of those interactions. However, the actors also embody previous situations, and thus, each situation is a creation and reproduction. Through this concept, situations in time and space can be compared while being protected against the risk of situationism.

Situation analysis sheds an original light on the processes and rules of rituals. It can detect consistency, shifts, loans, and misfires by comparing situations. Thus, while an analysis of a given ritual (e.g., an exchange of gifts) may adopt a macro-perspective, in striving to highlight the constituent features of a diplomatic gift as such, the focus on the situation brings out the singularity of an interaction, a diplomatic relation, an occasion, etc. Rituals are always performed in situation; thus, one cannot understand rituals without taking seriously what transpires between actors at the moment they are engaged in a ritual. In short, the diplomatic order that emerges from rituals is visible from situation to situation. In that sense, it is an "interactional chain of rituals" (Collins 2005).

* * *

Examining rituals can open up a whole new field of work in diplomatic studies. It can, for instance, help us understand how institutions develop a shared representation of the world. The existence of political communities, of tribes in the most complex international organizations, is both the product and the source of more or less elaborate rituals. Similarly, starting from rituals, one can reveal how institutions build and maintain their power and legitimacy over time, or how practices spread throughout the international system. Thanks to rituals, therefore, a whole set of practices can take on new meaning (e.g., deterrence, torture, military exercises, international summits, etc.). Here, we can see that ritual is not synonymous with an analysis of symbols.

References

Burke, Peter, "La reconstruction des rituels politiques au siècle de Louis XIV," in Yves Deloye, Claudine Haroche, Olivier Ihl (eds.), *Le Protocole ou la mise en forme de l'ordre politique*, Paris, L'Harmattan, 1999, pp. 171–183.

Certeau, Michel de, *L'Invention du quotidien*, vol. I, Arts et faire, Paris, Gallimard, 1980.

Chambon, Albert, *Mais que font ces diplomates entre deux cocktails?* Paris, Pédone, 1983.

Collins, Randall, *Interaction Ritual Chain*, Princeton (NJ), Princeton University Press, 2005.

Deloye, Yves, Haroche, Claudine, Ihl, Olivier (eds.), *Le Protocole ou la mise en forme de l'ordre politique*, Paris, L'Harmattan, 1999.

Dolcos, Sanda, "The Power of a Handshake: Neural Correlates of Evaluative Judgments in Observed Social Interactions," *Journal of Cognitive Neuroscience*, 24 (12), 2012: 2292–2305.

Durkheim, Émile, *Les Formes élémentaires de la vie religieuse. Le système totémique en Australie*, Paris, Presses universitaires de France, 1912.

Elias, Norbert, *La Société de cour*, Paris, Calmann-Lévy, 1974.

Geertz, Clifford, *Savoir Local, Savoir Global*, Paris, Presses universitaires de France, 1986.

Gluckman, Max, "Les rites de passage," in Max Gluckman (ed.), *Essays on the Rituals of Social Relations*, Manchester, Manchester University Press, 1966

Goffman, Erving, *The Presentation of Self in Everyday Life*, London, Penguin, 1959.
———, *Interaction Ritual: Essays into Face-To-Face Behavior*, Chicago, Aldine Publishing Company, 1967.
———, *Strategic Interaction*, Philadelphia (PA), University of Pennsylvania Press, 1969.
———, *Les Rites d'interaction*, Paris, Minuit, 1974.
Haroche, Claudine, "L'ordre dans les corps: gestes, mouvements, postures. Éléments pour une anthropologie politique des préséances (XVIe-XVIIe siècles)," in Yves Deloye, Claudine Haroche, Olivier Ihl (ed.), *Le Protocole ou la mise en forme de l'ordre politique*, Paris, L'Harmattan, 1999, pp. 213–229.
Harrison, Jane, *Ancient Art and Ritual*, London, Williams and Northgate, 1913.
Keck, Frédéric, "Goffman, Durkheim et les rites de la vie quotidienne," *Archives de philosophie*, 75 (3), 2012: 471–492.
Lomenie, L.H. de, Brienne, Comte de, *Mémoires*, vol. I, Paris, 1919.
Mauss, Marcel, *Essai sur le don. Forme et raison de l'échange dans les sociétés archaïques*, Paris, Presses universitaires de France, 2007.
Post, Emily, *Etiquette: The Blue Book of Social Usage*, New York (NY), Funk & Wagnall, 1940.
Rappaport, Roy, *Ritual and Religion in the Making of Humanity*, Cambridge, Cambridge University Press, 1999.
Roosen, William, "Early Modern Diplomatic Ceremonial: A System Approach," *The Journal of Modern History*, 52 (3), 1980: 452–476.
Schiffrin, Deborah, "Handwork as Ceremony: The Case of the Handshake," *Semiotica*, 12 (3), 1998: 189–202.
Serres, Jean, *Manuel politique du protocole*, Paris, Éditions de la Bièvre, 1992.
Stollberg-Rilinger, Barbara, "Zeremoniell, Ritual, Symbol. Neue Forschungen zur Symbolischen Kommunikation in Spätmittelalter und Früher Neuzeit ," *ZHF*, 27, 2000: 389–405.
Stollberg-Rilinger, Barbara, Althoff, Gerd, Goetzmann, Jutta, Puhle, Matthias (Hrsg.), *Spektakel der Macht. Rituale im Alten Europa (800–1800)*, Katalog und Essayband zur Ausstellung des Kulturhistorischen Museums, Magdeburg, Darmstadt, 2008.
Tambiah, Stanley J., "A Performative Approach to Ritual," *Proceedings of the British Academy*, 65, 1979: 113–169.
Wiquefort, Abraham de, *L'Ambassadeur*, La Haye, Jean & Daniel Steucker, 1680–1681.

PART II

The Actors

CHAPTER 9

States and Their Foreign Services

Christian Lequesne

THE ORIGINS OF THE FOREIGN SERVICE

Most diplomacy textbooks date the creation of the permanent foreign service to Western Europe in the late Middle Ages. Contemporary diplomatic administrations are thought to be a Western creation established as a universal frame of reference for other countries around the world. Despite Nehru's frequent calls for an Indian way in foreign policy, numerous studies have postulated that India's diplomatic service was formed in 1947 from the proto-organization set up by the British government to handle its colony's foreign policy. Recently, Indian authors driven by the postcolonial studies and connected histories movement began challenging Eurocentric explanations, asserting that ancient India had diplomatic institutions based on the same principles of representation and mediation as those in Europe, which were thus their legacy. Deep K. Datta-Ray traces contemporary principles of Indian diplomacy back to the Mughal Empire (Datta-Ray 2015). Historians and anthropologists of non-European civilizations still have a

C. Lequesne (✉)
Sciences Po, Paris, France
e-mail: Christian.lequesne@sciencespo.fr

© The Author(s) 2020
T. Balzacq et al. (eds.), *Global Diplomacy*,
The Sciences Po Series in International Relations and Political Economy, https://doi.org/10.1007/978-3-030-28786-3_9

huge range of material to explore in answering the question of the Western—or not—roots of the foreign service as it is used today.

Historians believe the function of the consul to be the oldest in Europe. In ancient Greek cities, the proxenus, chosen among the citizens of a city whose protection was sought, was in charge of representing foreigners in their relations with political bodies and local laws. Spartan proxeni were entitled to use seals engraved with the emblems and coat of arms of the country whose interests they represented. Eager to protect merchants' activities, starting in the tenth century Mediterranean and Hanseatic cities agreed to the presence of merchant consuls in charge of defending nationals from other countries in maritime and trade disputes. The situation began to change in the fifteenth century when the first ambassadors were sent between Italian cities (Genoa, Venice, and Florence). Contrary to consuls, ambassadors were no longer tasked merely with defending nationals involved in disputes, but also with representing their sovereign to political authorities. This formula became widespread in Europe in the sixteenth and seventeenth centuries. Thus, King Francis I sent the first permanent ambassador to the Sublime Porte in Istanbul in 1536.

It was also in the sixteenth and seventeenth centuries that European states began creating permanent diplomatic administrations within the machinery of government. In 1589, during the reign of Henri II, France saw the creation of the first post of secretary of state in charge of foreign affairs. It was entrusted to Louis de Revol, who became the first holder of the post of French Minister of Foreign Affairs. The post was subsequently made permanent in the organization chart of the French state, regardless of political persuasion. In Great Britain, the Foreign Office wasn't created until 1782. In the United States, the State Department was established in 1789. Finally, in the mid-nineteenth century, China, Japan, and the Ottoman Empire set up a permanent administration of foreign affairs. In the West, the nineteenth century was characterized by the emergence of a functional specialization of diplomatic statecraft when ministries of foreign affairs were endowed with geographical and thematic departments and offices.

After the Second World War, the process of decolonization, then the breakup of large federal states (URSS, Yugoslavia), saw a proliferation of countries and thus of embassies and consulates around the world. France thus had 163 bilateral embassies in 2017 compared to 47 at the end of 1945. In the second half of the twentieth century, ministries acquired many new departments in charge of multilateral negotiations, as well as permanent representation to international organizations (United Nations, European Union, African Union). Starting in the 1960s, diplomatic statecraft also became a new focus of public debate in democratic countries. Parliaments and the press began asking more frequent questions about their effectiveness, their cost, and the soundness of their methods, in particular those involving activities of social representation. In the early twenty-first century, this debate prompted a reduction in the scope of embassies and consulates by Western countries. Conversely, it was characterized by the creation of new diplomatic posts by emerging states (Brazil, China, and Turkey). Long ranked in second place worldwide after the United States for the number of its diplomatic posts, France was outstripped in 2017 by China, which opened embassies all over the world, particularly in regions considered more important for diplomacy such as Africa.

Institutional Design

Ministries of foreign affairs are generally quite limited in size compared to other departments. Thus, in 2015 the French Ministry of Foreign Affairs had only 14,000 agents, including 1650 senior civil servants. The Indian diplomatic service is even smaller. In 2015, it had only 900 senior civil servants running 119 embassies and consulates. Despite these small workforces, ministries of foreign affairs continue to occupy a high rank in the scale of government prestige, due to the symbolic weight of state representation in international relations. When a government is formed, it is not unusual for an influential political figure to be asked to run the country's diplomatic operations. Depending on the country and the period, ministries may be in charge of only foreign affairs, such as in Germany, the United States, and Brazil. They may also be assigned issues involving development aid, such as in France and Great Britain, foreign trade issues, such as in Australia, or both as is the case in Canada.

Ministers of Foreign Affairs rarely come out of the diplomatic administration. It does happen, as with Jean-François Poncet from 1978 to 1981 and Dominique de Villepin from 2002 to 2004 in France, but that is not the norm. Ministers of Foreign Affairs are usually politicians who discover the diplomatic system upon appointment. They are complemented by deputy ministers in charge of policy functions. Depending on the country, they are called vice-minister, deputy minister, or secretary of state. Thus, the Ministers of Foreign Affairs for all European Union countries have a deputy minister for European Affairs who focuses on matters negotiated in Brussels.

Ministries of Foreign Affairs are organized around different professional worlds: on the one hand, the central administration located in the country's capital and, on the other hand, its diplomatic and consular representation positioned in its partner states and international organizations.

Central administrations are generally structured into geographical (Asia, Europe, Africa, and the Americas) and thematic (economic, political, and legal) departments. The degree of specialization depends on the country's foreign policy agenda. The Ministry of Foreign Affairs for the Caribbean Island of Trinidad and Tobago has only three departments: one devoted to Caribbean affairs and the other two to bilateral and multilateral affairs. In many states, reforms begun in the 1990s have attempted to introduce new departments in charge of dealing with new foreign policy issues. This is the case, for example, with sustainable development and public diplomacy. Reforms have often called for strengthening crisis management structures within central administrations. In France, a 2008 white book on foreign and European policy led to the creation of a center in charge of managing humanitarian and security crises at the Quai d'Orsay. In Germany, the reform initiated in 2014 by Minister Frank-Walter Steinmeier resulted in few structural changes except for the creation of a new crisis prevention department. Finally, central administrations tend to delegate certain aspects of diplomacy (such as culture or the economy) to agencies endowed with some freedom of management. The Goethe Institute in Germany and the British Council in Great Britain are agencies responsible for the cultural diplomacy of the two countries. The reason for that autonomy is first of all budgetary: Cultural institutes are asked to self-finance their activities insofar as possible, in particular by selling language courses. But it is also political. Cultural diplomacy that seems to be run by an outside agency rather than directly by a ministry is assumed to produce greater influence in societies around the world, who see it as proof of pluralism. In France, the reform meant to create the French Institute in 2010, designed to handle cultural diplomacy, was shaped by similar arguments. It did not completely succeed, due to opposition from the French diplomatic corps eager to preserve its ministry's bureaucratic interests in that area.

Diplomatic and consular representations are administrative outgrowths of ministries of foreign affairs abroad. First and foremost, diplomatic representation is the institution that officializes an accredited state's presence to a receiving state or international organization. In the first case, it is a bilateral embassy. In the second case, it involves permanent representation (when the state is a member of the international organization) and a permanent mission or delegation (when the state is not a member of the international organization). Diplomatic representation is run by the ambassador. It enjoys privileges and immunities recognized by the Vienna Convention on Diplomatic Relations signed in 1961. In particular, the embassy and permanent representation remain an integral part of the territory of the accredited country in compliance with the legal principle of extraterritoriality. Any intervention by the receiving state inside the embassy is considered a violation of international law.

Consular representation is an institution established on the territory of a receiving state with the aim of fulfilling three missions: protecting the interests of its nationals; developing trade, cultural, scientific, and economic relations; and delivering administrative and travel documents. Contrary to an embassy, a consulate is not involved in political representation of the state. There is a hierarchy in how consular representation is designated: consulate general, consulate, vice-consulate, and consular agency, or honorary consulate. In the latter case, the task is often undertaken by a volunteer who may be an expatriate national or a citizen of the receiving country. The staff of a consular post enjoys privileges and immunities recognized by the Vienna Convention on Consular Relations signed in 1963.

The density of a country's diplomatic and consular network depends on its domestic resources, as well as its foreign policy ambitions. Looking only at bilateral embassies, five countries in 2017 had networks covering a vast majority of the 193 countries recognized by the UN: the United States (170 embassies), China (166 embassies), France (163 embassies), the UK (152 embassies), and Russia (146 embassies). Conversely, Malta, with 446,000 inhabitants, has only 23 embassies and 2 permanent representations around the world. Small countries, which are the most numerous, often give an ambassador multiple accreditation to better fulfill their diplomatic presence. In 2017, the Ghanaian ambassador to Prague was accredited in the Czech Republic, as well as in Slovakia, Hungary, Romania, and Macedonia. His services then involved diplomatic relations with five Central European and Balkan countries.

Budgets for ministries of foreign affairs are rarely posts that weigh most heavily on a state's public finances. However, in democratic countries they are easily subject to reductions in annual budget reviews. The budgets of the French and British Ministries of Foreign Affairs were reduced by 20% between 1990 and 2010. The relative ease with which the budgets of diplomatic administrations are reduced can be explained by two factors. The first is the lingering perception among parliamentarians and in the press that the work is largely limited to representation (cocktail parties and dinners). The second is that ministries of foreign affairs rarely have interest groups to support them, with the exception of diplomats themselves and expatriate communities. As a result of new public management practices, the idea that ministries of foreign affairs should evaluate their activities with performance indicators was introduced in many countries in the 2000s (Japan, Singapore, Great Britain, and France). This was the era when a host of quantitative criteria was invented to evaluate the effectiveness of diplomacy. Twenty years later, such procedures have proven very disappointing, diplomacy being a largely intangible activity that is hard to measure with quantitative criteria.

The Diplomatic Corps

The creation of permanent diplomatic missions starting in the seventeenth century gave rise to the diplomatic profession in Europe, usually pursued by representatives of the nobility who developed mutual codes. François de Callières, a diplomat for Louis XIV, and author in 1716 of a treatise entitled "On the Manner of Negotiating with Princes," speaks of the interests and common customs of European diplomats as a true "Freemasonry." These ties of sociability between well-born persons gave rise to the concept of a "diplomatic corps," whose practices were first institutionalized by the Vatican, then by various empires. In 1815, the Congress of Vienna recognized the title "dean" of the diplomatic corps, attributed to the ambassador with the longest posting in a country. It was not until the second half of the nineteenth century that admissions exams were established for embarking on a diplomatic career. In France, the first examination was held in 1880 during the Third Republic.

In 2017, the process for recruiting senior diplomats within ministries of foreign affairs varied from one state to another. In major countries (Brazil, China, the United States, France, Japan, and Great Britain), diplomats are recruited through exams. They become career diplomats, a term used by diplomats about themselves. In Germany, Brazil, and Norway, there is one pathway to enter the career. In other countries, there may be several different pathways. In France, diplomats at the Quai d'Orsay are recruited either through the École nationale d'administration or through the ministry's own exams, notably those for advisor and secretary for the "cadre d'Orient" requiring the knowledge of scarce languages. In the Gaimusho, the Japanese Ministry of Foreign Affairs, there are also two exams: one to recruit generalist diplomats and another for experts of a particular policy or country. In the United States, taking the State Department's foreign service exam requires choosing one of five branches that determine a diplomat's future specialization: management, consular affairs, economic affairs, political affairs, or public diplomacy.

After passing the exam, training differs from one country to another. In France, it only lasts three and a half months and is more akin to a program of socialization into the ways of the Quai d'Orsay than to any real acquisition of knowledge. Conversely, candidates in Brazil who have passed the exam take eighteen months of classes (in law, history, economics, languages, etc.) at the Rio Branco diplomatic academy in Brasilia before starting their first posting as third secretary in the Itamaraty, the Brazilian Ministry of Foreign Affairs. In general, the existence of career diplomacy goes hand in hand with substantial corporatism. This tendency is reinforced by the fact that ministries of foreign affairs have a small workforce compared to other administrations.

Democratic states may have mixed recruitment combining the career system with temporary appointments by the government. This is the case in France, Brazil, and the United States. Political appointments mainly involve ambassadorial posts and are often viewed highly negatively by career diplomats who see them as competition in obtaining the most important posts. In France, President Mitterrand, convinced that French diplomats were mostly right-wing, appointed several figures from outside the Quai d'Orsay to ambassadorial posts in May 1981 (to the United States, Italy, and the Netherlands), distressing career diplomats. In the United States, appointing ambassadors from outside the career track is viewed as more legitimate, as it occurs within the so-called spoil system, authorizing each newly elected president to appoint close associates to important government posts. About 30% of American ambassadors (probably more under the Trump administration) are recruited outside the State Department. It is generally a reward given to a large campaign donor, such as Jane D. Hartley, the American ambassador to France and Monaco from May 2014 to January 2017, who gave over 600,000 dollars to the Democratic National Committee for Barack Obama. In certain countries, such as Brazil, non-career diplomats appointed as ambassadors can never be part of the Ministry of Foreign Affairs. In France, they sometimes can, but are subject to highly restrictive procedural conditions.

In democratic countries where career diplomacy exists, governments are increasingly concerned about how the diplomatic corps is represented in society at large. This may manifest through affirmative action policies consisting in promoting women or social and ethnic diversity. With the exception of Northern European countries such as Finland and Norway, women are still under-represented in comparison with men in managerial positions in ministries of foreign affairs. This is particularly true for ambassadorial jobs. In 2015, women held 36% of ambassadorial posts in Norway and only 19% in Great Britain. In France, the 2012 Sauvadet law, aimed at promoting the hiring of women in the highest jobs in the civil service, led to a noticeable increase in the number of women ambassadors at the Quai d'Orsay: 30% in 2015 compared to 14% in 2013. The second reflection about the representative aspect of the diplomatic corps concerns social and ethnic origins. Countries like Germany, Brazil, France, and Norway set diversity goals for recruitment. In France, that objective is informal because the law does not allow the use of social and ethnic origins as a criterion for recruitment in the government. The situation is different in Norway, where juries for diplomatic exams show more official concern, at the last stage of the diplomatic exam, for recruiting Norwegian citizens with parents of immigrant origin. In Brazil, the Itamaraty traditionally recruits from the upper white echelons of society, showing little evidence of the country's social and ethnic diversity. This gap with social reality has been criticized in public debates because it manifests in a tiny proportion of black diplomats. It wasn't until 2011 that the first black career ambassador was appointed in the Itamaraty. In 2002, in response to criticism, the Brazilian government began giving out grants to candidates who identified as "Afro-descendants," enabling them to take the expensive courses to prepare for the diplomatic exam. In 2011, the left-wing government went a step further than affirmative action policies by reserving 10% of the spots in the Rio Branco Institute for Afro-descendants. However, in 2015 that 10% quota could be viewed from a relative perspective, due to the need to obtain a certain grade on the entrance exam. While societies have become actors of diplomacy in their own right, these measures show that ministries of foreign affairs can no longer avoid a democratic debate on how representative the social fabric really is.

But such considerations about exams in democratic countries should not overshadow the fact that in many non- or semi-democratic states, recruiting diplomats is still mainly a matter of how close one is to the political regime in power. This is the case in numerous countries on the African continent and in Central Asia. In certain states where the government is based on a multi-confessional compromise, as in Bosnia-Herzegovina and Lebanon, access to a diplomatic career requires the support of a community or faith-based political party. In China, belonging to the Communist Party remains an obligation in order to have a career in the Ministry of Foreign Affairs. The more the state is ruled by authoritarian political practices, the more recruiting diplomats is based on controlling their political dependability rather than on their expertise alone.

While practices vary from one state to another, a diplomat spends on average a third of his/her career at central headquarters and two-thirds on assignment abroad. When posted at an embassy or consulate, a diplomat is exempted from paying taxes in his/her country of residence, according to the terms of the two Vienna Conventions. Neither they themselves, their families or their private residence may be searched by the authorities in the country of residence. Likewise, a diplomat cannot be sentenced by a court, which can create tension between states in the case of criminal acts. Thus, some diplomats, responsible for a traffic accident in which citizens of their country of residence were killed, have never been tried. Diplomats are often better paid when posted abroad rather than at central headquarters, because they receive residence allowances. In countries with low civil service salaries, such as certain Central European states that are members of the European Union (Poland, the Czech Republic, and Slovakia), a job at an embassy may pay one to five times more than one at central headquarters. That large difference means few diplomats want to work in their home capital, creating human resource management issues for ministries of foreign affairs.

Ambassadors can only represent their country in another country after first obtaining accreditation, then presenting their credentials to the country's head of state. Requests for accreditation are usually answered within one month. A refusal—when no reply is given—is a highly rare procedure that blocks the appointment of a potential ambassador. The few recent cases of a refusal of accreditation were either due to political reasons, or for reasons strictly related to the person. A political refusal indicates a foreign policy disagreement. For instance, in 2015 the Brazilian government refused to give its consent to the appointment of Danny Cohen, the ambassador approached for the job by Israeli Prime Minister Netanyahu. In that instance, Brasilia did not want Tel-Aviv to be represented by an influential member of a committee of Israeli settlers in the West Bank. But there are other cases of refusals strictly related to the person. On two occasions, in 2008 and 2015, Vatican authorities refused to give their consent to French ambassadors because the candidates shortlisted in Paris were homosexuals. However, the real reason for the refusal was never officially explained by the Holy See, because international law does not require it. France in that case was reduced to acknowledging a failed approval that nonetheless raised questions in terms of all the conventions protecting human rights.

Diplomatic Practices

While technology enables faster diffusion of information, profound dynamics of change have affected diplomatic practices in all countries, in particular in terms of gathering and processing information. On the other hand, certain practices such as representation and negotiation have changed little since the nineteenth century.

Information gathering remains an essential part of the work of ministries of foreign affairs. Whether at central headquarters or posted abroad, diplomats continue to produce a huge volume of notes and reports to inform their governments. For them, it is a matter of deciphering events in other countries and within international organizations in order to facilitate foreign policy decisions. Exchanging with counterparts in other countries—and increasingly with non-governmental actors—is still the main source of information for diplomats, as well as participating in public meetings and analyzing the media. Code cables remain the favored mode of communication. In Western countries, numerous reforms in ministries of foreign affairs have called in vain for a reduction in the number of diplomatic cables. The WikiLeaks organization, which in 2010 illegally circulated several thousand cables written by American diplomats, has shown how precisely informed State Department agents are. The more diplomatic posts a country has, the more varied the information exchanged. With 37 embassies and permanent representations, Luxembourg's Ministry of Foreign Affairs does not have access to the same level of specific daily information as its German, French, and British counterparts. Thus, it has endorsed the creation of 150 delegations from the European Union around the world to complement its own information about countries in which it has no bilateral embassy. The fact remains that even ministries of foreign affairs in major countries can no longer claim a monopoly on information and intelligence in the international domain. A number of other actors (press agencies, large corporations, and international NGOs) are capable of gathering and disseminating information, sometimes at an even faster pace than ministries of foreign affairs.

Subject to competition from a number of other ministries, as well as from heads of state and government in creating foreign policy, diplomats are fond of saying their main added value remains expertise in international negotiations. Ministries of foreign affairs still negotiate a great deal on behalf of their governments in a format that can be bilateral (with another state) or multilateral (within international organizations). The development of multilateralism since the end of the Second World War has led to more proactive practices regarding the positions of multiple actors and to coalition-building. Within the European Union, multilateral negotiations are subject to another variable: majority vote in the Council of Ministers since the mid-1980s. In that institutional context, knowing they can no longer use their veto power, diplomats must learn to build blocking majorities or minorities. Although the departments in charge, respectively, of multilateral and bilateral diplomacy remain separate entities in most ministries of foreign affairs, their interaction in everyday affairs is a necessity. Thus, while 60% of UN Security Council resolutions concern Africa, the directorates dealing with UN issues or African issues within the five member states must work together. The same is true for permanent representation at the UN and bilateral embassies in African countries. Similarly, an increasing part of the work of European Union member state embassies in other member states consists in bilaterally deciphering the positions to be negotiated with the multilateral arenas of the European Union. Thus, the bilateral and multilateral formats for negotiating are deeply intertwined.

Furthermore, foreign policy (including in certain authoritarian states) is created by states that are rarely monoliths, but rather segmented entities based on continuous compromising between ministries of foreign affairs and other ministries, heads of state and government, parliaments, subnational authorities, and interest groups. The idea of foreign policy driven by Leviathan ministries of foreign affairs is largely a myth. Ministries of foreign affairs devote a great deal of time to foreign policy positions for their country even when it is considered a very centralized one. The 2000s saw an increase in inter-ministerial coordination within departments and state agencies. Foreign trade issues require working with the Finance Ministry, foreign military operations with the Ministry of Defense, and migration issues with the Ministry of the Interior. The ministries of foreign affairs in Germany and the United States must constantly check on positions taken by their national parliaments, given veto powers in international negotiations by their constitutions. In federal states like Belgium and Canada, the ministries of foreign affairs have increasingly included provinces, regions, and linguistic communities in international negotiations, to prevent them from refusing to ratify treaties.

Ministries of foreign affairs sometimes forfeit the power of coordination to central government bodies. In France and Great Britain, European Union affairs are directly coordinated by the prime ministers' offices (by the General Secretariat for European Affairs in Paris and by the Cabinet Office's European Secretariat in London). In some countries where the president has a great deal of power over foreign policy, tensions between the president's close circle and the ministries of foreign affairs are part of everyday decision-making. This is the case in the United States, where the president's national security advisor at the White House sometimes has more power than the secretary of state. This situation explains why theories of bureaucratic politics applied to the study of foreign policy were developed from the American experience, notably in Allison's founding book "The Essence of Decision." Furthermore, the rise of foreign policy coordination at the level of presidents and prime ministers is a widespread phenomenon linked to the development of summit diplomacy (G8, G20, European Council). Thus, Franco-German diplomacy tends to be coordinated by the entourages around the President of the Republic and the Federal Chancellor without the two countries' foreign affairs ministries and embassies playing a very prominent role. Thus, coordinating within their own country occupies foreign affairs ministries as much as negotiating with partners, echoing what Robert Putnam calls "two-level games."

In the public imagination, a diplomat is someone who spends a great deal of time entertaining, being invited out and going to social events. These activities, which have changed little since the nineteenth century, are often perceived as social affairs of little use. In ministries of foreign affairs, they are still taken seriously and go under the specific name of representation. The latter indeed remains an important practice in a posting, particularly in bilateral embassies where the head of the mission and his/her collaborators hold and attend many meals, cocktail parties, and receptions. In 2014, the French ambassador to the UK was required to attend at least one breakfast and cocktail party every day. Representation is not aimed solely at developing trust with the country of residence. It is directed at all social actors, in particular from the economic world. Ambassadors are increasingly involved in economic diplomacy designed to facilitate trade and investment for companies in the country of residence.

In order to grasp the real meaning of representation, one must go beyond observations about the social aspect. As James Der Derian so aptly explains, it consists in reducing the "estrangement" between separate worlds. Diplomats occupy the position of mediator, expressed through interpersonal relations. Representation is thus an integral part of a diplomat's job. Does it really generate influence? Interviews and archives have shown that a diplomat's assessment of interpersonal relations remains an important aspect in creating foreign policy. Diplomats continue to see as a resource what societies and analysts tend to view as outdated or even futile. Representation is one of the practical skills the social sciences must learn to understand better in their analysis of diplomacy.

Finally, ministries of foreign affairs should learn increasingly to forego secret negotiations and speak directly to social actors who are foreign policy actors in their own right. For a diplomat, the activity generally known as public diplomacy consists in communicating with diverse audiences, going to places as different as universities and trade fairs, dialoguing with the press, and using social media. Ambassadors today have blogs and send messages on Twitter and Instagram. Encouraged by their ministries, these exercises in public diplomacy also require regulation. A note in 2015 from the German Ministry of Foreign Affairs reminded agents using social media: "Always bear in mind that you are not communicating as a private person, but as a representative of the Federal Ministry of Foreign Affairs." Some authors have spoken of the development of "cyber diplomacy" or "digital diplomacy" as a revolution that has led ministries of foreign affairs to involve societies in the creation of foreign policy. Such conclusions are exaggerated. Reactions to social media have mainly enabled ministries of foreign affairs to assess the legitimacy of their partners' foreign policy decisions, as well as those in their own country. Ultimately, the increased reliance on public diplomacy has confirmed the new need for legitimacy (rather than mere effectiveness) in making foreign policy.

* * *

In a February 2017 policy paper, the Canadian scholar Andrew F. Cooper wrote that diplomacy—seen as a quest for mediation—has again become an increasingly contested activity lured by the opposite idea of "disintermediation": rejecting international trade agreements and the mobility of foreign populations and retreating behind state borders. Following Donald Trump's election in the United States and the Brexit victory in Great Britain, diplomatic tools have indeed been destabilized in Western countries. In Great Britain, the Foreign Office can be considered the defeated champion of British membership in the European Union. A question must then be asked: Will diplomacy continue to emphasize the soundness of the idea of mediation (and peace) in the international system or will it yield to public condemnation by adopting the disintermediation scenario?

Reference

Datta-Ray, Deep K., *The Making of Indian Diplomacy: A Critique of Eurocentrism*, Oxford, Oxford University Press, 2015.

CHAPTER 10

Intergovernmental Organizations

Cédric Groulier and Simon Tordjman

The *Yearbook of International Organizations* currently lists about 250 intergovernmental organizations (IOs) which all share three common features. They are all the result of a constituent, deliberate and formalized act, whether it involves a treaty, charter, or convention. They are also supported by the material existence of permanent headquarters. Lastly, they are a coordination mechanism aimed at facilitating the exchange of information, defining common objectives and implementing joint policies. Marie-Claude Smouts, Dario Battistella, and Pascal Vennesson stress this last aspect, seeing IOs as "a structured ensemble in which participants belonging to different countries coordinate their actions with the aim of reaching common goals" (2003).

The rise of international organizations is partly based on various sectorial coordination mechanisms that emerged in the late nineteenth century. The development of administrative unions was then aimed at resolving

---

C. Groulier (✉) · S. Tordjman
Sciences Po Toulouse, Toulouse, France
e-mail: cedric.groulier@sciencespo-toulouse.fr

S. Tordjman
e-mail: simon.tordjman@sciencespo-toulouse.fr

© The Author(s) 2020
T. Balzacq et al. (eds.), *Global Diplomacy*,
The Sciences Po Series in International Relations and Political
Economy, https://doi.org/10.1007/978-3-030-28786-3_10

coordination problems linked to the intensification and extension of international exchanges. For instance, in the areas of trade, transportation, and communication, bilateral treaties were not enough: It now involved agreeing on provisions that could be extended to other participants. The first international unions appeared at this time with a technical vocation to facilitate the exchange of information and the development of common standards—Telegraph Union (1865), Permanent Meteorological Committee (1873), Postal Union (1874), Metre Convention (1875), International Union for the Protection of Industrial Property (1883), the establishing of the Greenwich Meridian as the "prime meridian" (1884), Convention for the Protection of Literary and Artistic Works (1886), and concerning the Carriage of Goods by Rail (1890). This sectorial cooperation remained extremely fragile, however, with variable degrees of institutionalization, and often brought together technical experts rather than political representatives from member states.

Growing multilateralism in the twentieth century can be seen as part of the continuity of such initiatives. However, the creation of the League of Nations (LN) in 1919, and even more so the United Nations (UN) in 1945, signaled a new era of institutionalization and politicization of IOs. Multilateral discussions could no longer be reduced to mere functional ambitions and now involved a dynamic political principle of cooperation aimed at finding converging goals and shared interests. Since then, IOs have experienced a spectacular quantitative and qualitative rise as their numbers, composition, and missions have expanded simultaneously.

Guillaume Devin (2016, 104–110) distinguishes four crucial tasks pursued by IOs. The first consists in defining their members' rights and how they are exercised. Like the UN and the principle of sovereignty, or the International Maritime Organization and the Law of the Sea, IOs present themselves as guarantors of international law or certain aspects of it. The purpose of many organizations is also to enable cooperative management of the world's shared resources by facilitating the exchange, gathering and disseminating of information (World Health Organization [WHO], United Nations Educational, Scientific, and Cultural Organization [UNESCO]). Thirdly, certain IOs undertake aid and recovery missions, in particular in less advanced countries and/or post-conflict situations (International Monetary Fund [IMF], World Bank, European Bank for Reconstruction and Development [EBRD]). Lastly, they may have an insurance aspect by being a means of managing, if not preventing, conflicts (African Union, Economic Community of West African States [ECOWAS], etc.).

The diversification of IO missions raises an implicit question about their nature and degree of autonomy. Notably, Robert Cox and Harold Jacobson have distinguished between forum-organizations designed to facilitate negotiations among members and others exclusively devoted to providing services. While the former are basically arenas in which multilateral diplomacy takes place between their members (see the chapter by Franck Petiteville and Delphine Placidi-Frot, "Multilateral diplomacy"), the latter have more leeway in defining and pursuing their activities. The distinction between these two sides is, however, less pronounced than it may seem, and many institutions are both *places of* and *actors in* international governance (Thakur 2010). While a veil is often cast over the organizational aspect of IOs, these institutions should also be taken as bureaucracies in their own right which in practice cannot be reduced to the sum of their parts. Already in 1964, Inis Claude (1964, 174) indicated that an IO's secretariat "*is* the organization." In this regard, the emphasis put on their impartiality by the UN secretariat, the World Food Programme or the European Commission highlights how an organization's neutrality could appear to be the condition of possibility for its autonomy. Michael Barnett and Martha Finnemore (2004) have stressed that the authority of international organizations is founded on "their ability to present themselves as impersonal and neutral—as not exercising power but instead serving others" (Barnett and Finnemore 2004: 21). In practice, IOs are thus both established and establishing institutions which, in forming new spaces for interstate relations, can have an influence on negotiations between states.

And yet, devoting a chapter to IOs in a diplomacy textbook is not a given. Indeed, the literature on diplomatic practices often remains rooted in a state-centric perspective, which views IOs merely as negotiating arenas prolonging state foreign policies. Taking an opposing view to some analyses of the issue (see, e.g., Karnes and Mingst 2013, 142–159), this chapter is meant to grasp the contribution of IOs to diplomacy by focusing on diplomatic *practices* rather than on the—explicit or latent—*functions* attributed to IOs. The Vienna Convention on diplomatic relations (1961) is still the frame of reference for diplomatic practices. Its article 3 highlights the three main missions of diplomacy, namely *representation*, *observation*, and *negotiation*. In the first case, it involves representing the country of origin to a foreign country. This aspect, apart from consular activities of communication and assistance to nationals, usually involves a desire to promote and foster the country of origin's endeavors. The observation mission refers to information gathering, and the analysis and transmission of intelligence, in particular on the foreign country's domestic situation. Lastly, negotiation is traditionally at the core of the diplomatic profession, to such an extent that it is sometimes perceived as synonymous with diplomatic activity itself.

While diplomacy's traditional functions are a priori an imperfect fit with missions assigned to IOs, our intention is to show that they are highly interdependent. The legitimacy of these state-instituted organizations is often indexed to their political representativeness. However, while the legal personality of IOs has only been acknowledged belatedly, their autonomy and representative power have been increasingly asserted in recent times. Furthermore, the creation of IOs may be understood as a means for states to reduce the cost of information and thus foster the emergence of cooperative relations. Their cognitive resources also show prescriptive uses and a quest for more influence led by the IOs themselves. Finally, in terms of negotiations, these institutions very often go beyond the neutrality they may claim in order to help in more or less directly shaping negotiating objects and practices.

From Representativeness to Self-Representation

In state diplomacy, representation is considered a prerequisite to negotiations. The presence of a country's representatives in a foreign territory contributes to reinforcing the frequency and density of interactions between states. It is thus a condition that enables diplomatic interplay. When transposed onto the scale of IOs, the representative aspect of their diplomatic activity raises the question of their relative autonomy and ability to represent themselves as more than the sum of their components.

Representativeness as a Vector of Legitimacy and Object of Negotiation

As the number and scope of international organizations have increased, the representativeness of their decision-making processes has become a sensitive political issue, closely linked to the legitimacy and relative autonomy of the institutions in question. An IO's ability to "represent its members well" is indeed a compelling aspect of its legitimacy. Marieke Louis (2016, 27–48) showed how the International Labour Organization (ILO) has been driven since its creation by the claim of "well" representing the working world as a whole. Conversely, the perception of an organization's lack of representativeness affects its legitimacy and effectiveness (Devin 2016).

At the general level of an organization, the absence or underrepresentation of a member deemed indispensable to its proper functioning directly affects the results of its actions. This phenomenon is particularly visible in the case of universal or regional institutions faced with the withdrawal or non-membership of certain countries considered emblematic of the identity asserted by the organization. The institutional difficulties caused by Brexit are accompanied by more general fears about the spillover effects of the British withdrawal and about the sustainability of an organization divested of one of its most important members.

As attested by the criticism targeting the composition of the UN Security Council, representativeness perceived as dysfunctional may foster fears about the IO being manipulated by its most well represented and/or most powerful members. The debates prompted by IMF reforms in 2008 and 2010 also attest to the importance attributed to the political representativeness of different members within the institution. At the IMF, decision-making is based on an allocation of voting rights by shares indexed on a country's level of investment. Even so, the shares are not freely exchanged and their attribution is always the result of deals and negotiations between members of the organization, based on their preexisting voting rights. For example, the last reform approved in 2010 and ratified in 2015 by the American Congress authorized an increase in the total volume of shares (660 billion) and a revaluation of those of less well endowed economic powers (China, Korea, Mexico, Turkey). At the same time, it modified the voting rights of the United States, now set at about 17%. Nevertheless, the reform remained limited. Insofar as a majority of 85% of votes is still necessary for any modification of the fund's statutes, it does not call into question the possession of quasi-veto rights by the United States.

The powers and relative influence of member states in IO decision-making processes are often perceived as a means of validating what they see as their "rightful place" on the international scene. Representativeness then acts as a powerful vector of legitimacy, capable of affecting the relative autonomy of institutions.

The Legal Personality of IOs

Although belatedly, international law has helped to endorse IOs by recognizing their legal personality. In the early twentieth century, the prevailing opinion would never have considered it: Countries had a monopoly on international legal personality and IOs had no independent existence distinct from that of their members. While the principle remained deeply rooted, the International Court of Justice (ICJ) finally recognized that IOs could have a legal personality. In its April 11, 1949, advisory opinion, *Reparation for injuries suffered in the service of the United Nations*, it pointed out that "The Charter has not been content to make the Organization created by it merely a centre 'for harmonizing the actions of nations in the attainment of these common ends' [...]. It has equipped that centre with organs, and has given it special tasks. It has defined the position of the Members in relation to the Organization by requiring them to give it every assistance in any action undertaken by it [...], and to accept and carry out the decisions of the Security Council; by authorizing the General Assembly to make recommendations to the Members; by giving the Organization legal capacity and privileges and immunities in the territory of each of its Members; and by providing for the conclusion of agreements between the Organization and its Members.' Most recent founding treaties expressly recognize the legal personality of IOs. This is the case for the Treaty on European Union, where article 46 A provides that "the Union has a legal personality," or article 176 of the 1982 Montego Bay Convention on the law of the sea, regarding the International Seabed Authority. In the absence of explicit recognition in the treaties, the legal personality of IOs is presumed, until an examination of the terms of their founding treaty confirms or invalidates that presumption.

Thus, IOs, along with states, are legal entities, subject to public international law, with this double signification: They are endowed with legal capacity and are subject to the law. From their founding treaty, IOs derive their legal personality and competence, which entitle them to conclude treaties with their member states, third-party states and other IOs, to adopt unilateral legal acts, to file international claims for damages, etc. However, they are simultaneously circumscribed in their being and their prerogatives by those same treaties. Unlike states created by an event (bringing together a territory, a population, and an exclusive political authority) and which enjoy paramount and plenary legal capacity (linked to their sovereignty), IOs are the result of a legal act, which only gives them a functional capacity, finalized in relation to the goals they are assigned by the states that created them. IOs appear to be secondary subjects of law, whose competence is governed by a principle of specialty, which can be called upon when necessary. Thus in its opinion of July 8, 1996, *Legality of the Threat or Use of Nuclear Weapons by a State in an Armed Conflict*, the ICJ considered that the WHO was not competent to submit a question for an advisory opinion about the legality of the use of nuclear weapons, to the extent that its competence is limited to international cooperation regarding health protection. In opinion 2/94 on March 28, 1996, the Court of Justice of the European Union (CJEU) deemed that the European Community could not join the European Convention on Human Rights, given that it did not have the necessary competence according to article 235 CE (now 352 TFEU).

The areas of jurisdiction assigned, and the interpretation of the founding treaties on this point, represent major issues in the autonomy of IOs. The existence of a judicial body specific to IOs, competent in interpreting the treaty, can foster a broad reading of its competencies. CJEU rulings reflect this overall. In particular, the theory of implicit competencies has made it possible to recognize external competencies for the Community (allowing international agreements to be negotiated), not expressly stipulated by the treaties, where the latter had assigned it an internal competence (CJEU, March 31, 1971, *AETR*). However, states, as leading subjects of law and creators of IOs, always retain the power to interpret their own commitments (arbitral award of December 9, 1978, *Case Concerning the Air Service Agreement of 27 March 1946 Between the United States of America and France*). Thus, by virtue of their sovereignty, they always have the possibility of contesting interpretations of the founding treaties by the IOs' bodies, and in particular potential extensions of competencies. In so doing, they are attempting to give precedence to conventional logic over the institutional logic that governs the organization as an autonomous legal entity (Raspail 2013, 937–967).

Such controversies on the scope of IO competencies reveal a conflict of legitimacy between their components and the institutions to which they belong. They also attest to the ambivalence of relations between states and IOs. Established by states but irreducible solely to the sum of their own interests, IOs have gradually gained relative autonomy, also sustained by the specific use of the cognitive resources they are graced with.

The Gathering and Use of Information

The gathering and exchange of information are meant to encourage states to overcome their initial mistrust and take part in a cooperative action approach by enabling increased transparency in international politics and ensuring compliance with commitments undertaken. As vectors of predictability in international politics, these cognitive mechanisms are a crucial aspect in the mission of coordination for IOs. They also help transform the diplomatic practices of their members, subject to a double injunction of transparency and public disclosure. But the contribution of IOs to diplomatic activity should also be seen in the light of more prescriptive uses of information.

Information as a Condition for Cooperation

Whether they have a strictly technical dimension, like the administrative unions created in the nineteenth century, or a more political ambition, international organizations all provide a formal framework for interstate cooperation. This formalism cannot be reduced to a single procedural dimension. At odds with the established secret nature of bilateral meetings, the demand for transparency that comes with multilateral negotiations has helped to reduce its uncertainty and facilitate the emergence of cooperative behavior (Keohane 1984). Predictability is indeed a condition of cooperation: When actors are devoid of the capacity to anticipate and be sure of their interlocutors' future behavior, self-help prevails. Regarding disarmament, the absence of a sufficient guarantee about respecting mutual commitments may explain the resumption of a logic of escalation. Liberal approaches to international relations stress the ability of IOs to use information gathering and/or monitoring mechanisms as a means to foster trust and cooperative behavior. In the case of negotiations involving environmental, health, or economic questions, information sharing allows a better grasp of the problems dealt with. By creating monitoring and evaluation mechanisms, the IOs also help reinforce respect for agreements concluded. Multilateral peacekeeping operations illustrate the cooperative effects induced by information gathering and dissemination by IOs. Initially instituted to follow the application of a ceasefire between belligerent states, UN peacekeeping operations were not conceived as instruments of coercion but as neutral channels of observation and information exchange. The first peacekeeping missions in 1948 and 1949 were mainly tasked to follow troop movements, to investigate allegations about possible ceasefire violations and to publicize those infractions in order to encourage states to respect the agreement.

Information gathering and dissemination are thus at the core of the IOs' coordinating mission. The increase in the quantity of information and its greater accessibility also go hand in hand with a principle of disclosure and a demand for transparency that has significantly transformed procedures for interstate negotiations (Colson 2009, 31–41). In that respect, the rise of IOs has broken with an old tradition of diplomacy which held the secret nature of both the negotiating process and its outcomes as an undisputed paradigm. Starting in the eighteenth century, the Kantian hope for universal and everlasting peace and the criticisms from Enlightenment philosophers against any form of personal power helped to make public disclosure a new imperative in international politics. Furthermore, that demand was taken up again in the Covenant of the League of Nations which, in article 18, decreed that "Every treaty or international engagement entered into hereafter by any Member of the League shall be forthwith registered with the Secretariat and shall as soon as possible be published by it." That obligation was again evoked in 1945 in article 102 of the United Nations Charter. However, although the charter insisted on disclosing *results*, it nonetheless remained silent about the negotiation *process*. Since the end of the Cold War, the demand for public disclosure involved not just results but increasingly pertained to the processes themselves. Transparency was then presented as a way of curbing the "democratic deficit" and opacity of many organizations. Declaration no. 17 attached to the Maastricht Treaty highlighted that "the transparency of the decision-making process strengthens the democratic nature of institutions, as well as public trust toward the administration." More recently, article 15 of the Treaty on the Functioning of the European Union stipulated that "The European Parliament shall meet in public, *as shall the Council when considering* and voting on a draft legislative act" (*our italics*). This rejection of opacity is also related to the increasing mobilization of non-state actors that have called for more involvement in IO decision-making processes and demanded greater transparency in their operations.

Disseminating and supplying information is therefore at the core of establishing and running IOs. Yet these elements are not enough to deduce the organizations' passive neutrality. Indeed, the shift from information sharing toward prescription has enabled IOs to exert new forms of normative activity and influence.

Prescriptive Uses of Information

Contemporary ways of gathering and using information in IOs tend to exert a standardizing influence without legal standards having to be formally adopted. This evolution is one of the consequences of using managerial instruments founded on evaluative and evidence-based logic. In an approach meant to be neutral, the information gathered strives to objectify performances toward which actors are urged to orient their behavior and practices.

The combination of several techniques has given rise to informal quasi-normative sequences, through which IOs play a prescriptive role. Imported from the business world and largely used in national administrations as well as IOs, benchmarking consists in comparing practices and measuring agents' performances (in this case, members of the IO) based on indicators and predefined objectives. This information gathering and sequencing tool is frequently implemented among peers: As "reviewed reviewers," IO member states systematically compare and evaluate their performances for the purpose of optimization. This peer-review process is based on a voluntary approach in which states trust one another and the IO itself as the appropriate framework for it. The Organization for Economic Cooperation and Development (OECD 2003) has shown a penchant for this technique, also illustrated by the IMF's monitoring system, the trade policy review mechanism at the World Trade Organization (WTO), or the open method of coordination (OMC) for economic and social policies used by the European Union. Furthermore, peer-review goes hand in hand with peer pressure, which is none other than influence and persuasion exercised by other countries during the review process: From informal dialogue to publication of assessment reports, the one reviewed is urged to improve performance and above all play the game—including by submitting to monitoring—so as not to lose credit and to preserve its reputation. These tools, most commonly used among members of an organization, are also employed within IOs themselves. For instance, the European Union and its member states agree to an OECD review of their regulatory policy performance. Moreover, when the OECD assessed the "Better Regulation" program developed by the European Commission, it equated the latter with a "country" (OECD 2015).

The assessment approach has become so standard that, in addition to reports, IOs produce rankings that in fact make them powerful influencers. For example, the rankings from the World Bank's *Doing Business* reports began measuring business regulation and its effectiveness in 190 countries and several major metropolises starting in 2002. Comparing states' respective performances on the basis of ten indicators, the rankings established have helped orient international investors' strategic choices toward the most favorable legal environment and led national governments to carry out domestic reforms to enable them to rise up in the rankings (relaxed labor laws, secured investments, fiscal incentives, reduced administrative costs). In a similar way, the Programme for International Student Assessment (PISA), launched in 1997 by the OECD, has had a normative effect on members of the organization by providing information designed to compare the performances of educational systems.

These procedures and interventions usually take place before the adoption of binding standards. By influencing or seeking to influence the actors' behavior, the identification and dissemination of "good practices" (Klein et al. 2015) contribute to a normative *function*. Through the use of evidence, they are instrumental in orienting behaviors, legitimizing (new) standards, and defining shared policies. However, their normative *power* depends on their degree of institutionalization and the nature of the tools designed to ensure observance (regular follow-up, peer monitoring, etc.).

INTERNATIONAL ORGANIZATIONS IN THE NEGOTIATING PROCESS

While the terms "negotiation" and "diplomacy" may have overlapped etymologically and historically, the two practices need to be distinguished. By facilitating the quest for compromise, negotiations are both the means and the end of diplomacy. In that process, IOs play a double role. They are both the space where multilateral negotiations unfold and an increasingly autonomous actor capable of influencing the objects and practices of negotiation. This aspect emerges in particular when IOs ensure and implement mediation strategies through the agency of their secretariats.

IOs and Negotiating Standards

Although not all negotiations are designed to conclude legal agreements, adopting new standards is often a country's aim in negotiating. Moreover, *negotium* is the eloquent name used by jurists for the content of legal rules. With this in mind, IOs are places where states conduct these activities and for which their substantial contribution varies. At first glance, the definition of the agenda refers mainly to the diplomatic interplay between members. The United Nations General Assembly, both guarantor of the principle of legal equality among states and responsible for "discussing any questions or any matters within the scope of the present Charter" (Art. 10), is traditionally entrusted by member states—both large and small—with attempting to echo new concerns. But building on their growing autonomy and the knowledge they have gradually gained, IO bureaucracies and secretariats are also increasingly capable of driving, framing, and orienting negotiations.

A member of the secretariat of the United Nations Convention on Biological Diversity stated that: "As a national delegate, it was my greatest ambition to change at least one word in the text of the decision; as part of the secretariat, I can influence the whole text" (Biermann and Siebenhuner 2009, 322). However, the terms of that influence are rarely direct or explicit. The reports produced by IOs, the "good practices" they formalize, the potential recommendations they adopt often herald conventional commitments that subsequently link states. A classic example, United Nations General Assembly Resolution 1962 (XVIII) involving the Declaration of Legal Principles Governing the Activities of States in the Exploration and Use of Outer Space, adopted on December 13, 1963, was the source of the principles subsequently recognized by international treaties, such as the eponymous treaty concluded on January 27, 1967.

The expertise of/in IOs provides those with the most extensive powers with a quasi-legislative function (Alvarez 2005). This is naturally the case for regional integration organizations such as the European Union through the secondary legislation adopted by its institutions, as well as when specialized IOs are authorized to regulate certain sectors (see, e.g., the International Civil Aviation Organization's [ICAO][1] "standards and recommended practices" or the WHO Assembly "regulations").[2] The conventional horizontal logic that applies to legal relationships between states is then challenged by such institutional, unilateral, and vertical dynamics, through which IOs gain more autonomy.

Finally, IOs sometimes participate directly in international normative processes by taking part in negotiations as legal subjects. In the framework of their competencies, they may be bound to states and other IOs through formal agreements. For example, the European Union is involved in about 140 trade agreements; it has been a member of the WTO since January 1, 1995; recently, it ratified the Paris Climate Agreement adopted on December 12, 2015. Through article 6 § 2 of the Treaty on the European Union, the EU may also become a party to the European Convention on Human Rights.

---

[1] Annexes from the Convention on International Civil Aviation signed on December 7, 1944.

[2] Art. 21 of the WHO Constitution, July 22, 1946.

IO Influence on Framing Negotiations

Multilateral institutions do have an impact on negotiations, which they may initiate and/or take a more direct part in. Their involvement can also be assessed in light of more informal and practical aspects. By fostering actors' participation in the collective and constant interplay of multilateral negotiations, IOs help spread shared representations and legitimate practices. The effective appropriation of these norms is variable and may give rise to explicit resistance or to token support. However, constructivist approaches have highlighted how, by influencing the forms of this collective interplay, IOs are also able to affect their outcome. The spreading of common understandings and concepts (from "human security" to gender mainstreaming) has helped to build shared frames of reference that orient the definition of key issues and the appropriate answers to be provided.

For instance, these framing operations may occur during mediation and peacemaking activities in which IOs have increasingly participated. Such initiatives have proliferated since the late 1980s, along with a growing involvement of IOs in conflict management and peace building. Secretary-generals (or their representatives) of universal organizations such as the UN or of regional institutions (mainly the European Union, the Organization for Security and Cooperation in Europe [OSCE], the African Union, ECOWAS) (Tenenbaum 2009) have been tasked with facilitating the start of peace talks and coordinating actors of diverse status in the field (UN agencies, non-governmental organizations, experts, governmental actors, and [para-] military leaders, etc.). These "diplomats with non-national roles" (Leguey-Feilleux 2009) have thus had to muster up all the diplomat's skillfulness, daring, and caution to keep discussions going and identify points of consensus between belligerents. They may also take on a more active role by proposing preliminary versions of texts amended and negotiated by delegations afterward. In the case of the technical negotiations between Serbia and Kosovo from 2011 to 2012, Robert Cooper, the European Union representative entrusted with facilitating the negotiations, produced the first version of the text ultimately accepted by the two parties. In that capacity, he not only helped guide and sequence discussions, but also provided more substantial proposals regarding the text of the final agreement.

The contribution of IOs to the negotiating process is not limited to mere procedural aspects. In defining the behavior expected within them, they take part in the supervision and possible outcomes of the negotiations. They may also intervene more directly as mediators with third-party belligerents, making possible and orienting dialogues.

* * *

The malleable and ambivalent diplomatic power of IOs can be assessed in light of tensions that arise on two distinct levels. While they prolong and catalyze the power games and differentiated strategies in state foreign policies, they cannot be reduced to that. Through operations involving piloting, normative impetus and socializing effects, IOs affect both the nature of relations between states and the objects of world governance. Their contributions unfold in a continuum ranging from loose, implicit initiatives to more robust and legally formalized interventions. While some IOs may negotiate texts, ratify treaties and thus constitute influential actors on the international scene in their own right, their effective scope of action should always be seen through the capacity to use their particular position, linked both to their members' exercise of sovereignty and ability to act autonomously, in more or less formal registers.

References

Alvarez, José E., *International Organizations as Law-Makers*, Oxford, Oxford University Press, 2005.
Barnett, Michael, Finnemore, Martha, *Rules for the World: International Organizations in Global Politics*, Ithaca (NY), Cornell University Press, 2004.
Biermann, Frank, Siebenhuner, Bernd (eds.), *Managers of Global Change. The Influence of International Environmental Bureaucracies*, Cambridge, The MIT Press, 2009.
Colson, Aurélien, "La négociation diplomatique au risque de la transparence: rôles et figures du secret envers des tiers," *Négociations*, 1 (1), 2009.
Devin, Guillaume, *Les Organisations internationales*, Paris, Armand Colin, 2016.
Inis, L. Claude, Jr., *Swords into Plowshares: The Problems and Progress of International Organization*, New York (NY), Random House, 1964.
Karns, Margaret P., Mingst, Karen A., "International Organizations and Diplomacy," in Andrew F. Cooper, Jorge Heine, Ramesh Thakur (eds.), *The Oxford Handbook of Modern Diplomacy*, Oxford, Oxford University Press, 2013, pp. 142–159.
Keohane, Robert, *After Hegemony: Cooperation and Discord in the World Political Economy*, Princeton (NJ), Princeton University Press, 1984.
Klein, Asmara, Laporte, Camille, Saiget, Marie (ed.), *Les Bonnes Pratiques des organisations internationales*, Paris, Presses de Sciences Po, 2015.

Leguey-Feilleux, Jean-Robert, *The Dynamics of Diplomacy*, Boulder (CO), Lynne Rienner, 2009.

Louis, Marieke, "Un parlement mondial du travail? Enquête sur un siècle de représentation tripartite à l'Organisation internationale du travail," *Revue française de science politique*, 66 (1), 2016: 27–48.

OECD, "Peer Review: A Tool for Co-operation and Change," in *Development Co-operation Report 2002: Efforts and Policies of the Members of the Development Assistance Committee*, Éditions OCDE, Paris, 2003. https://doi.org/10.1787/dcr-2002-6-en.

OECD, *OECD Regulatory Policy Outlook 2015*, Éditions OCDE, Paris, 2015. https://doi.org/10.1787/9789264238770-en.

Raspail, Hélène, "Contrôle de validité des actes juridiques des organisations internationales," in Évelyne Lagrange, Jean-Marc Sorel (eds.), *Droit des organisations internationales*, Paris, LGDJ, 2013.

Smouts, Marie-Claude, Battistella, Dario, Petiteville, Franck, Vennesson, Pascal (ed.), *Dictionnaire des relations internationales*, Paris, Dalloz, 2003.

Tenenbaum, Charles, "La médiation des organisations intergouvernementales: un maillon essentiel," in Guillaume Devin (ed.), *Faire la paix. La part des institutions internationales*, Paris, Presses de Sciences Po, 2009, pp. 101–131.

Thakur, Ramesh, "Multilateral Diplomacy and the United Nations: Global Governance. Venue or Actor?" in James P. Muldoon, Joann F. Aviel, Richard Reitano, Earl Sullivan (eds.), *The New Dynamics of Multilateralism: Diplomacy, International Organizations, and Global Governance*, Boulder (Co), Westview, 2010.

CHAPTER 11

Supranational Diplomats

Stephanie C. Hofmann and Olivier Schmitt

Regional, international, and global organizations have established their position as major vehicles for producing and implementing public and club goods beyond the state. The proliferation of international organizations (IOs) as well as their increased scope has gone hand in hand with the continued emergence of diplomatic actors located outside national governments and operating within supranational and international structures.[1]

While diplomatic relations are generally understood as conducted by states, or more precisely by national governments—which set up diplomatic academies and curricula to train their diplomats before sending them to a posting, or formulate foreign policy from a ministry based in the

---

[1] The terms international bureaucrats and supranational bureaucrats are used interchangeably here.

S. C. Hofmann (✉)
Graduate Institute of International and Development Studies,
Geneva, Switzerland
e-mail: stephanie.hofmann@graduateinstitute.ch

O. Schmitt
University of Southern Denmark, Odense, Denmark
e-mail: schmitt@sam.sdu.dk

© The Author(s) 2020
T. Balzacq et al. (eds.), *Global Diplomacy*,
The Sciences Po Series in International Relations and Political
Economy, https://doi.org/10.1007/978-3-030-28786-3_11

capital—the number of international bureaucrats who also take on diplomatic functions with third countries or other IOs has steadily increased. It is thereby interesting to note that the number of IO temporary staff has decreased, and national secondment is far less frequent than in the early twentieth century. Today's international bureaucrats often swear allegiance to the international organization they are working for. They have developed expertise that can be complementary or not with member states. All in all, IO bureaucrats conduct diplomacy next to states and do not necessarily see eye-to-eye with them.

Existing scholarship has shown that international bureaucrats, that is, bureaucrats working for and representing an international organization, play an active role in formulating and implementing multilateral policies not only within the IO and its membership but also in relation to other countries, IOs, and NGOs (Haas 1958; Snidal and Thompson 2003; Hawkins and Jacoby 2006). However, their independence from their member states varies (Haftel and Thompson 2006), whether on the level of formal organizational structures or informal ones (Mérand et al. 2011). In addition, no matter the formal or informal delegated authority, not all international organizations have large bureaucracies.

This chapter presents major works dealing with supranational political diplomatic actors and action. In order to get a better grasp of the different ways of understanding supranational diplomacy, we focus on four approaches in international relations: neo-functionalism, principal-agent approaches, diplomatic practices, and international authority. Most of this work was initially developed and applied to developments in the European Union (EU), and we draw from this organization for our empirical illustrations. The EU's External Action Service is arguably the most well-known supranational diplomatic actor today although international bureaucrats from organizations such as the UN, NATO, and many others have also developed capacities that let them act outside member states' constraints. In other words, while the EU remains a prominent IO when looking for supranational diplomacy, the different approaches outlined in this chapter have been extended to different international organizations that operate either on the regional or the global level.

Neo-Functionalism and Integration of National Diplomacy

Neo-functionalism (conceptualized by Ernst Haas in his 1958 book, *The Uniting of Europe*) is an evolution of functionalism, an approach initially proposed by David Mitrany. The latter thought that an increasingly extensive system of international organizations run by experts could be a transformative force within the international system, going beyond a competitive nationalist mind-set. Haas reformulated this technocratic and elitist vision into a more political approach, studying the multiple ways in which sub-national sectorial interests, continuously competing and cooperating, could be reconciled through the creative intervention of technocratic supranational actors.

Neo-functionalism is a difficult approach to classify because it borrows from theories of both international relations and comparative politics. Neo-functionalism recognizes the fundamental importance of the role played by states, notably when international organizations are created, or treaties renegotiated. However, it also stresses two categories of non-state actors that initiate processes for more integration:

- interest groups and transnational social movements that form at the regional level;
- organizations' international secretariats.

Nation-states set up the terms of the initial agreements and may try to monitor their developments, but are not the only ones influencing the direction and pace of change. On the contrary, international bureaucrats—in cooperation (or not) with actors whose interests and values push for solutions incorporated into concrete problems—have a natural tendency to exploit *spillover effects*, which arise when states consent to a degree of supranationalism to settle a specific problem, but then realize that solving the problem requires extending that supranationalism to other connected areas.

According to this approach, regional integration is necessarily a conflictual and sporadic process, made of give-and-take. But the approach deems that democratic and pluralist governments running complex societies will gradually find themselves subjected to economic, political, and social dynamics on a regional scale and will resolve their differences by agreeing to delegate a certain number of competencies to supranational entities. Haas specified no temporal horizon for the empirical confirmation of his theory of increased integration, and a classic error consists in forgetting the conflictual aspect of the process he analyzes in favor of a teleological interpretation of a continuously ongoing integration. That error has led many studies to put forward the idea that neo-functionalism was "outdated" with each new difficulty in the process of European integration.[2]

Several researchers have attempted to go beyond Haas' empirical work (focused on the European Commission) by involving other actors in their analysis, and stepping outside an approach that could be seen as results-focused. In particular, Philippe Schmitter's "neo-functionalist" approach (1970) represents the process not as a continuum with ups and downs (or even a multitude of continua) as Haas does, but rather as successive cycles involving phenomena of integration or simultaneous slackening depending on the domain. Similarly, Sandholtz and Stone Sweet (1998) have stressed the importance of interaction among private economic actors, legislators, and judges in the European integration dynamic. The integration process has its source in the development of transnational economic, political, and social exchanges, which makes it costly to maintain a mode of national governance. Consequently, non-governmental actors engaged in these transactions are pressuring governments, often with the support of community institutions—for instance by the increasing number of appeals before the Court of Justice of the European Union (CJEU)—with the aim of establishing a mode of supranational governance where community institutions are capable of regulating a sector and constraining the behavior of the actors involved, including states. The emergence of these rules and organizations has led to the new development of transnational society. This approach has

---

[2] However, Haas himself recognized the limits of his approach. Studies from the 1970s, attempting to use neo-functionalism outside the European context, led to a highlighting of the European experience's exceptional nature, notably by the fact that it included democratic countries with a high standard of living, and whose security was largely taken care of by the United States through a designated organization (NATO). Moreover, the European Union was ultimately caught up by a phenomenon that Haas had anticipated: its gradual politicization. European citizens began paying attention to how the European Union affected their lives, and politicians realized they could win or lose elections over issues dealt with on a regional level rather than at the level of their own state. That politicization challenged the illustrative neo-functionalist mechanism based largely on discrete cooperation among international bureaucrats, national delegates, and representatives of interest groups.

been criticized particularly for its excessive generalization, as it cannot be applied to all sectors, but it provides a vivid illustration of the increasing role played by certain international bureaucrats in favor of greater integration.

This being so, how can one explain the creation of the European External Action Service in relation to the neo-functionalist approach? The creation of the EEAS can be interpreted as a consequence of the spillover effect responding to the weaknesses of foreign policy and security cooperation as attested in the Balkans: The states had decided at the time of the Maastricht Treaty to endow the European Union with a "foreign policy and shared security" pillar (run by a "high representative"), but realized its difficult institutional position with respect to the European commissioner in charge of external relations and to the president of the Council of the EU and his "foreign affairs" lineup. The three posts were merged during the adoption of the Treaty of Lisbon, and the new post of "high representative" was endowed with a designated administrative service, the EEAS, thereby illustrating the increasing integration dynamic. Thus, actors from the EEAS are always international experts, at the interface between states (since national diplomats are outposted there) and supranational organizations (hosting experts from the Council and the Commission).

Principal-Agent Approaches

Similar to neo-functionalist approaches, scholars working from a principal-agent perspective study how international bureaucrats (or "agents") can increase their turf and push IO member states toward new policy domains or issue areas (Littoz-Monnet 2017).[3] From the point of view of the state (or "principal"), this often involves agency slack. However, unlike neo-functionalism, this approach does not suppose an unequivocal teleological direction for integration and an increased supranationalization. Instead, it does not assume a priori that international bureaucrats necessarily work for the common good.

Researchers working in this tradition are more interested in understanding under what conditions states delegate authority to IO agents, and how agents translate their relative autonomy into actions not necessarily anticipated by their principal (Hawkins and Wade 2006; Pollack 2003; Nielson and Tierney 2003). States can anticipate and try to mitigate their agents'

---

[3] The principal-agent approach was imported to IR from domestic politics studies.

pursuit of their own preferences. When states set up structures for an international organization, they try to control agents by putting in place various mechanisms: The most common are resource management, institutional oversight, or decision-making procedures limiting the influence of bureaucrats. In these circumstances, we should not observe much supranational diplomatic capacity independent of member state preferences. But states can never control bureaucrats completely. In short, the agents' *degree* of autonomy and the discretion that these agents take, as well as the monitoring devices that principals can create to gain back their power, are the main area of investigation.

In principal-agent approaches, international bureaucrats are understood to be strategic actors: their objectives include material security and increasing their turf, legitimacy, and promoting their preferred policies. Variations in the agents' ability to act are often explained by the varying staff size and resources at their disposal, the importance states accord an issue, and the capabilities that states invest in controlling their agents. While most principal-agent approaches suggest that international bureaucrats gradually carve out their autonomous spaces over time, recently scholars such as Tana Johnson (2013) have suggested that even in the initial design stage of IOs, international bureaucrats contribute actively in the process.

This approach has been applied to a variety of international organizations (regional and global) covering a broad range of policy domains and issue areas. The EU has received disproportional attention, in particular how agents such as the European Commission and the European Court of Justice behave unpredictably with regard to their principals. Most recently the EU's EEAS has emerged as a new agent in Brussels which is at the forefront, next to the European Commission, in fostering relations with outside actors. Using the tools provided by principal-agent approaches to study the creation and operation of the EEAS, we can analyze its structures and its degree of freedom. The EEAS is composed not only of staff from the Commission and the Council, but a third of its personnel is supplied by member states. The EEAS had a hard time establishing itself as an actor between the Commission and the Council, but has slowly created its own area of operations. Member states are still reticent about using the EEAS to negotiate major policy outlines. However, as shown by the discussions on relations between NATO and the EU, once the main parameters have been set up, it is the EEAS's job to implement the joint declaration by the two institutions, thus having at their disposal a degree of interpretative flexibility for the directives established by member states (Hofmann 2019).

Diplomatic Practices and the Regionalization of Diplomacy

Increasing numbers of internationalists have taken an interest in the study of international "practices" over the past ten years, defined in the minimal sociological sense as socially meaningful patterns of behaviors. The origin of such practices is not to be found in individuals' rational choices, nor in mechanisms above or outside the agents imposed by the social structure, rather these practices are the result of repeated interactions which themselves become constitutive of the social world. This approach to the study of diplomacy is directly influenced by sociological work, inspired by Bourdieusian praxeology, the "communities of practices" theorized by Lave and Wenger, actor network theories (associated in particular with the work of Bruno Latour) and pragmatic sociology as conceived by Boltanski.

In international relations, the work of Emmanuel Adler (2008), Vincent Pouliot (2016), Rebecca Adler-Nissen (2014), and Iver Neumann (2012) is particularly linked to the study of diplomatic practices. This approach also pertains to epistemological commitment, since the practices are not seen merely as a dependent variable resulting from causes to be elucidated. On the contrary, the practices themselves are constitutive of international order. This approach makes it possible to go beyond positivist and theoretical analyses of how the international system operates (such as the neorealist approach), which tend to see diplomats as cogs implementing structural dynamics over which they have no influence or which they generally do not perceive. On the contrary, through a practice-based approach, the emphasis can be put back on the practitioners themselves, their interactions and professional rituals generating the social orders that constitute international relations.

Diplomatic relations are governed by a set of rituals (of which "protocol" is only the formalized aspect) including in particular specific forms of eloquence, shared symbols understandable by all members of the diplomatic corps, gift exchanging and at times even particular dress codes. Multilateral diplomacy is no exception to these rules, and international organizations are the site of many ritualized diplomatic practices which are the *result* of preexisting social orders, but which *reinforce* or *contest* that social order once implemented by diplomats. Thus, in NATO, being seen as a "reliable ally" involves a certain number of very concrete practices which contribute to establishing an informal status hierarchy within the organization, depending on whether or not they are successfully implemented by diplomats from the countries concerned (Schmitt 2017). At the UN, being a non-permanent member of the Security Council means those states joining must commit to a certain number of favorably perceived public policies (for instance, deploying troops on peacekeeping missions to show concerted engagement), but it also means the diplomats from those countries must adopt a set of practices (when to talk during Council meetings, how to comment on a resolution, whom to contact during preliminary meetings, etc.) that signal their status. Naturally, the permanent members on the Security Council also have their own diplomatic practices that signal (and justify) their status at the symbolic summit of the United Nations social space.

How to explain the emergence of the EEAS through a practices-inspired approach? First, by observing, as Christian Lequesne has shown (2015), that the creation of the service is the result of a compromise between representatives of four institutions (the European Commission, the European Parliament, the Secretariat General of the Council of the EU, and member states) each having different professional practices and attaching different meanings to the term "European diplomacy."

Secondly, since the EEAS was created, the study of practices has helped in observing the emergence (or not) of a shared professional culture within the EEAS. In particular, two "groups" can still be observed within the EEAS: on the one hand, the former members of the Commission or of the Council, and on the other hand, the national diplomats, each harboring suspicions about the other's competence. Members of the former group feel that national diplomats assigned to the EEAS do not understand how the EU operates, and in particular the budgetary implications of public policy proposals, tasks they do not deal with in their national ministries but that are part of the professional skill of European bureaucrats. Members of the latter group feel that members of the first group lack competence in writing effective and relevant reports on specific political situations (a classic diplomatic task). The study of practices also makes it possible to establish how diplomatic work is carried out in regional diplomacy, notably tasks such as coordinating tools, sharing information within the EEAS and strategic reflection on the tasks, and roles of European diplomacy. The study of diplomatic practices thus helps us see how regional diplomacy is built, through keen empirical analysis of the everyday elaboration of that diplomacy and the symbolic struggles that are the key issues for those designing and implementing it.

International Authority

Recently, there have been some important developments in the study of the supranationalization of diplomacy following the creation and publication of new datasets on international authority. Pioneering conceptual work has been conducted by Haftel and Thompson (2006), who have shown that many studies assume that international bureaucrats possess some independence from member states but had not conceptualized, or measured, formal or informal institutional features to support a theory of degree of autonomy. This call to systematically study institutional design features has been picked up by several research collaborations. In particular, Liesbet Hooghe, Gary Marks, and their collaborators, as well as the team working with Michael Zürn have drawn attention to ways of measuring authority in international organizations. Hooghe, Marks, and their collaborators have focused on measuring the degree of delegation and pooling, and Zürn et al. (2012) similarly have examined the definition of rules, as well as monitoring, interpretation, and enforcement.

This empirically grounded work provides opportunities for theoretical and conceptual synthesis. Neo-functionalism and principal-agent models look at the mechanisms through which supranational actors can establish (more and more) discretion for themselves. Here, it is important to know the preferences of member states and international bureaucrats in terms of policy content and institutional design. As the preceding section has shown, the study of practices focuses on everyday politics in supranational diplomacy and how it shapes international politics at large. On the contrary, the work focusing on international authority highlights the powers and functions of international bureaucrats in absolute terms: The core analysis is not necessarily about the kind of diplomacy conducted by international bureaucrats (aligned with states or not), but on the kinds of resources they have to potentially carry out autonomous policies, as well as on their degree of independence.

According to Hooghe and Marks (2014), international authority must be understood and measured by two conceptually and empirically distinct aspects: delegation and pooling. Delegation occurs when states want to reduce the transaction costs tied to cooperation, and pooling is linked to the possibility for states to keep their veto power. Delegation manifests itself through the existence and capacity of international secretariats, while indicators for pooling look into whether states have given international bureaucrats more leeway by reducing their veto opportunities during the decision-making and ratification stages. Via delegation, international bureaucrats can help states overcome issue cycling, sustain their commitments and provide information—in short, they reduce transaction costs.

Through these empirical measures, authors have analyzed how institutional design features enable or constrain international authority (Hooghe and Marks 2014), and how international authority can lead to IO scope expansion into unexpected fields (Haftel and Hofmann 2017). For their part, Zürn et al. (2012) have observed how high levels of authority go hand in hand with contestation, which is the expression of a high level of politicization. Thanks to this research agenda, largely driven by empirical questions, it is possible to show how the EEAS has and will develop over time, notably on issues of delegating authority and resource-sharing. Furthermore, this lens draws our attention to the potential of politicization that lies within the EEAS.

Concluding Remarks

The various approaches presented in this chapter highlight different explanatory factors and variables and do not share the same epistemological grounds. However, they all examine how interactions between structures in international organizations, the role and strategies of international bureaucrats and state preferences have helped redefine the contours of multilateral diplomacy. Some approaches focus more on the role of everyday practices, others are more interested in "major decisions." Some approaches highlight material factors, and others ideational ones. Thus, without minimizing the epistemological divergences, a degree of complementarity between approaches can be envisaged. Work inspired by the study of international authority (exploring institutional opportunities available to international bureaucrats) could be compatible for instance with research on diplomatic practices (studying how international bureaucrats use these institutional means in their daily work). The regionalization of supranational diplomacy is thus a major issue for both researchers and practitioners.

References

Adler, Emmanuel, "The Spread of Security Communities: Communities of Practice, Self-Restraint, and NATO's Post-Cold War Transformation," *European Journal of International Relations*, 2 (14), 2008: 195–230.

Adler-Nissen, Rebecca, *Opting Out of the European Union: Diplomacy, Sovereignty and European Integration*, Cambridge, Cambridge University Press, 2014.

Haas, Ernst B., *The Uniting of Europe*, Palo Alto (CA), Stanford University Press, 1958.
Haftel, Yoram Z., Hofmann, Stephanie C., "Institutional Authority and Security Cooperation Within Regional Economic Organizations," *Journal of Peace Research*, 54 (4), 2017: 484–498.
Haftel, Yoram Z., Thompson, Alexander, "The Independence of International Organizations: Concept and Applications," *Journal of Conflict Resolution*, 2 (50), 2006: 253–275.
Hawkins, Darren, Jacoby, Wade, "How Agents Matter," in Darren Hawkins, David Lake, Daniel Nielson, Michael Tierney (eds.), *Delegation and Agency in International Organizations*, New York (NY), Cambridge University Press, 2006.
Hofmann, Stephanie C. "The Politics of Overlapping Organizations: Hostage-Taking, Forum Shopping, and Brokering," *Journal of European Public Policy*, 26 (6), 2019: 883–905.
Hooghe, Liesbet, Marks, Gary, "Delegation and Pooling in International Organizations," *Review of International Organizations*, 10, 2014: 305–328.
Johnson, Tana, "Looking Beyond States: Openings for International Bureaucrats to Enter the Institutional Design Process," *Review of International Organizations*, 8, 2013: 499–519.
Lequesne, Christian, "EU Foreign Policy Through the Lens of Practice Theory: A Different Approach to the European External Action Service," *Cooperation and Conflict*, 50 (3), 2015: 351–367.
Littoz-Monnet, Annabelle (ed.), *The Politics of Expertise in International Organizations: How International Bureaucracies Produce and Mobilize Knowledge*, New York (NY), Routledge, 2017.
Mérand, Frédéric, Hofmann, Stephanie C., Irondelle, Bastien, "Governance and State Power: A Network Analysis of European Security," *Journal of Common Market Studies*, 49 (1), 2011: 121–147.
Neumann, Iver B., *At Home with the Diplomats: Inside a European Foreign Ministry*, Ithaca (NY), Cornell University Press, 2012.
Nielson, Daniel, Tierney, Michael, "Delegation to International Organizations: Agency Theory and World Bank Environmental Reform," *International Organization*, 57, 2003: 241–276.
Pollack, Mark, *The Engines of European Integration: Delegation, Agency, and Agenda Setting in the EU*, New York (NY), Oxford University Press, 2003.
Pouliot, Vincent, *International Pecking Orders*, Cambridge, Cambridge University Press, 2016.
Sandholtz, Wayne, Stone Sweet, Alec (eds.), *European Integration and Supranational Governance*, Oxford, Oxford University Press, 1998.
Schmitt, Olivier, "International Organization at War: NATO Practices in the Afghan Campaign," *Cooperation and Conflict*, 52 (4), 2017: 502–518.

Schmitter, Philippe C., "A Revised Theory of Regional Integration," *International Organization*, 24 (4), 1970: 836–868.

Snidal, Duncan, Thompson, Alexander, "International Commitments and Domestic Politics: Institutions and Actors at Two Levels," in *Locating the Proper Authorities*, Ann Arbor (MI), Daniel Drezner (ed.), University of Michigan Press, 2003, pp. 197–233.

Zürn, Michael, Binder, Martin, Ecker-Ehrhardt, Matthias, "International Authority and Its Politicization," *International Theory: A Journal of International Politics, Law and Philosophy*, 4 (1), 2012: 69–106.

CHAPTER 12

Sub-State Diplomacies: Regions, Parliaments, and Local Authorities

Benjamin Puybareau and Renaud Takam Talom

Diplomacy was long thought of as the "exclusive domain" of the sovereign. The term is associated with the idea of states maintaining relations, the main principles being sovereign equality and non-interference in domestic affairs. It was seen as the preserve of the executive, represented by heads of state or government and Ministers of Foreign Affairs. That restrictive understanding automatically excluded any actor from the diplomatic arena that did not meet this criterion of sovereignty. Thus, speaking about sub-state diplomacy might seem to be an oxymoron at first. And yet, this traditional and extremely old vision of diplomacy is clearly obsolete. For several decades, central governments have gradually lost their monopoly on external activity and must deal with a growing number of new actors occupying the international stage, among which sub-state territorial entities such as regions,

B. Puybareau (✉)
Sciences Po, Paris, France

B. Puybareau · R. T. Talom
University of Namur, Namur, Belgium

© The Author(s) 2020
T. Balzacq et al. (eds.), *Global Diplomacy*,
The Sciences Po Series in International Relations and Political Economy, https://doi.org/10.1007/978-3-030-28786-3_12

local parliaments, towns, and municipalities. Some refer to sub-state diplomacy, while others talk about "paradiplomacy," "protodiplomacy," or even "multilevel" diplomacy. This profusion of names comes with its own problems and even shows a kind of uncertainty faced with a rapidly expanding phenomenon that is not well understood. Are these terms synonymous? Do they have the same referent? How are these new forms of diplomacy deployed? We will first proceed with some conceptual clarification in order to analyze the specificities of sub-state diplomacy by situating them within their historical trajectory. We will then highlight the particularities of diplomatic practices for the three main kinds of sub-state actors.

Sub-State Diplomacy: Definition, Trajectory, and Tools

Sub-state actors' grasp of international matters is labeled by various concepts, depending on the author, and it is sometimes hard to really determine the nuances and differences. While this conceptual profusion may generate a wealth of terminology, it can be misleading and no doubt underscores how hard it is to understand this changeable phenomenon.

What Is Sub-State Diplomacy?

Sub-state diplomacy denotes the set of external activities undertaken by sub-state entities. It is the means through which regions, parliaments, and local and regional authorities implement their agendas beyond national borders. Some speak of paradiplomacy, multilevel diplomacy, protodiplomacy, or microdiplomacy.

Sub-State Diplomacy, Paradiplomacy and Protodiplomacy
"Paradiplomacy" and "sub-state diplomacy" are often used interchangeably. This is the case specifically when paradiplomacy is defined as "the international activities of sub-state entities" (Paquin 2004, 17). However, other authors have reduced its scope by defining it as "the external action of sub-state governments" (Massart-Piérard 2005). According to Soldatos Panayotis, it is "the direct pursuit of foreign activities to various degrees by federated states." It would thus involve international activities by executives of federated states.

A related concept, also used, is that of "protodiplomacy." This term describes the "foreign policy of a substate government that seeks to secede." It is distinguished from the preceding concept through its objective, which is to go from internal autonomy to international sovereignty. It is more conflictual, as it assumes antagonism between the federal executive and federated executive (Paquin 2004, 17). This conflictual dynamic inherent in protodiplomacy seems to exclude any framework for dialogue and projects an image of multi-tier foreign policy. However, one may be a way of reaching the other. In other words, traditional paradiplomacy may lead to protodiplomacy.

This means the two concepts cannot be considered synonymous with the concept of sub-state diplomacy. Rather, they reflect the specificities of a more general phenomenon. In that sense, "paradiplomacy and protodiplomacy" are used to describe phenomena characteristic of the federal system. This sidelines international activities undertaken by sub-state actors from a decentralized unitary system. Furthermore, the expression "sub-state government" is exclusive as it does not include exterior actions conducted in various frameworks by parliamentary entities. Thus, paradiplomacy includes the space of sub-state diplomacy without representing the entire phenomenon.

Sub-State Diplomacy, Parallel Diplomacy, and Multilevel Diplomacy
It is therefore common to find these terms in the literature representing the international involvement of sub-state entities. In a comparative perspective, parallel diplomacy supposes exterior actions conducted independently and not jointly by sub-state entities. It pertains to the idea of the splintering of a country's foreign policy. This is the case in particular when a regional executive takes a line that is different from and even contradictory to the one proposed by the central government.

On the other hand, the idea of multilevel diplomacy mainly developed by Brian Hocking (1993) presents a state's external activity as public policy that is thought out and unified, where different national and sub-national actors negotiate and agree on orientations. Each of the actors then plays a part without encroaching on the other's domain. This comes closer to shared competence in foreign policy matters. It reflects the idea that international relations of sub-national units are "the result of formally elaborated and convergent strategies" (Gagnon and Palard 2005). Foreign policy, like other public policies, cannot escape the dynamic of a redistribution of the national balance of power between central and local authorities: Initially hierarchical, the balance of power is now "connected in a partnership of negotiation between echelons of power and the different actors in internal politics" (Nagelschmidt 2005). This approach invites two remarks. First, it reduces the emancipation of sub-state actors and the competitive perspective while highlighting cooperation in implementing public policy. Then, it assumes the preponderance of the central government's diplomatic system; sub-state actors are merely included in the preexisting system and act under the central government's control. This concept tends to qualify and even negate any "autonomy" of sub-state actors. These last two concepts describe less the external activity of sub-state actors than the latter's relationships with central authorities. The goal is then to grasp the relationships these various actors have, more than the content of sub-state diplomacy itself.

SUB-STATE DIPLOMACY: HISTORICAL TRAJECTORY AND MAIN CATALYSTS

The incursion of sub-state entities on the supranational level is not a new phenomenon. Many authors agree that its development occurred after the Second World War. However, the intensity of the phenomenon and the broader horizon of activity seems quite recent and has arisen at the conjunction of various factors such as globalization, regional integration, and the crisis of the state.

Globalization and processes of regional integration are the crucial catalysts in the deployment of sub-national entities' international activities. Globalization, characterized by the free movement of people, goods, and services and by the digital revolution, has rendered the "internal/external" "border" all but inoperative and the dichotomy irrelevant. National territories are constantly crossed by a transnational flow of people, and activities are systematically deterritorialized and dematerialized. In this dynamic environment, it is easier for federated, regional, and municipal entities to forge ties abroad. Using digital resources, they strive to improve their territory's competitiveness and to conquer new market shares and international investments. As for regional integration, it has led to the downfall of various barriers, created formal supranational frameworks for consultation by sub-state entities, and furthermore has facilitated their integration within the international arena. Making the most of this favorable context, sub-state units have developed networks of relationships and solidarity with other national or sub-national entities. This solidarity goes beyond the mere framework of "economic promotion," developing on the religious, cultural, and even political levels. Thus, globalization, by offering local powers ever more possibilities, has facilitated their autonomy and emancipation from central governments and accelerated the internal fragmentation of states.

Another non-negligible catalyst in supranational investment by sub-state units is undoubtedly the fragmentation of states, "the transformation of national political systems in close contact with the territorial division of power" (Gagnon and Palard 2005) and the demand for new modes of governance based on "the shared exercise of power." Indeed, central governments, whether in federated or decentralized unitary systems, have constantly accorded increasing competence and even autonomy to sub-state entities. It is localism, understood as a form of good governance consisting in reinforcing attributions by regional and municipal federated authorities. These entities then strive to exercise their new competence on all levels, including beyond their borders. It is a matter of defending what one has acquired or even carving out new competencies: "The more competencies there are of sub-state entities, the more aspects of the international environment are liable to concern sub-state entities" (Paquin 2005).

Nationalism is also a factor to take into consideration. Indeed, several sub-state entities have become involved internationally in order to highlight their difference and assert their distinctive features vis-à-vis the nation-state to which they belong. This is known as "identity-based paradiplomacy," defined as the set of actions undertaken externally by a sub-state actor with the goal of "reinforcing regional identity within the framework of a multinational country" (Paquin 2005). International deployment is thus a means of legitimizing irredentist ambitions and international recognition. All this to say how much states seem to be facing real competition from subnational actors on the international stage. This competition has prompted some to say that the state has been supplanted on the international stage by new actors helping to make its word more irresolute, if not inaudible.

SUB-STATE DIPLOMACY AND CLASSIC DIPLOMACY: BETWEEN COMPLEMENTARITY, RIVALRY, AND RESILIENCE

The international activities of sub-national entities raise many questions. Thus, should sub-state diplomacy be seen as a "mere" renewal of the art of maintaining relations between states or as a "new form of diplomacy," fundamentally reshaping the principles and methods in how international affairs are managed? What is the relationship between traditional diplomacy and sub-state diplomacy?

Between Rupture and Conflict

Sub-national entities have in some ways introduced a true break with diplomatic practices. From a stylistic viewpoint, these non-conventional actors have moved onto the stage, leaving aside the ceremonial trappings, rituals, and formality considered inherent in state diplomacy. Their diplomatic style is characterized more by discretion and sobriety. Instead of the traditional well-defined and freighted language and gestural rigor, sub-state diplomacy substitutes a more direct approach that is less suffused with formalities. Furthermore, sub-state actors are less in search of power than of partners with whom to develop economic and political ties. They prefer a less aggressive, more consensual approach, closer to Realpolitik, where means are judged by ends. Enjoying more freedom, they seem more able to defend "international public goods," as they are not inclined toward strategic calculation. More in search of autonomy and cooperation over force, they elude conventional diplomatic codes (Badie, 1998, 50).

Such orientations are often in open conflict with the foreign policy choices made by central governments. This leads to "confusion" in the implementation of foreign policy, with discordant signals. Some see in it a "counter-diplomacy," an implosion in the unity between diplomacy and foreign policy. State diplomacy has adapted to this new presence and in the end has developed strategies for cooperation.

Resilience and Cooperation

Better than adapting, state diplomacy has shown remarkable resilience. The stiff competition from sub-nationals on the international stage notwithstanding, traditional diplomacy remains at the core of the international system. It is the favored means of "settling international conflicts" and "preserving the geopolitical balance" (Cohen 2005). Thus, only states within the UN Security Council can decide to use armed forces. Even areas in which sub-national diplomacy is highly active still rely on traditional diplomacy. Indeed, faced with a global issue like climate change, municipal and regional diplomacy have been more than remarkable. However, through their commitment capacity, nation-states alone are capable of achieving a true reduction in greenhouse gases.

Certain states, aware that paradiplomacy can be an added value in their international strategies, often agree with sub-national authorities. It may also enable a state to express its opinions implicitly on matters without taking complete responsibility for them. On that basis, central governments sometimes open up diplomatic channels to internal entities. There may also be a dividing of competencies. Sometimes it is even laid down by law. This was the case for Belgium which, by virtue of the principle of "*in foro interno, in foro externo*" written in its constitution, recognizes the right of federated entities to exercise competencies outside its territory that they exercise within their national territory. In so doing, there is a true dialogue and division of tasks. In the same vein, in 1994 the Belgian federal government signed an agreement with federated authorities settling issues of representation within groups in the Council of the European Union. This agreement involves federated entities in the decision-making process, but also defines particular situations in which federated entities have exclusive competence. However, while it reduces the risk of conflict, this "institutional flexibility" (Gagnon and Palard 2005) is not a panacea. At least that is what has been shown by the Walloon Parliament and French-speaking community blocking the UE-Canada (CETA) economic and commercial global draft agreement in October 2016. The draft agreement, desired by the federal executive branch, was not approved by the Walloon Parliamentarians, effectively preventing Belgium from ratifying the text. The situation challenged a long-negotiated agreement involving all member countries of the European Union (EU).

Sub-State Diplomacy: A Diversity of Actors and Tools

One cannot refer in a general and undifferentiated way to diplomatic actions of sub-state entities. A distinction must be made between local and regional authorities of unitary states and state entities brought together in federal states. One must also take into account how competencies are allocated and how state supervision is exercised, as it varies considerably from one state to another based on historical specificities. Finally, one must take into consideration the kind of power involved in these diplomatic exchanges: executive power if it concerns a local government or legislative power if it concerns a regional parliament.

In this chapter, we will look successively at three kinds of actors in sub-state diplomacy: regional governments, parliaments, and local authorities. Each of these actors is characterized by its specific diplomatic practices.

Regional Diplomacy

Among the different kinds of sub-state actors, regions—understood here as federated entities or territories with a specific autonomy status in certain unitary states (such as Catalonia in Spain)—are the first to have engaged in diplomacy parallel to that of governments and to have drawn the attention of researchers. Thus, regional diplomacy is most often associated with the term "paradiplomacy," all the more so as it may involve federated entities claiming greater autonomy on the international stage, or even independence.

Principal Actors and Intensity of Regional Diplomacy
In the early twenty-first century, some specialists reported 350 active regional entities on the international level. Canadian provinces, American states, German Länder, and Swiss cantons intensified their international presence starting in the 1960s, soon joined by Austrian Länder, Belgian regions and communities, Australian states, and Spanish autonomous communities (Paquin 2005, 131). There are also examples of regional diplomacy in Southeast Asia, Central Asia, Latin America, and Africa. The situations in these regions are highly variable from one country to another and sometimes even within the same country. It is difficult to describe it in a homogeneous manner, due to the intensity and extensiveness of the phenomenon. The ambition, real influence, and forms of international politics by regional entities vary greatly from one example to another. For instance, the annual budget that Quebec ascribes to its international policies is equal to half that of all American states. The budget for Flanders represents over twice as much as all American states combined (Paquin 2005, 133).

Instruments
Federated states have numerous kinds of foreign policy. Indeed, with the exception of recourse to military force, which remains the exclusive prerogative of a sovereign state, the range of diplomatic tools and instruments used by regional entities is as broad as that enjoyed by governments. The

most common instruments are the networks of representation and delegation abroad, enabling permanent contact with a country, region, or international institution. Networks of regional entities may at times be larger than those of some sovereign states. For example, among the most active regions on the international stage, Flanders has one hundred representations abroad, Catalonia has fifty, and Quebec twenty-six. By comparison, Israel has one hundred, while Côte d'Ivoire, Finland, and North Korea have fifty.

Treaties, agreements, or "ententes" may also be negotiated between regions or between a region and a sovereign state. Quebec, highly active in this area, has concluded over 755 international ententes, 388 of which are still active, such as the Franco-Quebec entente on recognizing professional qualifications, signed in 2008, or the entente on developing cooperation in industrial research and technological innovation signed in 2017 with Israel.

Furthermore, some regions take part in their country's delegation at meetings of major international organizations and institutions such as the United Nations (UN), the World Trade Organization (WTO), and the European Union. Sometimes, a federated entity may even be a full member of an international organization, like Quebec within the Francophonie (OIF), allowing them to directly influence decisions in many areas.

Fact-finding and outreach missions abroad, financing public relations campaigns to increase exports and attract investments, organizing official visits hosting leaders from other countries and regions, or setting up institutions for regional and transregional cooperation round out this non-exhaustive list of instruments used by regions to increase their influence on the diplomatic level.

Regional Parliamentary Diplomacy

Diplomacy has traditionally been considered a privilege of the executive, an area in which legislative power has little influence or levers of action. The argument often used to justify this allocation of roles is the opposition between deliberation, which is "done by more than one," and negotiation, which is "done by one" (Maus 2012, 14). Yet, while international relations was at first an area in which parliaments had limited leeway, the latter have gradually succeeded in occupying that arena. Indeed, many parliaments maintain external links nowadays, whether in a bilateral framework or within multilateral parliamentary institutions. Well known for their legislative function and for monitoring government actions on the internal level, parliamentary institutions have experienced a rapidly expanding role on the international stage, to the extent that one may now refer unquestionably to these parliaments' international activities. For the last thirty years, these activities, conducted on the sidelines and as a complement to governmental diplomacy, have constituted what is referred to as "parliamentary diplomacy." Although the academic literature on parliamentary diplomacy is still underdeveloped, and its definition still prompts questions and discussions (Maus 2012), its relevance as a topic of research has been established. One need only observe how frequently the concept is used by politicians and parliamentary civil servants throughout the world.

Parliamentary diplomacy is an interesting topic of study as it is not a prerogative of parliaments in sovereign states. Indeed, alongside supranational parliamentary diplomacy, which occurs notably in institutions such as the Inter-Parliamentary Union or the Parliamentary Assembly of the North Atlantic Treaty Organization (NATO), a diplomacy of regional parliaments has developed. National parliaments coexist with regional parliaments and complement one another, the former focusing on major national affairs while the latter exercise decentralized authority to legislate on important local and regional matters.

The development of parliamentary diplomacy by regional entities can be explained in part by the principle of the separation of powers, which forbids governments of sovereign states from interfering in the affairs of its constituent regional parliaments. The latter are therefore free to occupy the international stage or not. The absence of a hierarchy in interparliamentary relations is also an explanatory factor for the existence of what is sometimes called "paraparliamentary diplomacy," with many international parliamentary organizations opening their doors to regional parliaments as full-fledged members. Thus, the French-speaking communities in Belgium and Quebec are members of the Parliamentary Assembly of the Francophonie (APF), on an equal footing with Canada, France, and Luxembourg. Parliaments have a plethora of channels through which to exchange externally. They can be divided into two categories: bilateral channels and multilateral channels.

Bilateral Channels (Friendship Groups, Visits, Meetings)
Among the forms that diplomatic exchanges between parliaments may take, friendship groups are probably the most frequent. The purpose of these groups is to create diplomatic relations with parliamentarians from a

given state or region through exchanges, missions, symposiums, maintaining channels of influence, and interactions between leading figures and such groups. A friendship group generally strives to organize missions abroad during a term of office and at least once to host representatives from the country or region it is connected to. The goal of these mission exchanges is to strengthen personal ties, to promote one's region and become more familiar with a country or region, but it is hard to give an overview of the activities of friendship groups or to assess their true impact (Maus 2012).

The first recorded friendship groups were established after the First World War, when a France-Great Britain group was created at the Chambre des députés to establish ties of friendship and solidarity between parliamentary veterans in the two assemblies. Regarding regional parliaments, one could cite the example of the France-Quebec Friendship Group, formed in 1986, through which the National Assembly of Quebec created special ties with the French National Assembly and Senate. More recently, a Swiss-Catalan Parliamentary Group stirred up a commotion in Spain. In April 2016, three Swiss Parliamentarians took the initiative of creating a parliamentary friendship group to "draw the federal Council's attention to the Catalan issue."

More rarely, parliaments may also create interparliamentary commissions with the goal of developing cooperative initiatives led jointly by each assembly. Thus, the France-Quebec Interparliamentary Commission, formed in 1979 and composed of five Quebec *députés* and five French *députés*, meets alternately in France or Quebec every year to exchange on political events and predefined themes.

In addition to friendship groups and interparliamentary commissions, visits and meetings between parliamentarians from different countries and regions have multiplied in recent years, spurred by globalization and easy communications (Maus 2012). Generally, it is the President of the National Assembly and the President of the Senate who embody this form of parliamentary diplomacy. Presidents of parliamentary assemblies thus receive many leading figures on official trips or state visits and frequently go abroad on official visits to meet with their counterparts or to strengthen ties between parliaments. Here again, it is difficult to assess the influence and scope of these kinds of meetings, as they are often largely taken up by official interviews.

Multilateral Channels

Interparliamentary cooperation, in other words different actions that contribute in one way or another to parliamentary diplomacy, mainly goes through international parliamentary assemblies. These multilateral organizations are characterized by great diversity, both in terms of their thematic interest, their objectives, structures and working methods. The most senior of these international parliamentary assemblies is the Inter-Parliamentary Union which has acted since 1889 as the world organization of parliaments of sovereign states. The list of organizations in which parliaments of sub-state entities are particularly active could include notably the APF and the Conference of European Regional Legislative Assemblies (CALRE). The cantons of Jura and Vaud, Quebec, Manitoba, Nova Scotia, and Ontario are among the full-fledged members of the APF, an advisory body of the Francophonie whose objectives include promoting the French language, democracy, and human rights. CALRE includes presidents from regional parliamentary assemblies that all have legislative powers and belong to member states of the European Union, notably the Spanish autonomous communities, Italian regions, Belgian regions and communities, and Austrian and German Länder. Its goals range from promoting the role of regional parliaments within the European Union to defending the values and principles of regional democracy and fostering cooperation and experiential exchanges among its members.

DIPLOMACY BY LOCAL AUTHORITIES

The term "local authorities" may have slightly different meanings depending on the political culture and a state's degree of centralization. In the Anglosphere, one refers to local government. We are using a rather general definition here that includes local authorities as all parts of the territory of a state that enjoys a certain autonomy of management—even partial—some competencies being ascribed to it by the state in a process of decentralization. Local authorities may notably be towns or municipalities, *départements*, circles, or regions (if a unitary state).

Sometimes called "territorial diplomacy," diplomatic action by these authorities stems from the Franco-German twinning policy created after the Second World War, for the purpose of reconciliation. In studying twinning between towns on both sides of the Rhine, researchers highlighted the influence of private actors and local associations in bringing about a lasting rapprochement between the two countries, illustrating from the outset the important role that could be played by territorial diplomacy.

Furthered by globalization and the process of European integration since the 1980s, local authorities' international actions have developed a great deal in recent decades. Increasing numbers are acting on the world stage, in highly diverse areas. Some towns have developed economic strategies on an international level. Others, like the city of San Francisco, sanction countries that do not respect human rights.

Beyond bilateral relations with foreign local authorities—first in the framework of twinning then more broadly in decentralized cooperation (a term designating all friendly relations, from twinning to partnerships forged between local authorities in different countries)—local governments today are joining together in multiple International networks such as the International Association of Cities and Ports (AIVP), the Worldwide Network of Port Cities, and United Cities and Local Governments (UCLG), the main worldwide organization of twinned cities acting notably in the areas of local democracy, decentralization and decentralized cooperation. These local authorities and networks today are seeking international recognition from regional and international organizations. Thus, the UCLG is involved in different partnerships with the UN and some of its agencies.

"City diplomacy" is a particular category of "territorial diplomacy" which through its vitality has drawn a great deal of attention from researchers (Viltard 2010). At the first worldwide conference organized on the theme in The Hague in 2008, the UCLG, the city of The Hague, and the Association of Dutch Municipalities agreed on the following definition: "City diplomacy is a tool of local governments and their associations aimed at promoting social cohesion, conflict prevention and resolution, and post-conflict reconstruction, with the goal of creating a stable environment in which citizens can live together in peace, democracy and prosperity." This definition presents conflict resolution and peacebuilding as fundamental objectives in city diplomacy. Since the late 1990s, the number of local authorities that have provided support to cities affected by a violent conflict has constantly increased. Contacts have been established and links created with cities in the former Yugoslavia, in Palestine, Israel, Colombia, and Sri Lanka, as well as in Iraq and Afghanistan, for the purpose of furthering democracy in these areas. This evolution has gradually gained recognition on an international scale: Organizations in the UN and NGOs are increasingly inviting local authorities to take part in their peacemaking efforts.

It is interesting in this regard to highlight that the pacifist, universalist and human rights objectives local authorities have attributed to their international initiatives are identical to those that states habitually subscribe to within the framework of international organizations (Viltard 2010, 595). Contrary to the "paradiplomacy" of some federated entities, "territorial diplomacy" by local authorities should be seen above all as an extension of state diplomacy at the local level. Moreover, it is carried out in cooperation with and as a complement to the central government's foreign policy. Local authorities, lacking sovereign powers, "are obliged to promote universal values of peace and solidarity in order to affirm their acting in partnership with states and participating in the regulating of the international political order" (Viltard 2010, 604).

Nevertheless, in certain rare cases, local diplomacy may emerge to protest against the central government's foreign policy. In the United States, for example, international initiatives by local and regional authorities have greatly developed since local populations became mobilized during the 1980s against Ronald Reagan's international policies. Some municipalities boycotted investments deemed unethical in certain countries or helped to host illegal refugees fleeing conflicts in Latin America. More recently, hundreds of American cities signed the declaration submitted to the UN Secretary-General, in which they committed to respecting the objectives of the Paris Agreement on Climate Change, shortly after Donald Trump's decision to withdraw the United States from the treaty.

* * *

Ultimately, sub-state diplomacy is characterized above all by its diversity. The profusion of concepts attempting to describe this heterogeneous phenomenon attests to the wide variety of actors, forms, and instruments that compose it. But whether initiated by regions, local parliaments, or local and regional authorities, sub-state diplomacy finds consistency and unity in the idea of challenging state monopoly of international politics. In this, it is completely in line with the contemporary international dynamics of globalization and regionalization that are leading to the gradual elimination of the Westphalian state in the face of an increasing number of new actors.

REFERENCES

Badie, Bertrand, "De la souveraineté à la capacité de l'Etat," in M.C. Smouts (ed.), *Les nouvelles relations internationales*, Paris, Pressses de Sciences Po, 1998, pp. 35–58.

Cohen, Samy, "Les États face aux nouveaux acteurs," *Politique internationale*, 107, 2005: 409–424.

Gagnon, Bernard, Palard, Jacques, "Relations internationales des régions et fédéralisme. Les provinces canadiennes dans le contexte de l'intégration nordaméricaine," *Revue internationale de politique comparée*, 12 (2), 2005.

Hocking, Brian, *Localizing Foreign Policy: Non-Central Governments and Multilayered Diplomacy*, New York (NY), Palgrave Macmillan, 1993.

Massart-Piérard, Françoise, "Introduction à l'analyse des collectivités décentralisées et ses répercussions," in *Du local à l'international: nouveaux acteurs, nouvelle diplomatie, Revue Internationale de Politique Comparée*, 12 (32), 2005: 123–128.

Maus, Didier, "Le cadre institutionnel de la diplomatie parlementaire," *Parlement[s]. Revue d'histoire politique*, 1 (17), 2012: 14–36.

Nagelschmidt, Martin, "Les systèmes à niveaux multiples dans les régions transfrontalières en Europe. Le cas du Rhin supérieur et des nouvelles coopérations à la frontière est de la RFA," *Revue internationale de politique comparée*, 12 (2), 2005: 223–236.

Paquin, Stéphane, *Paradiplomatie et relations internationales. Théorie des stratégies internationales des régions face la mondialisation*, Brussels, PIE/Peter Lang, 2004.

———, "Les actions extérieures des entités sub-étatiques: quelle signification pour la politique comparée et les relations internationales?" *Revue internationale de politique comparée*, 12 (2), 2005: 129–142.

Viltard, Yves, "Diplomatie des villes: collectivités territoriales et relations internationales," *Politique étrangère*, 3, 2010: 593–604.

CHAPTER 13

Diplomacy by Non-State Actors

Auriane Guilbaud

Multinational corporations such as Total, an NGO like Médecins sans frontières (MSF), or a private foundation like the Bill and Melinda Gates Foundation are international actors. Their activities are carried out on a transnational scale (the Gates Foundation, for instance, conducts development projects in over a hundred countries), and they influence the international agenda (such as MSF calling on countries to mobilize against the Ebola epidemic in West Africa in 2014). And yet, does that mean they are undertaking diplomatic activities and conducting real diplomacy?

Diplomacy is traditionally understood as carrying out a country's external relations, implementing its foreign policy, above all through negotiations, except for war and military operations. A "government diplomat" fulfills three main functions: representation, communication (information and observation), and negotiation. This definition is in keeping with a state-centered approach of international relations (Devin 2016, 217), which sees states as the main actors in the international system. According to the French scholar Raymond Aron, interactions between states can be illustrated with the help of two structuring figures in international relations:

A. Guilbaud (✉)
University Paris 8, Saint-Denis, France

© The Author(s) 2020
T. Balzacq et al. (eds.), *Global Diplomacy*,
The Sciences Po Series in International Relations and Political
Economy, https://doi.org/10.1007/978-3-030-28786-3_13

the soldier, who intervenes in times of war, and the diplomat, who represents states in times of peace (Aron 1962).

This restrictive conception of diplomacy has been fine-tuned on several points, in particular by highlighting the existence of a continuum in conducting a country's external relations. Thus, negotiating activities continue in wartime, and diplomacy mobilizes techniques ranging from persuasion to coercion. Threatening the use of force is not the only coercive tool available to diplomats, and the area of diplomatic activity has also broadened considerably beyond issues of war and peace. Today, diplomacy is conceived of more as "the art of responding to any problem linked to the effects of separation and distinction between spaces of proclaimed sovereignty" (Badie 2008) and includes the resolution of territorial conflicts, climate negotiations, as well as debt cancellation and rescheduling for countries. Many actors other than states have now become involved in the "art of responding" to worldwide problems.

In the late twentieth century, there was an erosion of the purely regalian concept of diplomacy, due to the profusion and diversification of actors in international relations and to the rediscovery—mainly through the work of historians—of the historical contingency of the state's monopoly on diplomacy. So-called non-state actors, such as NGOs, multinational corporations, criminal groups, indigenous peoples, religious actors, think tanks, and private foundations may undertake diplomatic activities of representation, negotiation, and information gathering. There are numerous examples, but let us consider the Community of Sant'Egidio, a Catholic organization that works—among other areas—in conflict resolution, conducting mediation, and negotiation activities within the framework of resolving the civil war in Mozambique in 1992, and in recent years in the Central African Republic.

Different concepts have been forged bearing in mind this opening up of diplomacy. Diamond and McDonald (1996) have referred to "multi-track diplomacy," a system where various kinds of actors conduct parallel negotiations in distinct arenas: governments and leaders of quasi-governmental groups (such as rebel movements) negotiate officially in "track 1," representatives of influential institutions (political and religious organizations, academic institutions, etc.) are included in so-called track 2 negotiations, while "track 3" negotiations bring together actors working "in the field" such as local NGOs and community representatives. Wiseman (2010) has referred to "polylateral diplomacy" in considering relations conducted between state entities (a state or intergovernmental organization) and non-state entities. These relations are systemic in nature, thus characterized by regularity and reciprocity, especially in the areas of information exchange and communications, representation and negotiation, but in no way entail mutual recognition as sovereign entities.

Some actors seeking recognition as states or governments of a state (secessionist and rebel groups for example) may be considered quasi-states rather than non-states. This situation of challenging the "state" power of a government is what has characterized civil wars, the resolution of which is an important object of diplomatic activity. But due to their desire to be recognized as states and taken into account by "traditional" diplomacy, these actors are outside the purview of this chapter, as are supra and infra-state entities (which remain organically linked to the state), as well as individuals, dealt with in another chapter.

Nevertheless, the category of non-state actors remains porous, since it has a negative definition. It is highly diverse, encompassing all organized collective actors (in the sense of entities endowed with a certain autonomy, an identity, and its own resources, which thus has the capacity to act in pursuing its specific interests) which are not a state or constituted by states (i.e., an intergovernmental international organization like the UN). Moreover, this denomination only makes sense in a state-centered understanding of the international arena, within which only states, subjects of international law, have a clearly defined role—a conception that emerged in Europe in the seventeenth century.

However, since 1945 the number and visibility of these non-state actors have increased under the influence of three main phenomena: the democratization of states (giving people more freedom of association), the revolution in information and communications (increasing the capacity of individuals and groups to mobilize), and the increasing support of international intergovernmental organizations that include them in their activities (Devin 2016, 149). They have not only shaken up the diplomatic game, forcing states to take them into consideration, but have also developed their own diplomatic activities, sometimes delegated by states, at other times in competition with or in opposition to them. What is the nature of these diplomatic activities? Are we witnessing an overhaul of diplomatic practices? Do they form a system such that one might refer to diplomacy by non-state actors?

After analyzing the constitution and then the erosion of the regalian diplomatic monopoly, we will examine diplomatic activities that non-state actors have undertaken and practices they have revived, and then explore how governmental diplomacy has adapted, as well as the limits to forming a "diplomatic system" by non-state actors.

CONSTITUTION AND EROSION OF THE REGALIAN DIPLOMATIC MONOPOLY

International relations in various forms, that is relations between distinct political entities, are as old as the existence of human communities. But it was from the moment when the existence of independent political organizations stabilized and regular relations were established between them that one can speak of external relations conducted through the intermediary of diplomacy, which had already occurred in Antiquity (Allès and Guilbaud 2017). The state/non-state distinction became effective starting in the seventeenth century, when a new European political order grew out of the Thirty Years War (1618–1648). So-called modern states were consolidated, with a concentration of (political, economic, and religious) power in the hands of heads of state who gradually established a monopoly on conducting foreign relations.

Diplomatic activities by non-state actors are thus very old, developing from the seventeenth to the nineteenth centuries parallel to and in conjunction with the consolidation of modern states. These diplomatic activities could be undertaken either for their own sake (where non-state actors had "external relations" to maintain) or for political entities (states, city-states, empires), without necessarily a clear distinction between the two.

The discovery of the Americas, progress in means of transportation (navigation, then railroads) and communication (the perfection of printing) enabled increased contact between societies. Thus, the Society of Jesus, a Catholic religious order, reached China in the late sixteenth century, and at least two of its members took part in the negotiations between China and Russia to demarcate borders between the two countries (Treaty of Nerchinsk, 1689). New entities also developed, such as the different European companies in the East Indies. Created in the seventeenth century,[1] they may be seen as "proto-multinationals" authorized by sovereigns to

---

[1] The British created their East India Company in 1600, the Dutch in 1602, the Danish in 1616, the Portuguese in 1628, the French in 1664, and the Swedish in 1731.

trade with foreign powers. They granted these firms the power to represent them in negotiating trade routes and exchanges with local authorities and/or other states. One of the stakes in negotiations involved establishing areas where European law would be recognized in trade issues (respecting contracts, etc.) (Pigman 2013). For instance, from 1639 to 1799 (its date of dissolution), the Dutch East India Company was the only foreign company granted permission by Japanese authorities to engage in trade with Japan through the intermediary of the man-made island of Dejima located in Nagasaki Bay. Its director was treated like the representative of a state, paying an annual visit to the Shogun (political leader) in Edo (former name of the capital, now Tokyo) with a small Dutch delegation.

However, starting in the nineteenth century, the state monopoly on conducting external relations was established through the professionalization and bureaucratization of diplomacy. Its three main functions (representation, observation-information, and negotiation) were henceforth entrusted to "professional governmental diplomats," who were no longer merely temporarily accredited representatives but agents who spent their entire career within the foreign affairs administration. In France for instance, decrees were ordered in 1800 to define the rights of foreign affairs agents (recruitment, pay, advancement), the first step in the transformation of foreign affairs "clerks" subject to royal power into civil service agents (Outrey 1953, 499). Interactions with non-state actors continued to exist—in particular in the exchange of information—but were centralized by states. This "golden age" of traditional diplomacy was characterized by the primacy given to relations between states, a culture of secrets and an elitist aspect.

The two world wars and the development of human rights transformed these diplomatic practices, putting new emphasis on diplomacy by non-state actors. As of 1918, American President Woodrow Wilson championed "open diplomacy," more transparent, multilateral, and at odds with the secret, bilateral practices that had not been able to prevent deadly conflicts. This renewed diplomacy, which could even lead people to get involved in "public diplomacy," brought in non-state actors, better at addressing society and public opinion (this is the case, for instance, for the media, cultural, and athletic associations, etc.). The fact that the United Nations Charter recognized from 1945 that the Economic and Social Council (Ecosoc, a UN body) "may make suitable arrangements for consultation with non-governmental organizations which are concerned with matters within its competence" (chapter X, article 71) acted as a catalyst (NGOs with consultative status at Ecosoc have grown from 40 in 1946 to over 4000 today).

Finally, the deadly conflicts of the nineteenth and twentieth centuries also led to the creation of humanitarian organizations such as the International Committee of the Red Cross, formed in 1863 by Swiss citizens around Henry Dunant to provide relief for victims of conflicts. Interventions required diplomatic negotiations with the parties in conflict, whether during the Franco-Prussian War in 1870 or today in Syria for example.

Since 1945, the accelerating transnational flow of trade and people and densification of interdependencies on a global scale has led to a transformation in international modes of action, with a predilection for operating in partnership with non-state actors now recognized as "stakeholders" in global public policies. That mode of operation has been explicitly promoted by the Millennium Development Goals (2000–2015) and the Sustainable Development Goals (2015–2030) that have set orientations for development. At the same time, states have seen a transformation in their administrative operations, notably through the application of "new public management" principles striving for bureaucratic reorganization according to a cost-effectiveness calculation. State action is now characterized by more delegating to external actors in traditionally regalian public service initiatives, through contractualization in the form of public-private partnerships. The increased movement of individuals and the multiplication of short contracts (internships, temporary fixed-term contracts), including within regalian administrations such as foreign affairs, has also helped to spread diplomatic practices between different types of actors. Non-state actors are now engaged in diplomatic activities within that framework.

Sustained Diplomatic Activities and Renewed Practices

Non-state actors are still engaged in the "traditional" diplomatic activities of representation, communication (information and observation), and negotiation. With respect to how they were once conducted, in the seventeenth century for instance, what has changed is the regularity, visibility, and at times institutionalized recognition of their activities.

The most salient change may be with respect to their participation in international negotiations. That participation does not just involve their consultation in the implementation phase of the decisions adopted, but also their inclusion in the processes leading to the creation of international standards. Thus, NGOs like Handicap International or Human Rights Watch took part in launching an international campaign to ban land mines, the first step toward the adoption in 1997 of the Ottawa Anti-Personnel Mine Ban Convention. These NGOs did not settle for media coverage to have the topic put on the international agenda and to convince certain countries (Canada, Germany) to follow through on their demand for a ban with a treaty; they were also present at the negotiating conferences alongside experts and members of civil society (such as mine victims).

Non-state actors' legitimacy in participating in international negotiations is based on their capacity for expertise, enabling them to provide information acknowledged as necessary for negotiations to run smoothly, and on their role in representing populations (organizations from civil society representing the sectorial interests of groups of people, for-profit organizations championing trade interests tied to the interests of consumers and shareholders). While the quality and validity of that representative function is at times the subject of debate (see below), international negotiations are now open to the explicit consideration of diverse interests, no longer expressed solely through the intermediary of states.

With the increased global flow of trade, information, data, etc., and densifying interdependencies, more and more non-state actors are engaged in diplomatic activities for their own sake and are developing organizational structures to that end. Indeed, when a non-state actor initiates transnational activities, it must interact with multiple interlocutors and represent its own interests. Firms, NGOs, and well-endowed private foundations have developed offices or departments to handle these relations (usually an office/department of "government relations" or of "public affairs"), true equivalents of government foreign affairs ministries. Multinational corporations are used to negotiating with other actors to obtain access to markets and import/export licenses, and to handle crises, but relations with governments, international or regional organizations, and civil society have multiplied. Thus, in 2010, Total grouped together different departments within a "public affairs division" to handle relations internationally, in Europe and with the firm's NGOs. The Bill and Melinda Gates Foundation has 1400 employees between its headquarters in Seattle and offices in Washington DC, New Delhi, London, Beijing, Addis Ababa, Abuja, and Johannesburg. They conduct international programs through the foundation's three departments: "Global Development," "Global Health," and "Global Policy and Advocacy," a department of external relations that builds relationships with the foundation's partners (governments, public policy experts, and philanthropists). Furthermore, the Gates Foundation is the second-largest contributor to the World Health Organization's budget, amounting to 18%, after the US government. This has given it an important place within the organization, enabling it to drive certain health priorities like a member state—for instance, its financing mainly directed at the global program of the World Health Organization (WHO) in fighting polio. Non-state actors may also organize summits to discuss global problems, such as the World Economic Forum, formed by 1000 major corporations, which organizes the Davos Summit every year (that government representatives may attend) or the World Social Forum that brings together members of civil society.

Does this mean that non-state actors are now behaving like states in the diplomatic arena? While one may observe diplomatic activities and similar structures, new practices have also been developed by using their own negotiating tools. For instance, NGOs may engage in coercive diplomacy, not through the intermediary of traditional tools like economic sanctions or threatening the use of force, reserved for states, but by shaming/denunciation, and boycotting. Non-state actors also have greater recourse to public diplomacy tools: circulating information, advertising campaigns, appeals to public opinion through the media and social networks on the Internet. This non-state diplomacy is also carried out in networks: by forming coalitions of NGOs, transnational social movements, business associations, etc. Thus, it was through ties established between an American lobbying group, the Intellectual Property Committee (composed of twelve heads of major American companies in the sectors of pharmaceutics and chemicals, new information and communications technologies and entertainment), and Japanese and European business associations that the firms developed a shared position in the late 1980s, forming the basis for negotiations on the Agreement on Trade-Related Aspects of Intellectual Property Rights (TRIPS), adopted by WTO member states.

CONSTRAINTS AND INFLUENCE OF GOVERNMENTAL DIPLOMACY

States have adapted to a certain extent to this increased diplomatic activity by non-state actors. Thus, Denmark has announced the creation of a "digital ambassador" to handle the kingdom's relations with Silicon Valley's digital companies (Google, Airbnb, Facebook, Netflix, Apple), ultimately treating them as new states with which the country must maintain diplomatic relations. Anne-Marie Slaughter, an American academic and director of policy planning at the State Department under Hillary Clinton (2009–2011), considers this adaptation to be unfinished, that the organization of non-state actors into networks has not been sufficiently taken into account, and that the key issue now is to integrate them into state networks (Slaughter 2016).

In the great majority of cases, states have settled for opening certain places up to non-state actors, such as major global UN conferences. For instance, the so-called Earth Summit conferences to promote sustainable development (Stockholm, 1972; Rio, 1992; Johannesburg, 2002; Rio+20, 2012) that have brought together a very high number of non-state actors (about 10,000 in 2012). Meetings of governing bodies of international organizations (annual assemblies of member states, board meetings, and executive boards) have also opened up to their presence, but one limited to observer status. For example, after a reform was adopted in 2016, WHO developed a framework for engaging with non-state actors, which recognizes a status for corporations, private foundations, and academic institutions distinct from the already existing one for NGOs. This presence in the international arena is characterized not only by taking part in negotiations (notably beforehand, during preparatory meetings, see above), but also by organizing side events (nearly a hundred are organized yearly during the World Health Assembly, an annual meeting of WHO member states in Geneva), and even counter-conferences (like the People's Summit for Social and Environmental Justice organized by and for civil society in 2012 at Rio+20). Beyond the creation of ties with government diplomats, organizing these side events and counter-conferences has encouraged the development of non-state actors' own diplomatic activities and organization into networks to set up structures and find financing to enable these events to be held.

But states have also created new international institutions that are hybrid in nature, with non-state actors that sometimes have voting rights and are entitled to take decisions like a state. For example, the Global Fund to Fight AIDS, Tuberculosis and Malaria is a funding mechanism to fight those three diseases (in other words, it mobilizes, manages, and distributes funds but is not an organization that carries out programs in the field) created in 2001 on the model of public–private partnership. This means that participation of non-state actors is envisaged from the outset (moreover, in December 2001 thirty representatives from major corporations—Pfizer, Merck, Novartis, GSK, Anglo American, ExxonMobil, etc.—participated in a working meeting on the organization's structure) (Guilbaud 2015).

The Global Fund's board, the organization's "supreme body" according to its statutes revised in 2016, is composed of 20 voting members: 7 representatives of developing countries (DCs); 8 representatives of donor countries; 5 representatives of civil society and the private sector (1 NGO from DCs, 1 NGO from developed countries, 1 private foundation, 1 company from the private sector and 1 representative from the communities living with the diseases). These representatives are chosen by constituencies from each sector (NGOs, companies, etc.), which define a procedure to do so. Within the Global Fund, non-state actors have thus established real diplomacy in order to participate (prior discussions within the groups to designate a representative to the council, elaborating positions for negotiating, voting, etc.).

This is also the case within the Committee on World Food Security (CFS) which, contrary to the Global Fund, is a UN committee, created in 1974 and reformed in 2009 so that non-state actors could participate. Organizations from civil society and the private sector sit on the advisory group, the CFS's strategic body, allowing them to intervene during meetings and thematic working groups, to contribute to the agenda, and to present documents and proposals. This participation is undertaken autonomously, through the intermediary of a "civil society mechanism" and a "private sector mechanism" that organizes coordination and consultation of members. For instance, the civil society mechanism gathers together organizations divided into 11 "social sectors": small farmers and breeders, small-scale fishermen, indigenous peoples, workers in farming and the food industry, landless farmers, women, youth, consumers, food insecure urban populations, and NGOs. They then each elect one member on the coordinating committee, which makes policy decisions. Setting up that mechanism required major diplomatic work: establishing regular, steady relations between members, coordinating mechanisms (mainly by Internet), developing common interests, discussions on representativeness (thus, NGOs are only one part of civil society along with representatives of workers, indigenous peoples, etc.). However, neither organizations from civil society nor those from the private sector have voting rights, a competence reserved for states.

It is not merely due to member states that want to keep their privileges as international actors within the UN. Certain organizations from civil society are not favorable to it, arguing that they only represent sectorial interests, that only states can represent their entire population, and that it is necessary not to water down the responsibility of states then charged with respecting and implementing decisions made within the CFS. The case is interesting because it highlights one of the limits in the institutionalization of non-state actor participation within diplomatic arenas: the problem of representation, tied to the issue of accountability, to the ability to be accountable to the individuals represented. While states have delegated certain diplomatic activities and recognized the legitimacy of non-state actor participation in international bodies, and some non-state actors have developed true diplomacy for themselves in order to manage and develop their transnational relations, there are limits to what that "delegation without sovereignty" can achieve.

* * *

Diplomatic activity by non-state actors is not a recent phenomenon, and the regalian diplomatic monopoly stems from the distorting effect of analyses focusing on the consolidation of nation-states and their bureaucratic apparatus. What is new, however, is the systemic aspect of the phenomenon: the multiplication and diversification of non-state actors developing diplomatic activities, the structuring of their organizations to do so (creating departments devoted to external relations, appointing representatives equivalent to ambassadors, etc.), the densification of interdependencies and thus the regularity of interaction (ties between transnational actors: between non-state actors, with states, etc.), and recognition from other actors in the international system (institutionalizing the participation of non-state actors in international intergovernmental organizations, delegation by states in public–private partnerships/contractual procedures, etc.). These changes have legitimized the existence of diplomacy by non-state actors in promoting their own interests and have been developed both toward other non-state actors and states. Thus, talking about diplomacy by non-state actors means recognizing that the international system is not merely between states, even if the issue of representation has not been resolved, as it remains fragmented between different kinds of actors (states, social movements, NGOs, firms, etc.) while states continue to be the depositary of sovereignty.

References

Alles, Delphine, Guilbaud, Auriane, "Les relations internationales: genèse et évolutions d'un champ d'étude," in Christophe Roux, Eric Savarese (eds.), *Manuel de science politique*, Brussels, Larcier, 2017, pp. 239–254.

Aron, Raymond, *Paix et guerre entre les nations*, Paris, Calmann-Lévy, 1962.

Badie, Bertrand, *Le Diplomate et l'Intrus. L'entrée des sociétés dans l'arène internationale*, Paris, Fayard, 2008.

Devin, Guillaume, *Les Organisations internationales*, Paris, Armand Colin, 2016.

Diamond, Louise, Mcdonald, John, *Multi-Track Diplomacy: A System Approach to Peace*, West Hartford, CT, Kumarian Press, 1996.

Guilbaud, Auriane, *Business Partners. Firmes privées et gouvernance mondiale de la santé*, Paris, Presses de Sciences Po, 2015.

Outrey, Amédée, "Histoire et principes de l'administration française des Affaires étrangères," *Revue française de science politique*, 3, 1953: 491–510.

Pigman, Geoffrey Allen, "The Diplomacy of Global and Transnational Firms," in Andrew F. Cooper, Jorge Heine, Ramesh Thakur (eds.), *The Oxford Handbook of Modern Diplomacy*, Oxford, Oxford University Press, 2013, pp. 192–208.

Slaughter, Anne-Marie, "How to Succeed in the Networked World: A Grand Strategy for the Digital Age," *Foreign Affairs*, 95 (6), 2016: 76–89.

Wiseman, Geoffrey, "'Polylateralism': Diplomacy's Third Dimension," *Public Diplomacy Magazine*, 4, 2010: 24–39.

CHAPTER 14

Individuals and Diplomacy

Pierre Grosser

Meir Dagan, the head of Mossad from 2002 to 2011, explained that assassinations have an effect on morale, as well as a practical impact: "I don't think there were many people that could have replaced Napoleon, or a President like Roosevelt, or a Prime Minister like Churchill" (quoted by Bergman 2019). Similar assessments have been made to justify decapitating terrorist groups; mention is frequently made of Abimael Guzman in Peru, whose arrest in 1992 led to the rapid decline of the Shining Path Maoist group. In May 2011, the cover of *Time* magazine featured a photograph of Bin Laden marked by a red cross, like the one in 1945 when Hitler died. There is a whole "What if?" literature that takes as its branch point the premature death of "great" men (Hitler assassinated), the non-death of others (would America have become involved in the Vietnam War if Kennedy had not been assassinated?), or someone's non-election (would Al Gore, the Democratic candidate, have attacked Iraq if he had been elected in 2000 and been president on 9/11?).

Indeed, the most traditional way of approaching international relations is by focusing on great men. History has long chronicled their deeds and

P. Grosser (✉)
Sciences Po, Paris, France

© The Author(s) 2020
T. Balzacq et al. (eds.), *Global Diplomacy*,
The Sciences Po Series in International Relations and Political Economy, https://doi.org/10.1007/978-3-030-28786-3_14

portrayed their character. At the same time classical realism, a frequent point of reference in political science emphasizes their responsibilities. As the embodiment of national interests, they steer the ship that popular passions and special interests must not lead astray. Raymond Aron stressed the importance of individuals in history, thwarting any general science of international relations, and their passions that lead to wars. The burden of responsibility does not weigh on the head of state alone; many diplomats and those in the military have had to take serious emergency decisions without any clear instructions from their hierarchy.

And yet, philosophy has questioned the omnipotence of great men in making history: Either they are only a product of deeper forces (such as the class struggle), or they do not understand the history they are making, or their desire to make history produces above all tragedies (particularly in the twentieth century), or again their power has now been diluted in the flood of actions by millions of anonymous people who vote, produce, communicate and are increasingly mobile. In fact, from the 1950s to the 1970s, the Annales school mocked the agitation of supposed great men who epitomize but the froth of history made in the depths of time and in waves like economic cycles. Structuralism and systemic analyses, especially in political science, have favored the unity of the state, interactions between unities, and the determinism of everything over the particular. The polarizing mode of the international system constrains—and even determines—foreign policy choices.

The "rediscovery" of the individual has occurred within the framework of a challenge to statism, a crisis of Marxism, a standstill in systemism's ability to explain history's bifurcations and surprises, and of postmodernism promoting the latter's indetermination. Beginning in the 1970s, historians rediscovered the joys of biography and narrative, political scientists opened up the state's black box and began exploring political psychology, while sociologists focused on the subject or on that of individuals maximizing their interests. Appeals to political analysts to rethink the idea of what constitutes a leader came just before a super-empowered individual, Osama Bin Laden, became the most wanted man after the 9/11 attacks, when the president of the world's greatest power, George W. Bush, launched a "war of choice" in Iraq; but it was also after a generation of American best-sellers had claimed to reveal the secret of how to become a successful leader in business and society, often by example.

The individual became the purview of international law, long focused on states. International criminal law highlights the victim, but above all targets the victimizer as a responsible individual. For historians, the First World War was no longer the inevitable product of deep forces (militarism, nationalism, or imperialism), or the deadly spiral sweeping away actors behind the times, but the result of decisions and non-decisions by leaders who led the world into the abyss. World history and microhistory have delighted in following noteworthy individuals. The "charisma" of various leaders (particularly Hitler) has been studied over and over, and there is great interest in "the century of leaders" (Cohen 2013), corresponding to the high modernism of the first half of the twentieth century.

This "return" of the great man also reflects a certain nostalgia for the great architects of the international order and the men who had the courage to take great steps to achieve peace, such as Gorbachev or Rabin, at a time when conflicts have dragged on and international competition seems to be on the rise again. In France, nostalgia for de Gaulle (and even for Napoleon) among supporters of renewed enthusiasm for the presidency, and for Jean Monnet among advocates of increased European integration, attest to that demand. In France, Emmanuel Macron spoke of a "Jupiter-like" presidency, which could continue to lead on and inspire people. Indeed, there is a demand for heroism in the face of technocratic governance, admired outside the political world (athletes, especially of extreme sports, trailblazing entrepreneurs, media celebrities, anonymous heroes in catastrophes), but also an increasingly widespread passion for strongmen (from Putin to Dutertre or Erdogan), while the personality cults for Hitler and Stalin, Kim Il-sung or Bokassa seem to belong to another age. In those days, the major powers were already relying on leaders in the South whose virtues they extolled (particularly in Asia for the United States and in Africa for France), while revolutionaries, and then dissidents, were turned into heroes (from Solzhenitsyn to Aung San Suu Kyi). During the 1990s–2000s, the rhetoric on democratization suggested that eliminating a "bad shepherd" (Milosevic, Saddam Hussein), would inevitably lead populations toward democracy, as was the case when Nazi leaders were eliminated in Germany after 1945. In reality, the issue is to know whether a head of state can still meet people's expectations without favoring symbolism over effectiveness, at a time when issues are more numerous and complex, bureaucracies heavier, the media more prompt to react; the issue has been raised for American presidents, whose mistakes and inadequacies commentators are quick to point out.

"Summit meetings" continue to exert fascination, like major historical events such as the Yalta conference in February 1945, the Soviet-American summits in the 1970s–1980s, or Nixon's trip to China in 1972. The end of the Cold War cannot be understood without observing that the West was run by a handful of leaders who respected, spoke and wrote to one another, and remained in power for a long time in the 1980s (Reagan, Thatcher, Kohl, Mitterrand, and Nakasone). But it is also clear that direct means of communication, particularly phone calls, dramatically increased the number of interactions between heads of state and between other decision-makers. The election of Donald Trump showed how important personalization can be, using twitter diplomacy.

As a result, studying individuals in diplomacy has to be approached from three angles: First, focusing on the actor, knowing who he is; second, broadening the focus to the major challenges of decision-making and leadership, in a comparative mode; and third, expanding the focus onto various actors engaged in diplomacy in one way or another.

Anatomy of the Individual as Actor

Policy-makers receive files on a regular basis from diplomats and intelligence services about foreign interlocutors or new figures in charge of countries or their administrations. An individual's biography and personality are therefore considered important. Databases on Soviet personnel were compiled on computers in the United States (by Rand) or on index cards in France (by journalist Michal Tatu) during the Cold War. Psychology experts were sometimes called upon. In 1943, the Office of Strategic Services (OSS), ancestor of the Central Intelligence Agency (CIA), asked psychoanalyst William Langer to draw a psychological portrait of Hitler from the piles of sources he was supplied with; his booklet wasn't published until 1972. The "remote profiling" method was employed. Within the framework of the Office of Net Assessment, created in 1973 at the instigation of Andy Marshall, the Americans tried to accumulate as much data as possible on the perceptions of Soviet leaders; they deemed that the elite in power would feel vulnerable if they were specifically targeted by strikes. A new American strategy was formulated to heighten those fears. Remote psychobiography and psychoanalysis gained a new impetus in the 1990s in order to understand the behavior of Saddam Hussein and the North Korean leader Kim Jong-il. The Bosnian Serb leader, Radovan Karadzic, was all the more interesting as he himself was a psychiatrist.

An individual's development is based on his experiences. Individual trajectories are thus scrutinized. The individual's place of origin and background, the nature of his studies, professional career, and current social environment (family, networks, party) are so many clues in trying to grasp his personality. However, these deterministic factors are often misleading, such as when hope was placed in Bachar Al-Assad or Kim Jong-un because they had spent time in the West, notably for their studies. These trajectories and experiences are often evoked in discussing the "worldviews" of major actors in diplomacy. That expression, vying with "operational code" and "mind mapping," assumes there is a set of prisms through which an individual can analyze reality, in particular internationally. President Wilson may have promoted internationalism, spread democracy and peoples' right to self-determination, but swayed by racism in the southern United States, he restricted those benefits to "civilized" nations and did not challenge colonial domination, contrary to Roosevelt. The latter had a rather romantic vision of China and quite a negative one of the Japanese; his mother's family had made their fortune in China. It is impossible to think of Stalin's foreign policy without taking into account his Georgian origins and above all his Eurasian vision of security and Soviet interests. There has been a slew of studies in recent years on the religious convictions of American presidents and of several Secretaries of State (such as John Foster Dulles). There are more and more book titles nowadays starting with the words "Inside the mind of," for Putin, Erdogan, Xi Jinping, or Kim Jong-un.

An individual's "complete" biography involves exploring two sensitive areas: their personal life and health. Their personal life is often a delicate subject, since intelligence services see it as a vulnerability factor. In the early 1950s, McCarthyism went after members of the State Department for being homosexuals, pointing out their vulnerability to blackmail by Soviet espionage. The impact of one's personal life on decision-making remains hard to assess. It may have been a factor in the hawkish attitude of Austrian chief of staff Franz Conrad von Hötzendorf in 1914, obsessed by a victory that would enable him to "break down the barriers" separating him from his mistress, a married woman. Statesmen's physical and mental health cannot be disregarded, since it affects their judgment and availability. In the final months of his life, Roosevelt was unable to focus on his work for more than two or three hours a day, and the Republicans felt that he had been weak in dealing with Stalin at Yalta due to his health issues. When Churchill once again became Prime Minister in 1951, he was in ill health, like Anthony Eden, in charge of foreign policy. As a result, the

Bermuda Conference, meant to bring together the Americans, the British and French to deal with the consequences of Stalin's death in March 1953, was postponed several times and was not held until December, in a very different context. Eden himself has been accused of being involved in the Suez intervention in 1956, in a rather solitary manner, under the influence of drugs that altered his temperament and judgment. Particularly since the Cuban Missile Crisis, the issue of stress during a major crisis has been an important topic of study.

Questions around an individual's socialization are raised at an earlier stage. Mention is often made of the Ivy League, Oxbridge, and the École nationale d'administration (ENA) to explain a shared worldview and the personal relations of American, British, and French diplomats and decision-makers. Major universities today are vying to attract future leaders, while fostering their geographical mobility in rhetoric about cosmopolitanism, shared values, and the ability to be a global leader. During negotiations on the North American Free Trade Agreement (NAFTA) in the early 1990s, a number of Mexican negotiators were fully acquainted with their American interlocutors' procedures as they had gone to the same universities in the United States. Likewise, the Israelis were faced with a new generation of Palestinian negotiators in the 1990s that had been trained in law and negotiating techniques at American universities. There are programs in the United States and France, for instance, to bring in promising young leaders by leveraging the sustainability of the contacts they establish. Cooptation within the Bilderberg Group—a discreet conclave of transatlantic elites created in 1954 that has inspired many global conspiracy fantasies—works more as a confirmation than as an incubator.

Regular participation in negating bodies later on creates a form of socialization. Mastering the "codes" and techniques of multilateral negotiation explains why there is a specialization in UN and European Union affairs. French diplomat Pierre Sellal is an example of that "Brussels-based" continuity as he has been involved in many occasions in France's Permanent Representation in Brussels, which he has headed twice. Similarly, there are "development" professionals, although their profile changes based on how the subject is viewed: Within the European Economic Community (EEC), it was first former "colonial bureaucrats" that filled the Directorate-General devoted to development and aid policies. Diplomats had to be specialists in environmental questions as they became more important on the international agenda. Indeed, along with mastering codes, many issues require technical expertise. During the Cold War an arms control "community" was formed, specialized in complex negotiations in conventional and nuclear arms control. Specialists on strategic questions, in particular nuclear ones, also formed a community within the North Atlantic Treaty Organization (NATO) and with certain closely aligned countries like Israel. The heads of central banks around the world include many individuals who have worked at the International Monetary Fund (IMF). Increasing interactions and everyday practices are a guarantee of predictability, therefore, of mutual trust, and even of personal relations. However, one must beware of rhetoric about "big families," of international legal experts, for instance, as the degree of internationalization in national communities of jurists is unequal, being greater in the UK than in France or Russia.

Cognition, Decisions and Emotion

Since the 1970s, the very notion of rational decisions by decision-making individuals has been challenged. The latter are thought to be dependent on their (often biased) perceptions and beliefs. New information is filtered based on confirmation bias, which discards whatever challenges beliefs. The filter's density depends on the individual's cognitive openness: Among Israeli leaders, Yitzhak Shamir was not very open, while Yitzhak Rabin was more so, deeming it necessary to negotiate with the Palestine Liberation Organization (PLO). Even when the individual's beliefs change, he is not always aware of the fact and remains convinced that he has always thought what he now thinks. Since so-called rational choices are always rooted in convictions (beliefs), we must find out how they were built up and what points of reference they provide. The Hitlerian analogy, not shared by decision-makers all over the world, interprets a state's aggressive actions based on Hitler's conquests. George H. W. Bush's caution regarding the rapid changes in people's democracies in Eastern Europe in the fall of 1989 can be largely explained through analogies: In 1956, when American radio stations based in Germany encouraged the Hungarian rebellion against the Red Army's tanks, giving them false hopes; and in June 1989 when Chinese leaders used force against protesters, which Communist regimes in Europe might have done, arguing that it was interference by the United States. Since the 1970s, American historians and highly mainstream practitioners have tried to find a way to teach decision-makers how to use history "correctly," notably to avoid mirror imaging, namely the belief that other decision-makers are acting the way you would, in short ethnocentrism (Brands and Inboden 2018).

Interactions between adversaries prompt negative perceptions. Individual A thinks he is acting in a reactive way, while individual B would act above all based on who he is rather than in reaction to A's actions. On the other hand, when B changes his behavior in a positive way, it is considered by A to be a validation of his own actions. Thus, in an escalation phase, B is driven by who he is, not by what A does, while during the de-escalation phase the causality of B's behavior would be the opposite. These biases have been confirmed by studying crises, such as the negative perceptions of the Soviets and Chinese during their short border clash in 1969, where neither side understood that they did not perceive each other as moderates, and both exaggerated the potential threat. In overplaying the Hitler analogy, Western leaders have tended to "orientalize" Middle Eastern leaders (from Nasser to Saddam Hussein) who for their part have often exaggerated Western hostility. Negative perceptions do not necessarily produce negative results; the two superpowers partly misjudged each other's intentions during detente, but it made it possible to limit tensions and provide more predictability to foreign policy.

Because of predetermined convictions, the truth can easily turn into whatever one wants it to be. As a result, decision-makers are frequently overconfident in their own judgment. It is hard for them to acknowledge a mistake because it would challenge their convictions. Furthermore, they rarely take convictions seriously when they do not share them, notably those of their adversaries. And yet, understanding those convictions is essential in interpreting and anticipating their actions. Like most individuals, decision-makers are more aware of losses than of gains. They internalize the "domino effect": A loss will have a series of repercussions. There is thus a temptation to take big risks in order to avoid a small loss. One must therefore be firm in anticipation, because of the possible consequences on events elsewhere. That is why it was hard for the French to abandon Indochina (the Communists would have advanced throughout Southeast Asia, North Africa would have wanted to shake up colonial dependence like Vietnam, and France would have lost its status), then for the Americans to abandon South Vietnam. Decision-makers only rarely think about those receiving the signals they send out and may be mistaken in their interpretation. The Americans thought, mistakenly, that the nuclear threat had led the Chinese to agree to end the Korean War in 1953. Conversely, policy-makers and bureaucracies tend to overestimate their own capacity to decipher clues about the intentions of others, to see "signs" everywhere, and often to be wrong in interpreting them.

The ability to learn is therefore a key issue. In the area of intelligence, learning and "lessons learned" explain why success sometimes arrives after failure—which is often highlighted to shed light on why there have been no more catastrophic terrorist events in the United States since 9/11. But, for that, the specialists advise leaders to encourage their decision-making circles to reflect on the reasons for failure in an environment where they are not afraid to admit mistakes without risking their job (or even their life). Narcissism, as well as the certainty of having experience and knowing better than others, can make people blind and deaf. These days, modesty, and systematic doubt have been espoused in analyzing intelligence and increasing counter-intuitive hypotheses that enable one to "think outside the box." However, there are still questions about decision-makers' appetite for intelligence, their willingness or not to hear what does not fit in with their cognitive patterns, and the everyday reality of making decisions amid uncertainty, as they are based on information that is necessarily incomplete and ambivalent.

This alludes to the very nature of an individual actor's leadership, whether a head of state, of an international organization, a major corporation or an NGO. Leadership styles have been studied "scientifically" for a century now, but the literature providing advice to rulers and handbooks for good ambassadors that have flourished in the modern era should also be taken into account. A distinction is often made between situational leadership, capable of grasping the ins and outs of a given situation, and relational leadership, which focuses on people, whether through having followers (charismatic leadership) or by creating consensus. Another distinction is made between transactional leadership, which negotiates with a certain flexibility, seeking optimal solutions to preserve stakeholders' interests, and transformational leadership, which motives and stimulates, creating emulation and above all striving to transform what exists, both domestically and in the international arena. Leadership styles result in certain pathologies: On the one hand, the delicate balance between intuition and effectiveness, and on the other hand, consulting different even opposing—views from those of the leader. Too much thinking leads to procrastination, too much haste to mistakes. "Groupthink," as in the Israeli war in Lebanon in 1982, is pack behavior or the herd instinct, while "polythink" is cacophony because there are too many voices in the leader's entourage.

An important factor in decision-making is the concern for one's reputation, internally, and internationally, which seems to have had pride of place in old Europe and to be an equivalent of "face" in Asia, which obsessed diplomats and the military posted in the Far East. Reputation has been associated with credibility regarding allies and enemies ever since President Obama chose not to bomb the Syrian regime in the summer of 2013, after it had crossed a red line defined by Washington as the use of chemical weapons. It is unclear whether not going through with a threat really harms one's credibility with adversaries, as there is uncertainty about the next blow that might come as an overreaction. With regard to allies, it could prompt a feeling of abandonment, but could also involve another pathology in alliances, namely the fear of being dragged into a venture unwillingly. If the alliance is solid and the cost of non-execution not too high, one's credibility may not suffer. Wanting to preserve credibility can lead to military undertakings; Johnson became mired in the Vietnam War by comparing himself to Kennedy (who was also thinking about his own credibility during the Cuban Missile Crisis). Nixon's "madman theory" was not successful, since Moscow did not budge, but it was destructive in Vietnam and risky for the world. It attested to the president's narcissism, impatience, and desire to "save face" in an "honorable" retreat from Vietnam.

Behind the separation often assumed between rational and irrational actors, between reasoned acts and emotional reactions, it now appears that cognition and affect cannot really be separated, which has been confirmed by neurobiology. Pure rationality is only a fantasy, and it would be absurd to judge a decision by its degree of distortion from constructed rationality. Still, anger or even enmity contribute to perception biases, since they often prevent one from taking into account arguments uttered by someone loathed or despised. A lack of empathy prevents one from knowing the enemy and may lead one to misjudge their intentions and not anticipate their choices: As Stalin did with regard to Hitler, or the North Vietnamese leader Le Duan with regard to American presidents. Optimism and pessimism regarding nuclear proliferation and the possibility of dissuading a nuclear state are important variables for understanding the choice to use or not use preventive strikes on nuclear installations. Jacques Hymans has highlighted the "oppositional nationalism" of certain leaders (combining anxiety over an external threat and pride in having the modern capacity to face one) to explain why certain countries have initiated nuclear weapons programs.

For constructivists, humiliation, frustration, fear, the will to restore one's status or honor, or to reassert forms of masculinity are important aspects nowadays in the march to war, in civil conflicts and revolutions. Hatred and disgust should not be forgotten: In Indochina, then in Algeria, "colonials" showed officials from Paris (Marius Moutet, then Jacques Soustelle) the horrors committed by "rebels" in order to create an insurmountable gap and toughen policies on the mainland. Firsthand accounts flood in to show the barbarism of a tyrant when he becomes an enemy or after he has been killed, as with Saddam Hussein or Gaddafi. Henceforth, the shift is clear even regarding the emotional aspect, which can be used as an explanation and as an excuse, since it is not a loathsome passion harmful to reason but an unavoidable reality that can lead to the best or to the worst. It is not an excuse for one's adversary (the impact of massive American bombing on North Korea from 1950 to 1953, and the Iran–Iraq War for Iran), but for oneself, when one must "understand" the instant reaction of the United States after 9/11, or the lasting impact of the Jewish genocide on the psyche of Israeli leaders.

While trust has been built up as the cardinal virtue of resilient capitalism, it also appears to be the lubricant crucial to international relations. Multilateralism and international institutions partly ensure this lubricating function, facilitating relations between states with different degrees of power and values. Specific processes (track-two, confidence-building, transparency and verification measures) must make it possible to build a lasting bond and limit negative perceptions. Lies in diplomacy, like the improper interpretation of an agreement, may create lasting rifts. But trust and mistrust also involve emotions. Mistrust is hard—and at times almost impossible—to overcome: As a result, the adversary's smile and handshake are perceived as traps, and taking the slightest risk is considered too costly. Trust is often founded on interpersonal bonds. Roosevelt tried to create one with Stalin during the Second World War. The power of first impressions is lasting, often from a person's face (coming from a highly specialized part of the brain, FFA, the fusiform face area); it is very difficult to change subsequently and also to decipher someone's facial expressions in a sure way. The chemistry that creates trust, and even friendship, is very complex. In 2001, in Slovenia, Bush looked Putin in the eye and saw his soul ("I was able to get a sense of his soul. He's a man deeply committed to his country and the best interests of his country," he said after their first meeting in 2001), and therefore, trusted him. There are however numerous cases showing that personal contacts have made it possible to create a climate of trust, and even to speak frankly, leading to the resolution of tense situations that appeared to be dead ends (Wheeler 2018). Personal relations between Reagan and Gorbachev, Schultz and Shevardnadze, and on both sides of the Iron Curtain, played a definite role in ending the Cold War. In particular, trust allows a greater understanding of the constraints of domestic politics that weigh on others, where they are traditionally minimized. Nevertheless, trust is always fragile, subject to faux pas and symbolic wounds.

THE INDIVIDUALS THAT COUNT INTERNATIONALLY

These reflections on state policy-makers could be transposed onto the many other individuals that count in international relations. The history of the UN "galaxy" shows that general secretaries and directors have counted in promoting ideas and policies. The movement of international elites—between administrations, think tanks, missions in high-level groups, academic positions and foundations they have created, or companies whose undertakings they have facilitated—outlines modes of power more intricate than a mere hierarchy of authority of high modernism. The term "governance" can help explain this transnational action, which often relies on networks of "socialized" actors. Similarly, it is often believed that individuals further international initiatives through their internationally impacting work, through all their forms of mobility—temporary or permanent—through their consumption patterns, communications, and relationships, etc. The importance of anonymity, in situations of peace and conflict, has been highlighted through recent globalization, especially involving networks of mobilization and expertise and is now attracting interest in the study of terrorist networks.

Historians have shifted their gaze onto older forms of internationalism and transnational interactions, and onto individual actors out of the traditional spotlight (Grosser 2013). There is a profusion of biographies of ambassadors and veterans of diplomacy, stressing the role of individuals that have had an important function in foreign policy, such as the private secretary for Foreign Affairs to the Prime Minister in the UK or legal advisors to ministries of foreign affairs. It appears that some policy choices are compelled by the actions and documentation produced at intermediate levels of bureaucracy: It is hard to understand the start of the Indochina War without seeing the role of the colonial colonels, in the field and in Paris.

In the United States, the generals in charge of theater commands, in particular of the United States Central Command (CENTCOM, the Greater Middle East) and the United States Pacific Command (PACOM), play a real diplomatic role. Statesmen use parallel networks and special envoys who sometimes short-circuit the bureaucracy in place, like the Foccart networks in Africa at the time of General de Gaulle. The national security advisor in the United States has at times played a major role, whether with Kissinger or Brzezinski, the former striving ceaselessly to circumvent the State Department. Laurence Tubiana played an important role in the COP 21 in Paris in 2015, alongside ministers Laurent Fabius and Ségolène Royal. Central bankers are seen as major actors: Already in the 1920s, the American Benjamin Strong and the Briton Montagu Norman appeared to be the masters of the international financial system due to their relationships and activities. The clash between the Briton Keynes and the American White at Bretton Woods in 1944 weighed heavily on the post-war monetary and financial order.

Norm entrepreneurs are being increasingly studied. There are countless studies on Henri Dunant, the "inventor" of the Red Cross, on Raphael Lemkin, who played a fundamental role in drawing up the Convention on the Prevention and Punishment of the Crime of Genocide, and on the individuals who created international criminal law—including the chief prosecutor of the International Criminal Court, Luis Moreno Ocampo, given star status before being beset by numerous affairs. Some of these entrepreneurs are members of a government, like William Hague, who worked for the Foreign Office from 2010 to 2014 on the issue of sexual violence in conflicts. Experts from academia have also played important roles (Lowenthal and Bertucci 2014): Thomas Biersteker for targeted sanctions, and the political analyst John G. Ruggie for the UN Global Compact. Progress in the humanitarian arena and in human rights was driven after the Great War by René Cassin for veterans' rights, Albert Thomas for workers' social rights, Fridtjof Nansen for the status of refugees, and Eglantyne Jebb for children's rights. It is difficult to tell the story of humanitarian work and the right to intervene without going into the biographies of Bernard Kouchner and Rony Brauman. Legal experts have praised the major role played by colleagues at the beginning of the previous century who, in promoting the Kellogg–Briand Pact of 1928, are seen as working toward a "Copernican" revolution, namely making war abnormal and even criminalizing it.

Finally, there is an inexhaustible interest in super-empowered individuals. In the past, it may have involved revolutionary icons (Mao, Ho Chi Minh, Che Guevara, Malcolm X), who inspired protest movements and revolutions around the world in the 1960s, or icons of non-violence (Gandhi, Martin Luther King, John Lennon) whose global influence has been displayed from South Africa to Communist Eastern Europe. Megaphilanthropy was not always associated with a particular individual, despite eponymous American foundations (Carnegie, Rockefeller, Ford); today, however, the men running them are seen as both heroes and threats, like Bill and Melinda Gates for global health issues or George Soros for democratization. The involvement of show-business celebrities has been frequently criticized, in particular through reproducing a colonial situation by wanting to "save" victims in countries in the South; yet, like major philanthropists, they do have preferential access to many heads of state and government, and international organizations. They symbolize an agenda (Angelina Jolie and refugees, George Clooney and the Darfur issue, Leonardo Di Caprio and environmental issues), popularize ideas (thus, Jeffrey Sachs' idea on development, as one who had previously been an icon of free-market "shock theories" in Latin America and post-Communist Europe), and create expectations for politicians through their use of social networks (Grosser 2013).

References

Brands, Hal, Inboden, William, "Wisdom Without Tears: Statecraft and the Uses of History," *Journal of Strategic Studies*, 4 (7), 2018: 916–946.

Bergman, Ronen, *Rise and Kill First: The Secret History of Israel's Targeted Assassinations*, London, John Murray Press, 2019.

Cohen, Yves, *Le siècle des chefs. Une histoire transnationale du commandement et de l'autorité (1890–1940)*, Paris, Éditions Amsterdam, 2013.

Grosser, Pierre, *Traiter avec le diable? Les vrais enjeux de la diplomatie au XXIe siècle*, Paris, Odile Jacob, 2013.

Lowenthal, Abraham F., Bertucci, Mariano E. (eds.), *Scholars, Policymakers, and International Affairs. Finding Common Cause*, Baltimore, MD, John Hopkins University Press, 2014.

Wheeler, Nicholas J., *Trusting Enemies: Interpersonal Relationships in International Conflict*, Oxford, Oxford University Press, 2018.

PART III

Sectors

CHAPTER 15

Economic and Corporate Diplomacy

Laurence Badel

Brought to the forefront in France in May 2012 by the Minister of Foreign Affairs, Laurent Fabius, who declared it "a priority for France" (Fabius 2012), economic diplomacy was an instrument of state foreign policy that had been established in the late nineteenth century as a tool for projecting power in the world in the context of rising imperial rivalries. During the First World War, it was the focus of multilateral reflection and practices aimed at working in concert to stabilize international economic and financial relations in the aftermath of the conflict. In the first case, economic diplomacy designates the mobilization of public, semi-public, and private actors under the supervision of public authorities, at the national, regional, and local levels to champion national economic interests by endorsing the commercial and financial expansion of national companies into foreign markets and by promoting the appeal of the national territory to foreign investors. It involves bilateral procedures and reflects an approach fluctuating between patriotism and economic warfare. In the second case, it designates the practice of multilateral negotiations in the economic and financial

L. Badel (✉)
University of Paris I Panthéon Sorbonne, Paris, France
e-mail: Laurence.Badel@univ-paris1.fr

© The Author(s) 2020
T. Balzacq et al. (eds.), *Global Diplomacy*,
The Sciences Po Series in International Relations and Political Economy, https://doi.org/10.1007/978-3-030-28786-3_15

arena and is based on a cooperative approach to international relations. As a fundamentally ambivalent notion, economic diplomacy conveys both a warring approach and one of economic cooperation. How can the national interest be reconciled with the necessary regulation of global markets to ensure collective security and prosperity and, as a result, the stability of the international system? The answers provided were conditioned by the growing interdependence between economies, the capacity of companies to face international competition, and national diplomatic cultures.

Economic diplomacy as a field of study fell into a relative decline during the 1980s. It was doubly doomed, due to the "cultural shift" that impacted the choice of new subjects and promoted approaches opposing realist interpretations of the international arena. Economics, which had saturated historiographical discussions in the 1960s and 1970s, was fading as a topic of study. Diplomacy, expressing the essence of state sovereignty, was regarded from afar with disdain. In France, only former practitioners still dealt with economic diplomacy (Carron de La Carrière 1998). Nearly alone during the 1980s, respectively, in the fields of history and in international political economics, books by Marc Trachtenberg (1980) and Georges-Henri Soutou (1989), and by Susan Strange (1988), developed a strong and unique reflection on these subjects. The former reexamined the concept of French economic diplomacy driven by revenge against Germany, the second highlighted among other things the importance of the first interallied economic conferences in building a new world order. Susan Strange analyzed the transformation in relations between companies and states in the new phase of globalization impacted by deregulation and the rise of foreign investing. Since the 2000s, there have been many studies dealing with both the rise in multilateral economic diplomacy between the two wars (Fink et al. 2002) and its diversification beginning in the 1970s (Woolcock and Bayne 2007; Mourlon-Druol and Romero 2014), with arms and economic sanctions (Dobson 2012; Zhang 2014), and with policies for penetrating developing markets, a practice that states instituted during the Cold War (Bagnato 2003; Lorenzini 2003; Badel 2010). Finally, the issue of the autonomy of economic actors vis-à-vis public actors, the core of historical reflection in the 1960s and 1970s, has been reexamined by researchers in diplomatic studies, as well as international management and international business studies. Subsequent to a pioneering article by Susan Strange (1992), they developed the notions of corporate and business diplomacy (Muldoon 2005; Saner and Yiu 2008; Ruël and Wolters 2016) and of "private multilateralism" (Harvie et al. 2005). Talking about economic diplomacy in the early twenty-first century, one cannot exhaust the variety of relations that exist between private economic actors and public actors. Moreover, the notion of corporate diplomacy has now been equally established.

Economic diplomacy, shaped gradually in the late nineteenth century by the major European powers, joined later by Japan and the United States, was both an instrument for imperial dominance in the East, the Far East and Africa, for penetrating newly independent markets in Central and South America, and a means for smaller European states to assert themselves in a competitive world. The strengthening of multilateral economic diplomacy around the First World War confirmed the increased interdependence of economies and societies set in motion during the first phase of contemporary globalization in the 1860s, the diversification of objects of negotiation, and the fundamental interconnectedness of economic questions with cultural, social, and strategic issues. Economic diplomacy became a tool in the hands of certain developing states in the late 1960s, and emerging ones in the 1990s and 2000s, still trying to find a place in the international structure built after 1945 by the Allied powers. Asserting themselves through realist policies where the quest for wealth dovetails with a desire for power, emerging countries have forced developed states to rethink their own approach to economic diplomacy. Studying the latter represents a vital marker in thinking about new power hierarchies that do not always correspond to the ones passed on after the Second World War.

A Tool for Economic and Financial Dominance

Economic diplomacy, or just plain diplomacy, began as trade diplomacy: Thus in Venice, the Republic's first representatives were consuls invested with trade and administrative functions. It became more structured with gradual state control of consular functions starting in the mid-seventeenth century in England and France. This intensification of international economic and financial relations between Western states, and between those states and those under their domination (Ottoman Empire, Asian, and South American states), was characterized by trade treaties, then financial agreements and monetary conventions. European states built the first public structures designed to implement their economic diplomacy in the context of the first wave of globalization in the contemporary era, marked by a technological revolution of transportation and telecommunications, as well as by human migration and an unprecedented circulation of capital.

From its development in the 1880s, economic diplomacy has emerged as a public support scheme for gathering information on foreign markets, negotiating tariff agreements, encouraging direct investments abroad, and promoting national interests. Networks of public agents—whether local (consulates), semi-public, or private (chambers of commerce and industry, chambers of commerce abroad, employers' associations)—appeared insufficient and states undertook a preliminary rationalization of the system. In all European countries, certain consulates were eventually focused specifically on their commercial mission, then a new position was created within embassies: the commercial attaché. In Great Britain, the first British commercial attaché was the former Consul General in Westphalia, who was appointed to Berlin in 1880 with jurisdiction over Germany and Austria-Hungary. In France, the law of December 7, 1908, created six commercial attaché positions. For smaller European states, some of which were neutral (Sweden, Switzerland), active commercial diplomacy conducted by consuls was a means of asserting oneself in the international arena to compensate for an absence of political power. Thus, the consular network of the Swedish-Norwegian Union (1814–1905) expanded considerably in the second half of the nineteenth century. Before the First World War, two extra-European states (Japan and the United States) earned their stripes as regional powers due to active economic diplomacy. Under the Roosevelt and Taft presidencies, the United States inaugurated "dollar diplomacy," a policy of investing in economically weaker countries in Central America. The island of Santo Domingo was a laboratory for US reform methods to restore the failing finances of foreign states, the State Department working closely with economists and bankers (Rosenberg 2003). The scheme, theorized for France by a "finance-industry-diplomacy triptych" (Thobie 1974) consolidated at the end of the century, could be extended to other European powers, with modulations depending on the government's degree of leverage in dealing with economic affairs.

The First World War intensified relations between business and government circles on behalf of the war effort and in formulating goals (Soutou 1989). To the extent that Foreign Affairs Ministries did not create departments devoted to foreign economic expansion until the 1920s, it was the Ministries of Commerce and Finance that developed and reinforced their vocation as international actors during the First World War. After the war, foreign affairs ministries were now obliged to create real departments in charge of economic issues, such as the Sub-Directorate of Trade Relations in France (Sous-direction des Relations Commerciales) in 1919, the Foreign Trade Office (Außenhandelsstelle) in Germany, which became an independent department in July 1920, or to create hybrid structures such as the Department of Overseas Trade in the UK in 1917, attached to the Foreign Office and the Board of Trade. Foreign networks were growing (there were about fifty French commercial attachés in 1930). Governments also set up credit insurance systems designed to cover the political risk taken by those exporting to foreign markets (Great Britain, 1919; Belgium, 1921; Denmark, 1922; The Netherlands, 1923; Germany, 1926; Italy, 1927; France, 1928) (Badel 2010). Halted in their hegemonic ambitions, Japan and Germany recovered by strengthening their dynamic economic diplomacy, the former by reinforcing its major *zaibatsu* (Mitsui, Mitsubishi, etc.), business conglomerates close to political parties, the latter supported by its cartelized industries and major businessmen (Hugo Stinnes, Walther Rathenau) convinced that the interdependence of economies would lead the Allies to accept revising the Treaty of Versailles. By giving currency a new central place in international relations, the war also put the United States, now the Allies' creditor, in a position to expand dollar diplomacy to Europe by affecting its reconstruction through the adoption of the Dawes Plan (1924) tying the reimbursement of the war debt owed by the Allies to the payment to them of reparations owed by Germany. Finally, the war made people aware of the vital nature of raw material resources and, among them, oil was to occupy a special place in the twentieth and twenty-first centuries due to its strategic aspect. Its use by countries in the Organization of Petroleum Exporting Countries (OPEC) in 1973 highlights the coercive, and even punitive, dimension that economic diplomacy can have. There are indeed different kinds of sanctions: blockades, boycotts, and embargos (Dobson 2012). The twentieth century was characterized by major examples in this vein: The blockade used as a weapon by the Entente against the Central Powers in 1915, against the USSR in Berlin in 1948–1949, against Cuba by the United States in 1962; the embargo on exporting strategic material to Communist countries and China during the entire Cold War through the creation of the Coordinating Committee for Multilateral Export Controls 1949–1994 (COCOM) and the China Committee (CHINCOM) set up in 1952 (Cain 2007; Zhang 2014). Boycotts are another weapon frequently used by raw materials producers. This was the case in 1956 (Suez crisis) and in 1967 (Six-Day War) when the governments of Arab producer countries started a boycott against aggressor countries.

After 1945, public mechanisms were reinforced in numerous countries—in 1950 France even created a new body of civil servants for economic development, the "corps de l'Expansion économique"—which continued to be promoted by heightened development aid policies during the 1960s. These policies were highly ambivalent: The aid was often "tied to" something. Gifts and loans, whether public or benefiting from public support, were used to finance the purchase of goods and services only in the donor country, or in a group of countries that was not comprised of all the countries receiving the aid. States included development aid instruments in an overall strategy of national economic expansion designed to ensure growth, an equilibrium of the balance of payments, and starting in 1973, employment. Thus, development aid policies had complex motivations blending international solidarity and a concern with lifting societies in the South out of poverty, as well as the goal of selling abroad both industrial products and technical expertise, and ensuring the influence, or even the dominance, of the creditor country (Badel 2010). This was particularly true for the two Germanies after 1945 (Lorenzini 2003).

A Tool for Global Governance: Multilateral Arenas of Economic Diplomacy

Multilateral cooperation blossomed during the 1860s. Currency and customs being two regalian prerogatives, monetary and trade policy have historically been two major areas in the hands of European states and preferred areas for intergovernmental dialogue. International monetary relations involved multilateral cooperation starting in 1865, the year when the Latin Monetary Union was created (Thiemeyer 2009). The First World War led to the creation of interallied economic cooperation destined to continue after the war in the League of Nations (Soutou 1989). Monetary issues became a central focus of cooperation between Europe and the United States. In 1922, the Genoa Conference pursued that vision by reorganizing the international monetary system (Fink et al. 2002). To facilitate the return to fixed parities and save world gold reserves, the gold exchange standard was substituted for the old gold standard. The economic crisis of October 1929, and the impossibility of finding a global solution during negotiations at the London Economic Conference in July 1933, defined the limits of that dynamic, shattered by resistance from national interests, starting with those of the United States and the withdrawal to protected markets.

The purpose of intergovernmental cooperation was also to promote trade and investments. This was the case for the Genoa international economic conference in 1922, following the customs wars that marked the end of the previous century, remembered as the height of free trade efforts in the 1920s. Beginning in 1947, the General Agreement on Trade and Tariffs (GATT) became the framework for international trade negotiations, and in particular for the confrontation between the United States and the European Economic Community on the issue of trade liberalization (Dillon Round, Kennedy Round, Tokyo Round, and Uruguay Round). As states re-engaged politically, there was a profusion of ministerial meetings and gatherings of heads of state and government leading to the creation of the European Council in 1974 and of the G6 in 1975, which became the G7 in 1976, then the G8 in 1998, after the admission of Canada, then Russia alongside the founding countries: Germany, the United States, France, Italy, Japan, and the UK (Mourlon-Druol and Romero 2014). The countries also agreed on regulating the use of export credits, and in 1978 signed the first Arrangement on Guidelines for Officially Supported Export Credits with public support, in the framework of the Organization for Economic Cooperation and Development (OECD). The European Economic Community is a regional negotiating arena in which the European Commission has specific powers to enforce free competition. Rule No. 17 passed in 1962—the so-called 17/6214 rule—requires the Commission to be notified regarding any agreements between corporations that could affect trade between countries in the common market (Warlouzet 2016). It was the basis for reinforcing competition policies during the 1980s.

Starting with the creation of the World Trade Organization (WTO) in 1995, multilateral economic diplomacy has been characterized by a diversification of objects of negotiation (environmental and social norms, etc.) extending the first expansion of those (technology, health, etc.) issues undertaken as of the mid-nineteenth century through the participation of formerly Communist states, the assertion of emerging states and the redefinition of the relationship between states and private actors. Other intergovernmental arenas emerged thanks to the rise of interregional dialogues in the 1990s and free trade agreement negotiations: Thus, the European Union established frameworks for special dialogues with the United States, Canada, Latin American, and Asian countries. Since 1989, relations between Pacific-rim countries have been structured around Asia Pacific

Economic Cooperation (APEC). Another significant change can be mentioned: As their financial resources faded, states have sought the participation of private actors (banks, NGOs) and are increasingly including their representatives in delegations to international conferences. Furthermore, while NGOs may organize counter-demonstrations at international negotiations such as in Seattle in 1999, they are involved at the same time in negotiations on the environment with the UN and on development with the World Bank. Moreover, business circles have created their own arenas for parallel negotiations: the Transatlantic Business Dialogue (TABD), Asia-Europe Business Forum (AEBF), etc. (Badel 2013). There has also been an increased demand for transparency in negotiating methods: On October 9, 2014, the negotiating mandate for the Transatlantic Treaty entrusted to the European Commission in 2013 was declassified.

Negotiations have also attempted to "untie" the issue of aid to poor countries. Gifts or loans from the public sector, designed to support development in third-world recipient countries, are subject to the securing of contracts by companies from donor countries or small groups of donor countries. In 1991, signatories to the 1978 Arrangement accepted a regulatory framework called the Helsinki Rules, which drastically restricted the use of tied aid credits. Subsequently, during the 1990s, the issue of untying aid was the focus of discussions between OECD countries. After discussions held in 1998, the OECD achieved recognition of the need to move toward the end of the tied aid mechanism, in the framework of contract procurement, in a DAC recommendation on untying ODA to the least developed countries and heavily indebted poor countries. It is estimated that between 1999–2001 and 2008, the percentage of untied bilateral aid gradually went from 46 to 82%. However, the debate was sparked again during the 2010s around the idea of untied aid, along with a low level of concessionality to support long-term infrastructure financing.

Economic Diplomacy in Emerging Countries

With the exception of Japan, non-Western countries have only developed tools to promote their economic diplomacy relatively recently. The 1973 oil crisis led the Indian government to construct an economic diplomacy policy focused on the Persian Gulf and based on sending well-trained Indian experts and technicians (Rana 2007). After 1978, China asserted itself as a key player within the international community by conducting active economic diplomacy. Like Japan, it has been a provider of development aid and a major investor both regionally and globally. It joined the WTO in 2001.

During the 2000s, the fundamental realism of emerging countries fostered innovative practices in public diplomacy and nation-branding designed to support their economic expansion abroad. The democratization of international relations forced all states, including authoritarian ones, to set up structures in charge of their public diplomacy, to develop public–private partnerships and apply them not only to their cultural relationships but also to economic ones. Following the economic sanctions taken by the United States, Germany, and Japan against India due to its nuclear tests in May 1998, the Confederation of Indian Industry and the Indian Ministry of Commerce created an India Brand Equity Fund to help Indian companies build their brand image abroad, and in 2006 the Indian government established a Public Diplomacy Division within the Ministry of Foreign Affairs to orchestrate rather spectacular advertising campaigns with the Ministry of Tourism (Rana 2007). China's economic strategy is also a diplomacy of influence, based since 2004 on the Confucius Institute networks. This is also the case for Russia and Turkey.

The assertion of economic diplomacy by emerging countries corresponds to a phase of intensification in interregional relations. The structuring of national strategies has been coupled with flourishing multilateral economic diplomacy, whose two main arenas are the Trans-Pacific Partnership (TPP), launched in 2008 between twelve countries including the United States but not China, and the Asian Regional Comprehensive Economic Partnership (RCEP), set up in 2012 between sixteen member countries including China but not the United States. South Africa was not starting from scratch when the African National Congress (ANC) came to power in 1994. The Afrikaanse Handelsinstituut was created in 1942 to fight British predominance in the business world (Pfister 2005). Rapid trade liberalization in the 1990s went hand in hand with multilateral engagement, as illustrated by the Millennium African Recovery Programme presented by South African President Thabo Mbeki at the 2001 Davos Forum, one of the sources of the New African Initiative (NAI) adopted by the Organization of African Unity Summit in Lusaka in 2001, and renamed Nepad, New Partnership for Africa's Development. At the same time, a framework agreement was signed in 2000 by South Africa and the Southern Common Market (Mercosur), leading to a preferential trade agreement signed in 2008 between Mercosur and the Southern African Customs Union (SACU).

Often driven by internal budgetary constraints, Western countries also had to adapt to the arrival of these new competitors and to modify their own strategies as a result. They may cross a new threshold by resorting to nation-branding consultants. It is no longer so much about promoting a country, as it is of "selling" it to tourists, foreign investors and industrialists, a practice that was actually established in the nineteenth century. Finally, public mechanisms were restructured during the 1990s and 2000s, and for some countries, such as France, the transformation was long and hard. Canada, a member of the group of seven major industrialized countries (G7), was a groundbreaker in this area. In 1993, the Ministry of Foreign Affairs became the Department of Foreign Affairs and International Trade (DFAIT), renamed in June 2013 Department of Foreign Affairs, Trade, and Development (DFATD), then in November 2015, Global Affairs Canada, by the government of Justin Trudeau. Canada is, moreover, highly active in multilateral economic diplomacy, both in the area of development aid and in trade. It is the G8 country with preferential access to the US market (North American Free Trade Agreement—NAFTA, December 1992) and, more recently, to the European Union. The Free Trade Agreement with the EU—the Comprehensive Economic and Trade Agreement (CETA)—was ratified in October 2016 and approved by the European Parliament in February 2017.

During the 2000s, major agencies emerged, embodying the "New Look" economic diplomacy of many post-modern and emerging states. In May 1999, the Blair government created a new body that centralized commercial diplomacy functions, which until then had been scattered between several agencies: information gathering, promoting British products, and developing contacts in host countries. Jointly answerable to the Foreign and Commonwealth Office and to the Department of Trade and Industry, the body (British Trade International—BTI) was composed of two parts: Trade Partners UK for trade diplomacy and Invest UK for foreign investments. In 2003, the two internal departments merged and the BTI took the name of UK Trade and Investment (UKTI) (Lee 2004). In Germany, the Gesellschaft für Außenwirtschaft und Standortmarketing, or GTAI (Germany Trade and Invest MBH), was established in 2009 to ensure the "marketing of Germany as an economic, investment and technology site, including the active acquisition of investors (location-based marketing), as well as assistance for foreign companies wanting to expand their activities to the German market and for German companies engaged in exporting and capturing foreign markets."[1] Restructuring in Austria gave rise to Außenwirtschaft Austria in 2012. By attaching foreign trade and tourism to the ministry in April 2014, Laurent Fabius normalized the French economic diplomacy mechanism (Badel 2010), completing the merging begun twenty years earlier of the various bodies in charge of foreign trade and investments. The Business France agency was created on January 1, 2015, from the merger of Ubifrance (2003) and the French Agency for International Investment (AFII, 2001), with the goal of supporting the internationalization of small and mid-sized French companies and attracting foreign companies to France. The Brazilian Trade and Investment Promotion Agency (ApexBrazil) emerged in 2003, the Moroccan Investment and Export Development Agency for (AMDIE) in December 2017.

Lastly, Belgium's case is a reminder that economic diplomacy has never solely involved states, but can also be orchestrated at the sub-national level. This was already the case in the nineteenth century for chamber of commerce missions, for the Hanseatic cities and German Länder. Belgium has never had a Ministry of Foreign Trade (contrary to France, which created one in the mid-1970s), an area that has always fallen within the remit of the Ministry of Foreign Affairs. But it is the regions (Flanders, Wallonia, Brussels) that are most competent in matters of commercial diplomacy. In the early 1990s, they created their own agencies for promoting exports: the Walloon Exports and Foreign Investment Agency (AWEX), Brussels Invest & Export (BIE), and Flanders Investment & Trade (FIT). Each one has its own network of economic and commercial attachés to rely on, as well as the network of Belgian embassies around the world (Coolsaet 2004). The federal government has retained control over multilateral trade policies.

CORPORATE DIPLOMACY *VERSUS* ECONOMIC DIPLOMACY: PUTTING THE STORY IN PERSPECTIVE

After observing the steep increase in foreign direct investment (FDI) during the 1990s, many studies date the arrival of multinational corporations in the diplomatic arena from that decade, as they have attempted to take into account various local, national, and international laws and regulations, and,

---

[1] https://www.gtai.de/GTAI/Navigation/EN/Meta/About-us/Who-we-are/history.html.

above all, to deal with states and local authorities where they want to be established, and to respond to highly incisive NGOs. In other words, they have faced a double constraint: obtaining the support of public authorities and trying to have their arrival seen as legitimate by the public at large. Also, they have often had to answer for actions that have prompted transnational movements of condemnation, such as Total's activities in Burma in the early 2000s or Volkswagen's dieselgate in 2015.

In this context, major corporations have created services, directions, or departments with varying names: institutional relations, public relations, etc., in charge of "corporate diplomacy" that enable them to intervene in two major areas: society and the environment. Thus, in 2016, Total oil company's Internet home page proclaimed its commitment to "protecting people, meeting environmental challenges, contributing to shared development," and encourages us to become aware of three fundamental values in the company's "ethical code": "respect, responsibility, and exemplariness." Total has also published a code of conduct in nineteen languages monitored by an ethics committee since 2001. Similarly, the communications and entertainment company Vivendi's home page declares its "social responsibility" and has a "List of extra-financial indicators"[2] that can be downloaded displaying its partner relationships.

Thus, these companies appear to be inaugurating new practices by setting up specific representation structures, which neither their in-house communications departments nor their marketing or advertising services can really ensure (Muldoon 2005). There are two new concepts designating them, sometimes distinct, at other times used interchangeably (this is the case for Ruël and Wolters 2016). The notion of corporate diplomacy can be used for the process aiming to reinforce the company's internal cohesion. It involves the company head's ability to master both the company's global culture and that of subsidiaries run in various countries, and other cultures that also impact the company's culture. The second concept, business diplomacy, covers the firm's relations with its foreign partners (Saner and Yiu 2008). Many multinational corporations today employ diplomats for such positions. This is the case for the United States and also for France. Christophe Farnaud, the French Ambassador to Athens, was laid off from 2012 to 2016 to take on the function of vice-president of international relations for the Thalès group before running the French Embassy in Pretoria.

---

[2] In French, "Cahier des indicateurs extra-financiers."

Sylvie Forbin started out at the Quai d'Orsay in 1983, was appointed Vice-President for Institutional and European Affairs at Vivendi in 2001 before becoming executive director for the culture and creative industries sector at the World Intellectual Property Organization (WIPO) in July 2016. The role of these "corporate diplomats" cannot be reduced to one of representing the corporation to public authorities and local entrepreneurs and businessmen (Lucas 2012). It fluctuates between leveraging communications, lobbying, gathering strategic information, and cultural action in the broad sense.

And yet, the adaptation of major corporations to international and societal changes, their conduct of "firms as diplomats" (Strange 1988) must be put in perspective in light of the preliminary in-depth historical studies that are starting to be made available. The Compagnie française des pétroles (CFP), which later became Total, was the French government's vanguard in the Persian Gulf when it was still under British domination, playing a role of informal diplomacy not only in supporting the rise of French exports in the region, but also through cultural initiatives developed as of 1954 by a civil mining engineer, Jean Rondot—whose title was "CFP representative to the Levant states" (Wursthorn 2017). His post was institutionalized when taken over in 1958 by François de Laboulaye, a career diplomat who created a department of foreign relations in the company. In 1970, Roger Chambard, the former French Ambassador to Seoul, became director of the information and public relations department for Pechiney–Ugine–Kuhlmann, in a decade in which the consortium established itself as one of the two main French investors in South Korea along with Rhône-Poulenc (Fauvet 2016). Employers' associations also assumed functions of representation and negotiation. This was the case for the National Council of French Employers, created in 1945. In West Germany, the German Eastern Economic Committee (Ost-Ausschuss der Deutschen Wirtschaft), created in the fall of 1952 (Jüngerkes 2012), played a key role in establishing ties with Eastern European and Asian Communist states with which the GDR had no official diplomatic relations. It signed the first trade treaty with the People's Republic of China in 1957, fifteen years before diplomatic relations were established between the two countries (Jüngerkes 2012). When the United States would not allow Japan to appoint any diplomats abroad between 1945 and 1952, members of *zaikai*, or employers' unions—including the *Keidanren*, created in 1946, which continues to play a crucial role even today—stood in for diplomats in handling the resumption of foreign economic relations and played a role in negotiating the San Francisco Treaty in 1951 (Bryant 1975). Thus, well before the 1990s, corporations set up structures and individuals designed to develop channels of representation, information, negotiation, and promotion of their national interests, either to serve as a palliative for a function the government could not fulfill structurally, or did not wish to maintain politically, or to promote their own interests.

At issue is the potential conflict between the goals pursued by corporate diplomacy and those of the country the corporation comes from. Through pressure exerted on public authorities, the corporation may try to put on the agenda the negotiation of topics serving its interests at the expense of the government's. The debates in the 2010s surrounding negotiations for the "Transatlantic Treaty" (Transatlantic Trade and Investment Partnership—TTIP), begun in June 2013 between the European Union and the United States, are a good example of the complexity that prevailed in economic negotiations in the early twenty-first century. It was at the request of the US Department of Commerce and the European Commission that several heads of corporations—Allaire (Xerox), Trotman (Ford), Mead (Tenneco), Luke (Westvaco), Hudson (AMP Incorporated), Murphy (Dresser Industries), Strube (BASF), Sutherland (Goldman Sachs International), etc.—agreed to take part in establishing the Transatlantic Business Dialogue (TABD) in 1995, one of the main development forums for the TTIP. Today that dialogue between American and European corporations falls within a broader authority, the TABC (Transatlantic Business Council) created from the merger in 2013 of the TABD and the EABC (European-American Business Council). This renewed form of "public-private" partnership is a new example through which to explore the notion of "private multilateralism" and its limits, given the obvious permeability of these spheres.

* * *

Addressing economic diplomacy thus requires not being boxed in by a compartmentalized vision of external action. In this early twenty-first century, economic diplomacy is closely connected to public diplomacy as a strategic vision for international relations. Perhaps more than other areas of external action, the issue of the independence of private actors with respect to public actors was vigorously debated in the early 2000s, fueling the debate on the "harmful effects" of globalization. It has led to a reflection on the possibility of conducting economic diplomacy without diplomats.

REFERENCES

Badel, Laurence, *Diplomatie et grands contrats. L'État français et les marchés extérieurs au XXe siècle*, Paris, Publications de la Sorbonne, 2010.

———, "CNPF-International, acteur du dialogue Asie-Europe (ASEM): jalons pour une recherche historique sur les interrégionalismes," in Pierre Tilly, Vincent Dujardin (eds.), *Hommes et réseaux. Belgique, Europe et Outre-Mers. Liber amicorum Michel Dumoulin*, Brussels, Peter Lang, 2013, pp. 193–202.

Bagnato, Bruna, *Prove di Ostpolitik. Politica ed economia nella strategia italiana verso l'Unione Sovietica (1958–1963)*, Florence, Leo S. Olschli, 2003.

Bryant, William, *Japanese Private Economic Diplomacy: An Analysis of Business Government Linkages*, New York, NY, Praeger, 1975.

Cain, Frank, *Economic Statecraft During the Cold War: European Responses to the US Embargo*, London, Routledge, 2007.

Carron de La Carrière, Guy, *La Diplomatie économique. Le diplomate et le marché*, Paris, Économica, 1998.

Coolsaet, Rik, "Trade and Diplomacy. The Belgian Case," *International Studies Perspectives*, 5 (1), 2004: 61–65.

Dobson, Alan P., *US Economic Statecraft for Survival (1933–1991): Of Embargoes, Strategic Embargoes, and Economic Warfare*, London, Routledge, 2012.

Fabius, Laurent, "La diplomatie économique, une priorité pour la France," *Les Échos*, 23 August 2012.

Fauvet, Anne, "Au cœur des réseaux d'affaires français en Asie du Nord-Est. Roger Chambard, premier ambassadeur de France en Corée du Sud (années 1950–1980)," *Relations internationales*, 3 (167), 2016: 113–126.

Fink, Carol, Frohn, Axel, Heideking, Jürgen (eds.), *Genoa, Rapallo, and European Reconstruction in 1922*, Cambridge, Cambridge University Press, 2002.

Harvie, Charles, Kimura, Fukunari, Lee, Hyun-Hoon, *New East Asian Regionalism: Causes, Progress and Country Perspectives*, Northampton, Edward Elgar, 2005.

Jüngerkes, Sven, *Diplomaten der Wirtschaft. Die Geschichte des Ost-Ausschusses der Deutschen Wirtschaft*, Osnabrück, Fibre, 2012.

Lee, Donna, "The Growing Influence of Business in UK Diplomacy," *International Studies Perspectives*, 5, 2004: 50–54.

Lorenzini, Sara, *Due Germanie in Africa. La cooperazione allo sviluppo e la competizione per i mercati di materie prime e tecnologia*, Florence, Polistampa, 2003.

Lucas, Didier (ed.), *Les Diplomates d'entreprise. Pouvoirs, réseaux, influence*, Paris, Choiseul, 2012.

Mourlon-Druol, Emmanuel, Romero, Federico (eds.), *International Summitry and Global Governance: The Rise of the G-7 and the European Council*, London, Routledge, 2014.

Muldoon, James P., Jr., "The Diplomacy of Business," *Diplomacy & Statecraft*, 16 (2), 2005: 341–359.

Pfister, Roger, *Apartheid South Africa and African States: From Pariah to Middle Power (1961–1994)*, London, Tauris Academic Studies, 2005.

Rana, Kishan, *Asian Diplomacy: The Foreign Ministries of China, India, Japan, Singapore and Thailand*, Genève, DiploFoundation, 2007.

Rosenberg, Emily, *Financial Missionaries to the World: The Politics and Culture of Dollar Diplomacy (1900–1930)*, Durham, Duke University Press, 2003.

Rüel, Huub, Wolters, Tim, "Business Diplomacy," in Costas Constantinou, Pauline Kerr, Paul Sharp (eds.), *The SAGE Handbook of Diplomacy*, London, Sage, 2016, pp. 564–576.

Saner, Raymond, Yiu, Lichia, "Business-Government-NGO Relations: Their Impact on Global Economic Governance," in Andrew F. Cooper, Brian Hocking, William Maley (eds.), *Global Governance and Diplomacy: Worlds Apart?* New York, NY, Palgrave Macmillan, 2008, pp. 85–103.

Soutou, Georges-Henri, *L'Or et le Sang: Les buts de guerre économiques de la première guerre mondiale*, Paris, Fayard, 1989.

Strange, Susan, *States and Markets*, London, Pinter Publishers, 1988.

———, "States, Firms and Diplomacy," *International Affairs*, 68 (1), 1992: 1–15.

Thiemeyer, Guido, *Internationalismus und Diplomatie. Währungspolitische Kooperation im europäischen Staatensystem (1865–1900)*, München, Oldenbourg, 2009.

Thobie, Jacques, "L'emprunt ottoman 4% (1901–1905): le triptyque finance-industrie-diplomatie," *Relations internationales*, 1, 1974: 71–85.

Trachtenberg, Marc, *Reparation in World Politics: France and European Economic Diplomacy (1916–1923)*, New York, NY, Columbia University Press, 1980.

Warlouzet, Laurent, "The Centralization of EU Competition Policy: Historical Institutionalist Dynamics from Cartel Monitoring to Merger Control (1956–1991)," *Journal of Common Market Studies*, 2016: 725–741.

Woolcock, Stephen, Bayne, Nicholas (eds.), *The New Economic Diplomacy: Decision-Making and Negotiation in International Economic Relations*, Ashgate, Aldershot, 2007.

Wursthorn, Kévin, "La Compagnie française des pétroles au Moyen-Orient: une diplomatie d'entreprise à l'avant-garde de la présence française dans les années 1950," *Relations internationales*, 171 (3), 2017: 85–96.

Zhang, Shuguang, *Beijing's Economic Statecraft During the Cold War (1949–1991)*, Baltimore, MD, Johns Hopkins University Press, 2014.

CHAPTER 16

Cultural Diplomacy

Marie-Christine Kessler

In order to talk about cultural diplomacy, it first has to be defined. Officially, it is a sector of foreign policy. Cultural diplomacy is indeed a public policy that strives to export data representative of the national culture and to promote interactions with other countries in the cultural arena, within the framework of foreign policy. Since foreign policy, a regalian prerogative, is formulated by a state seeking to defend its own interests in the international arena, it is not surprising that the cultural sector is dealt with through cultural cooperation agreements signed between representatives of both countries to undertake a joint operation enjoying mutual consent. Thus, France and Germany hold "cultural summits" where problems are settled and paired actions organized. Targeted actions may also be undertaken, such as the creation of the Louvre Abu Dhabi, stemming from an intergovernmental agreement signed on March 6, 2007, between France and the United Arab Emirates.

M.-C. Kessler (✉)
Centre National de la Recherche Scientifique, Paris, France
e-mail: kessler.mc@wanadoo.fr

© The Author(s) 2020
T. Balzacq et al. (eds.), *Global Diplomacy*,
The Sciences Po Series in International Relations and Political Economy, https://doi.org/10.1007/978-3-030-28786-3_16

Nevertheless, this definition of cultural diplomacy tied to a traditional concept of the results of state action has its limits. First, because in practical terms states do not always appear in a visible or official way. Cultural diplomacy increasingly involves cooperative action, where the state relies on other forces that are spotlighted. Cultural diplomacy comes from what Joseph Nye called soft power, in other words a quest for power (or influence) through means other than force (Nye 1990). Cultural diplomacy is a weapon of choice from the standpoint of increasing power of attraction and influence.

External cultural policy is destined for a foreign public that it strives to win over, influence and attract through various means. The range of potential interventions is quite broad, as the word "culture" is vague and its vectors have diversified, notably with audiovisual media, the press, the Internet, and social networks. There may be many actors hosting these spaces, and their outlines may be unclear. The word "culture" could then serve as an alibi, and notions of propaganda, destabilization and psychological effects may hang over such activities. But the word "culture" is also used in a more noble sense: of preserving heritage, of artistic, intellectual and literary development, of the free movement of ideas, respecting norms that go beyond personal interests. This cultural diplomacy relies on international efforts to preserve public goods and share resources of intelligence and human creativity. It may fall within the scope of bilateral diplomacy, but increasingly within the multilateral vocation of international organizations, the foremost of these being the United Nations Educational, Scientific and Cultural Organization (UNESCO).

Cultural Diplomacy Actors in National Government

Cultural diplomacy actors are part of the state system and of state diplomacy, with a view toward resolute government interventionism. There are, however, diverse configurations depending on the political regimes involved (Roche 2006).

The Particular Case of Authoritarian Regimes

Mention should be made first of the approach taken by authoritarian regimes before going more directly into the traditional contemporary sense of the term "cultural diplomacy," more characteristic of democracies. The most classic example is the USSR and the popular democracies which, during the bipolar period (1947–1991), were endowed with a highly centralized diplomatic system that supervised how official negotiations were carried out in the cultural arena. For instance, in the post-Stalin era (1953–1991), Eastern European popular democracies conducted cultural relations with France through joint committees that carefully regulated the number of grant holders and missions constituting cultural and artistic exchanges. In some countries, networks of cultural organizations have been superimposed onto this diplomatic system, for the purpose of organizing meetings, courses, and seminars designed for the public in the host country. Shortly after its creation, the USSR also established VOKS—the All-Union Society for Cultural Relations With Foreign Countries—(Fayet 2013), subsequently imitated by Warsaw Pact countries (European capitals were filled with cultural institutes and libraries, such as the GDR Cultural Institute on Boulevard Saint-Germain in Paris).

Since the fall of the USSR, and especially in the Putin era inaugurated in 2000, Russia has upheld these practices between cultural relations and state propaganda. Russian television channels (Russia Today) or those with Russian allegiance (Sputnik TV), and Web sites and activists ("trolls") in favor of the Kremlin's theories attest to it, to the extent that a debate has emerged in Western democracies over their impact on major electoral processes.

China, another authoritarian regime, can also count on its effective system and diplomatic network (the world's second diplomatic network in terms of bilateral embassies) in developing targeted cultural diplomacy, also controlled by the state and favorable toward its theories. Since 2004, it has worked at setting up Confucius Institutes, often perceived as emanating directly from the political powers that be. They are run by the Hanban in Beijing (National Office for Teaching Chinese as a Foreign Language), which finances the institutes and coordinates their activities. The People's Republic of China's Ministry of Education chooses their location. In 2010, there were 316 institutes in 94 countries. The institutes develop nonprofit partnerships with universities and other institutions, which can be controversial since several Western universities have refused to get involved with an organization viewed as emanating from the Chinese Communist Party (Arodirik 2015) and not playing by the rules of disinterested cultural diplomacy as envisaged by liberal democracies.

The Case of France, an Example of Democratic State Cultural Diplomacy

France is the only democratic country that conducts its foreign cultural policy through specific state and administrative structures and devotes a significant part of its state budget to it. A government system of foreign cultural policy has been in place since the late nineteenth century that illustrates in many respects the "omnipresent state" strategy. That legacy goes back to Francis I and the Capitulations in 1536, which gave him the right and duty to protect his merchants, clergymen, and Christians in the Near East (Kessler 1999).

Since 1840, the Ministry of Foreign Affairs has provided free boat passage to teaching missionaries. The first official bilateral cultural agreements were signed at the time by French diplomats. The Alliance française, a network of private local committees abroad coordinated in Paris and devoted to teaching French and spreading French culture, was founded in 1883 by several administrative, political, and academic figures (with support from the Ministry of Foreign Affairs).

A specific administrative structure was set up in the early twentieth century, endowed with public funds and dedicated to developing and managing French cultural establishments abroad. It expanded between the two wars, when a "works department" was created to oversee cultural affairs at the Ministry of Foreign Affairs, and with the founding of the French Association of Artistic Development and Exchanges Abroad. Increasing numbers of French cultural institutes and lycées were established in foreign countries (Roche and Piniau 1995).

In the aftermath of the Second World War, the state's predominant hand in cultural action abroad increased. The Department of Cultural Affairs was created in 1945 (ruling of April 13 and decree of July 17) to "show the vitality of French thought." Its scope continued to expand. France is the only country that combines a very broad range of areas of intervention under the supervision of the Ministry of Foreign Affairs. In 1967, the Department of Cultural Relations became the Department of Cultural, Scientific and Technical Relations. It was in charge of promoting the language and teaching of French abroad, artistic exchanges, scientific and technical cooperation, a large part of development aid and of audiovisual media abroad. It was allocated substantial funds. From 1960 to 1980, its resources represented 53% of the budget for the Quai d'Orsay. This central apparatus relied on a solid infrastructure abroad. Cultural advisors began to appear in embassies in 1949. The French "network," already long-established, has grown to become one of the largest in the world. In 1996, it included 300 lycées, 132 centers and cultural institutes, 1060 Alliances françaises, 25 research institutes, 200 archeological dig missions, and a workforce composed of 9000 French and 15,000 local recruits. This system was criticized, however, within the institution itself. Numerous reports viewed it as needing modernization and simplification. The obsolete nature of French language learning methods and programing in cultural institutes were blamed, as well as turf wars between Alliances françaises and cultural institutes.

But the vital role of government and of the Ministry of Foreign Affairs in cultural relations has never been challenged. The doctrine of direct government intervention in cultural policy abroad is an official postulate that has been practically unchanged over the years and shared by all political and administrative actors. It also falls within the scope of the defense of Francophonie. Teaching French remains the priority of French cultural diplomacy in 2017. Dwindling funds and the reduced foreign affairs budget have affected it less than other sectors of cultural action abroad, heavily impacted. In 2017, there were 492 establishments accredited by the Ministry of Education, 74 directly run by the AEFE (Agency for Teaching French Abroad), a public establishment placed under the supervision of the Ministry of Foreign Affairs.

Its cornerstone is the need to uphold French language learning abroad in order to preserve France's prestige and influence in the world, and to champion the democratic ideals created in 1789 through promoting its culture. In addition to this, there is the certainty of the ties between culture and commerce. That belief, the basis for the creation of the Alliances françaises network, has endured for over a hundred years. The following notice was featured on the first page of the *Alliance française Bulletin* in 1884: "The French language induces French customs; French customs lead to the purchase of French products. Whoever speaks French will become a client of France" (Rosselli 1996). This presentation—which probably would not be promoted in the same way today—clearly shows one of the key issues in cultural diplomacy, namely economics in addition to politics.

Furthermore, another tool in this kind of diplomacy involves initiating paired operations for "artistic and economic promotion." One example is the *Saisons*, which have initiated exchanges between France and over sixty countries since 1984. Originally focused solely on the arts and culture, they now involve research, higher education, education, sports, tourism, the economy and gastronomy. From three to six months (*Saison*) or from six to twelve months (*Année*), the paired *Saisons* and *Années* are decided at the highest level of government, reflecting France's orientations in cultural matters.

Since 2008, when a new plan was implemented, the French model of cultural diplomacy has moved closer to foreign European models that are less state-run and more prone to sub-contracting agencies, and above all private actors. Thus, new media (global news channels for instance), useful for their vast circulation but with content that is difficult to apply within the framework of democratic diplomacy, as well as influential private companies (luxury, and well-known French brands), and personalities (artists, intellectuals, athletes) contribute to promoting French culture without the Foreign Affairs office being involved. In the field, the embassy and cultural advisors are increasingly involved in promoting or accompanying initiatives, and less as sole organizers of events. Cultural diplomacy is under the jurisdiction of the Directorate-General of Globalized Development and Partnerships (the Directorate-General of Cultural Relations no longer exists). Three new agencies are connected to it with the status of industrial and commercial public undertakings: The French Institute is devoted to promoting French culture, Campus France to enhancing and promoting the French higher education system, and Expertise France is devoted to promoting technical assistance and international expertise.

European Models of Cooperative Cultural Diplomacy

Working with operators that are dependent on the government but have varying degrees of autonomy is indeed the most frequent model of cultural diplomacy in the world today (Roche and Piniau 1995), partly inspired by practices in English-speaking cultures. Such operators may be quite numerous and have different specializations within the same country.

Germany, for example, with its Goethe Institutes for language learning and cultural exchanges; DAAD (Deutscher Akademischer Austauschdienst), created in 1925, for grants and young artists; foundations that are private but receive state subsidies like the Friedrich Ebert Stiftung or the Konrad Adenauer Stiftung, which finance and publish studies of a more political nature (Dakowska 2014). Elsewhere, a major actor may occupy a commanding position in the cultural system, such as the British Council in the UK and the Cervantès Institutes in Spain (Jacques 2015).

Dependence on the government may take various forms. The most common formula is public/private co-financing. Control by government and political authorities may be more or less strict. In certain cases, such as DAAD, there is near-total autonomy. In others, like the British Council, it is less real than often supposed, since its major orientations are decided by the Foreign and Commonwealth Office, and there is parliamentary budget monitoring (Haize 2012).

The American Model of Masked State Cultural Diplomacy

The final model is of apparent government non-intervention, which chiefly characterizes the case of the United States. Officially, American cultural diplomacy has no formal state or para-state structure, but relies on the private sector, corporate underwriting, private foundations and collectors. And yet, it would be inaccurate to presume an absence of cultural diplomacy in the United States. The government intervenes through protective standards, overlapping cultural policies abroad and trade and industrial policies. Cultural and entertainment industries (leisure, culture, information) may benefit from market organization and commercial and customs systems. The United States is highly conditioned in its film industry for instance, structured around a commercial mind-set, by which American companies have conquered and controlled the national, then the international market through anti-competitive practices.

Cultural policy also exists as a weapon in the United States, beyond this private mind-set. The use of intellectual diplomacy as a tool for fighting Soviet ideological expansionism after the Second World War attests to it. The Congress for Cultural Freedom—CCF, founded in 1950 and located in Paris—was an anti-Communist cultural association that was totally apolitical in appearance (Grémion 1995). Its instruments of action were indirect and sophisticated: Creating networks of European intellectuals welcomed at American universities, scientific meetings, and publishing high-level revues (*Preuves*, in France). In 1967, it was revealed that the CIA was secretly financing the CCF through screen foundations like the Ford Foundation. At its height, the CCF was active in thirty-five countries and was assisted by major European anti-Communist intellectuals (Charpier 2008).

INTERNATIONAL ACTORS

To be sure, cultural diplomacy is state public policy, and for that reason involves national ambitions formulated at the government level. But due to the profusion of actors, and the interweaving of key political, intellectual and commercial issues, its international interactions are characterized by complex interdependence.

Cultural Diplomacy and International Negotiations

Since the end of the Second World War, international organizations have been engaged in international cultural interplay. This was the case first for UNESCO, the only organization in the UN system explicitly dedicated to culture. According to its founding charter, its purpose is "to contribute to peace and security by promoting collaboration among the nations through education, science and culture in order to further universal respect for justice, for the rule of law and for the human rights and fundamental freedoms which are affirmed for the peoples of the world, without distinction of race, sex, language or religion, by the Charter of the United Nations."

Subsequently, other international institutions acquired competency in the field, such as the European Council and the Francophonie. Culture is also on the agenda of the European Union. It slipped into negotiations on television and film conducted by the European Commission. It has officially become one of the components of foreign policy and joint security. The "EU strategy in the area of international cultural relations," presented by the European Commission and the High Representative of the Union for Foreign Affairs and Security Policy, is aimed at encouraging cultural cooperation between the EU and its partner countries, and at promoting a global order founded on peace, the rule of law, freedom of expression, and understanding.[1] Culture is also a recurring theme in major international meetings, such as those concerning development and the environment (Matsuura 2006).

The specific procedures and practices of these actors have compelled governments to develop a kind of "diplomacy of cultural diplomacy," in other words a strategy to define their political objectives, their interests, means and behavior in and regarding these international organizations. This is attested by American reversals with respect to UNESCO (the statement from the Trump administration in November 2017 that the United States was going to leave the organization, viewed as lacking structural reforms and accused of an anti-Israeli bias), and by competition over their control (the election of a Franco-Moroccan to head UNESCO in October

---

[1] https://ec.europa.eu/culture/policies/strategic-framework/strategyinternational-cultural-relations_en.

2017 over at least two Arab candidates). The international cultural arena can no longer—or still cannot—avoid political power struggles, diplomatic maneuvers, alliances, and government strategies.

Going Beyond the National Game of Soft Power

The official intention of these bodies is for cultural diplomacy to go beyond its reputation as a vector of soft power, and for it not to be used by states as an instrument of influence. Conversely, there is a desire for peaceful dialogue between cultures, whose diversity would be respected and preserved through multilateral diplomacy. In 1945, UNESCO's initial core vocation was preserving world heritage and building a global universal education base. To that end, exchanges between countries meeting in work sessions and general assemblies have led to rules of good conduct to structure a new international rule of law. Today, culture has also become a constituent element in sustainable development, in social cohesion, and in environmental protection. It appears frequently in themes evoked in core international diplomacy and should ideally lead to founding principles and norms for a more peaceful future.

Thus, international organizations strive to avoid being pawns of states, attempting to make culture a shared resource of mankind, a cross-disciplinary issue also driven by transnational actors. This endeavor is often caught up in state political manipulation of culture.

Culture as an Object of Power

Cultural action remains central to recurrent conflicts between a country and groups of countries. Sometimes these conflicts are directly linked to power narratives, or to commercial and industrial concerns. How to organize the film and television industries was the focus of intense discussions in several international arenas: the World Trade Organization (WTO), the Organization for Economic Cooperation and Development (OECD), the European Union, and UNESCO. Jack Lang, François Mitterrand's Minister of Culture during the 1980s, started a European and international diplomatic battle, taken up by French authorities since then, for film not to be considered a traditional industry, which would have led to a ban on government aid in the name of free trade principles. This is when the idea emerged of cultural exception to guarantee that France could subsidize its film industry.

The debate was triggered again due to pressure from the United States and its film industry. That pressure was held at bay at UNESCO, partly thanks to French and Canadian diplomacy. Cultural exception, advocated by both countries in diplomacy and multilateral negotiations, was resisted by others as a term that symbolized French and European protectionism. It was replaced by the duty to protect all cultures, called the universal principle of respect and cultural diversity. In 2001, the principle of cultural diversity was enshrined in positive law. The Francophonie adopted the principle. Cultural diversity was included as one of the organization's missions in the Declaration of Ouagadougou on November 27, 2004.

Material and commercial interests are not alone in explaining cultural tensions. Since the end of the Cold War, opposing foreign policies have continued to clash even within international cultural organizations, where they have found a sounding board. Among the many significant examples, at its ninth congress in 2014 the UNESCO committee to protect cultural goods in wartime denounced "deliberate and repeated attacks against cultural patrimony, notably in Syria and Iraq." Irina Bokova, then director-general of UNESCO, asserted that the destruction of Mosul constituted a violation of UN Security Council Resolution 2199 and considered the destruction of Nimrud a war crime; the UN General Assembly unanimously passed a resolution on it, proposed by Germany and Iraq and endorsed by ninety-one member states. And yet, on the legal level the subject is debatable, and UNESCO is sometimes accused of not condemning other phenomena—such as not taking in war refugees in Europe—as vigorously as crimes damaging patrimony perpetrated by fundamentalists in the Near East. It is thus thought to be "fetishizing patrimony" to the detriment of other causes whose cultural implications apply equally.

* * *

These last examples, like older rivalries during the Cold War, highlight an obstacle familiar to the social sciences: the difficulty of defining culture. Transposed to an analysis of diplomacy and sectorial developments, this difficulty paves the way for multiple strategies. Cultural diplomacy has been analyzed here as a public foreign policy, in other words as an action integrated into a state political and administrative system. Private actors may nonetheless undertake projects involving a framework of private diplomacy, by taking part in initiatives that boost their image and interests in any given country, through underwriting. From state propaganda to underwriting, from multilateral protection of shared resources to the intellectual discovery of the Other and language learning, cultural diplomacy has significantly diversified in the hands of increasingly numerous actors. State diplomacy can hardly afford to do without careful deliberation over the implications of this sector of activity in the modern era, between competition and cooperation and the means to be implemented in order to enable foreign policy-makers to remain strategic stakeholders.

REFERENCES

Arodirik, Hakan D., "La diplomatie culturelle comme un instrument de la diplomatie publique: la diplomatie culturelle chinoise dans le contexte d'institut Confucius," 2015. independent.academia.edu/arodirikhakandavid.
Charpier, Frédéric, *La CIA en France. 60 ans d'ingérence dans les affaires françaises*, Paris, Seuil, 2008.
Dakowska, Dorota, *Le Pouvoir des fondations. Des acteurs de la politique étrangère allemande*, Rennes, Presses universitaires de Rennes, 2014.
Fayet, Jean-François, "VOKS: The Third Dimension of Soviet Foreign Policy," in Jessica C. E. Gienow-Hecht, Mark C. Donfried (eds.), *Searching for a Cultural Diplomacy*, New York (NY) and Oxford, Berghahn, 2013, pp. 33–50.
Grémion, Pierre, *Intelligence de l'anticommunisme. Le congrès pour la liberté de la culture à Paris (1950–1975)*, Paris, Fayard, 1995.
Haize, Daniel, *L'Action culturelle et de coopération de la France à l'étranger. Un réseau, des hommes*, Paris, L'Harmattan, 2012.
Jacques, Julien, "L'Espagne en France. Les centres culturels espagnols dans l'Hexagone au XXe siècle," Paris, Université Paris-I Panthéon-Sorbonne, Masters Dissertation in History, 2015.
Kessler, Marie-Christine, *La Politique étrangère de la France. Acteurs et processus*, Paris, Presses de Sciences Po, 1999.
Matsuura, Koïchiro, "L'enjeu culturel au cœur des relations internationales," *Politique étrangère*, 4, 2006: 1045–1057.
Nye, Joseph, "Soft Power," *Foreign Policy*, 80, 1990: 153–171.
Roche, François, Piniau, Bernard, *Histoires de diplomatie culturelle des origines à 1995*, Paris, Ministère des Affaires étrangères/ADPF, 1995.
———, "La diplomatie culturelle dans les relations bilatérales. Un essai d'approche typologique," *Sens public*, revue web, Université de Montréal, 2006.
Rosselli, Mariangela, "Le projet politique de la langue française. Le rôle de l'alliance française," *Politix*, 9 (36), 1996: 73–94.

CHAPTER 17

Environmental Diplomacy

Amandine Orsini

International environmental diplomacy is recent compared to other kinds of diplomacy and only became official during the 1970s. However, it has stood out from the beginning due to its exemplary, unfailing dynamism over time. In 2013, Rakhyun Kim (2013) already counted 747 multilateral environmental agreements. Add to those the new agreements regularly adopted by states, like the 2013 Minamata Convention on Mercury that strives to reduce the harmful effects of mercury or the 2015 Paris Agreement related to the United Nations Framework Convention on Climate Change (UNFCCC), one of whose goals is to limit climate change and its effects. Driven by that dynamism, the scope of certain events in environmental diplomacy has grown exponentially. For instance, 25,903 participants took part in the 22nd Conference of the Parties to the UNFCCC in Marrakech in December 2016. Nearly a quarter of them were non-state observers.

But, first and foremost, what is environmental diplomacy? In theory, environmental diplomacy is understood as diplomacy that deals solely with

A. Orsini (✉)
Université Saint-Louis – Bruxelles, Brussels, Belgium
e-mail: amandine.orsini@usaintlouis.be

© The Author(s) 2020
T. Balzacq et al. (eds.), *Global Diplomacy*,
The Sciences Po Series in International Relations and Political
Economy, https://doi.org/10.1007/978-3-030-28786-3_17

environmental issues. But in practice, environmental diplomacy deals on a regular basis with many other themes related to trade (trade in endangered species, for example), intellectual property (such as rights of indigenous and local populations regarding the use of natural genetic resources), energy (reaching goals for reducing greenhouse gases, use of biofuels, etc.), health (among others, the health impact of consuming genetically modified organisms—GMOs), and even security (the consequences of global warming on transnational migration, for instance).

Initially understood by decision-makers with regard to its primary sense, environmental diplomacy was long seen as secondary by governments. That sidelining gave it more freedom and helped it to develop distinctive features that explain its current dynamism, as detailed in this chapter. The first part looks at the content of environmental diplomacy and the second part at its rules.

The Content of Environmental Diplomacy

Environmental diplomacy developed cautiously from the fourteenth century on the European continent through bilateral agreements (between England and Portugal, England and France, etc.) to manage fishing resources. In the seventeenth and eighteenth centuries, several of those agreements investigated access to certain territories and rivers in Europe and North America. Apart from these agreements on specific resources and territories, it was only in the nineteenth century that the environment took on a decidedly multilateral dimension. Indeed, bilateral actions are often insufficient in managing non-exclusive, non-rival threatened public goods. Furthermore, most resources (such as fish) and core environmental issues know no borders. In 1857, the first multilateral agreement—involving more than three countries—committed states bordering Lake Constance to handle pumping the lake's waters. During the nineteenth century, multilateral agreements gradually developed and began dealing more directly with environmental problems such as transporting hazardous substances or protecting endangered species.

Following the gradual development of environmental agreements in the nineteenth and twentieth centuries, it took major environmental summits, in particular the Stockholm Summit in 1972, for the environment to assume its truly global sense and for environmental diplomacy to turn toward protecting the world's natural resources rather than merely managing them.

After the 1972 summit, other summits, held every ten years, set the tone for environmental diplomacy (Morin and Orsini 2015: 133–156), providing an opportunity to take stock, propose general principles embedded in official declarations, and create international institutions devoted to the environment (Death 2011).

The 1972 Stockholm Summit, or United Nations Conference on the Human Environment, was the first multilateral summit devoted to the environment. Thanks to the active participation of developing countries, the summit was one of the largest international conferences ever held. Delegations from 114 countries participated, while at the time the United Nations only had 131 member states and the environment had not yet become a key issue in international relations. Subsequent to the participation of developing countries, the summit highlighted environmental concerns as a priority, but recognized in the same breath the importance of economic development. This association between environment and development objectives has remained highly present at other summits on environmental protection. In particular, it gives a quick answer to developing countries concerned about implementing measures that are technologically costly or restrictive for their economic development. While developing countries were initially suspicious of multilateral initiatives to protect the environment, the summit showed that compromise was possible. The final declaration stated twenty-six general principles on the environment. It endorsed in particular the creation of the United Nations Environment Programme (now known as UN Environment) and advised states to create the first national ministries specialized in the environment.

To consolidate the gains made in Stockholm, a second summit, the United Nations Conference on Environment and Development, was held in Rio in 1992. The summit affirmed the ties between environment and development. Indeed, it was decided that the conference would be held in a developing country this time, in this instance Brazil (Tolba 1998). It was a large-scale summit that brought together 108 heads of state, 187 delegations, around 10,000 governmental delegates, over 1400 officially accredited non-governmental organizations (NGOs), and nearly 9000 journalists. It was particularly productive. Countries endorsed a political declaration that clarified general principles inherited from those adopted in Stockholm and agreed on an ambitious plan of action, named Action 21, to identify problems, define goals, and specify the means of action on themes as diverse as chemical substances, access to safe drinking water and transportation. A major principle adopted was the principle of common but differentiated responsibilities. According to this principle, all states must commit to make an effort to protect the environment, but that effort must be calculated proportionally to their responsibility and capacities. In other words, in line with these criteria, efforts required of developed countries must be far greater than those asked of developing countries. The summit also saw the adoption of two international treaties: the UNFCCC and the Convention on Biological Diversity (CBD), while two international diplomatic processes were put into effect on desertification and forests. With regard to institutional arrangements, the summit saw the creation of the Global Environment Facility and the Commission on Sustainable Development, to ensure the follow-up to Action 21. Lastly, the summit confirmed a major trend: liberalism in the field of environmental protection. That trend emphasized the economic value of the environment which, by establishing markets, would help preserve it, as in the carbon market approach, or through payments for ecosystem services.

In 2002, the World Summit on Sustainable Development held in Johannesburg shifted partly from environmental priorities, opening the door to non-state actors. Indeed, the summit's organizers actively encouraged concluding "Type II partnerships," or agreements made not only between states but between partners of various kinds, including companies, intergovernmental organizations, NGOs, and states. More than two hundred Type II partnerships were reached in Johannesburg, for investments totaling over 23 million dollars. That trend developed within the dynamic of environmental liberalism, but also marked a desire to improve the effectiveness of environmental measures, by delegating their implementation to actors in the field.

Twenty years after the Rio Summit, UN members tried for a new diplomatic breakthrough by organizing a summit on sustainable development in Rio de Janeiro, the Rio + 20 summit (Foyer 2015). Despite a less favorable international context (with the 2008 economic crisis and the rise of emerging economies), Rio + 20 was again innovative in several respects, introducing the concept of "green economy." According to "The Future We Want" declaration adopted at the Rio + 20, the green economy is "one of the important tools available for achieving sustainable development" (paragraph 56). A flexible instrument, it would not be "a rigid set of rules" (paragraph 56). Another major innovation of the summit was to insist on the importance of information gathering and dissemination to incite behavior that is more respectful of the environment. From the standpoint of institutional innovations, the Commission on Sustainable Development, created in Rio in 1992, was replaced by the High-level Political Forum on Sustainable Development involving "high-level decision-makers," in order to give it greater visibility and decision-making power. "The Future We Want" also called on the UN General Assembly to reinforce the institutional structure of UN Environment.

Parallel to these major summits, a multitude of environmental treaties has been signed on highly varied themes such as hazardous wastes, chemical products, and marine pollution to cite but a few. These treaties have no single institutional affiliation (e.g., to UN Environment) because the institutionalization of environmental treaties in the international organizational landscape happened step by step. In certain cases, preexisting international organizations preferred expanding their own areas of action rather than delegating that role to international environmental institutions. For instance, the United Nations Educational, Scientific, and Cultural Organization (UNESCO) took under its wing the 1972 Convention Concerning the Protection of the World Cultural and Natural Heritage, thus also managing natural sites. Furthermore, organizations and their treaties, which initially had no environmental objectives, have gradually adopted some. This is the case for the International Tropical Timber Organization and the International Whaling Commission, which had quite commercial objectives when created, namely ensuring respectively the sustainability of the timber trade and whale hunting, and gradually shifted toward the protection of the corresponding natural species. In these two cases, the treaties adopted fall outside the United Nations system. Finally, numerous environmental treaties have a regional dimension and therefore go hand in hand with regional organizations. This is the case for example with the Protocol on Environmental Protection to the Antarctic Treaty adopted in 1991. Due to their very different levels of institutionalization, environmental treaties have in any case tended to become independent, for example, by setting up their own secretariats.

Despite their different origins and institutional ties, environmental treaties form a family of treaties, in which certain provisions have lasted through various agreements (Kim 2013). These include provisions that reflect the major orientations emphasized at environmental summits (sustainable development, the importance of development, partnerships, etc.) as well as a certain number of more specific principles such as the precautionary principle, the principle of advance informed agreement, and of common but differentiated responsibilities.

Furthermore, the absence of a single institutional affiliation for these different environmental treaties has helped extend environmental standards and principles to diplomatic bodies outside the environmental field. Thus, environmental diplomacy has spread to other fields in a dual dynamic: First, it is expanding its competency and its applicability to non-environmental themes; second, it is involved in disseminating its own principles.

On the one hand, environmental diplomacy has repeatedly spoken out on issues beyond its core competence. Several environmental treaties have thus been developed in opposition to the principles of the World Trade Organization (WTO) and/or its Agreement on Trade-Related Aspects of Intellectual Property Rights (TRIPS). For instance, the 1992 CBD recognized the sovereignty of states over their natural resources (open access until then), in order to oppose the development of patent-type intellectual property rights within the TRIPS agreement, through which innovations coming from those resources could be privatized. Also, the 2000 Cartagena Protocol on Biosafety, pertaining to GMOs, took a stand against the WTO's principle of scientific evidence by adopting the precautionary principle. Where the former recognized the harmlessness of GMOs until proven otherwise, the latter recognized the potential risks tied to GMOs until they are proven harmless. The Cartagena Protocol is also opposed to the principle of free trade by adopting the principle of advance informed agreement that requires states to be informed of any transfer of GMOs intended for direct release in the environment on their territory and for this transfer to be validated before being effective. That principle has also been used by several environmental treaties involving the transport of hazardous substances.

On the other hand, environmental diplomacy has tried to have its goals adopted by diplomatic actors beyond the environmental field. Since the 1980s, the World Bank has been accused of environmental degradation after granting loans of several million dollars for development projects with disastrous environmental impacts. For example, the construction project for the Polonoroeste road through the Amazon, which began in 1981, had a catastrophic impact on biodiversity and on living conditions for indigenous populations in the region. The Bank was then criticized by NGOs as well as states and in particular the American Congress, which threatened to suspend its contributions. It had to modify its practices and today is striving to be more consistent with sustainable development goals. Another example is climate issues, which turned up at the UN Security Council for the first time in 2007, when countries evoked the consequences of climate change on worldwide security with threats such as sea levels rise and the increase in climate refugees.

The result of this tangled institutional web is that, since the 2000s, for each sub-theme dealt with, environmental diplomacy has formed a pluri-institutional structure that cannot be summed up by one single international regime. On the contrary, it lies at the crossroads of several regimes, often forming regime complexes. For example, the question of investment in biofuels is located at the intersection of four international regimes: climate change with, among others, the UNFCCC's clean development mechanism; trade, represented by the WTO; development, represented by the World Bank; and energy, represented by the European Renewable Energy Directive. Similarly, the issue of access to natural genetic resources is interwoven with the regimes of environmental protection with the Nagoya Protocol; intellectual property rights with the World Intellectual Property Organization; health with the World Health Organization; and agriculture, notably with the Food and Agriculture Organization of the United Nations.

These regime complexes can present different, more or less coherent structures which consequently may create synergies or conflicts. In any case, the price to be paid in terms of participation in environmental diplomacy is relatively high. Efforts have to be intensified nowadays, whereas in the 1990s it was still possible to follow a single arena of negotiation in order to remain informed and influence a theme. Furthermore, once they have paid for admission into the game of diplomacy, actors must also invest in understanding its rules.

The Rules of the Environmental Diplomacy Game

Environmental diplomacy is based on three main tacit rules that shape governmental decisions.

First, environmental diplomacy is based on the rule of consensus, in a game where collective actions are important. Thus, the vast majority of decisions are presented to all diplomats and adopted, unless there is an opposing reaction from any government. Voting is very rare. The consensus rule and the corresponding "silence means consent" practice allow any interests at stake to be expressed, in theory. It is therefore a rather inclusive rule. But, in practice, it prevents those absent from expressing their potential opposition (when the profusion of arenas of negotiation poses a problem simply in terms of one's presence at discussions). It also puts some pressure on diplomats, since the impact on one's reputation could be substantial for a country that raises its voice against all the others.

Second, in environmental diplomacy, every negotiation is divided into sub-themes, while the final agreement pertains to all of them, a global package combining different possibilities for each sub-unit. This enables package deals and tradeoffs, according to the formula "nothing is agreed until everything is agreed" (Jepsen 2013). Agreements usually follow a similar structure whose main elements are a general preliminary declaration, followed by definitions, a description of measures, control mechanisms, and legal procedures for implementation. For each of these points, negotiations are subdivided into different working groups, often themselves subdivided into contact groups, regarding issues that often become highly technical and varied: economic as well as legal, ethical, etc. For example, during the negotiations at the 12th session of the United Nations Forum on Forests, countries set up two working groups. One was to work on drawing up a ministerial declaration, and the other was to work on a shared resolution. The second working group created a contact group to discuss possibly setting up a committee on application and technical opinions. That contact group had to envision the committee's functions, modalities, and possible competencies. Since each point, even technical ones, is important, diplomats only give their opinion once they feel they have a precise enough vision of all modalities.

Third, multilateral environmental negotiations correspond very closely in game theory to the game of chicken. It is a non-zero-sum game involving two players, in which cooperation is rewarded. The game draws on scenes of car duels in several major American films. Two drivers are facing each other on two sides of the same track. They race toward each other. The first one to jump out of his vehicle to avoid a crash loses and is a "chicken." Each driver's goal is thus to show his determination and act tough, to make his adversary give up as quickly as possible. This allows the two drivers to stay alive. In the opposite case, the game would be counterproductive because they would both lose their lives. If you replace the drivers with diplomats, and the action of jumping out with accepting an agreement, then the game truly does reflect the dynamics of environmental diplomacy.

On the one hand, states see the value in adopting a joint agreement. Indeed, they invest time and money in numerous international meetings. Although official meetings for each treaty are often held no more than every two years, and only last two weeks, they are the result of dozens and even hundreds of preparatory meetings all over the world. The absence of a final agreement would not enable states to maximize the return on these material investments. Furthermore, such investments indicate that some states acknowledge the urgency of the problems to be dealt with and recognize that environmental themes can only be resolved collectively. Handling radioactive waste only makes sense on a multilateral basis, so as to avoid the dumping of such waste in countries that do not have the means to participate in environmental diplomacy, without, furthermore, solving the environmental problems of such waste. Efforts to limit climate change only make sense if all states commit to it (Aykut and Dahan 2015). Consequently, the outcome of environmental diplomacy must be a global agreement.

On the other hand, none of the negotiators wants to take the first step toward cooperation. Concerns about economic competitiveness have slowed down the momentum of most developed countries. Conversely, small delegations have either had trouble following the discussions, or been unable to find satisfactory solutions. Furthermore, segmentation of negotiations into working and contact groups has led all the diplomats to wait as long as possible before reaching an agreement, because often they only know at the last minute what it will consist of. As a result, agreements are reached at the very end, late at night after real diplomatic marathons. It is not uncommon to find negotiators asleep at their desks, on sofas in the corridor or even on the floor of negotiating rooms. Moreover, negotiating sites are arranged like miniature towns to allow the diplomats to be ever present, complete with catering, rooms for prayer, meditation, and yoga.

Most delegations understand this dynamic and use their best diplomats sparingly, only sending them in for the second week of negotiations.[1] But some smaller delegations make out well thanks to their representatives' physical strength and force of character. Tewolde Berhan Gebre Egziabher, an Ethiopian delegate, impressed the negotiators of the Cartagena Protocol on Biosafety due to his active presence, day and night, at all the negotiation meetings. The legend of the Ethiopian marathoners seems to have been confirmed in international diplomacy.

---

[1] This dynamic is also important for anyone wanting to plan fieldwork during international environmental negotiations. In order to meet the most people and conduct interviews, it is preferable to be involved during the first week when diplomats have more time. To understand the outcome of negotiations or try to meet important political actors, it is better to be involved in the second week of negotiations and expect to have feedback a day or two after the official closing date announced at the beginning of the meetings, constantly postponed.

If environmental diplomacy follows the game of chicken, how are agreements reached? In addition to states' motivation, two elements in the negotiating procedure do increase the chances of an agreement being adopted: transparency in discussions and the importance of session chairs.

Environmental diplomacy is in many respects a transparent diplomatic game followed by numerous non-state actors who play the role of safeguards. Not only is the number of countries involved in environmental diplomacy impressive, but the diversity of actors is equally so, with the significant participation of various kinds of non-state actors (Canal-Forgues 2015; Kuyper and Bäckstrand 2016). Since the Rio Summit, actors as diverse as mayors, indigenous leaders, farmers, representatives of student organizations, heads of multinational companies, and union delegates have taken part in discussions.

In addition to the number and diversity of actors, there is also a diverse range of political roles they may play. Whereas observers are traditionally confined to a passive role, several procedures in environmental diplomacy provide a chance for them to have their voices heard. Already at the Rio Summit, certain actors from civil society attended the preparatory meetings, where they were able to convey documents to government representatives and take the floor during plenary sessions. Furthermore, observers have the possibility of expressing themselves during environmental negotiations, but only after state diplomats have spoken. Along with these official statements, non-state actors engage in everyday lobbying interactions that influence final decisions (Orsini 2010).

Other official events may be planned in order to foster interactions between observers and official diplomats. This is the case for side events that generally take place in rooms adjacent to official negotiations, but also for an increasing number of spaces used for exhibitions, discussions, and meetings. During the twenty-first session of the Conference of the Parties, in Paris, many exchanges occurred at the "alternative village" in Montreuil, the "climate generation spaces" at Le Bourget, the "climate action zone" at CentQuatre, the "global landscapes forum" at the Palais des Congrès, and at the two "solutions galleries" at the Grand Palais and Le Bourget. There are many borders that get blurred between the "main" (official diplomacy) and "fringe" (informal diplomacy) events.

In addition to on-site transparency, most multilateral environmental diplomatic meetings have detailed records available online and more recently webcasts. Since the 1992 Rio Summit, the Earth Negotiations Bulletin (IISD, n.d.) has produced bulletins on a regular basis about major negotiations in progress, presenting highly detailed summaries of official negotiations while also valuing corridor discussions. Since COP21, real virtual participation in the UNFCCC's COP has been possible through live streaming and later on webcasts. This transparency has intensified civil society's focus on environmental diplomacy and has worked favorably in adopting agreements, even though it complicates decisions by multiplying the interests at stake.

The second procedural element that fosters decision-making has been the gradual increase in importance of session chairs who are traditionally designated at the beginning of every official meeting, or for an entire negotiating process, and whose role has become more and more vital. There are often two of these negotiation ambassadors, traditionally representing two countries with opposing interests regarding the themes dealt with. For instance, for the negotiations on the Nagoya Protocol on Access to Genetic Resources, the co-presidents were a Canadian diplomat, Canada being a user country of genetic resources, and a Colombian diplomat, Colombia being a supplier country of genetic resources. The co-presidents are chosen by the secretariats of the institutions the negotiations are tied to, and their choices are then approved by all the parties at the start of negotiations.

The role of session chairs is officially to handle the diplomatic processes in order to bring them to a successful conclusion. In practice, these key actors often write drafts of future agreements. It is also not uncommon for them to use innovative negotiating techniques to foster a positive conclusion to discussions. For example, during the final negotiations of the Cartagena Protocol in September 1999 and January 2000, diplomats could not reach an agreement. Discussions were impossible between pro- and anti-GMOs. The session chair, Juan Mayr, Colombian environmental minister, decided to use colored balls to coordinate slots for speakers. Not finding anymore colored balls for the last negotiating session, he chose five different-colored teddy bears that he named Justice, Testaverde, Brown, Rodriguez, and Smith. Like colored balls, teddy bears were used to manage the order of diplomats' interventions. No diplomat had the right to speak before choosing a teddy bear and hugging it. The teddy bears helped to ease tensions by adding some humor and a human touch (the teddy bear as a symbol of something sweet and childlike). The Cartagena Protocol was adopted on January 29, 2000, and the teddy bears were present when it was signed. When session chairs do not succeed in reaching an agreement, the country hosting the meetings may also play an important role. For instance, "The Future We Want," adopted at Rio + 20, was drawn up at the last minute by Brazilian diplomats.

* * *

As has already been explained in detail in this chapter, environmental diplomacy is dynamic, innovative, and inventive. For this reason, it is worth being used more often as a model for other areas of diplomacy, even if its performance could also be improved (Susskind and Ali 2014). In terms of content, others could learn from environmental diplomacy through its constant ability to provide new ideas and willingness to challenge existing models in the interest of effectiveness. In terms of rules, others could learn from environmental diplomacy the importance of transparency in discussions, participation by all, and collective dynamics allowing highly diverse interests to be taken into account: of developed and developing countries, of present and future generations, of mankind and of all living beings, etc.

And yet, rather than being a model for others, the environmental diplomacy described above is threatened due to its increasing politicization. This is the case notably for the subject of climate change. As an attentive observer at COP21 stated: "the climate change arena has become the place to speak, to be heard and to seek funds" (Foyer 2016, 4). To be sure, this politicization has given more visibility to the environment on the international stage, but it also risks paralyzing negotiations. The expanded audience dilutes environmental imperatives, and generalist decision-makers, contrary to diplomats specialized in the environment, are not always favorable to environmental policies. Thus, for better or worse, environmental diplomacy has become more dependent on the interests of the major powers.

References

Aykut, Stefan, Dahan, Amy, *Gouverner le climat? 20 ans de négociations internationales*, Paris, Presses de Science Po, 2015.
Canal-Forgues, Éric, *Démocratie et diplomatie environnementales. Acteurs et processus en droit international*, Paris, Pedone, 2015.
Death, Carl, "Summit Theatre: Exemplary Governmentality and Environmental Diplomacy in Johannesburg and Copenhagen," *Environmental Politics*, 20 (1), 2011: 1–19.
Foyer, Jean (ed.), *Regards croisés sur Rio+20. La modernisation écologique à l'épreuve*, Paris, CNRS Éditions, 2015.

———, "Dans les coulisses de la COP 21," *La Vie des idées*, 23 February 2016.

Jepsen, Henrik, "Nothing Is Agreed Until Everything Is Agreed," *Issue Linkage in the International Climate Change Negotiations*, Århus, Politica, 2013.

Kim, Rakhyun E., "The Emergent Network Structure of the Multilateral Environmental Agreement System," *Global Environmental Change*, 23 (5), 2013: 980–991.

Kuyper, Jonathan W., Backstrand, Karin, "Accountability and Representation: Non State Actors in UN Climate Diplomacy," *Global Environmental Politics*, 16 (2), 2016: 61–81.

Morin, Jean-Frédéric, Orsini, Amandine, *Politique internationale de l'environnement*, Paris, Presses de Sciences Po, 2015.

Orsini, Amandine, *La Biodiversité sous influence? Les lobbies industriels face aux politiques internationales d'environnement*, Brussels, Éditions de l'université de Bruxelles, 2010.

Susskind, Lawrence E., Ali, Saleem H., *Environmental Diplomacy: Negotiating More Effective Global Agreements*, Oxford, Oxford University Press, 2014.

Tolba, Mostafa K. (ed.), *Global Environmental Diplomacy, Negotiating Environmental Agreements for the World (1973–1992)*, Cambridge, MIT Press, 1998.

CHAPTER 18

Humanitarian Diplomacy

Elise Rousseau and Achille Sommo Pende

The destruction of Aleppo, the Western African Ebola virus epidemic, the migration crisis in Europe, floods in Bangladesh, internal displacements in Iraq, and the civil war in Sudan are situations in which millions of people's lives are in danger and which require an immediate response. A proliferation of local and international actors comes into play to prevent these dangers, to rescue and protect vulnerable people, or to promote respect for fundamental rights. These events are not straightforward, however. In most cases, in order to carry out their work on the ground, humanitarian actors must acquire the approval of state or non-state entities, whether they are of a civilian or (para)military nature. For many years, these types of interactions have been described as "humanitarian actions." However, in their everyday practices, humanitarian practitioners develop a special kind of expertise, and they draw on innovative methods to achieve their goals and, in fact, demonstrate real diplomatic skills. This phenomenon is now so widespread that some mention the emergence of a new form of diplomacy, labeled "humanitarian diplomacy."

E. Rousseau (✉) · A. S. Pende
University of Namur, Namur, Belgium
e-mail: elise.rousseau@unamur.be

© The Author(s) 2020
T. Balzacq et al. (eds.), *Global Diplomacy*,
The Sciences Po Series in International Relations and Political Economy, https://doi.org/10.1007/978-3-030-28786-3_18

The concept of "humanitarian diplomacy" has scarcely been theorized in international relations, and its relevance to the field is sometimes even disputed. The label itself is an oxymoron (Smith 2007). Indeed, while proponents of a certain humanitarian ideal tend to reject political games, diplomacy dominates the political relations between states. When a humanitarian actor takes on the role of diplomat, she/he enters by default into political action, and the question of his/her impartiality may sometimes arise. This chapter is an entry point for grasping the contours of humanitarian diplomacy and the increasingly important role it is playing in the field of diplomacy. It addresses the following sets of questions: What is the definition of "humanitarian diplomacy?" What are the foundations of this concept? Who are its actors? What are their practices?

Definition

Most authors tend to agree that humanitarian diplomacy refers to all the negotiation activities undertaken by various actors with governments, (para)military organizations, or public figures in order to intervene in a context where humanity is in danger. Its purpose may also be to persuade decision-makers and opinion leaders to act in accordance with the fundamental principles of human rights. This definition remains vague, however, because it says little about the actors carrying out these negotiation and advocacy activities. Two rival conceptions coexist, the restrictive and the extensive views. According to the *restrictive* view, these activities are specific to humanitarian private organizations and to some United Nations bodies (Minear and Smith 2007). For the *extensive* view, humanitarian organizations, personalities, states, and international organizations engage in humanitarian diplomacy whenever the purpose of their actions is to preserve human dignity (Veuthey 2012).

This debate tends to mask the more general question of the relevance of the concept of "humanitarian diplomacy" itself. Indeed, the majority of actors involved in these negotiation and advocacy activities do not see themselves as being "diplomats" (Minear and Smith 2007). For many of them, these activities are just the ordinary tasks falling within their humanitarian mission. Furthermore, there is no "international regime" of humanitarian diplomacy equivalent to that of the 1961 and 1963 Vienna Conventions for so-called traditional diplomacy. Indeed, actors involved in humanitarian missions do not follow a prescribed set of rules, principles, and procedures organizing their interactions.

However, humanitarian diplomacy is gradually becoming a field of its own, mainly because it relies on a particular foundation and on specific practices.

"The Imperative of Humanity": The Foundation of Humanitarian Diplomacy

Humanitarian diplomacy is based on one foundation, namely the imperative of humanity. The imperative of humanity is the recognition that the other, whoever she/he may be, is a human being whose dignity deserves to be protected (Dunant 1862). This imperative is outlined in a set of principles embedded in international humanitarian law (IHL) and international human rights instruments (see Table 18.1).

Table 18.1 The main instruments of international human rights and international humanitarian law

International human rights	*International humanitarian law*

• The Universal Declaration of Human Rights
• The International Covenant on Civil and Political Rights
• The International Covenant on Economic, Social, and Cultural Rights
• The United Nations Conventions:
  – against Torture and Other Cruel, Inhuman or Degrading Treatment or Punishment;
  – on the Rights of the Child and its two optional protocols;
  – on the Elimination of All Forms of Racial Discrimination;
  – for the Protection of All Persons from Enforced Disappearance;
  – on the Elimination of all Forms of Discrimination Against Women;
  – on the Rights of Persons with Disabilities
	• The four Geneva Conventions and their three additional protocols
	• The Hague Convention for the Protection of Cultural Property in the Event of Armed Conflict
	• The Biological Weapons Convention
	• The Chemical Weapons Convention
	• The United Nations Convention on Certain Conventional Weapons and its four protocols
	• The Convention on Cluster Munitions
	• The Convention on the Prohibition of the Use, Stockpiling, Production, and Transfer of Anti-Personnel Mines and on their Destruction
	• The 2013 Arms Trade Treaty

Source Authors

IHL is the branch of international law that governs the conduct of international and non-international armed conflicts and aims to limit their consequences. The Geneva Conventions of 1949 and their three additional protocols are the cornerstone of IHL. These texts provide a framework for the protection of those who do not partake in hostilities, such as civilians, the sick, and the wounded, but also those who are shipwrecked, prisoners of war, and members of medical and/or humanitarian organizations that come to help. More importantly, the principle of selfless and indiscriminate assistance to any victim or vulnerable person in a conflict is enshrined in these texts. Recently, IHL had to adapt to the changing forms of wars, which are affected by technological advances and the active involvement of civilians in conflicts. Now, IHL regulates the course of combats in order to limit the violence of war on soldiers and its consequences on the environment and nonmaterial goods.

At first sight, the principles of IHL essentially involve the state parties to the different texts. This commitment consists of a negative obligation (refraining from committing a violation of the right or encouraging a violation) and a positive obligation (acting collectively or individually to stop violations). In our view, this double obligation has two limitations. First, the conventions bind only states that have legally consented to it through a process of ratification. This excludes, de facto, the enforceability against states that have not ratified them. Second, the ratification of these texts is not synonymous with compliance. Their application remains subject to the will of political leaders who can exhibit the argument of sovereignty either to avoid obligations, or to implement the texts following their own interpretation. These two limitations—illustrated by the tragedies in Biafra (Nigeria, 1967–1970), Rwanda, and the Balkans in the 1990s—prompted the UN to adopt the responsibility to protect principle (R2P) in September 2005 (Bettati 2007). This principle approves the right of the international community to override national sovereignty in the event of a humanitarian crisis, within the framework of a mandate emanating from a supranational authority. This principle was first invoked by the Security Council on March 17, 2011, to authorize a collective armed intervention in Libya (resolution 1973) and, then, on March 30, 2011, to authorize an individual intervention in Côte d'Ivoire (resolution 1975).

However, the abovementioned cases and other arenas of conflict (e.g., Somalia, Darfur, East Timor, Iraq, and Syria) have shown that states are no longer the only actors perpetrating violence. Since the end of the Cold War, indeed, conflicts have involved armed non-state actors (ANSAs) operating within one or more states. Similar to states, these actors are encouraged to respect the imperative of humanity. Since 2000, the NGO "Geneva Call" has urged ANSAs to respect the principles of IHL. This initiative circumvents the legal incapacity of ANSAs to ratify international conventions by offering them the ability to sign "acts of engagement." These acts concern, for example, the prohibition of anti-personnel mines, the protection of children in armed conflict, the prohibition of sexual violence in armed conflict, and the elimination of gender-based discrimination. Although nonbinding, they enable ANSAs to demonstrate their adherence to some humanitarian standards (Veuthey 2012).

Despite the existence of a link between humanitarian diplomacy, human rights, and IHL, one needs to beware of conflating two things. First, humanitarian diplomacy is not the prerogative of international lawyers (Veuthey 2012). Some perpetrators are aware of the unlawfulness of their actions but show their determination not to comply. Addressing these violations with legal arguments would therefore be useless, if not counterproductive. Second, the spectrum of humanitarian diplomacy cannot be reduced to interventions in conflicts. The imperative of humanity—the foundation of humanitarian diplomacy—also implies intervening in locations where people are vulnerable because of natural disasters, health, or even social crises.

Actors and Diplomatic Practices

In this section, we present the actors of humanitarian diplomacy and their practices according to what we previously called the "extensive" concept. This does not mean that we are taking a stand in the debate. Our goal is rather to offer a broad panorama of the different agents who could be put in the category of "humanitarian diplomats," according to researchers studying the concept. In the following subsections, we describe the practices of the International Committee of the Red Cross (ICRC), those of some NGOs, and those of states and the United Nations.

The ICRC: A Key Player in the Humanitarian Field

The ICRC is a private association established under Swiss law in 1863 and a unique diplomatic actor. This special identity results from the Geneva Conventions by which state parties entrusted the ICRC with the specific mandate to assist and protect victims of armed conflict. This mandate also means preventing suffering by promoting and reinforcing the principles of IHL. Furthermore, state parties to the Geneva Conventions have endowed the ICRC with an international legal personality. This allows the association to obtain a diplomatic status similar to that of representatives of a state, of the United Nations, or of the European Union. For example, the ICRC enjoys privileges such as exemption from taxes and customs duties, the inviolability of its offices and documents, and immunity from jurisdiction. Moreover, since a resolution adopted on October 16, 1990, the ICRC enjoys observer status in the UN General Assembly similar to that of Palestine or the Holy See. The Swiss association enjoys similar status in other international institutions, such as the Council of Europe, the Organization of American States, the African Union, the Organization of the Islamic Conference, and the Non-Aligned Movement. Given this particular legal status, and the rights and privileges associated with it, it would be tempting to equate the ICRC with a traditional diplomatic actor, such as an intergovernmental organization. This impression may be heightened by the fact that the ICRC online job portal regularly offers diplomatic adviser posts.

However, the international legal personality of the ICRC is strictly functional (Harroff-Tavel 2005). In other words, the ICRC's diplomatic activities are limited to assisting or protecting victims of conflict and to promoting IHL. The ICRC representation in various international institutions is motivated by the opportunity provided by these spaces to interact with states' delegations on the issues falling within its mandate. This allows the ICRC to engage with all parties involved in a conflict, including ANSAs, without this being considered as interference and without having to disclose the substance of these exchanges. Furthermore, the ICRC is exempted from the obligation to testify or to provide evidence in national and international criminal courts. This is a requirement under Rule 73 of the Rules of Procedure and Evidence of the International Criminal Court and following the decision of the International Tribunal for the Former Yugoslavia on July 27, 1999, in the case of *The Prosecutor c / Simiç et al.* This privilege is granted on the basis of the "general interest" at the heart of ICRC's actions.

The ICRC's humanitarian diplomacy has two main objectives. The first goal is operational and consists of extending the acceptability of the ICRC (and of its mandate) to all actors involved in armed conflict. This provides the ICRC with access to victims in order to give them necessary assistance and protection as well as access to prisoners of war. It enables the association to deliver family messages and to help in finding missing persons in war zones. The second goal is legal and consists of promoting IHL among states and ANSAs. Within this framework, the ICRC organizes the International Conference of the Red Cross and Red Crescent every four years to discuss contemporary humanitarian issues and the evolution of IHL. The conference brings together the bodies of the International Red Cross and Red Crescent Movement, the state parties to the Geneva Conventions, most international organizations, the United Nations and some of its specialized agencies, NGOs, and academic institutions.

According to Harroff-Tavel, to achieve these two objectives, the ICRC favors persuasion through discreet and confidential negotiations. To some extent, the ICRC can mobilize potential allies (states, international organizations, NGOs, religious or economic actors, and political, sports or cultural personalities) that are able to "influence [discreetly] the parties of a conflict in order to make them respect humanitarian law" (Harroff-Tavel 2005, 78). In regard to soliciting the help of third-party states, the ICRC only has to remind them of their commitment to uphold IHL in accordance with Article 1, which is common to the four Geneva Conventions. Concerning the other actors, the ICRC gives them the freedom to define their means of intervention, as long as it is in accordance with IHL. To some extent, however, the choice to call on allies risks undermining the ICRC's principle of independence.

Non-Governmental Organizations: Two Humanitarian Approaches to Diplomacy

The ICRC was at the forefront of international humanitarian action during the first half of the twentieth century. In the 1960s, voices began to oppose the vision of humanitarianism endorsed by the association and, more specifically, the principle of confidentiality. A few human rights NGOs emerged, and the creation of Doctors Without Borders (MSF) by fourteen French doctors after the Biafran War (1967–1970) marked a sharp break from some of the ICRC's practices. A few years later, a larger transnational human rights network was operating on the international stage (Sikkink 1993). At the turn of the 1980s, MSF was divided between two opposing visions of humanitarianism and its relationship to politics (Maillard 2008). This division, we contend, illustrates a tension dividing the world of humanitarian non-governmental action, which led to two different humanitarian approaches to diplomacy: one public and the other pragmatic.

The *public* approach to humanitarian diplomacy is the one that was championed by Bernard Kouchner at MSF. Proponents of this approach thought the principle of confidentiality that characterized humanitarian action before the 1960s should be rejected. Under the influence of Kouchner, MSF—and later Doctors of the World—refused to remain silent in the face of abuses and started to relay the crimes committed during conflicts. Accordingly, violations of human rights were denounced and made public. More than ever, humanitarianism interfered in the political sphere: By forging the concept of the right of interference (*droit d'ingérence*), Bernard Kouchner and Mario Bettati wished to theorize humanitarian actions undertaken by *state* actors. In addition to the activities of this historical branch of MSF, this approach also includes those of human rights NGOs such as Amnesty International or Human Rights Watch. At least five types of practices characterize the *public* approach to humanitarian diplomacy.

A first diplomatic practice is the launching of international awareness-raising campaigns. In this context, NGOs frame a situation in which humanity is in danger with the hope of arousing emotion, attention, and most importantly compelling third-party states to act.

A second strategy is the organization of naming and shaming campaigns denouncing the complicity of states that do not act in the territory where abuses are committed. During these campaigns, states and institutions are reminded of their liberal democratic identity as well as their commitment to human rights and humanitarian law (Risse and Sikkink 1999, 23). During these campaigns, NGOs communicate information they alone possess (Keck and Sikkink 1998). Indeed, when a government blocks traditional channels of communication, local organizations can get their message through via contacts with international NGOs. These international NGOs would then urge other states and intergovernmental organizations to pressure the norm-violating state into changing its behavior. These actions may take the form of international condemnations, sanctions, or interventions. This strategy has been called the "boomerang pattern" by Margaret Keck and Kathryn Sikkink (Keck and Sikkink 1998).

It should be noted that in these two types of strategies, NGOs lobby governments and international institutions to put the identified problem on the agenda. These humanitarian diplomatic practices are indirect, primarily about pressuring other actors to act in order to influence the perpetrator's behavior.

A third practice implemented by non-governmental "humanitarian diplomats" is the establishment of public actions aimed directly against the deviant actor, again by launching naming and shaming campaigns. This time, the campaigns denounce the norm-violating action without going through other actors. These actions can be seen as David's weapon against Goliath, the weapon of the weak non-governmental actor against the powerful state actor. However, the results are mixed (Friman 2015).

Another direct diplomatic practice seems to have a bright future ahead of it: participation in the elaboration of international treaties. In addition to putting a humanitarian problem on the international agenda, NGOs can sometimes participate fully in the negotiation of a treaty. This fourth practice is illustrated, for example, by the negotiations leading to the 1997 Ottawa Convention on the Prohibition of Anti-Personnel Mines, which has been presented as "one of the most iconic cases of humanitarian diplomacy" (Ryfman 2010, 573). Indeed, NGOs *directly* participated in the negotiations of the treaty, thanks to the support of a series of states. For example, the NGO Handicap International was able to accompany the French delegation to the first international conference on the subject organized in Canada. In this context, humanitarian diplomats participated in the redaction of the treaty.

Finally, a fifth practice is monitoring the implementation of international treaties. For example, NGOs have endorsed this role in the framework of the Ottawa Convention, but also in the Kimberley Process, an international forum regulating the international rough diamonds trade in order to prevent the diffusion of conflict diamonds.

The second approach to humanitarian diplomacy by non-governmental actors is the *pragmatic* approach. This approach follows the vision advocated by Rony Brauman, president of MSF from 1982 to 1994. Refusing to ban the principle of confidentiality from humanitarian thinking, and thus remaining close to the ICRC's vision of humanitarianism, Brauman considered that care must override the duty to testify. By denouncing abuses committed in the territories where they work, NGO members risk losing access to the victims. Here, "know-how" runs counter to the duty to inform (Maillard 2008).

The pragmatic approach has two foundations, urgency and neutrality, understood as "a restraint that is exercised in showing our sympathies or rejections" (Brauman 2009, 107). The humanitarian logic is distinct from the logic of economic, political, and emotional actions. First, humanitarianism is different from the economic logic of development aid agencies that advocate economic transformations in impacted areas (Calhoun 2010). Indeed, humanitarian workers act in a context of emergency. Their purpose is to save lives, not to evaluate which structural transformations should be implemented in states facing a disaster. Second, those who adhere to this vision reject the political logic underlying the public approach to humanitarian diplomacy mentioned earlier. Neutrality is what grants humanitarian workers access to the victims of crises: If NGOs are not perceived as threats, the states in which they operate will not hinder their actions (Calhoun 2010). Third, in addition to rejecting the political logic, this conception of neutrality implies a refusal of any emotional logic: "People have emotions, but a humanitarian institution must help smooth over emotions, to escape their grasp in order to act according to the situations observed rather than to temporary outbursts" (Brauman 2009, 111). Indeed, for those advocating this approach, humanitarian diplomacy should not indulge in international campaigns aimed at arousing public emotion.

Here, diplomatic practices are implemented at the operational level. NGOs deal with the government to negotiate the transporting of materials and humanitarian personnel, delivering food, gaining access to victims, obtaining visas for humanitarian actors, or coordinating aid (Veuthey 2012, 95–196). In such contexts, humanitarian workers demonstrate real diplomatic skills, negotiating through the use of diplomacy techniques, methods, and tools to achieve their goals (Smith 2007).

Diplomatic Approaches to Human Rights and Humanitarianism

After the ICRC's foundation at the end of the nineteenth century, most states lost interest in humanitarian and human rights issues in the pursuit of foreign policy. It was only after the Second World War that these issues returned to the forefront of the international scene, as shown by the promulgation of the four Geneva Conventions (1949) and the Universal Declaration of Human Rights (1948). After this key moment, some European countries developed a regional regime for the protection of human rights by, *inter alia*, establishing the European Court of Human Rights in 1959. Within the framework of the United Nations, humanitarian aid was introduced with the creation of the United Nations Children's Fund (Unicef) in 1946 and that of the United Nations High Commissioner for Refugees (UNHCR) in 1950.

In the United States, the doctrine of containment began to precedence in the foreign affairs agenda and trumped all considerations related to humanitarianism and the protection of human rights abroad. It was not until the 1970s, after Jimmy Carter's election and in response to the growing influence of NGOs, that the United States would return to considerations linked to the respect of human rights in their foreign policy decision-making. Around the same time, some European states, such as Norway and the Netherlands, explicitly developed a foreign policy agenda directed toward the protection of human rights. A few years later, in the framework of the United Nations, the organization of humanitarian action became more institutionalized through the creation of the Office for the Coordination of Humanitarian Affairs (OCHA) in 1991. In the remainder of this section, we will start by presenting state humanitarian diplomacy before turning to that of the United Nations.

The inclusion of human rights considerations in foreign policy decision-making has led some states to redefine their approach to their national interest by incorporating moral elements (Brysk 2009). This evolution does not mean, however, that decision-makers forsake any notion of interest in favor of unconditional altruism: The respect of human rights abroad is only one factor among others influencing foreign policy decision-making (Hafner-Burton 2013). The humanitarian diplomacy of these actors, usually liberal democratic states, would thus combine national interest and the promotion of human rights values. In her book on the foreign policy of these actors, Alison Brysk highlights five ways through which humanitarian diplomacy could be exercised (Brysk 2009, 20–22). First, states can opt for the multilateral path and join fundamental rights bodies, participate in the drafting of treaties, or promote IHL. Second, humanitarian diplomacy can be part of bilateral relations between states. For example, a government may try to improve the humanitarian situation in another country through mediation processes or through rewards and sanctions. Third, development assistance mechanisms can help improve the humanitarian situation of states unable to support themselves. Fourth, the humanitarian situation abroad could also be improved through mechanisms promoting peace, such as conflict prevention or post-conflict reconstruction. Finally, a form of humanitarian diplomacy can also be found in the reception of refugees.

In addition to these practices, some states have explicitly located the concept of "humanitarian diplomacy" at the heart of their foreign policy agenda. For example, in a text published in 2013, the former Turkish Minister of Foreign Affairs announced that he intended to develop the humanitarian diplomacy of his country along three axes: the well-being of Turkish citizens, the promotion of a human approach to conflict resolution, and proactive action within the UN (Davutoglu 2013). The concept of "human security," dear to the promoters of Canadian and Japanese foreign policy, is similar to that of "humanitarian diplomacy." Indeed, at a symposium on Turkish-Japanese relations in 2016, some researchers said the two countries shared a common vision of humanitarian diplomacy (ORSAM 2016).

Next to the ICRC, NGOs, and state diplomats, the UN is a key player in contemporary humanitarian diplomacy. The help provided by the organization can be divided into four domains of action: humanitarian crises (natural disasters and armed conflicts), relief of victims, protection of vulnerable people, and crisis prevention. More concretely, humanitarian help is supported by five bodies: the UNHCR, UNICEF, the United Nations Development Program (UNDP), the World Food Program (WFP), and the World Health Organization (WHO). As mentioned previously, their work is coordinated by the OCHA. For Larry Minear and Hazel Smith (2007), the staff of these organizations are among the only people who can truly be called "humanitarian diplomats." Unlike state humanitarian diplomacy, UN humanitarian diplomacy occurs at a very operational level. Indeed, UN agencies must establish their presence and that of their staff in the field, monitor assistance programs, and encourage respect for IHL. Like state diplomats, some UN personnel may have special *laissez-passer*, diplomatic immunity, and may negotiate with political figures (Minear and Smith 2007). However, unlike state diplomats, they must not take into account issues raised by national interests. The most important thing for them is to protect humanity at risk.

* * *

Humanitarian diplomacy already generates less skepticism than it did in the early days. While some authors perceive it as a limited and discrete enterprise (Smith 2007, 38), others see it as a form of alternative diplomacy (Ryfman 2010, 576). Humanitarian diplomacy is unique in that it is able to cope with emergencies and overcome deep divisions in order to reach solutions to situations previously considered inextricable. The negotiation and persuasion techniques of humanitarian diplomats are relatively unknown to practitioners of traditional diplomacy. This is mainly because humanitarian actors are not even aware that they possess diplomatic skills which could elicit interest and be passed on. That being said, to speak of humanitarian diplomacy as a homogeneous unit would be a mistake. So far there have been no absolute rules. While some major players, such as the ICRC, are extremely regular in their diplomatic practices, this is less clear for others. The practice of humanitarian diplomacy varies from one context to another, but it always keeps the imperative of humanity at its core. The diversity of actors, the different fields of intervention, and the variety of practices surely mean that humanitarian diplomats will face continuing challenges. In particular, they should avoid the pitfalls of instrumentalizing humanitarian action and problems due to competition between people in places where coordination of efforts should instead be encouraged.

References

Bettati, Mario, "Du droit d'ingérence à la responsabilité de protéger," *Outre-terre*, 20 (3), 2007: 381–389.

Brauman, Rony, *Humanitaire, diplomatie et droits de l'homme*, Paris, Éditions du Cygne, 2009.

Brysk, Alison, *Global Good Samaritans: Human Rights as Foreign Policy*, Oxford, Oxford University Press, 2009.

Calhoun, Craig, "The Idea of Emergency: Humanitarian Action and Global (Dis)order," in Didier Fassin, Mariella Pandolfi (eds.), *Contemporary States of Emergency: The Politics of Humanitarian Interventions*, New York (NY), Zone Books, 2010, pp. 29–58.

Davutoglu, Ahmet, "Turkey's Humanitarian Diplomacy: Objectives, Challenges and Prospects," *Nationalities Papers: The Journal of Nationalism and Ethnicity*, 41 (6), 2013: 865–870.

Dunant, Henry, *Un souvenir de Solférino*, Genève, Comité international de la Croix-Rouge, [1862] 1990.

Friman, H. Richard (ed.), *The Politics of Leverage in International Relations. Name, Shame, and Sanctions*, New York (NY), Palgrave Macmillan, 2015.

Hafner-Burton, Emilie M., *Making Human Rights a Reality*, Princeton (NJ), Princeton University Press, 2013.

Harroff-Tavel, Marion, "La diplomatie humanitaire du Comité international de la Croix-Rouge," *Relations internationales*, 121 (5), 2005: 73–89.

Keck, Margaret E., Sikkink, Kathryn, *Activists Beyond Borders: Advocacy Networks in International Politics*, Ithaca (NY), Cornell University Press, 1998.

Maillard, Denis, "1968–2008: le Biafra ou le sens de l'humanitaire," *Humanitaire*, 18, 2008, https://journals.openedition.org/humanitaire/182, accessed 24 February 2017.

Minear, Larry, Smith, Hazel, "Introduction," in Larry Minear, Hazel Smith (ed.), *Humanitarian Diplomacy: Practitioners and Their Craft*, New York (NY), United Nations University Press, 2007, pp. 1–4.

ORSAM, "Symposium Japan-Turkey: Dialogue on Global Affairs," *Meeting Evaluation*, 8 August 2016.

Risse, Thomas, Sikkink, Kathryn, "The Socialization of International Human Rights Norms into Domestic Practices: Introduction," in Thomas Risse, Stephen C. Ropp, Kathryn Sikkink (eds.), *The Power of Human Rights: International Norms and Domestic Change*, Cambridge, Cambridge University Press, 1999, pp. 1–38.

Ryfman, Philippe, "L'action humanitaire non gouvernementale: une diplomatie alternative?" *Politique étrangère*, 3, 2010: 565–578.

Sikkink, Kathryn, "The Power of Principled Ideas: Human Rights Policies in the United States and Western Europe," in Judith Goldstein, Robert O. Keohane (eds.), *Ideas and Foreign Policy: Beliefs, Institutions, and Political Change*, Ithaca (NY), Cornell University Press, 1993, pp. 139–170.

Smith, Hazel, "Humanitarian Diplomacy: Theory and Practice," in Larry Minear, Hazel Smith (eds.), *Humanitarian Diplomacy: Practitioners and Their Craft*, Tokyo, New York, and Paris, United Nations University Press, 2007, pp. 36–62.

Veuthey, Michel, "Humanitarian Diplomacy: Saving It When It Is Most Needed," in Alexandre Vautravers, Yivita Fox (ed.), *Humanitarian Space and the International Community: 16th Humanitarian Conference*, Geneva, Webster University, 2012, pp. 195–209.

CHAPTER 19

Defense Diplomacy

Frédéric Charillon, Thierry Balzacq and Frédéric Ramel

There are few academic studies devoted explicitly to defense diplomacy, whereas the complementarity between soldiers and diplomats is well known (Aron 1962, 770), and there are specialists of the relationship between the tools of diplomacy and those of the military (Doise and Vaïsse 2015). The term has only recently gained ground in the vocabulary of practitioners, with a very particular connotation.

The idea of defense diplomacy in its contemporary sense emerged during the 1990s and suggests (more than it "designates," as no official or final definition has been acknowledged) the desire to use military channels, or those of experts on defense issues, to help create a climate of trust and

---

F. Charillon (✉)
University of Clermont Auvergne,
Clermont-Ferrand, France

T. Balzacq · F. Ramel
Sciences Po, Paris, France
e-mail: thierry.balzacq@sciencespo.fr

F. Ramel
e-mail: frederic.ramel@sciencespo.fr

© The Author(s) 2020
T. Balzacq et al. (eds.), *Global Diplomacy*,
The Sciences Po Series in International Relations and Political
Economy, https://doi.org/10.1007/978-3-030-28786-3_19

a convergence of interests. Thus, as its name indicates, it is dedicated to diplomacy more than to military efficiency strictly speaking (Hills 2000). With respect to more distant times, it is a considerable reversal of perspective: Collaborating in the military arena is what now helps political rapprochement, not maintaining political relations to assist in forging military alliances.

This dynamic grew out of the context of the double imperative of reconstructing Europe. First, reconstructing the relationship between Western powers and former Communist countries. The latter's armies, trained to fight against the North Atlantic Treaty Organization (NATO), were now being asked to join it (as well as the European Union). The 1998 British strategic defense review was one of the first official sources to explicitly mention as one of its "new missions"[1] the goal of "defense diplomacy," designed to "dispel hostility, build trust, and take part in developing armed forces under democratic control (thus helping conflict prevention and resolution)," mainly with post-Communist Europe (House of Commons 1998). Germany quickly engaged in a defense dialogue with Central and Eastern Europe, as did Norway with Russia, Finland, and Sweden with the Baltic countries (Cottey and Forster 2004).

Reconstruction was also crucial in the Balkans after the Yugoslavian tragedy, during which grave abuses were committed by national militias and armed forces from ex-Yugoslavian countries, defying all ethical notions and international injunctions. The post-war period and prospects of the new Balkans joining the European Union (EU) or NATO raised the issue of reforming the military and security sector in the region.

Subsequently, the use of military and defense channels to facilitate political dialogue became widespread throughout the world, going beyond the mere framework of democratic countries, always with the same goal of cooperation and diplomatic gains (Matsuda 2006). China engaged in military dialogue with India, Australia with Indonesia, and ASEAN countries with each other.

---

[1] Three "military tasks" were mentioned: arms control (including non-proliferation, confidence-building, and safety measures), a policy of engagement toward former Communist Europe, including Russia, and "other overseas military cooperation activities."

After the 9/11 attacks, defense diplomacy gained new momentum (Blannin 2017), and in 2002, a new chapter was added to the abovementioned 1998 British strategic defense review, highlighting defense diplomacy as a tool in the fight against terrorism by establishing trust between armies (Ministry of Defence 2002).

The concept of defense diplomacy reflects several distinct levels in terms of practices. In terms of theory, it involves several sets of issues. Finally, the sociology of the actors driving it has changed constantly, raising the question of the concept's future.

Defense Diplomacy: The Concept's Limits, Variations in Practices

The contemporary context, characterized by the idea of confidence-building, has led us to dismiss other uses of the concept of defense diplomacy, which are ongoing but in fact obsolete or anachronistic. Defense diplomacy remains above all a channel for military dialogue and an area of expertise shared by a community of actors of different nationalities.

What Defense Diplomacy Is Not

First, we have ruled out a rather common usage that alludes to the use (or threat) of force in support of diplomacy. This is in fact the old "gunboat diplomacy" that consists in making a show of military strength to lead a given power to make concessions, the exact opposite of the soft power category that contemporary defense diplomacy would like to fit into.

We will also not discuss "defense diplomacy" when foreign policy is implemented by actors that happen to be in the military but are acting as leaders. This is the case for military regimes (Burmese junta, South American military dictatorships) or where the army has a strong influence (Algeria, Pakistan, Egypt). It may also be the case for democratic civilian regimes in which an individual, admittedly one with military training, temporarily performs the civil functions of head of state (the United States under General Eisenhower, France under General de Gaulle), head of government (Israel under Yitzhak Rabin, Ehud Barak, and Ariel Sharon), or of a minister (Alexander Haig, American Secretary of State from 1981 to 1982). Their diplomacy is one of the whole state and not merely defense diplomacy.

We will also not confuse defense diplomacy with "defense communications," an activity in which communications services communicate in a purely informational manner (and naturally in a favorable light) about life in the army, its military exploits, and ongoing military operations.

The traditional (and still valid) custom of sending military advisors—or financial military assistance—to foreign armies also does not reflect the post-Cold War imperative of a military dialogue for diplomatic purposes, where the sole objective is increasing military efficiency in a conflict or in preparing one.

We adhere more to the spirit of the definition proposed by Juan Emilio Cheyre in his contribution to the Oxford Handbook of Modern Diplomacy (Cheyre 2013), where defense diplomacy is seen as "employment, without duress [or without urgent international or national constraints], in time of peace of the resources of Defence to achieve specific national goals, primarily through relationships with others"[2] (defense actors, located abroad).

We are still refining this line of thought, distinguishing several expectations regarding this kind of practice.

Defense Diplomacy as a Channel for Military Dialogue

The use by a given country of its military actors (mainly officers or high-level actors) for diplomatic purposes, to establish a dialogue and a network of confidence with soldiers from other countries, constitutes the essence of defense diplomacy. That dialogue is kept up during peacetime through military cooperation, a foreign army being trained by another, visits or stopovers by the army in a given country, joint military exercises used as learning exchanges to create a climate of mutual awareness and trust between authorities and personnel from two or several armies, and through increasing interpersonal ties between soldiers. To be sure, military aims cannot be excluded from that objective (greater efficiency of joint operations for example), but it remains diplomatic and political, in that it facilitates the use of military channels to establish a dialogue, notably in a crisis.

Thus, during the Arab uprisings in 2011, American soldiers did not fail to notice Tunisian chief of staff General Rachid Ammar's refusal to obey President Ben Ali's orders, turning him into a key actor in the situation (Atkinson 2014, 2). At that specific moment, the past history of personal

---

[2] F. Sanz Roldán, "La diplomacia de defensa: una aproximación desde España," *Revista Arbor*, CLXV (651), 2000: 519–527 cited in Cheyre (2013).

relations between American and Tunisian soldiers (as later between Americans and Egyptians) and prior training of Tunisian soldiers in the United States fostered channels for dialogue that traditional civil diplomatic relations could not explore in the same way. The issue was not reinforcing the Tunisian army, but leveraging contacts with key actors to influence the political situation.

This is indeed the challenge for defense diplomacy: to capitalize on ties woven or made possible by the soldiers' awareness of belonging to the same community—the latter at times depicted, if not as a closed society, then as a highly differentiated environment (Gresles 2003) aware of its specificity (Joana 2012) with its codes and hierarchies—in order to create a special channel for political or diplomatic purposes. With this in mind, while some tools long used in a purely military framework may be reutilized, it is only by being converted to the aims of political convergence. Thus, military cooperation—as conceived by France toward its former colonies, in order to form African armies in the 1960s—has given way to more multilateral security dialogues on the African continent (such as the "G5 Sahel" since 2014), where the accent is on exchanges and shared values. Rather than striving for increased military capacities (formerly, military aid or advisors), defense diplomacy now emphasizes conflict prevention and fostering a culture of stability.

Defense Diplomacy as an Area of Expertise

When military actors share not only the same community (the army) but also training and knowledge of certain specific areas (armaments, strategy, combat techniques), themselves customizable by the armed forces (army, air force, navy), it is possible to enlist the shared codes of a real epistemic community.

By adding arms engineers or civilian defense specialists, defense diplomacy borders on the sectorial (Devin 2002). It can then serve political goals tied to sectors of activity that demand particular technical skills. Two cases are worth mentioning in this regard: the arms industry sector and reforming the security sector.

The arms industry contains an essential goal fraught with economic ramifications for state diplomacy: exporting or importing arms. For the main exporting powers (United States, Russia, China, France, Germany, UK, Spain, Italy), the issue amounts to a specialized kind of foreign trade. For the main purchasing countries (India, Saudi Arabia, United Arab Emirates,

Australia), the expertise is expressed in terms of capability requirements (Sorenson 2008). The choice of materials to purchase, the conditions for the transfer of arms technologies to be exported or imported, and competitive tendering for suppliers all demand expert knowledge of the needs of purchasing countries and of the technologies involved, which soldiers will be using. During the various stages of this import/export process, contacts between soldiers and defense specialists are brought into play to facilitate exchanges, not only as members of the same professional community here but also as experts.

Another specific area: Reforming the security sector (or RSS) has been an important activity since the 1990s (Hills 2000). By providing external training and advice, its goal is to reform third-state institutions tied to security enforcement (armed forces, police, and possibly intelligence services, customs, justice), so as to increase their effectiveness in accordance with democratic principles (transparent operations, parliamentary monitoring, moderate use of force). The role of security actors (soldiers, police) from democratic countries in training their counterparts, less accustomed to these democratic practices, is thus key in this process, even though many private actors (NGOs, think tanks like the center for Democratic Control of Armed Forces [DCAF]—in Geneva) have largely taken up this RSS question. The expertise of security and defense professionals is sought in support of an important political issue: the evolution of foreign security forces toward practices that are more ethical and create less strained relations.

THEORETICAL CHALLENGES: A LIBERAL FOCUS

An academic analysis of these practices spans several key issues in international relations. We will address two of them here: public diplomacy (which may also connect more broadly to the discussion on soft power) and collective security.

Public Diplomacy and Soft Power

If by public diplomacy one means a given state developing initiatives aimed at informing and favorably influencing a foreign public, for the purpose of improving or keeping up the image of its external actions, then defense diplomacy plays a full part in it. It informs communities of specialists and segments of international opinion about a country's defenses and armed forces and promotes the capability of military tools, benefitting the image of diplomacy as a whole.

External operations with a humanitarian or democratic purpose and peacekeeping operations play a key role in this respect. The favorable image of an army, its generals and soldiers, may help a country's reputation and/or government. Examples abound of national armies being showcased and through them a foreign policy shown to be determined in its goodwill. Examples range from the memories of allied troops landing in Normandy in 1944 to images of French President François Hollande given a triumphant reception in Bamako a few months after Operation Serval was launched, pushing back jihadist combatants from Northern Mali. Subsequently, it is up to defense professionals in specific circles to capitalize on the reputational impact thus acquired, to convince others of their country's role in international security. Thus, in June 2013, a meeting was held at the Chinese Ministry of Defense in Beijing between French officers at the Centre for Advanced Military Studies (CHEM) and Chinese officers, designed as an exchange on several subjects, including the success of France's Operation Serval in Mali.

By enabling enough people to intervene so as to exert the most influence and foster mutual understanding between "soldiers," the use of established networks between military personnel also fits into the definition of soft power as summarized by Joseph Nye: "the ability to reach the desired results by developing an agenda of cooperation, persuasion, and attraction" (Nye 2011, 17). This construction is achieved over the long term and can be analyzed on the micro-social level, being the work of individuals (here, the officers). After socialization in temporary collective units (American military schools for instance), they are the ones who, upon returning, transform and socialize approaches, ideas, and norms of broader and now permanent macro-political units: their own countries (Atkinson 2014, 5). Thus, the American State Department stated in 2009 that over 1500 military personnel trained in American military schools occupied national functions of responsibility at the highest level in their country of origin (State Department 2010, 282).

An International Field of Collective Security Established by the Actors Themselves

More generally, the ultimate goals of defense diplomacy partly coincide with the liberal idea of peace and security through dialogue and with the belief according to which the institutionalization of political exchanges applied through a regular framework contributes to stability through cooperation (along with democracy and, for free-market liberals, trade). In this respect, it is assumed that defense professionals who dialogue, exchange with, and know one another will engage in confidence-building together rather than in a dynamic of mistrust generated by compartmentalized military communities, as was the case during the Cold War.

The specificity of defense diplomacy in this regard again lies in the fact that it is driven by defense actors themselves. Whatever brings that community together is therefore encouraged and routinized wherever possible, in order to reproduce opportunities for dialogue at regular intervals, from joint military exercises to international conferences on security. This means soldiers and defense specialists implementing the liberal principle of cooperation and institutionalized dialogue, applied to a community characterized by its own codes. The main goals promulgated in brochures, or work produced by institutional actors and think tanks specializing in security issues, borrow broadly from liberal international relations vocabulary: reducing levels of tension or hostility, confidence-building, transparency of abilities and intentions, transforming cultures and perceptions for the purpose of peace and cooperation, encouraging a dynamic of trust through incentives and rewards, democratic and global responsibility of armies...[3]

The Sociology of Defense Diplomacy in the Twenty-First Century: Is the Concept Finished or Being Transformed?

The concept of defense diplomacy has not escaped criticism, notably on two points: its optimism inherent in the period immediately after the Cold War and its limited use when international tensions upset its good intentions. But its main challenge today comes from the possible relativization of its military specificity. There are two aspects to this change: the dilution of the defense field in the more vast one of "security" and civil actors in diplomacy taking defense activities in hand.

---

[3] A case in point: Centre for Strategic Studies, "Regional Defence Diplomacy: What Is It and What Are Its Limits," *Strategic Background Paper*, 21, Auckland, New Zealand, CSS, 2015.

From Defense to Global Security?

The now frequent embedding of defense within broader security concerns,[4] but also in an international civilian-military strategy devoted to a "global approach" (Wendling 2010), raises the question of military specificity. The fusion between defense, domestic security, intelligence, and diplomacy accelerated after the 9/11 terrorist attacks inaugurated an era characterized by the link between domestic security and the need for external military action. Yet they are different professions with specific cultures and purposes, among which the military profession which, as we have seen, has many unique features (ranging from its non-civilian nature to its specific relationship to death, its ranks, physical training, mastery of certain techniques, career paths, etc.) The question therefore arises of knowing if defense diplomacy is soluble through the action of global security, in other words whether or not the specific contribution to state diplomacy of a channel for dialogue between soldiers can be maintained in this new context.

Rhetoric in the late 2010s alluded to "integrated diplomacy," often inter-ministerial and including a "defense brick." References have been made in the UK to a fusion doctrine expressing *bricks* of expertise, or different areas of ministerial action coalescing around particular themes (cybersecurity for example) or regions of the world, the whole piloted by the Cabinet Office of the National Security Secretariat. The Ministry of Defense, the Home Office, the Department for International Development, the Foreign and Commonwealth Office and others meet regularly over priorities defined, and supervision is attributed to one of the ministries. Within the Ministry of Defense, the Defense Engagement Department (which works hand in hand with the British Military Chief of Staff) is involved in this process. Here, the defense—or military—specificity is expected to be combined with others.

Major international security meetings initiated to bring together civilians and soldiers are another interesting case. As tools of parallel defense and security diplomacy, they assemble a wide range of actors and observers and tend to water down the specific nature of a dialogue among soldiers. From the ADMM (ASEAN Defence Ministers' Meeting, created in 2006)

---

[4] Since 2008, French White Papers on Defense (*Livres blancs français de la défense*) have stressed "defense and national security." Other countries such as the UK have experienced the same evolution.

to the Conference of Central American Armed Forces (CFAC) established in 1997, institutional summits (of NATO for instance) as well as meetings initiated over the years by think tanks (such as the Shangri-La Dialogue in Singapore every year, at the initiative of the International Institute for Strategic Studies in London), these forums are numerous and have a powerful media impact on the international political scene (consider also the annual conferences on security in Munich and Geneva). Some are known as "track 1" meetings, where only official actors are brought in (such as the ASEAN Regional Forum Inter-Sessional Meeting on Maritime Security), and others are "track 1.5," blending official and academic actors (like the Expanded ASEAN Maritime Forum).

Military Diplomacy Without Soldiers?

The concept's ambiguity becomes apparent here: While defense diplomacy is the result of the Ministry of Defense and its different departments playing on the specificity of defense specialist networks, it must nevertheless fit into the broader framework of state foreign policy and its main priorities and guidelines (Cheyre 2013). Whose job is it to reflect upon, supervise, and drive it? On the one hand, the "defense" card would have the optimization of this specific channel of dialogue left up to the military and its common codes. On the other hand, conducting diplomacy requires civilian supervision, through a concern for both coherent action and democratic principles.

In France, for example, military and defense cooperation is under the control of the Department of Military Cooperation and Defense at the Ministry of Foreign Affairs (DCMD), while supervision of bilateral diplomatic defense networks in French embassies falls to the Department of International and Strategic Relations (DGRIS) at the Ministry of Defense, the latter run by a diplomat but with a high concentration of military personnel. As with any similar situation from an organizational sociology standpoint, this configuration may illustrate full complementarity or confusion (Zipper de Fabiani 2002).

A core issue here involves the figure of defense attachés posted to embassies, whose number around the world first rose sharply during the 1990s, then began to shrink in the late 2000s due to budgetary constraints, just when challenges were increasing: reforming the defense and security sector in countries transitioning to democracy, supporting peacekeeping and civil emergency operations, fighting terrorism, etc. Thirdly, increased control of attachés and how their mission, appointment, and administrative performance are defined—by civil rather than military authorities—were set up in certain countries (such as France since the mid-2010s). This raises the question of whether defense diplomacy remains as such when no longer implemented or driven by military personnel.

A defense attaché's role was summarized as follows by a research institute in Geneva (DCAF 2007): (1) representing (and defending) his/her country's military and security interests; (2) representing military authorities and establishing contacts with those in the host country; (3) setting up a security and military policy network also capable of operating during times of friction or restricted bilateral political relations; (4) acting as an advisor to ambassadors and personnel from one's country; (5) observing conditions impacting security in the host country; (6) supervising activities in the area of military assistance, defense diplomacy, and security cooperation; (7) fostering the host country's arms industries; and (8) playing a role in emergency situations and in support efforts when crises arise.

While the defense attaché is a key actor in a defense diplomacy system, he is thus acting both within a specific channel for dialogue and as an expert on technical issues. An affiliation with military or defense spheres (as a weapons engineer for instance) constitutes an added value. Autonomy of action to play this card fully will be a key issue in diplomacy in the coming years.

* * *

Has the concept of defense diplomacy occurred during an interlude at the end of the Cold War that is ending, as multipolar competition and Realpolitik reclaim their place in the international system? Or, on the contrary, does it have a bright future ahead of it, at a time when a new public diplomacy is developing in which it has a definite part to play? After a period of liberal priorities focusing on democratization and reforming the security sector, should we turn defense diplomacy into a diplomacy of global security and far less one of military diplomacy? Is it relevant, given the prospect of a profusion of new conflicts and the extent to which the military balance of power has changed? On the doctrinal and practical levels, as well as on the more academic one of the concept's definition, this has opened a much broader agenda for reflection, which is evolving in ways that are sure to impact international relations practices.

REFERENCES

Aron, Raymond, *Paix et guerre entre les nations*, Paris, Calmann-Lévy, 1962.
Atkinson, Carol, *Military Soft Power: Public Diplomacy Through Military Educational Exchanges*, New York (NY), Rowman & Littlefield, 2014.
Blannin, Patrick, *Defence Diplomacy in the Long War*, Leyde, Martinus Nijhoff, Brill Research Perspectives, 2017.
Cheyre, Juan Emilio, "Defence Diplomacy," in Andrew F. Cooper, Jorge Heine, Ramesh Thakur (eds.), *The Oxford Handbook of Modern Diplomacy*, Oxford, Oxford University Press, 2013.
Cottey, Andrew, Forster, Anthony, "Reshaping Defence Diplomacy: New Roles for Military Cooperation and Assistance," *Adelphi Papers*, 44 (365), 2004: 1–84.
Devin, Guillaume, "Les diplomaties de la politique étrangère," in Frédéric Charillon (ed.), *Politique étrangère. Nouveaux regards*, Paris, Presses de Sciences Po, 2002.
Doise, Jean, Vaïsse, Maurice, *Diplomatie et outil militaire. Politique étrangère de la France (1871–2015)*, Paris, Seuil, 2015.
Geneva Centre for the Democratic Control of Armed Forces (DCAF), "Defence Attachés," DCAF Backgrounder series, July 2007.
Gresles, François, "La 'société militaire': son devenir à la lumière de la professionnalisation," *Revue française de sociologie*, 44 (4), 2003: 777–798.
Hills, Alice, "Defence Diplomacy and Security Sector Reform," *Contemporary Security Policy*, 21 (1), 2000: 46–67.
House of Commons, *The Strategic Defence Review White Paper*, London, House of Commons, 1998.
Joana, Jean, *Les Armées contemporaines*, Paris, Presses de Sciences Po, 2012.
Matsuda, Yasuhiro, "An Essay on China's Military Diplomacy: Examination of Intentions in Foreign Strategy," *NIDS Security Reports*, 7, 2006.
Ministry of Defence, *The Strategic Defence Review: A New Chapter*, London, Ministry of Defence, 2002.
Nye, Joseph, *The Future of Power*, New York (NY), Public Affairs, 2011.
Sorenson, David, *The Process and Politics of Defense Acquisition: A Reference Handbook*, New York (NY), Praeger, 2008.
State Department, *Congressional Budget Justification for Foreign Operations*, Washington (DC), SD, 2010.
Wendling, Cécile, "L'approche globale dans la gestion civilo-militaire des crises: analyse critique et prospective du concept," *Cahiers de l'Irsem*, 6, 2010.
Zipper de Fabiani, Henry, "La 'diplomatie de défense,' composante essentielle de la diplomatie préventive. Vers une nouvelle symbiose entre diplomatie et défense," in Centre Thucydide (ed.), *Annuaire français des relations internationales*, Paris, Bruylant, 2002, pp. 614–629.

CHAPTER 20

Entertainment Diplomacy

Maud Quessard

In January 2017, just as power politics were making a comeback (Mandelbaum 2016), the CSIS (Center for Strategic and International Studies) and the CPD (Center on Public Diplomacy) made public a report on the evolution and role of governmental soft tools ("Public diplomacy and national security in 2017"), stressing the complementarity of initiatives led by private and paragovernmental actors in their missions to strengthen alliances (transgovernmental cooperation) and "fight violent extremism and terrorism." At a time of "strategic chaos" (Hassner 2003) and the growing power of non-governmental actors in the game of international relations, the United States could no longer afford to promote forms of engagement that only fostered interstate relations. It would have to support all initiatives to enhance its image, because the resulting positive impact—whether political or economic—was important for maintaining power. This is not a recent observation; indeed it is characteristic of modern public diplomacy in the twentieth and twenty-first centuries.

The following analysis examines the evolution of foreign policy engagement and more specifically the role and typology of non-state and parastate

M. Quessard (✉)
IRSEM, Paris, France

soft tools characteristic of the twentieth and twenty-first centuries liable to promote national security interests. This analysis focuses on three key concepts in reassessing the relationship between entertainment (as an American cultural phenomenon) and diplomacy: soft power, public diplomacy, and nation branding. In an international context of increasing competition among powers, soft diplomacy fosters pop culture (entertainment, sports, infotainment, national traditions, and celebrities) in order to promote a country's image and highlight foreign policy objectives; in this context, entertainment could therefore be defined as an essential part of any nation's public diplomacy (Burns and Kanji 2016). However, entertainment as a twenty-first-century American cultural phenomenon has emerged as a preferred tool in US nation branding (Anholt 2013), involving all private actors liable to promote the "American brand" image, whereas public diplomacy requires the participation of institutional actors (Melissen 2005, 19).

The evolution in American soft power calls for a historical perspective on interactions between propaganda, public diplomacy and entertainment, leading to a reassessment of the role and power of institutional actors in American diplomacy (White House, State Department, Pentagon) and of private and non-governmental actors, particularly those in charge of promoting a certain idea of the United States and its values, as these actors may play complementary or contradictory roles (as individuals and economic actors). Consequently, it is a reflection not on one but on the many projection(s) of America that have emerged, an America conceived and perceived in an internationalist perspective, no longer as a nation-state but as a network state, a twenty-first-century state (Slaughter 2009) projecting the success of the American model, notably through entertainment and the society of leisure, enabling the pursuit of happiness beyond America's borders; happiness being the fundamental American ethos, an inalienable right asserted in the Declaration of Independence that sees individuals as naturally oriented toward felicity.

The American model of entertainment diplomacy grew out of the privatization of twentieth-century US public diplomacy designed to serve strategies of American influence in all-out warfare or in the Cold War. The end of the American century and increasing competition between powers introduced more explicit qualifiers—competing (Iran, Qatar), emerging (India), emerged (China), or re-emerging (Russia)—to highlight soft power, contributing to the diversification and globalization of forms of entertainment. And yet it is arguable whether the diplomatic and strategic interests of these competing powers as a whole have been fostered in a sustainable way through paradiplomatic strategies for influence, which require mastering issues of reception by the targeted public.

The American Model of Entertainment Diplomacy in the Twentieth Century: The Privatization of Public Diplomacy in the Service of Strategies of Influence

Diplomacy and Entertainment in Wartime(s): The Precedents of the CPI and OWI, American Democracy in Propaganda

In the aftermath of the First World War, Harold Lasswell, a renowned political science professor at Yale, predicted that, given the way governments involved in the twentieth century's first total war had mobilized the masses, propaganda would undoubtedly become one of the characteristic features of modern life. Propaganda was the dawn of a new era, of public relations experts, specialists of psychological warfare, image counselors, and other mentors. These upheavals were part of a revolution in the media and in communications techniques and applications. The concomitance of the First World War and the revolution in international communications indeed transformed international relations and foreign policy practices. Before the conflict, diplomacy was above all considered, particularly by the United States, as the formal relationship between governments. With a few rare exceptions, it was not seen as necessary or appropriate to reach out to the population of another nation outside of official channels.

Exceptions to the rule were necessary when the United States became the preferred target of a propaganda war between the British and Germans, in an attempt to prevent military or financial aid from across the Atlantic going to the adversary. British superiority in terms of communication networks and information warfare gave London a distinct advantage in the fight to win over American public opinion. For Washington, it meant that once American troops joined the conflict, they would have to be capable of competing with British communications media in order to ensure American interests (Taylor 1990).

President Wilson felt that it was necessary to end the control of information by foreign nations, and in particular the Europeans, in order to implement his vision of a new world order based on notions such as democratic governments, free exchange, "open" diplomacy, and collective security.

He had to make communications a national priority, and for that purpose, he encouraged industries in the private sector to improve American power in the areas of telegraph transmission, information services, film production, air transportation, and cable communications (Rosenberg 1982, 79).

Immediately after the United States entered the war, President Wilson created the American government's first official propaganda agency and appointed progressive journalist George Creel to run it. His goal in supporting the war effort was to make the intentions of the United States in the conflict as widely known as possible by using modern information techniques and utilizing propaganda and censorship when necessary. The Committee on Public Information (CPI) quickly became a large organization of twenty units with offices and services spread throughout America and abroad. The CPI employed hundreds of professionals from the worlds of advertising, journalism, and public relations (Creel, *How We Advertised America*, 1920) and was composed of three main services: the Wireless Cable Service (for broadcasting radio messages to friendly countries), the Foreign Press Bureau (for transmitting texts and photographs to the foreign press), and the Foreign Film Division, in charge of circulating the CPI's propaganda films to foreign distributors fond of Hollywood productions, which they would be deprived of if they refused to also distribute George Creel's productions (Green 1988, 13–14).

Despite the CPI's considerable efforts abroad and the positive outcome of the conflict for the Americans, Congress remained highly suspicious of any collusion between George Creel and President Wilson, and once the war was over, it deemed this kind of activity unacceptable in peacetime (Lasswell 1927, 216–217). By eliminating the CPI's financing in 1919, it dismantled what was known by then as the Creel Committee (Mock and Larson 1939, 193) and blocked the creation of any official structure devoted to international information during the entire isolationist period between the wars.

Yet the clear success of propaganda during the conflict had opened the eyes of a class of informed people from all spheres of society on the many possibilities of governing public opinion. During this period, the advertising and public relations professions developed considerably in numerous private sector industries, while real specialists of propaganda emerged from the social sciences and journalism (Bernays 1928, 27). Among them, Walter Lippmann and Edward Bernays, both ex-members of the CPI, may be considered the archetypes of the rise of propaganda in the United States during the period between the wars.

Competition in European Cultural Diplomacy and the Rise of Fascist Propaganda from the Interwar Years to the Second World War

Until the 1930s, Washington was indeed reluctant to provide financial support for cultural activities abroad. The American government preferred to leave the matter of intellectual and educational exchanges to foundations and that of propagating American values to Hollywood. But, faced with the growing influence of clearly anti-American fascist and Nazi propaganda in Argentina, Brazil, and Chile where many Italian and German immigrants were supporters of those regimes, the Roosevelt administration became aware that American security depended on its ability to speak to other nations and gain their support. In Latin America, public and university libraries were brimming with books, magazines, and newspapers from Italy and Germany. America's presence was limited to a few Hollywood films. If the United States wanted to compete in a world where culture was increasingly tied to foreign policy and involved in developing the national image, then Washington had to adopt strategies identical to those of totalitarian states. In 1938, President Roosevelt championed the creation of an Interdepartmental Committee for Scientific Cooperation and a Division of Cultural Cooperation within the State Department; its immediate purpose was to implement the Good Neighbor policy toward Latin America (Pells 1997, 32–33).

The American government was thus the last great power to enter the game of intergovernmental cultural relations, until then the preserve of the private sector due to strong political determination. With the creation of the OWI (Office of War Information) in 1942 modeled on the CPI, the Second World War significantly accelerated this process and demonstrated that the Hollywood cultural industry had become a diplomatic asset for America. Moreover, this vector of influence did not escape the British, who joined Hollywood productions in vaunting the merits of their commitment against fascism (the archetypal film being William Wyler's 1942 *Mrs. Miniver*). Just after the conflict, the Truman government got the IMG (Informational Media Guarantee, 1949) passed by Congress, enabling a wide range of American films to be exported to Europe in support of the Marshall Plan. Hollywood was to become an asset in American Cold War diplomacy (Cull 2008).

Entertainment and Cold War Public Diplomacy: The Hollywood Model Serving American Lobbying Strategies

It was during the 1950s that the culture of entertainment took center stage in strategies to promote the American Cold War model. Contrary to the compartmentalized Soviet communications system, American entertainment knew no borders. President Eisenhower was highly aware of the power of Hollywood images, and collaboration was thus encouraged with certain heads of major studios to foster the production of militant films (NA RG 306, Streibert files, entry 1069, box 29). Early initiatives were indeed run directly by the executive and the State Department via the USIA— United States Information Agency, created by President Dwight Eisenhower in 1953. Drawing on the experience of the Second World War and lobbying strategies implemented at a time of open warfare, the Republican president initiated the first contracts between Hollywood and the federal government. At the time, the special counselor at the USIA for film production (the USIA's chief motion picture consultant) was the famous director Cecil B. DeMille. Between 1953 and 1954, the studios supported President Eisenhower's fight against Communism by producing *Path to Peace* (MGM), *Falcon Dam* (RKO), *Atomic Power for Peace* (Universal), *Life of President Eisenhower* (20th Century Fox), and *The Korea Story* (Warner Bros); Paramount went as far as supporting a film project entitled *The Poles are a Stubborn People*, featuring two Polish survivors of Communism fleeing in search of freedom. American diplomatic services facilitated the diffusion of American films destined in particular for people in Eastern and Western Europe. Subsequently, the US Information Services abroad (USIS) furthered the majors' desire to gain a foothold in North Africa and the Middle East, as well as in Iran, at a time when the United States was worried about the emergence of a pro-Communist nationalist government led by Mohammad Mossadegh (Mingant 2011).

However, despite presidential rhetoric, few Hollywood films truly helped the anti-Communist crusade of freedom policies conducted by official organs of information such as Radio Free Europe, Radio Liberty, and Voice of America. Hollywood entertainment only began to contribute significantly to the gradual Westernization of East European populations after works were commissioned by the Kennedy administration and its attendant mystique and above all when cross-border television and video were developed in the Reagan years. To attract the interest and enthusiasm of people in the East, the State Department and Hollywood united their efforts to produce and diffuse entertainment programming with a message (Snyder 1995). These two Cold War examples from the 1960s and 1980s are key moments when entertainment was used as a tool of American public diplomacy.

Edward Murrow's Public Diplomacy During the 1960s

Under the direction of Edward Murrow, a famous CBS journalist, television and communications professional, the use of films, documentaries, and images in general reached an unprecedented level in the Kennedy administration's public diplomacy activities (NA RG 306, Murrow files, 1962, box 18). No opportunity was missed to expose the most somber aspects of the Soviet adversary's policies to the world, and, conversely, those in charge of public diplomacy had to make sure that the image of the United States abroad was not too damaged, in particular by Hollywood productions. Post-war Europe had indeed been swamped with gangster films from Hollywood. The violence, crime, and corruption featured in such American films projected an image abroad that was incompatible with the USIA's mission, which included promoting the American way of life. To raise awareness about the issue among film industry professionals, Edward Murrow proposed financing documentary theses and films by students from UCLA and USC as of 1961. In exchange for their government-paid training, these students from prestigious film schools in California had to become official filmmakers with the USIA and serve American public diplomacy (NA RG 306, Murrow files, 1962, box 18).

Furthermore, to encourage the production of "quality" films liable to be appreciated and acknowledged by foreign populations, collaboration between the Agency and Hollywood film circles led to the creation of an international film festival in Washington meant to rival Cannes, Venice, and Moscow. It was important not to overlook the influence this kind of event could have, especially to people in Europe. An international film festival in Washington was intended to display the cultural power of the United States (NA RG 306, Murrow files, 1962, box 18).

As a result, the USIA produced a large number of propaganda documentaries commissioned by the White House, the most remarkable being *The Five Cities of June* by Bruce Herschensohn (1963), then the following year, *The March* by James Blue (1964) (Cull 1998). In the early 1960s, the paragovernmental agency indeed poached Hollywood's best documentary filmmakers: Bruce Herschensohn, who created true educational essays on US foreign policy in his films, and the son of one of Hollywood's most well-respected directors, George Stevens Jr., who was head of the USIA Film Department. Operationally, agents in the Film Department in Washington examined and corrected a large number of films and documentary screenplays liable to be distributed abroad. A case in point, the content of films on the issue of civil rights at the time was rigorously scrutinized and perhaps subjected to severe cuts, such as *The Negro American: A Progress Report*, in 1961, where the scenes were cut of the Freedom Riders or the events in Little Rock and Birmingham (NA RG 306, Murrow files, 1962, box 18).

Furthermore, Stanley Kramer's *On the Beach* (1959) and, in a more caustic style, Stanley Kubrick's *Dr. Strangelove* (1963) were part of a dual strategy to make movie-goers in America and across the Atlantic more aware of the dangers of a far greater threat than ideological warfare, that is, the nuclear power possessed by both the United States and the USSR. The films produced only by the USIA were prohibited in America due to their highly controversial nature. Although certain elected officials thought it questionable to deprive the American public of excellent films such as *John F. Kennedy: Years of Lightning, Days of Drums*, most members of Congress believed that official propaganda films, if broadcast in the country, would undermine the foundations of American democracy (Human Events 1965, 6).

But to the astonishment of certain hardened cold warriors, and in a much more prosaic way far from science fiction and political communications, it was representations of the wealth of the American people, and particularly of the "working class," that Communist authorities in the East feared above all. As the director of the MPIC (Motion Picture Industry Council) Eric Johnston recounted, broadcasting an image of a factory parking lot in California or Wisconsin filled with cars belonging to the workers was immediately labeled propaganda. For the Ministers of Culture concerned, there was no question of allowing the Polish or Czech people to believe that a mere worker in America could afford a car (Schweizer 2002, 23).

Jazz music, however, was the real Trojan horse of American entertainment in terms of its impact on Eastern Europeans, notably the Czechs and Slovaks (Von Eschen 2004). President Eisenhower considered jazz to be "America's greatest diplomat," and the best strategy for promoting American culture on the other side of the Iron Curtain was undoubtedly Willis

Conover's jazz program, *Music USA*, broadcast six days a week from Washington (Dizard 1961, 76).

Virtually unknown in the United States, this Voice of America radio host embodied the voice of entertainment from the West in the hearts and minds of thousands of people in the East for over forty years (Heil 2003). The broadcasts, whose precursor in the West was radio officer Sim Copans (Oriano 2001), allowed over thirty million people to enjoy jazz music again after it was banned by Communist regimes until the early 1950s and thus to get to know American culture (Nelson 1997, 197). Moreover, the feeling of transgression experienced by Czech, Hungarian, Rumanian, and Polish youth was all the stronger due to the Communist authorities constantly branding jazz and rock 'n' roll as decadent music leading to the subversive behavior of Western youth who, they said, were getting drunk on Coca-Cola. The people's infatuation can be gauged especially in light of the numerous crowds that gathered in Poland when Willis Conover came in 1959 and in Czechoslovakia at the first jazz festival allowed by the Communist authorities in 1964 (Cull 2008, 139–140).

The Explosion of the Soviet Bloc: The Impact of New Technologies and the Culture of Entertainment

The first major feat in the new era of public diplomacy occurred after the Helsinki Accords, the defining moment of Detente (at the Conference on Security and Cooperation in Europe, held in Helsinki from 1973 to 1975, the United States, USSR, Canada, and Eastern and Western European states reached major agreements promoting cooperation among countries and asserting the obligation to respect human rights and basic freedoms such as freedom of movement). In 1981, the USIA's first satellite broadcast, entitled *Let Poland Be Poland*, was rebroadcast all over Europe including on the other side of the Iron Curtain (thanks to the Worldnet satellite). The televised show, featuring among others Frank Sinatra and Glenda Jackson, was conceived by Charles Wick, a Hollywood producer and friend of President Reagan, and director of the USIA at the time. It was designed to destabilize the Soviets as the strikes orchestrated by the Polish dissident union Solidarnosc were being repressed (ADST, Morand 1994). Wick was firmly convinced that the broadcast was the most spectacular way to condemn the violence in Poland (Tuch 1990, 49).

But this use of entertainment had to fit in with new strategies for liberalizing the Eastern bloc. During the decade following the Helsinki Accords, the United States indeed used entertainment as a weapon, all the less conventional as it was not considered to be potential propaganda (Ellul 1990, 76). It was during this period that those in charge of the USIA's audiovisual media department fostered the creation of video clubs and the circulation of hundreds of (replicable) video cassettes from libraries in Eastern European diplomatic posts. Charles Wick came up with the idea of starting video clubs in the East in 1984, and a catalog of over 250 documentary and fiction films was offered to Eastern European populations. Given the program's huge success, the director of the USIA was convinced that USIS branches could become true centers of entertainment and, with that in mind, saw the contribution of leaders in Hollywood to public diplomacy strategies as a tremendous opportunity. With the open support of President Reagan, he contacted the majors to set up an advisory panel of Hollywood professionals headed by Leo Jaffe, director of Columbia Pictures and one of the most influential figures in Hollywood (RRPL entry 11425 Rusthoven Files 1981–1989). According to accounts by certain diplomats posted abroad, films such as *Kramer vs. Kramer* and *The Texas Chain Saw Massacre* could be seen as credible representations of American life by Eastern Europeans (Snyder 1995, 144–147).

In the USSR, there was widespread smuggling on the black market of American film videos that were hugely successful, such as *Doctor Zhivago*, and especially *Rambo* and *Rocky* (specifically symbolizing the Cold War struggle). But the rise of these clandestine films was a terrific weapon of persuasion for dissident movements. The Polish film *The Interrogation* (Ryszard Bugajski, 1982), censored by the authorities, was picked up by clandestine culture activists and copied hundreds of times. This fictional film illustrates human rights violations in Polish prisons through the suffering of a cabaret actress wrongly imprisoned and interrogated in an attempt to make her accuse one of her friends of treason and espionage. The film had a significant impact on the population and, once censorship was removed, it was awarded many prizes, by the Polish Film Festival (1990), as well as the Cannes and Chicago Film Festivals (1990). The technological revolution of video can be seen as a fundamental vector of liberalization in the East at the time.

But these traditional forms of entertainment liable to reach wide audiences beyond America's borders were followed by other forms and tools characteristic of the twenty-first century that often escaped the control of official diplomacy.

Competing Soft Powers: Diversification and Globalization of Entertainment in the Service of Twenty-First-Century Diplomatic Interests

Entertainment and Celebrity Diplomacy Used for Smart Power Operations: Non-institutional Ambassadors of Nation Branding

Since Daniel Boorstin's early analyses (1961), transdisciplinary work on the role of celebrities in international relations has developed to the point where Celebrity Studies has emerged as a field of study in its own right (Bennett 2010), represented by Andrew Cooper's definitive 2008 reference work, *Celebrity Diplomacy*. When official actors of American diplomacy no longer fulfill their role as ambassadors of exemplary democracy, as was the case for the George W. Bush administration at the time of the Iraq War, and more recently for the Trump administration when it withdrew from the COP 21, Hollywood actors, such as "Brangelina" or Leonardo DiCaprio, may act as ambassadors representing a different image of America. They do so in a private capacity for major international institutions such as the United Nations Organization (UN) and its agency, the United Nations Children's Fund (UNICEF), giving them an official function and an image of safeguarding the values of American exceptionalism. But, as impact assessments and opinion polls have shown, these show business ambassadors use their brand image to serve American interests. They have thus garnered record rates of positive perceptions among foreign populations throughout the world, whatever the context of diplomatic tensions at work involving the United States (Wike et al. 2017).

Conversely, this field of study is a potential provider of expertise for institutional actors, career diplomats, and heads of state to increase their capacity to influence foreign populations and become themselves celebrity diplomats projecting and embodying happiness. Barack Obama was the epitome of this (Kellner 2010), conveying the image of a "cool" president on the cover of major news and entertainment magazines (*Rolling Stone, Time, GQ*), and in the field, there was former American ambassador to Russia Mike McFaul, an ambassador who used social networks and digital diplomacy in the service of freedom of expression, a fundamental component of American happiness and its projection abroad.

Sports Diplomacy, Celebrities, and Anti-diplomats?

At the same time, the globalization of the society of leisure and entertainment has fostered the emergence of another category of entertainment diplomacy, pertaining to the projection and endorsement of a form of success through sports that is different from official delegations. American sports delegations were a mainspring of Cold War public diplomacy. President Nixon's trip to Beijing in 1972 was without a doubt the archetypal example, after the American Ping-Pong team's invitation from the Chinese government a few months earlier in a totally unexpected gesture of opening up dialogue with the United States. This famous example has been frequently highlighted in an attempt to specifically identify the actors of twenty-first-century Ping-Pong diplomacy (Griffin 2014). Notably, the State Department's Bureau of Educational and Cultural Affairs had a special program until the advent of the Trump administration that was devoted to athletic exchanges and promoting American culture through basketball, a "classic" cultural diplomacy program, modernized and adapted for foreign populations and their infatuation with NBA sports stars.

Parallel to these official examples, private ambassadors of a new kind have helped elucidate the limits and excesses of the role of non-governmental actors. The controversial role played by former NBA star Dennis Rodman in North Korea illustrates particularly well the limits of private initiatives in terms of sports and celebrity diplomacy. A great NBA champion, the Chicago Bulls' "Worm" was invited by Kim Jong-un in 2013, when the United States and North Korea had no diplomatic relations. The visit prompted a great deal of criticism, to the point of accusing Dennis Rodman of providing more propaganda for the North Korean regime than for American public diplomacy. All the more so because the meeting had been arranged by private media, in this case HBO and Vice Media, and Dennis Rodman, now notorious for his vehement speech and violent outbursts. In befriending the North Korean dictator, this impromptu ambassador, meant to represent the "magic" of American basketball, appeared to embody the archetype of the anti-diplomat. But ironically, in 2017, through his friendship with President Trump, this unconventional figure unknowingly became the only link between the two adversarial states, although no official dialogue was opened up (Hunter, September 14, 2017).

This confusion of roles and categories, which can lead to a contradiction and obstruction of official diplomatic interests, may also be explained in the twenty-first century by the reappropriation of soft power concepts and practices by powers competing with the United States.

Globalized Entertainment Versus Post-globalization Entertainment: Competing Soft Power Models

Despite the profusion of types of conflict, and of levels and venues of warfare, the twenty-first century also seems to be the century of power rivalries through soft tools, including the most authoritarian states using these tools and assets to reassert the presence of nation-states. Broadening the scope of early definitions by Joseph Nye, a political analyst at Harvard's Belfer Center, powers competing with the United States have increasingly invested in soft power tools over the past decade; the Chinese are unquestionably the best example of this particular interest in aspects of power other than military or economic strength.

Since the early twenty-first century, China has increasingly explored and invested in its soft power. This is evidenced by the growing number of university research centers and think tanks devoted to studying and developing public diplomacy activities on Chinese territory (Xie 2015). Only recently, Joseph Nye questioned any possible comparison between China and the United States in the area of soft power, for three reasons: the Chinese government's over-involvement in instruments of official outside communication such as CCTV, the meager budgets devoted to public and cultural diplomacy compared to the State Department (10 million dollars versus 660 million), and above all the Communist regime's lack of appeal for foreign populations. But these analyses have not taken into account the development of Chinese investments in numerous foreign entertainment activities.

For several years, Chinese entrepreneurs supported by the government have been investing in distribution strategies by breaking into Hollywood companies, following the example of the e-commerce company Alibaba, which acquired a stake in Steven Spielberg's studios, Amblin Partners (ex-DreamWorks), in September 2016. This epiphytic commercial strategy has enabled the Chinese giant to control content (through film coproduction), while giving American studios access to the huge Chinese market which, although highly regulated and censored, remains significant (Xie 2015). However, this commercial investment strategy, to some extent reminiscent of the strategies of major Japanese corporations like Sony during the 1980s, has not considered the need to produce exportable content liable to contribute to Chinese soft power. The most recent effort to produce mainstream Chinese films has mainly targeted the domestic market through attempts to reproduce the codes of Hollywood blockbusters from the 1980s extolling the qualities of their American adversary's B-movie heroes. Thus, for the 90th anniversary of the creation of the People's Liberation Army, Chinese authorities felt that the propaganda film *The Founding of an Army* (July 2017) would arouse enthusiasm in the public comparable to American archetypes like *The Avengers* and *Captain America*. In a total paradox, the American culture of entertainment may have helped promote a propaganda film by the Chinese government to the local population.

Aware of the need to enlist entertainment in enhancing their national brand to foreign populations and powers, other authoritarian states have been quick to invest in a wide range of public diplomacy strategies, often targeted but blurring the lines between broadcasting capacity and the ability to attract and persuade. For most of these regimes, it is a matter of showcasing progress in the modernization of civil society. For their sports diplomacy, the Qataris are banking on Western sports and entertainment such as soccer games and rebroadcasts on cable television channels like BeIn Sport, at times claiming a monopoly on diffusion, and confusing broadcasting capacity and drawing power. As for Russia under Vladimir Putin, contrary to Soviet Russia it has not invested in cultural outreach, which involves "highbrow culture" as well as pop culture and entertainment, preferring news channels such as Sputnik and RT, Russia Today (Audinet 2017), inclined at times to produce a kind of infotainment.

Furthermore, for nations like Qatar and South Korea, the choice of entertainment diplomacy reflects a desire on the part of small states—potentially threatened by their Middle Eastern or Asian neighbors' military might—to exist and assert themselves on the international stage by currying favor with Westerners and absorbing their culture. The economic ripple effects of sports power for Qatar, which purports to be a world capital of sports and soccer, go beyond mere profits linked to broadcasting and retransmission rights for sports events; they also include the possibility of developing infrastructures inside the country and envisaging a post-hydrocarbon economic transition (Boniface et al. 2012). As for South Korea, it has opted for pop cultural diplomacy, fostering a rapprochement with its American ally through pop icons that have adopted and distilled West Coast American cultural codes and above all through its KCON music festival illustrating the Korean wave, which Americans are particularly keen on, to the point of becoming a case study for public diplomacy experts at universities in California (Norman Lear Center 2017).

It should be pointed out that, for these emerging soft powers, the US model is not the only benchmark for public diplomacy blending culture, information, and entertainment. The British model, which often ranks close to the US in terms of soft power (Portland), has continually maintained its drawing power for foreign populations by combining the "highbrow culture" of independent news and entertainment programs on the BBC, as well as pop culture, sports, soccer in particular, and celebrities from pop culture, film, and literature such as Adele and Harry Potter.

In this context of nation-states reasserting themselves through soft power, the current academic debate around American soft power contradicts Joseph Nye's early analyses. The latter viewed the contemporary "American cultural empire"—established in particular by the oligopoly of American cultural industries supplying video games, global stars of pop music, film, and television—as a reassertion of the nation-state and a form of cultural nationalism; the latter would replace the ambitions of liberal internationalists regarding the power of a "twenty-first century state" capable of becoming a "network state" and champion global influence through the various actors and tools of soft power (Mirrelees 2016).

* * *

While entertainment, its practices and actors remain a key asset of American soft power enabling it to maintain its top Portland ranking for influence and cultural diplomacy, it has not been well used as a tool in globalized twenty-first-century showbiz society, a consequence of the digitalization of modes of communication and the resulting balkanization of public opinion at a time when the main content providers (such as Netflix) are increasingly fostering "à la carte entertainment."

And yet, projecting a random image and values could lead in a dystopian way to a kind of balkanization of cultural diplomacy, by advocating happiness or individual satisfaction with no guarantee of wider impact. Assessing the effective degree of influence of these paradiplomatic practices clearly depends on the thorny issue of their reception, a true challenge for the social sciences even in the most accomplished studies such as the Portland ranking.

References

Anholt, Simon, "Beyond the Nation Brand: The Role of Image and Identity in International Relations," *Exchange: The Journal of Public Diplomacy*, 2 (1), 2013: 6–12.

Audinet, Maxime, "La voix de Moscou trouble le concert de l'information internationale," *Le Monde diplomatique*, April 2017.

Bennett, James, "Historicising Celebrity Studies," *Journal of Celebrity Studies*, 1 (3), 2010: 358–359.

Bernays, Edward L., *Propaganda*, New York (NY), Liveright Publishing, 1928.

Boniface, Pascal, Verschuuren, Pim, Billion, Didier, Aby, Romain, "La diplomatie sportive qatarie. Le 'sport power': le sport au service de la reconnaissance internationale du Qatar," *Diplosport*, IRIS/CSFRS, 2012.

Boorstin, Daniel, *The Image or What Happened to the American Dream*, London, Weidenfeld & Nicolson, 1961.

Burns, N., Kanji, L., "Illustrations and Influence: Soft Diplomacy and Nation Branding Through Popular Culture," *Harvard International Review*, 18 April 2016.

Creel, G., *How We Advertised America*, New York (NY), Harper & Brothers, 1920.

Cull, Nicholas J., "Auteurs of Ideology: USIA Documentary Film Propaganda in the Kennedy Era," *Film History*, 10, 1998: 298–310.

———, *The Cold War and the United States Information Agency: American Propaganda and Public Diplomacy (1945–1989)*, Cambridge, Cambridge University Press, 2008.

Dizard, Wilson P., *The Strategy of Truth: The Story of the US Information Service*, Washington (DC), Public Affairs Press, 1961.

Ellul, Jacques, "Les caractères de la propagande," in *Propagandes*, Paris, Économica, 1990.

Green, F., *American Propaganda Abroad*, New York (NY), Hippocrene Book, 1988.

Griffin, Nicholas, *Ping-Pong Diplomacy: Ivor Montagu and the Astonishing Story Behind the Game*, London and New York (NY), Simon & Schuster, 2014.

Hassner, Pierre, *La Terreur et l'Empire, vol. II, La Violence par la paix*, Paris, Seuil, 2003.

Heil, Alan, L., Jr., *Voice of America: A History*, New York (NY), Columbia University Press, 2003.

Hunter, Felt, "How NBA Star Dennis Rodman Came to Stand Between the World and Nuclear War," *The Guardian*, 14 September 2017.

Kellner, Douglas, "Celebrity Diplomacy, Spectacle and Barack Obama," *Journal of Celebrity Studies*, 1 (1), 2010: 121–123.

Lasswell, Harold, *Propaganda Techniques in the World War*, New York (NY), Alfred A. Knopf, 1927.

Mandelbaum, Michael, *Mission Failure: America and the World in the Post Cold War Era*, Oxford, Oxford University Press, 2016.

Melissen, Jan (ed.), *The New Public Diplomacy: Soft Power in International Relations*, New York (NY), Palgrave Macmillan, 2005.

Mingant, Nolwenn, "Hollywood et le Département d'État: une liaison dangereuse?" *Géo-économie*, 58 (3), 2011: 67–73.

Mirrelees, Tanner, *Hearts and Mines: The US Empire's Culture Industry*, Vancouver, Toronto, UBC Press, 2016.

Mock, James R., Larson, Cedric, *Words That Won the War: The Story of the Committee on Public Information* (1917–1919), Princeton (NJ), Princeton University Press, 1939.

Morand, James L., *Interview, Foreign Affairs Oral History Project Information Series*, Arlington (VA), Association for Diplomatic Studies and Training, 9 June 1994, ADST, 1998.

Nelson, Michael, *War of the Black Heavens: The Battles of Western Broadcasting in the Cold War*, Syracuse (NY), Syracuse University Press, 1997.

Norman Lear Center, USC, "The Cultural Diplomacy of KCON," https://learcenter.org/cultural diplomacy kcon, accessed 13 June 2018.

Oriano, Michel, "'Play It Again, Sim': Sim Copans ambassadeur de la musique américaine en France," *Revue française d'études américaines (RFEA)*, Special Issue, 2001: 6–15.

Pells, Richard, *Not Like US: How Europeans Have Loved, Hated and Transformed American Culture Since World War II*, New York (NY), Basic Books, 1997.

Rosenberg, Emily, *Spreading the American Dream: American Economic and Cultural Expansion (1890–1945)*, New York (NY), Hill & Wang, 1982.

Schweizer, Peter, *Reagan's War: The Epic Story of His Forty Years Struggle and First Triumph over Communism*, New York (NY), Doubleday, 2002.

Slaughter, Anne-Marie, "America's Edge: Power in the Networked Century," *Foreign Affairs*, 88 (1), 2009: 94–113.

Snyder, Alvin, *Warriors of Disinformation*, New York (NY), Arcade Publishing, 1995.

Taylor, Philip M., *Munitions of the Mind: War Propaganda from the Ancient World to the Nuclear Age*, Glasgow, Patrick Stephens, 1990.

Tuch, Hans, *Communicating with the World*, New York (NY), St. Martin's Press, 1990.

"USIA: Films for Export Only," *Human Events*, 27 February 1965, p. 6.

Von Eschen, Penny M., *Satchmo Blows Up the World. Jazz Ambassadors Play the Cold War*, London, Harvard University Press, 2004.

Wike, Richard, Stokes, Bruce, Poushter, Jacob, Fetterolf, Janell, "US Image Suffers as Publics Around World Question Trump's Leadership, America Still Wins Praise for Its People, Culture and Civil Liberties," *Pew Research Center*, 2017, pp. 1–108.

Xie, Tao, "China's Soft Power Obsession," *The Diplomat*, 2015: 27–34.

CHAPTER 21

International Expertise and the Diplomacy of Influence

Nicolas Tenzer

International expertise is at the same time one of the least defined and most multiform concepts in international politics. The term is rarely used in official speeches and is often confined to only one of its aspects when employed by administrative structures. As public policy, international expertise lacks substance, unity, and visibility due to having so many different facets. It is above all a means, but in the service of highly dissimilar goals. The strength and relevance of expertise initiatives in various countries are closely linked to the prior assessment of targeted policies.

To summarize the nature of the politics of expertise, it consists in mobilizing experts, national or otherwise, in the service of predefined objectives. These experts wield their influence or undertake specific jobs which, intentionally or not, serve a set of goals linked to a state's foreign policy in all its dimensions. Expertise is the primary aspect of diplomatic influence and counterinfluence and one of the main components of economic diplomacy.

N. Tenzer (✉)
PSIA (Sciences Po), Paris, France
e-mail: nicolas.tenzer@wanadoo.fr

© The Author(s) 2020
T. Balzacq et al. (eds.), *Global Diplomacy*,
The Sciences Po Series in International Relations and Political Economy, https://doi.org/10.1007/978-3-030-28786-3_21

Anatomy of International Expertise

International expertise covers five main dimensions that are only rarely perceived as a whole and even more rarely coordinated. The scale on which they are implemented depends on what priorities the state has assigned itself and how serious it is about its soft power. These modalities may be immaterial or material in nature, but their success depends on the quality and strength of the infrastructure supporting them.

The first kind of action pertains to what is generally known as international technical expertise. Multilateral institutions (the European Union, the World Bank, the United Nations Development Programme, etc.), states (notably major emerging countries and those with raw material resources), important local and regional authorities, and certain large NGOs solicit international bids relating to expertise. They cover a wide range of areas, from urban planning and public safety, justice and health, government reform and democracy assistance to academic development, and the fight against climate change. Public, private, and academic organizations may respond to bids, and experts employed within this framework also involve highly varied professions, levels, and affiliations, from hydraulics technicians all the way to Nobel Prize-winning economists, from policemen and soldiers up to judges, from doctors specialized in tropical diseases to experts in local finances. Theoretically, these bids for expertise, estimated at around 100 billion euros per year, have an indirect impact on future works and supply contracts, even though in legal terms the entities involved must be different.

The second kind of action is tied to strategies in international organizations, covering several aspects. First, most of these institutions assemble committees of experts who help to strategize or provide opinions on technical issues. They then convene regular conferences to supply ideas the organizations may adopt. They also recruit experts who help determine action plans and the terms of reference for bids, at headquarters or in their delegations. Finally, these organizations use work carried out by experts elsewhere, in particular in think tanks and universities, not to mention action by experts in lobbying firms who sometimes introduce their ideas covertly.

The third kind of action involves an exchange of ideas. Particularly in the area of state security and foreign strategy, it is largely produced by think tanks and certain world-class universities, mainly in English. Although there is a certain gap between intellectual output and state action, the expertise is often relayed by the specialized and global press, providing food for thought to the advisors of those in power. Taking part in this work, either as an expert of such bodies or as a debater during conferences, has become a prerequisite to having one's voice heard. While most experts are independent from governments, their action contributes to a country's global advocacy and image.

A fourth type of action involves diplomatic strategies. The latter always come from key elements—notably in terms of values—defined by the head of the executive. Experts play a major role in applying them—negotiating positions, analyzing indirect effects, modifying the balance of power, allotting respective shares to bilateral and multilateral, etc.—that can lead to inflection points, as well as to influence regarding "talking points" to be dissected by diplomatic chancelleries. This expertise is also crucial in assessing how negotiating parties, whether allies or adversaries, will react. Consequently, it involves not only foreign policy, but also the sociological and psychological elements that structure the parties' positions. At the assessment and decision-making stages, the expertise may result in influencing leaders, who must often rely on their intuition to distinguish truth from fallacy and determine the certitude of a hypothesis.

A fifth type of action is necessary in a response initiative, on both economic and strategic levels. In itself, disinformation is nothing new: Fake news has long been used in diplomacy and in war. But it has acquired an unprecedented dimension with the diffusion of mass media and social networks. With economic actions, companies are thwarted in their development by rumors spread about the quality of their products or the way they were made. In the diplomatic arena, manipulation of information is a distinct tool, either for trying to prove to opinion leaders or the general public that their cause is just and that their adversary is indefensible, or to anesthetize public opinion about the true dangers. Expertise then consists in proving the falsehood of the news circulated and in making that widely known. It is a rectification of facts to demonstrate the truth. This work may be carried out by journalists, particularly investigative journalists, as well as by government experts. It is all the more necessary due to hostile countries often having facilitators in target countries, in academic spheres, think tanks, and among top social networkers, as well as in political circles.

A priori, international expertise is a broad and infinitely diverse notion in view of the tasks it implies, the skills it requires, the organizations it involves, and the objectives governing it. At the same time, expertise manifests necessary continua when the concept is approached with the aim of taking action or simply of building public policy: a continuum between an expert in the field in environmental engineering and an expert writing an article on good practices in that field in an international journal; the continuum between a police officer training forces in a country emerging from a dictatorship, or a journalist training others in countries where freedom of the press has long been muzzled, and human rights action in international arenas; lastly, a continuum between an expert in nuclear strategy in a think tank and a government consultant negotiating an agreement with Iran or defining positions on North Korea.

In every instance, promoting expertise means that prior definition of international priorities has clearly been undertaken and that the government—as well as private and academic actors—is willing to devote the means required and to be united in its intentions.

Expertise and the Coordination Challenge

Three patterns emerge for anyone following expertise on a global level, if confining it to states with the means and will to carry out their intentions, although none of the countries ticks off all the boxes for promoting expertise in all its aspects.

A first category includes offensive/proactive countries. These countries have not only become aware of the political, economic, and intellectual need for an influence and self-promotion strategy, but have also made sure they have the means to do so. Due to its power, the United States is the champion across the board, despite not having a comprehensive plan or fully developed strategy. Its action is the work of think tanks that have international networks and invite foreign experts who may form the future elite in certain countries, thus guaranteeing strong ties. Major universities sometimes act according to the same model. Several large American corporations, in particular in the area of consulting and auditing, bid on international contracts and advise foreign governments and certain multilateral organizations, not to mention the corporations themselves. Foundations for humanitarian work (the Bill and Melinda Gates Foundation, the Clinton Foundation) and advocacy (the different organizations under the umbrella of the National Endowment for Democracy—NED) have a real influence in the area of development aid and democracy assistance. The same is true for the United States Agency for International Development (USAID) and the Millennium Challenge Corporation (MCC). In the field of legal lobbying, the American Bar Association's power in international legal negotiations is beyond compare. The myth about a plan to "conquer" the world can be dismissed in light of an absence of overall coordination and the variety of orientations in these different organizations, but given its might, the all-out deployment of these various American bodies has unquestionable drawing power.

The case of Germany is the second example of an extensive network of expertise. Although it cannot boast the global scope of the United States, particularly in the area of security and international affairs, it makes use of two unique tools on that scale. The first is the presence of an exceptional network of technical experts, broadly unified by the Gesellschaft für internationale Zusammenarbeit (GIZ), and supplementary funding provided far beyond developing countries under the authority of the Kreditanstalt für Wiederaufbau (KFW). The second instrument is composed of the six German political foundations that engage in lobbying, notably by training future elites in nearly all areas around the world. Coordination in the field between government services and representatives from economic spheres is constant, in particular for invitations to tender and advance advice from regional representatives of international organizations. Finally, German industrialists and state bodies have not balked at spending considerable amounts on donations to illustrate the excellence of their expertise.

The UK is the third example of a proactive approach in this area. More discreet, but present in a wide range of fields of expertise, from the exchange of ideas to a subtle strategy to have experts appointed in key positions in international organizations, as well as lobbying and developing networks of experts. To date, even in periods of budget restrictions, the Department for International Development (DFID) has never experienced severe cuts. There is no strict coordination as such between different actors, but on the one hand, there is a broad flow of information, and on the other hand, UK involvement in global affairs has produced a kind of shared mind-set.

A second category is composed of the new conquerors. Without having the force of action of the three previous countries, Japan, Canada, Italy, and increasingly Korea have developed coherent and effective diplomatic expertise and lobbying. Japan, in particular, has defined priority territories for its expertise for over two decades largely tied to its economic interests, reaching beyond the region of Asia and Africa, and involving parts of Europe and Latin America. Security aspects are not foremost in Tokyo's mind, but the desire to counterbalance Chinese power is not foreign to it. Japan has also invested significantly in the exchange of ideas, notably on issues linked to development and technological and social transformations. As for China, while it has developed an ambitious strategy for being present in all markets, its regime undoubtedly prohibits it from being as active in creating concepts; and Chinese soft power is still struggling to find takers, with the possible exception of the Belt and Road Initiative. Over the next decade, India and Turkey, already on the offensive in third-country markets, should develop more thorough tools for intervening. Sweden also has policies that are highly targeted geographically, but effective and values-based.

A third category is made up of the hesitant. These are potential regional powers that have begun to explore expertise markets and tried to sell their image: Morocco, Brazil, or even Senegal. It is the case for France which, on the one hand, has the world's third largest diplomatic network and exceptional diplomatic status and has shown its ability to undertake diplomatic initiatives on a worldwide scale (notably the Paris Agreement), but, on the other hand, it remains disproportionately weak compared to equivalent countries in the exchange of ideas and on strategic issues, does not have a tool for expertise of sufficient scope, has not defined a plan of action per country, field, or area, and struggles to unify the efforts of public, private, and academic spheres. France is an example of a country where insufficient budget investment, both private and public, has affected the impact of its economic assets.

Conditions for a Global Influence Strategy

Theoretically, developing expertise all over and in multiple fields is the prerequisite for lobbying strategies. There is a continuum between intellectual and academic expertise applied to strategic and technical issues and its market development.

An influence strategy must focus on four aspects: time frame, strategic purpose, targets, and actors. These aspects are valid both for winning over markets involving technical expertise and for international politics, which often demands implementing initiatives to convince upstream.

Influence and advocacy initiatives may take place over three time frames: short-, medium- and long-term. Their success depends on how the three temporalities are structured and in particular the latter. Without any long-term in-depth policy, short- and medium-term lobbying runs the risk of being imperfect. This is true in the economic arena, through the use of image strategies, for companies as well as for countries with their internal and external components, and experts in the field with no guarantee of an immediate return; as well as in intellectual spheres, where building up the credibility of a university or think tank takes time; and in diplomatic circles, by creating advance messages and endeavors to convince opinion leaders and the wider public. The final stages in trade or diplomatic negotiations are far easier when the groundwork has been laid.

The second aspect is strategy, also on the economic, intellectual, and diplomatic levels. If not guided by specific goals—the opposite of indiscriminate "outreach"—influence policies are bound to fail. Deploying experts without a critical mass or prioritization leads to limited and unsustainable results. Those in charge of influence policies must therefore specify their goals, define targets, and set up human and financial resources in advance. All too often, lobbying initiatives lack this kind of strategic professionalism.

Third, it is important to define "targets" within the framework of this strategic thinking. After asking the question, "lobbying for what purpose?" comes that of "lobbying whom?" While lobbying was once aimed mainly at diplomatic chancelleries and political actors liable to relay state policies or private interests, it now involves more numerous and diverse categories that all require specific modes of action: opinion leaders, corporate executives, academics, members of think tanks, officials of international organizations, political parties, unions, NGOs, journalists, and even the broader public. To say nothing of the illegal means (corruption) employed by some states, policy tools have also become highly varied: articles in the international and specialized press, direct contacts with "targets," lobbying, massive presence on social networks, interventions during international and regional conferences, advance lobbying of international organizations (helping to define priorities and international invitations to tender), as well as grants for talented students from target countries, visits by academics and opinion leaders, in-kind equipment donations, etc. These initiatives require adapting one's stance toward targets.

Finally, influencers have evolved in a fashion largely analogous to their targets. Embassies and business executives must find facilitators among experts in the field, NGOs, academics, journalists, professional and union organizations, bloggers, key figures on social networks, etc. All these actors must be expanded upon in all places of potential influence, and while each must retain his own freedom and ethical code, a form of flexible coordination must be developed. Countries that have implemented successful lobbying strategies and established influential expertise on all levels are the ones where all these stakeholders are working more or less in the same direction.

Expertise to Counter Disinformation

The last aspect of expertise, whether strategic or economic, is counterattack. It requires identifying in advance possible threats and modes of action used by adversaries, in particular regarding disinformation, but also preparing the conditions for a counteroffensive, by nature a form of expertise that requires influence to make its full impact felt. Threats linked to disinformation have a triple impact that is economic, intellectual, and strategic.

On the economic level, many companies have been victims of competitors with varying degrees of honesty that have tried to undermine their reputation and cast doubt on the services they provide. To be sure, certain denunciations appear to be fully justified when proven: toxic products, defective services, various violations of the law including social and environmental standards, or indulging dictatorial countries and even terrorist groups. Others, however, involve disinformation: false accusations to international organizations of supposedly illegal practices in order to have them removed from short-lists or authorized bidders, media campaigns, rumors spread on social networks, etc. Counterattack involves constant vigilance and, if necessary, legal action and various means of crisis communication, as well as expertise initiatives. Targeted companies must not only defend the incriminated products and services, but also develop lobbying strategies toward decision-makers and the wider public. Here too, advance lobbying and communications strategies may render disinformation maneuvers less invasive.

On an intellectual level, disinformation strategies by states have several aspects, notably false information about a country, fake news, covering up embarrassing realities, false historical "narratives" aimed at concealing the truth, relativizing, as well as offensives against rival nations with the intention of discrediting or defaming them. These actions are relayed by opinion leaders, politicians, intellectuals and journalists, and naturally in social media that may target gullible populations receptive to propaganda themes. The rhetorical techniques used in this kind of propaganda have also been well documented: *whataboutism* (denunciation that immediately triggers an opposing denunciation in order to produce a relativizing effect), putting forward themes that can lead to undermining a national consensus, economic arguments (notably for countries under a regime of sanctions), playing on sentiments, and narratives often summarized by "after-the-fact" expressions and alternative facts. Here too, counteroffensives have borrowed from expertise and lobbying: correcting lies, notably historical ones, proof supported by facts, revealing offenses committed by criminal states, or supporting such groups. Due to the weakened credibility of official rhetoric, this counteroffensive requires the mobilization of intellectuals and journalists specialized in tracking down false information and a massive presence on social networks. It means exposing or even investigating bodies and people that relay propaganda and, if there is free speech, disclosing their affiliation. While some in the press, academic circles and think tanks have started putting such tools in place in addition to cybersecurity, democratic states are often still stalling, reflecting a lack of resolution on their part regarding the actions of undemocratic nations.

Finally, on a strategic level, the response must employ the intellectual tools alluded to earlier. It also means explaining the arguments underlying our positions and alliances, having an increased presence internationally and domestically, and connecting geopolitical vision and values. Just as technical expertise is not neutral in terms of principles—it may or may not foster development, respect for environmental and social standards, good governance, and preeminence of the rule of law—our foreign and even military policies remain founded on principles that propaganda initiatives strive to undermine, if not discredit. Perhaps the ultimate meaning of expertise and the legitimization of lobbying can be found here: connecting action to rules that we impose on ourselves because we consider them to be good

CHAPTER 22

Conclusion: Drowning Diplomats

Frédéric Ramel, Thierry Balzacq and Frédéric Charillon

"Being educated and intelligent, knowing about Negotiations and treaties, Writing and keeping one's master well informed" (Danès 1914–1915, 608). In the eyes of Pierre Danès, Bishop of Lavaur and Francis I's ambassador to the Council of Trent in 1542, these were the abilities required of posted diplomats. In his *Conseils à un ambassadeur* published in 1561, he associated each of them with specific qualities: "diligence and dexterity," "prudence and candor," "judgment and knowledge." His *Conseils* were admired by the poet Ronsard, proof that literary style was an integral aspect of the diplomatic profession. The book is part of a series of treatises (*trattatistica*) devoted to ambassadors and the art of negotiating, starting with Bernard de Rosier's *Ambaxiatorum brevilogus* (1436). They came under a

F. Ramel (✉) · T. Balzacq
Sciences Po, Paris, France
e-mail: frederic.ramel@sciencespo.fr

T. Balzacq
e-mail: thierry.balzacq@sciencespo.fr

F. Charillon
University of Clermont Auvergne, Clermont-Ferrand, France

© The Author(s) 2020
T. Balzacq et al. (eds.), *Global Diplomacy*,
The Sciences Po Series in International Relations and Political
Economy, https://doi.org/10.1007/978-3-030-28786-3_22

new genre that ranged from modalities of the right of ambassadorial representation to instructions on behavior (Andretta et al. 2015). Theoreticians and practitioners in Europe became interested in diplomacy later than those from non-Western traditions, particularly in the Iranian and Arab worlds. The latter drew on the *Secretum Secretorum*, a text with advice formulated by Aristotle when he was tutor to Alexander the Great, including several passages that already provided a set of recommendations regarding the use of messengers abroad, such as ensuring their loyalty and their sobriety with respect to alcohol. But his *Conseils* and treatises published in the fifteenth and sixteenth centuries[1] remain embedded in a modern concept of diplomacy conceived as a practice reserved for representatives of the state. The latter was not based solely on a monopoly of legitimate physical coercion. It involved both confiscating and concentrating the means allocated for conducting foreign affairs. Aron crystallized this idea by making diplomats, along with soldiers, one of two symbolic figures in international relations, both employed by the state.

Yet this way of seeing diplomatic activity deserves consideration, regarding both past configurations and especially the present context. In this respect, current diplomatic reconfigurations extend well beyond bureaucratic transformations impacted by new public management. They involve equally the instrument—no longer restricted to ministries of foreign affairs—and the increasingly competitive environment in which diplomats move. The chapters in this textbook examine the state monopoly on diplomatic activity. States, their embassy staffs and delegations have become diplomatic actors among many others. This transformed international arena means that functions involving information, negotiation, and nowadays even representation are no longer completely appropriated by state actors. This is evident in expressions such as plural diplomacy (Cornago 2013) and polylateralism (Wiseman 2010).

The three parts of the textbook detail all these reconfigurations, respectively, describing what can be summarized as the 3 Ds of contemporary diplomacy:

---

[1] From the late Middle Ages, although *Mirrors for Princes*—aimed at clarifying the function of rulers—remained silent as to diplomacy, some writings based on diplomatic experiences began to show a growing interest in external affairs. Between 1250 and 1440, "in Portugal as well as in Castille, France, the crown of Aragon and the Empire, under diverse formulations, loyalty, dedication, discernment and knowledge of the resulting effective *manners* are recurring demands, which must guarantee the proper execution of the assigned mandate, for the benefit, honor and utility of the prince represented" (Péquignot 2015, 110).

- the development of new diplomatic frameworks (part one);
- the increasing diversity of diplomatic participants (part two); and
- the growing density of diplomatic subject matter (part three).

However, these three processes are not totally unprecedented in the history of diplomacy, particularly the first two (Moeglin and Péquignot 2017). Venues for developing diplomatic relations have never been restricted to official visible settings. Informal meetings also play an important part in diplomatic relations. As for the formats in which the latter occur, they were already numerous in the nineteenth century, including group or club diplomacy such as the Concert of Europe established in 1815 in Vienna. Regarding the plurality of actors, it is also evident over the long term. Admittedly, states drew on a monopolization of diplomatic activity beginning in the Renaissance thanks to the transfer of innovations from city-states on the Italian Peninsula starting in the fifteenth century, particularly after permanent embassies were introduced. Nevertheless, other actors also became involved in interstate relations, whether it was trading companies, churches, or political parties.

Two new elements have arisen however. The first lies in the densification process due to the increased technicization and sophistication of diplomatic discussions. Subjects extend far beyond the stakes of high politics, that is to say those of war and peace among states. Economic, financial, trade, ecological, and cultural issues are also objects of bilateral and multilateral negotiations. They require a particularly astute understanding of both the positions championed by interlocutors, and scientific and expert interpretations in the fields involved. The second new element stems not only from the overlapping of the three processes but also their intensification. The development of new frameworks, diversity of participants and density of subject matter have created new pressure on state actors and more generally on how the state conducts diplomacy. Steeped in the "chancellery spirit," career diplomats must show unfailing loyalty to the governments they serve. The literary figure of the Marquis de Norpois imagined by Marcel Proust in *In Search of Lost Time* is frequently cited in describing these character traits: conservative, a master in the art of entertaining and conversing, while remaining concerned with the "constant interests" of the state. Such a description might evoke someone living the "high life" (Delcorde 2014, 51) in gilded reception rooms. Nothing could be further from the truth because diplomacy does not take place *In the shadow of young girls in flower* but in fact during crises and armed conflicts. The pressure exerted by the three processes highlighted above results in major tensions and a compelling need for diplomatic action by governments.

The main tension lies between the practice of secrecy (or discretion) and a concern for transparency regarding "public opinion." In crisis and conflict management, contacts with key players often benefit from an absence of official communications. Remaining in the shadows is thus an asset. At the same time, no chancellery can afford to obscure public diplomacy or the dissemination of official positions, whatever the international arena concerned. The French graphic novel *Quai d'Orsay* (Blain and Lanzac 2010) is a perfect illustration of this tension. While Minister of Foreign Affairs Alexandre Taillard de Worms, obsessed with explaining relations to the broader public, practices his Security Council speech with tremendous theatrics, his chief of staff asks not to be disturbed for an hour in order to find a solution to a major international crisis. Moving silently and with great economy of gesture, he makes use of a safe full of secret defense documents and a secure telephone line to connect with people abroad.

The compelling need is none other than the coordination efforts incumbent on ministries of foreign affairs (Hocking 1999). Such efforts are not limited to inter-ministerial cooperation objectives, which are central in times of crisis when one must intervene abroad, striving to turn the ministry into a flagship sailing through global turmoil. Diplomats provide substance to government orientations in all kinds of negotiations and existing diplomatic frameworks. Their primary function today consists in making positions coherent, either to reassure an ally, to inform a partner, or to clarify the interpretation of a legal text during negotiations. But with this type of configuration, such coordination is a highly perilous exercise. State diplomacy has proven increasingly delicate as it is beset by exceptionally intense challenges, which all have the particularity of highlighting an exposure to deficiencies and even to a total absence:

– *Diplomacy without a pilot?* The development of sectorial diplomacy sometimes leads to self-determination with respect to general foreign policy goals. This trend is due to the limits of coordination between ministries of foreign affairs facing "the internationalization of *domestic* bureaucracies" (Karvonen and Sundelius 1987). It also arises from entangled negotiating forums, which challenge the coherence of state positions in a given field.

- *Diplomacy without policies?* As a result of social norm entrepreneurs and their ever-increasing formal and editorial participation in diplomatic negotiations, the degree of freedom enjoyed by states is being redefined. Choices are made under the observation and even the constraint of these actors, who aim to confer their way of conceiving of the milieu's interests beyond those of states.
- *Diplomacy without prospects?* State leaders are subject to the dictatorship of immediacy that forces them to react quickly to emergencies, crises, and unanticipated events. This struggle to frame diplomatic action in the long-term also comes from the effects of electoral agendas. A potential beating at the ballot box then acts as a specter that dissuades political actors from formulating their objectives over the long term.
- *Diplomacy without diplomats?* The dwindling role of ambassadors is not only the result of increasing competition from new participants in civil society (from international nonprofits to multinational corporations), whether they are acting for their own sake (as with business and corporate diplomacy) or engaging in pre-diplomatic initiatives from which states may benefit in the shorter or longer term. Including or recruiting individuals from the private or nonprofit sectors within diplomatic administrations challenges the singularity of diplomatic practices, and thus the preservation of a specific state activity with diplomats specially trained for that function.
- *Diplomacy with no impact?* Diplomacy has undeniably impacted the very structure of the international order as an activity shared by its members (this is one of the major theories of the English school of international relations). This structure is not limited to the politico-strategic sphere through peace negotiations. It is also present in other areas ranging from the environment and trade to establishing cultural arenas for example (Ramel and Prévost-Thomas 2018). That effectiveness is being questioned today with regard to any number of issues, from wars that break out or continue to environmental degradation.

Over and above these challenges stemming from diplomatic practices, there is a specter haunting international relations—the end of diplomacy itself. Several contemporary phenomena, not necessarily connected through any explanation or manifestation, have altered diplomatic activity. From populist temptations to expressions of nationalism (Badie and Foucher 2017), from Brexit to Donald Trump's election, it is the very institution of diplomacy that is vacillating. We are in the throes of disintermediation (Cooper 2017), that is to say the opposite of diplomacy conceived as a network of ties between political actors, which has brought anti-diplomatic movements to the surface: challenging and insulting diplomatic personnel within governments themselves, the presence of powerful figures in media spheres acting in their own name, the failure of certain state leaders to perform customary diplomatic practices, and the violation of the bodily integrity of diplomats through assassinations. Is it not the "*raison de système*," which is contrary to the *raison d'État* and recognizes diplomacy as the "ultimate goal of any international society of independent states" (Watson 1984, 203), that is being challenged? Have we now gone beyond the counterrevolutionary phase of diplomacy as described by G. R. Berridge (2011)?[2]

Nevertheless, this pessimistic scenario of the end of diplomacy does not call into question certain invariables in how diplomacy is conducted, since the latter transcends the categories of actors involved, from agents employed by the state to experts in non-governmental organizations and heads of corporations. Beyond representational procedures, methods of communication and conflict-management tools (Bjola and Kornprobst 2013), diplomacy as a practice involves three cumulative arts: adjustment, recognition, and listening.

In 1953, before members of the Foreign Policy Association, United Nations Secretary-General Dag Hammarskjöld stressed that technique must always be adjusted to fit diplomacy. To a certain extent, doing so corresponds to "the real substance of diplomacy" according to him (Hammarskjöld 1953). The adjustment is multiple. It is not restricted to identifying resources made available to diplomats. It also involves relevance to the world they operate in. In that respect, contemporary adjustment entails the reasoned and reasonable use of social networks. Digital diplomacy (Bjola and Holmes 2015) is a necessity for all participants.

The practice of diplomacy also involves the art of recognition. This characteristic resonates with "what makes diplomacy." For Rebecca Adler-Niessen, it is about relationalism (Adler-Nissen 2015). For James der Derian, it is about estrangement, namely reconciling separation (Der

---

[2] Berridge perceives three major periods in the modern history of international relations: old diplomacy founded on secrecy, the new diplomacy that Wilson called for after the First World War, based on intergovernmental organizations and transparency, and counterrevolutionary diplomacy since 1960, whose distinctive feature is a partial return to the old diplomacy.

Derian 1987). These two ways of viewing diplomacy clearly show that it lies first and foremost in recognizing alterity. Diplomacy consists in creating ties with another who may prove to be very different and distant in terms of values. Accepting that alterity and engaging in communication with it are the necessary basis for all diplomacy.

As Holbein's famous painting *The Ambassadors* (1533) shows, diplomacy involves astute observation, since key information is often hidden. Knowing how to see from another perspective (*da dicosto* as suggested by Machiavelli and Guicciardini) proves to be fundamental.[3] Training them how to look is thus a necessity. But there is another quality that should not be overlooked in diplomacy: the art of listening. As a Japanese diplomat once emphasized in a rather radical but no less significant way: a diplomat "must use his ears rather than his mouth" (quoted in Freeman 1994, 117). Diplomacy is thus not merely an oratory art founded on the authority of speech. In reference to the semantic origin that Robert de Rosier attributes to the word "ambassador," whose task is to clear up ambiguities (*ambigua*) in order to achieve peace, it would seem that one of the main sources of discernment in diplomacy involves being a good listener.

References

Adler-Nissen, Rebecca, "Relationalism or Why Diplomats Find International Theory Strange," in Ole J. Sending, Vincent Pouliot, Iver B. Neumann (eds.), *Diplomacy and the Making of World Politics*, Cambridge, Cambridge University Press, 2015, pp. 284–308.
Andretta, Stefano, Péquignot, Stéphane, Waquet, Jean-Claude (eds.), *De l'ambassadeur. Les écrits relatifs à l'ambassadeur et à l'art de négocier du Moyen Âge au début du XIXe siècle*, Rome, Collection de l'École française de Rome, 2015.
Badie, Bertrand, Foucher, Michel, *Vers un monde néo-national?* Paris, CNRS, 2017.
Berridge, Geoffrey R., *The Counter-Revolution in Diplomacy and Other Essays*, New York (NY), Palgrave Macmillan, 2011.
Bjola, Corneliu, Kornprobst, Markus, *Understanding International Diplomacy: Theory, Practice and Ethics*, London, Routledge, 2013.
Bjola, Corneliu, Holmes, Marcus (eds.), *Digital Diplomacy: Theory and Practice*, London, Routledge, 2015.
Blain, Christophe, Lanzac, Abel, *Quai d'Orsay*, Paris, Dargaud, 2010.

---

[3] Only after moving around and looking at the painting "from another perspective" does the observer see the human skull drawn on the ground as an anamorphosis.

Cooper, Andrew F., *The Disintermediation Dilemma and Its Impact on Diplomacy*, Project "Diplomacy in the 21st Century," Stiftung Wissenschaft und Politik (SWP)/German Institute for International and Security Affairs, 2017.

Cornago, Noé, *Plural Diplomacies: Normative Predicaments and Functional Imperatives*, Leiden and Boston, Martinus Nijhoff Publishers, 2013.

Danès, Pierre, "Conseils à un ambassadeur," *Revue d'histoire diplomatique*, 28–29 [1561] 1914–1915: 607–612.

Delcorde, Raoul, "L'évolution du métier de diplomate," in Tanguy de Wilde d'Estmael, Michel Liégeois, Raoul Delcorde (eds.), *La Diplomatie au cœur des turbulences internationales*, Louvain, Presses de l'UCL, 2014, pp. 41–54.

Der Derian, James, "Mediating Estrangement: A Theory of Diplomacy," *Review of International Studies*, 13 (2), 1987: 91–110.

Freeman, Chas W., Jr, *The Diplomat's Dictionary*, Institute for National Strategic Studies, Washington (DC), National Defense University Press, 1994.

Hammarskjöld, Dag, "Address by the Secretary General, Foreign Policy Association," Press Release SG/344, 21 October 1953.

Hocking, Brian, *Foreign Ministries: Change and Adaptation*, New York (NY), Palgrave Macmillan, 1999.

Karvonen, Lauri, Sundelius, Bengt, *Internationalization and Foreign Policy Management*, Gower, Aldershot, 1987.

Moeglin, Jean-Marie, Péquignot, Stéphane, *Diplomatie et 'relations internationales' au Moyen Âge (IXe-XVe siècle)*, Paris, Presses universitaires de France, 2017.

Péquignot, Stéphane, "Figure et normes de comportement des ambassadeurs dans les documents de la pratique. Un essai d'approche comparative (Ca. 1250–Ca. 1440)," in Stefano Andretta, Stéphane Péquignot, Jean-Claude Waquet (eds.), *De l'ambassadeur. Les écrits relatifs à l'ambassadeur et à l'art de négocier du Moyen Âge au début du XIXe siècle*, Rome, École française de Rome, 2015, pp. 87–111.

Ramel, Frédéric, Prévost-Thomas, Cécile, *International Relations, Music and Diplomacy*, New York (NY), Palgrave Macmillan, 2018.

Watson, Adam, *Diplomacy: The Dialogue Between States*, London, Eyre Methuen, 1984.

Wiseman, Geoffrey, "'Polylateralism': Diplomacy's Third Dimension," *Public Diplomacy Magazine*, 4, 2010: 24–39.

Correction to: Global Diplomacy

Thierry Balzacq, Frédéric Charillon and Frédéric Ramel

Correction to:
T. Balzacq et al. (eds.), *Global Diplomacy*, The Sciences Po Series in International Relations and Political Economy, https://doi.org/10.1007/978-3-030-28786-3

The original version of the book was inadvertently published without the translation copyright statement. This has now been updated in the copyright page of the book.

The updated version of the book can be found at
https://doi.org/10.1007/978-3-030-28786-3

© The Author(s) 2020
T. Balzacq et al. (eds.), *Global Diplomacy*,
The Sciences Po Series in International Relations and Political
Economy, https://doi.org/10.1007/978-3-030-28786-3_23

References

Adler, Emmanuel, "The Spread of Security Communities: Communities of Practice, Self-Restraint, and NATO's Post-Cold War Transformation," *European Journal of International Relations*, 2 (14), 2008: 195–230.

Adler-Nissen, Rebecca, *Opting Out of the European Union: Diplomacy, Sovereignty and European Integration*, Cambridge, Cambridge University Press, 2014.

———, "Relationalism or Why Diplomats Find International Theory Strange," in Ole J. Sending, Vincent Pouliot, Iver B. Neumann (eds.), *Diplomacy and the Making of World Politics*, Cambridge, Cambridge University Press, 2015, pp. 284–308.

Aldecoa, Francisco, Keating, Michael (eds.), *Paradiplomacy in Action: The Foreign Relations of Subnational Governments*, London, Frank Cass Publishers, 1999.

Alles, Delphine, Guilbaud, Auriane, "Les relations internationales: genèse et évolutions d'un champ d'étude," in Christophe Roux, Eric Savarese (eds.), *Manuel de science politique*, Brussels, Larcier, 2017, pp. 239–254.

Allison, Graham T., Zelikow, Philipp, *The Essence of Decision: Explaining the Cuban Missile Crisis*, London, Longman, 1999.

Alvarez, José E., *International Organizations as Law-Makers*, Oxford, Oxford University Press, 2005.

Andretta, Stefano, Péquignot, Stéphane, Waquet, Jean-Claude (eds.), *De l'ambassadeur. Les écrits relatifs à l'ambassadeur et à l'art de négocier du Moyen Âge au début du XIXe siècle*, Rome, Collection de l'École française de Rome, 2015.

Anholt, Simon, "Beyond the Nation Brand: The Role of Image and Identity in International Relations," *Exchange: The Journal of Public Diplomacy*, 2 (1), 2013: 6–12.

Archetti, Cristina, "The Impact of New Media on Diplomatic Practice: An Evolutionary Model of Change," *Hague Journal of Diplomacy*, 7 (2), 2012: 181–206.
Arndt, Richard T., *The First Resort of Kings: American Cultural Diplomacy in the Twentieth Century*, Washington (DC), Potomac Books, 2005.
Arodirik, Hakan D., "La diplomatie culturelle comme un instrument de la diplomatie publique: la diplomatie culturelle chinoise dans le contexte d'institut Confucius," 2015. independent.academia.edu/arodirikhakandavid.
Aron, Raymond, *Paix et guerre entre les nations*, Paris, Calmann-Lévy, 1962.
———, *Peace and War: A Theory of International Relations*, Transaction Publishers, 2003.
Atkinson, Carol, *Military Soft Power: Public Diplomacy Through Military Educational Exchanges*, New York (NY), Rowman & Littlefield, 2014.
Audinet, Maxime, "La voix de Moscou trouble le concert de l'information internationale," *Le Monde diplomatique*, April 2017.
Axelrod, Robert, *The Complexity of Cooperation*, Princeton (NJ), Princeton University Press, 1997.
Aykut, Stefan, Dahan, Amy, *Gouverner le climat? 20 ans de négociations internationales*, Paris, Presses de Science Po, 2015.
Azema, Jean-Pierre, Bedarida, François, *1938–1948. Les années de tourmente de Munich à Prague*, Paris, Flammarion, 1995.
Badel, Laurence, *Diplomatie et grands contrats. L'État français et les marchés extérieurs au XXe siècle*, Paris, Publications de la Sorbonne, 2010.
———, "CNPF-International, acteur du dialogue Asie-Europe (ASEM): jalons pour une recherche historique sur les interrégionalismes," in Pierre Tilly, Vincent Dujardin (eds.), *Hommes et réseaux. Belgique, Europe et Outre-Mers. Liber amicorum Michel Dumoulin*, Brussels, Peter Lang, 2013, pp. 193–202.
Badie, Bertrand, "De la souveraineté à la capacité de l'Etat," in M.C. Smouts (ed.), *Les nouvelles relations internationales*, Paris, Pressses de Sciences Po, 1998, pp. 35–58.
———, *Le Diplomate et l'Intrus. L'entrée des sociétés dans l'arène internationale*, Paris, Fayard, 2008.
Badie, Bertrand, Foucher, Michel, *Vers un monde néo-national?* Paris, CNRS, 2017.
Bagnato, Bruna, *Prove di Ostpolitik. Politica ed economia nella strategia italiana verso l'Unione Sovietica (1958–1963)*, Florence, Leo S. Olschli, 2003.
Bail, Christoph, Falkner, Robert, Marquard, Helen (eds.), *The Cartagena Protocol on Biosafety: Reconciling Trade in Biotechnology with Environment and Development?* London, RIIA/Earthscan, 2002.
Balzacq, Thierry, Ramel, Frédéric (eds.), *Traité de relations internationales*, Paris, Presses de Sciences Po, 2013.
Barber, Brian, *What Diplomats Do: The Life and Work of Diplomats*, Lanham (MD), Rowman & Littlefield, 2016.

Barnett, Michael, Finnemore, Martha, *Rules for the World: International Organizations in Global Politics*, Ithaca (NY), Cornell University Press, 2004.
Bennett, James, "Historicising Celebrity Studies," *Journal of Celebrity Studies*, 1 (3), 2010: 358–359.
Bercovitch, Jacob, *Theory and Practice of International Mediation: Selected Essays*, London, Routledge, 2014.
Bergman, Ronen, *Rise and Kill First: The Secret History of Israel's Targeted Assassinations*, London, John Murray Press, 2019.
Bernays, Edward L., *Propaganda*, New York (NY), Liveright Publishing, 1928.
Berridge, Geoffrey R., *Diplomacy: Theory and Practice*, New York (NY), Palgrave Macmillan, 2010.
———, *The Counter-Revolution in Diplomacy and Other Essays*, New York (NY), Palgrave Macmillan, 2011.
———, *Diplomacy: Theory and Practice*, New York (NY), Palgrave Macmillan, 2015.
Bettati, Mario, "Du droit d'ingérence à la responsabilité de protéger," *Outre-terre*, 20 (3), 2007: 381–389.
Biermann, Frank, Siebenhüner, Bernd, "The Influence of International Bureaucracies in World Politics: Findings from the MANUS Research Program," in Frank Biermann, Bernd Siebenhüner (eds.), *Managers of Global Change: The Influence of International Environmental Bureaucracies*, Cambridge, MIT Press, 2009.
———, (eds.), *Managers of Global Change. The Influence of International Environmental Bureaucracies*, Cambridge, The MIT Press, 2009.
Bjola, Corneliu, Holmes, Marcus (eds.), *Digital Diplomacy: Theory and Practice*, London, Routledge, 2015.
Bjola, Corneliu, Jiang, Lu, "Social Media and Public Diplomacy: A Comparative Analysis of the Digital Diplomatic Strategies of the EU, US and Japan in China," in Corneliu Bjola, Marcus Holmes (eds.), *Digital Diplomacy: Theory and Practice*, London, Routledge, 2015.
Bjola, Corneliu, Kornprobst, Markus, *Understanding International Diplomacy: Theory, Practice and Ethics*, 2nd edn., London, Routledge, 2018.
Bjola, Corneliu, Cassidy, J., Manor, I., "Public Diplomacy in the Digital Age," *Hague Journal of Diplomacy*, 14 (1–2), 2019: 83–101.
Blain, Christophe, Lanzac, Abel, *Quai d'Orsay*, Paris, Dargaud, 2010.
Blannin, Patrick, *Defence Diplomacy in the Long War*, Leyde, Martinus Nijhoff, Brill Research Perspectives, 2017.
Bogart, Leo, *Cool Words, Cold War*, Washington (DC), American University Press, 1995.
Boniface, Pascal, Verschuuren, Pim, Billion, Didier, Aby, Romain, "La diplomatie sportive qatarie. Le 'sport power': le sport au service de la reconnaissance internationale du Qatar," *Diplosport*, IRIS/CSFRS, 2012.

Boorstin, Daniel, *The Image or What Happened to the American Dream*, London, Weidenfeld & Nicolson, 1961.

Borger, Julian, Rankin, Jennifer, Lyons, Kate, "The Rise and Rise of International Diplomacy by WhatsApp," *The Guardian*, 4 November 2016, www.theguardian.com/technology/2016/nov/04/why-do-diplomats-use-this-alienwhatsapp-emoji-for-vladimir-putin, accessed 13 June 2018.

Brands, Hal, Inboden, William, "Wisdom Without Tears: Statecraft and the Uses of History," *Journal of Strategic Studies*, 4 (7), 2018: 916–946.

Brauman, Rony, *Humanitaire, diplomatie et droits de l'homme*, Paris, Éditions du Cygne, 2009.

Brown, Katherine A., Green, Shannon N., Wang, Jian "Jay", "Public Diplomacy and National Security in 2017: Building Alliances, Fighting Extremism, and Dispelling Disinformation," CSIS, 2017, pp. 1–17.

Bryant, William, *Japanese Private Economic Diplomacy: An Analysis of Business Government Linkages*, New York (NY), Praeger, 1975.

Brysk, Alison, *Global Good Samaritans: Human Rights as Foreign Policy*, Oxford, Oxford University Press, 2009.

Buhler, Pierre, *La Puissance au XXIe siècle. Les nouvelles définitions du monde*, Paris, CNRS, 2011.

Burke, Peter, "La reconstruction des rituels politiques au siècle de Louis XIV," in Yves Deloye, Claudine Haroche, Olivier Ihl (eds.), *Le Protocole ou la mise en forme de l'ordre politique*, Paris, L'Harmattan, 1999, pp. 171–183.

Burns, N., Kanji, L., "Illustrations and Influence: Soft Diplomacy and Nation Branding Through Popular Culture," *Harvard International Review*, 18 April 2016.

Cain, Frank, *Economic Statecraft During the Cold War: European Responses to the US Embargo*, London, Routledge, 2007.

Calhoun, Craig, "The Idea of Emergency: Humanitarian Action and Global (Dis)order," in Didier Fassin, Mariella Pandolfi (eds.), *Contemporary States of Emergency: The Politics of Humanitarian Interventions*, New York (NY), Zone Books, 2010, pp. 29–58.

Callières, François de, *De la manière de négocier avec les souverains*, Genève, Droz, 2002.

Campbell, Brian, "Diplomacy in the Roman World (c. 400 BC–AD 235)," *Diplomacy and Statecraft*, 12 (1), 2001: 1–22.

Canal-Forgues, Éric, *Démocratie et diplomatie environnementales. Acteurs et processus en droit international*, Paris, Pedone, 2015.

Carron de La Carrière, Guy, *La Diplomatie économique. Le diplomate et le marché*, Paris, Économica, 1998.

Centre for Strategic Studies, "Regional Defence Diplomacy: What Is It and What Are Its Limits," *Strategic Background Paper*, 21, 2015.

Certeau, Michel de, *L'Invention du quotidien*, vol. I, Arts et faire, Paris, Gallimard, 1980.

———, *The Practice of Everyday Life*, Berkeley, University of California Press, 1980.

Chaloux, Annie, Paquin, Stéphane, Séguin, Hugo, "Federalism and Climate Change Negotiations: The Role of Québec," *International Negotiations*, 15 (1), 2015: 291–318.

Chambon, Albert, *Mais que font ces diplomates entre deux cocktails?* Paris, Pédone, 1983.

Charpier, Frédéric, *La CIA en France. 60 ans d'ingérence dans les affaires françaises*, Paris, Seuil, 2008.

Chatin, Mathilde, Gallarotti, Giulio (eds.), *Emerging Powers in International Politics: The BRICS and Soft Power*, London, Routledge, 2017.

Cheyre, Juan Emilio, "Defence Diplomacy," in Andrew F. Cooper, Jorge Heine, Ramesh Thakur (eds.), *The Oxford Handbook of Modern Diplomacy*, Oxford, Oxford University Press, 2013.

Cohen, Samy, "Les États face aux nouveaux acteurs," *Politique internationale*, 107, 2005: 409–424.

Cohen, Raymond, Westbrook, Raymond, *Amarna Diplomacy: The Beginning of International Relations*, Baltimore (MD), Johns Hopkins University Press, 2000.

———, "The Great Tradition: The Spread of Diplomacy in the Ancien World," *Diplomacy and Statecraft*, 1 (1), 2001: 23–38.

———, "Diplomacy Through the Ages," in Pauline Kerr, Geoffrey Wiseman (eds.), *Diplomacy in a Globalizing World: Theories and Practices*, New York (NY), Oxford University Press, 2017, pp. 21–36.

Cohen, Yves, *Le siècle des chefs. Une histoire transnationale du commandement et de l'autorité (1890–1940)*, Paris, Éditions Amsterdam, 2013.

Collins, Randall, *Interaction Ritual Chain*, Princeton (NJ), Princeton University Press, 2005.

Colonomos, Ariel, *La Politique des oracles. Raconter le futur aujourd'hui*, Paris, Albin Michel, 2014.

———, *Selling the Future: The Perils of Predicting Global Politics*, London, Hurst, and New York, Oxford University Press, 2016.

Colson, Aurélien, "La négociation diplomatique au risque de la transparence: rôles et figures du secret envers des tiers," *Négociations*, 1 (1), 2009.

Commission Européenne, "Une nouvelle stratégie pour placer la culture au cœur des relations internationales de l'UE," Bruxelles, Communiqué de presse, 8 juin 2016.

———, *A New Strategy to Put Culture at the Heart of EU International Relations*, Press release, 2016.

Constantinou, Costas M., *On the Way to Diplomacy*, Minneapolis (MN), University of Minnesota Press, 1996.

Constantinou, Costas M., Kerr, Pauline, Sharp, Paul (eds.), *Sage Handbook of Diplomacy*, London, Sage, 2016.
Coolsaet, Rik, "Trade and Diplomacy. The Belgian Case," *International Studies Perspectives*, 5 (1), 2004: 61–65.
Cooper, Andrew F., *Celebrity Diplomacy*, New York (NY), Routledge, 2008.
———, *The Disintermediation Dilemma and Its Impact on Diplomacy*, Project "Diplomacy in the 21st Century," Stiftung Wissenschaft und Politik (SWP)/German Institute for International and Security Affairs, 2017.
Cooper, Andrew F., Heine, Jorge, Thakur, Ramesh (eds.), *The Oxford Handbook of Modern Diplomacy*, Oxford, Oxford University Press, 2013.
Copeland, Daryl, *Guerrilla Diplomacy: Rethinking International Relations*, Boulder (CO), Lynne Rienner, 2009.
Cornago, Noé, *Plural Diplomacies: Normative Predicaments and Functional Imperatives*, Leiden and Boston, Martinus Nijhoff Publishers, 2013.
Cottey, Andrew, Forster, Anthony, "Reshaping Defence Diplomacy: New Roles for Military Cooperation and Assistance," *Adelphi Papers*, 44 (365), 2004: 1–84.
Creel, G., *How We Advertised America*, New York (NY), Harper & Brothers, 1920.
Criekemans, David (ed.), *Regional Sub-State Diplomacy Today*, Leiden and Boston, Brill, 2011.
Cross, David, Mai'a, K., *The European Diplomatic Corps: Diplomats and International Cooperation from Westphalia to Maastricht*, New York (NY), Palgrave Macmillan, 2007.
Cull, Nicholas J., "Auteurs of Ideology: USIA Documentary Film Propaganda in the Kennedy Era," *Film History*, 10, 1998: 298–310.
———, *The Cold War and the United States Information Agency: American Propaganda and Public Diplomacy (1945–1989)*, Cambridge, Cambridge University Press, 2008.
Cull, Nicholas J., Cowan, Geoffrey, "Public Diplomacy in a Changing World," *Annals of the American Academy of Political and Social Science*, 616 (1), 2008: 6–8.
Dakowska, Dorota, *Le Pouvoir des fondations. Des acteurs de la politique étrangère allemande*, Rennes, Presses universitaires de Rennes, 2014.
Danes, Pierre, "Conseils à un ambassadeur," *Revue d'histoire diplomatique*, 28–29 [1561] 1914–1915: 607–612.
Daniels, Alison, Childs, Rosie, "A Digital Campaign Like No Other: Supporting the Preventing Sexual Violence in Conflict Initiative," *Foreign and Commonwealth Office*, 2014.
Datta-Ray, Deep K., *The Making of Indian Diplomacy: A Critique of Eurocentrism*, Oxford, Oxford University Press, 2015.
Davutoglu, Ahmet, "Turkey's Humanitarian Diplomacy: Objectives, Challenges and Prospects," *Nationalities Papers: The Journal of Nationalism and Ethnicity*, 41 (6), 2013: 865–870.

Death, Carl, "Summit Theatre: Exemplary Governmentality and Environmental Diplomacy in Johannesburg and Copenhagen," *Environmental Politics*, 20 (1), 2011: 1–19.
Dejammet, Alain, *L'Archipel de la gouvernance mondiale. ONU, G7, G8, G20*, Paris, Dalloz, 2012.
Delcorde, Raoul, "L'évolution du métier de diplomate," in Tanguy de Wilde d'Estmael, Michel Liégeois, Raoul Delcorde (eds.), *La Diplomatie au cœur des turbulences internationales*, Louvain, Presses de l'UCL, 2014, pp. 41–54.
Deloye, Yves, Haroche, Claudine, Ihl, Olivier (eds.), *Le Protocole ou la mise en forme de l'ordre politique*, Paris, L'Harmattan, 1999.
———, "Protocole et politique. Formes, rituels, préséances," in Yves Deloye, Claudine Haroche, Olivier Ihl (eds.), *Le Protocole ou la mise en forme de l'ordre politique*, Paris, L'Harmattan, 1999, pp. 11–18.
Der Derian, James, "Mediating Estrangement: A Theory of Diplomacy," *Review of International Studies*, 13 (2), 1987: 91–110.
———, *On Diplomacy: A Genealogy of Western Estrangement*, Oxford, Basil Blackwell, 1987.
Devin, Guillaume, "Les diplomaties de la politique étrangère," in Frédéric Charillon (ed.), *Politique étrangère. Nouveaux regards*, Paris, Presses de Sciences Po, 2002.
———, "Paroles de diplomates: comment les négociations multilatérales changent la diplomatie," in Franck Petiteville, Delphine Placidi-Frot (eds.), *Négociations internationales*, Paris, Presses de Sciences Po, 2013, pp. 77–104.
———, *Les Organisations internationales*, Paris, Armand Colin, 2016.
Diamond, Louise, Mcdonald, John, *Multi-Track Diplomacy: A System Approach to Peace*, West Hartford (CT), Kumarian Press, 1996.
Dizard, Wilson P., *The Strategy of Truth: The Story of the US Information Service*, Washington (DC), Public Affairs Press, 1961.
Dobson, Alan P., *US Economic Statecraft for Survival (1933–1991): Of Embargoes, Strategic Embargoes, and Economic Warfare*, London, Routledge, 2012.
Doise, Jean, Vaïsse, Maurice, *Diplomatie et outil militaire. Politique étrangère de la France (1871–2015)*, Paris, Seuil, 2015.
Dolcos, Sanda, "The Power of a Handshake: Neural Correlates of Evaluative Judgments in Observed Social Interactions," *Journal of Cognitive Neuroscience*, 24 (12), 2012: 2292–2305.
Drouhaud, Pascal, "L'UMP et les relations internationales," *Revue internationale et stratégique*, 55 (3), 2004: 11–18.
Duchacek, Ivo D., "Perforated Sovereignties: Towards a Typology of New Actors in International Relations," in Hans J. Michelmann, Panayotis Soldatos (eds.), *Federalism and International Relations: The Role of Subnational Units*, Oxford, Oxford University Press, 1990, pp. 1–33.
Dunant, Henry, *Un souvenir de Solferino*, Genève, Comité international de la Croix-Rouge, [1862] 1990.

Duncombe, Constance, "Twitter and Transformative Diplomacy: Social Media and Iran–US Relations," *International Affairs*, 93 (3), 2017: 545–562.
Dupont, Christophe, *La Négociation post-moderne. Bilan des connaissances, acquis et lacunes, perspectives*, Paris, Publibook, 2006.
Durkeim, Émile, *Les Formes élémentaires de la vie religieuse. Le système totémique en Australie*, Paris, Presses universitaires de France, 1912.
———, *The Elementary Forms of Religious Life*, New York, Oxford University Press, 2001.
Dyer Maccann, Richard, "Film and Foreign Policy: The USIA (1962–1967)," *Cinema Journal*, 1969: 23–42.
Eilers, Claude, *Diplomats and Diplomacy in the Roman World*, Leiden and Boston, Brill, 2009.
Elias, Norbert, *La Société de cour*, Paris, Calmann-Lévy, 1974.
Ellul, Jacques, "Les caractères de la propagande," in *Propagandes*, Paris, Économica, 1990.
Fabius, Laurent, "La diplomatie économique, une priorité pour la France," *Les Échos*, 23 August 2012.
Faure, Guy Olivier, Zartman, William I., *Negotiating with Terrorists: Strategy, Tactics and Politics*, London, Routledge, 2010.
Fauvet, Anne, "Au cœur des réseaux d'affaires français en Asie du Nord-Est. Roger Chambard, premier ambassadeur de France en Corée du Sud (années 1950–1980)," *Relations internationales*, 3 (167), 2016: 113–126.
Fayet, Jean-François, "VOKS: The Third Dimension of Soviet Foreign Policy," in Jessica C. E. Gienow-Hecht, Mark C. Donfried (eds.), *Searching for a Cultural Diplomacy*, New York (NY) and Oxford, Berghahn, 2013, pp. 33–50.
Fink, Carol, Frohn, Axel, Heideking, Jürgen (eds.), *Genoa, Rapallo, and European Reconstruction in 1922*, Cambridge, Cambridge University Press, 2002.
Fitriani, Evi, *Southeast Asians and the Asia-Europe Meeting (ASEM)*, Singapore, ISEAS, 2014.
Fletcher, Catherine, *Diplomacy in Renaissance Rome: The Rise of the Resident Ambassador*, Cambridge, Cambridge University Press, 2015.
Fletcher, Tom, *Naked Diplomacy: Power and Statecraft in the Digital Age*, London, William Collins, 2016.
Fontana, Alessandro, "Les ambassadeurs après 1494. La diplomatie et la politique nouvelles," *Cahiers de la Renaissance italienne*, 3, 1994: 143–178.
Foret, François, *Légitimer l'Europe. Pouvoir et symbolique à l'ère de la gouvernance*, Paris, Presses de Sciences Po, 2008.
Foyer, Jean (ed.), *Regards croisés sur Rio+20. La modernisation écologique à l'épreuve*, Paris, CNRS Éditions, 2015.
———, "Dans les coulisses de la COP 21," *La Vie des idées*, 23 February 2016.
Freeman, Chas W., Jr, *The Diplomat's Dictionary*, Institute for National Strategic Studies, Washington (DC), National Defense University Press, 1994.

Friman, H. Richard (ed.), *The Politics of Leverage in International Relations. Name, Shame, and Sanctions*, New York (NY), Palgrave Macmillan, 2015.

Fry, Earl H., "The Role of US State Governments in International Relations and International Negotiations (1980–2016)," *International Negotiation*, 22 (1), 2017.

Gagnon, Bernard, Palard, Jacques, "Relations internationales des régions et fédéralisme. Les provinces canadiennes dans le contexte de l'intégration nordaméricaine," *Revue internationale de politique comparée*, 12 (2), 2005.

Geertz, Clifford, *Local Knowledge: Further Essays in Interpretive Anthropology*, Basic Books, 1983.

———, *Savoir Local, Savoir Global*, Paris, Presses universitaires de France, 1986.

Geneva Centre for the Democratic Control of Armed Forces (DCAF), "Defence Attachés," DCAF Backgrounder series, July 2007.

Geneva Centre for the Democratic Control of Armed Forces, *Les Attachés de défense*, Genève, DCAF, 2008.

Gerolymatos, Andre, *Espionage and Treason: A Study of the Proxeny in Political and Military Intelligence Gathering in Classical Greece*, Amsterdam, Brill, 1986.

Gilboa, Eytan, "Digital Diplomacy," in Constantinou Costas, Pauline Kerr, Paul Sharp (eds.), *The SAGE Handbook of Diplomacy*, London, Sage, 2016.

Gluckman, Max, "Les rites de passage," in Max Gluckman (ed.), *Essays on the Rituals of Social Relations*, Manchester, Manchester University Press, 1966.

Goff, Patricia M., "Cultural Diplomacy," in Andrew F. Cooper, Jorge Heine, Ramesh Thakur (eds.), *The Oxford Handbook of Modern Diplomacy*, Oxford, Oxford University Press, 2013.

Goffman, Erving, *The Presentation of Self in Everyday Life*, London, Penguin, 1959.

———, *Interaction Ritual: Essays into Face-To-Face Behavior*, Chicago, Aldine Publishing Company, 1967.

———, *Strategic Interaction*, Philadelphia (PA), University of Pennsylvania Press, 1969.

———, *Relations in Public: Microstudies of the Public Order*, New York (NY), Basic Books, 1971, pp. 62–94.

———, *Les Rites d'interaction*, Paris, Minuit, 1974.

———, *Interaction Ritual: Essays in Face-to-Face Behavior*, New Brunswick, Transaction Publishers [1967] 2008 (4th printing).

Gomart, Thomas, "La relation bilatérale: un genre de l'histoire des relations internationales," *Matériaux pour l'histoire de notre temps*, 65–66, 2002: 65–68.

Grandpierre, Véronique, *Histoire de la Mésopotamie*, Paris, Gallimard, 2010.

Green, F., *American Propaganda Abroad*, New York (NY), Hippocrene Book, 1988.

Gremion, Pierre, *Intelligence de l'anticommunisme. Le congrès pour la liberté de la culture à Paris (1950–1975)*, Paris, Fayard, 1995.

Gresles, François, "La 'société militaire': son devenir à la lumière de la professionnalisation," *Revue française de sociologie*, 44 (4), 2003: 777–798.

Griffin, Nicholas, *Ping-Pong Diplomacy: Ivor Montagu and the Astonishing Story Behind the Game*, London and New York (NY), Simon & Schuster, 2014.

Grosser, Pierre, *Traiter avec le diable? Les vrais enjeux de la diplomatie au XXIe siècle*, Paris, Odile Jacob, 2013.

Guilbaud, Auriane, *Business Partners. Firmes privées et gouvernance mondiale de la santé*, Paris, Presses de Sciences Po, 2015.

Haas, Ernst B., *The Uniting of Europe*, Palo Alto (CA), Stanford University Press, 1958.

Hafner-Burton, Emilie M., *Making Human Rights a Reality*, Princeton (NJ), Princeton University Press, 2013.

Haftel, Yoram Z., Thompson, Alexander, "The Independence of International Organizations: Concept and Applications," *Journal of Conflict Resolution*, 2 (50), 2006: 253–275.

Haftel, Yoram Z., Hofmann, Stephanie C., "Institutional Authority and Security Cooperation Within Regional Economic Organizations," *Journal of Peace Research*, 54 (4), 2017: 484–498.

Haize, Daniel, *L'Action culturelle et de coopération de la France à l'étranger. Un réseau, des hommes*, Paris, L'Harmattan, 2012.

Hajnal, Peter, *The G8 System and the G20: Evolution, Role, Documentation*, London, Routledge, 2013.

Hammarskjold, Dag, "Address by the Secretary General, Foreign Policy Association," Press Release SG/344, 21 October 1953.

Hanson, Fergus, "Baked in and Wired. eDiplomacy@State," in *Foreign Policy Paper Series*, Washington (DC), Brookings Institution, 2012, p. 30.

Haroche, Claudine, "L'ordre dans les corps: gestes, mouvements, postures. Éléments pour une anthropologie politique des préséances (XVIe-XVIIe siècles)," in Yves Deloye, Claudine Haroche, Olivier Ihl (ed.), *Le Protocole ou la mise en forme de l'ordre politique*, Paris, L'Harmattan, 1999, pp. 213–229.

Harrison, Jane, *Ancient Art and Ritual*, London, Williams and Northgate, 1913.

Harroff-Tavel, Marion, "La diplomatie humanitaire du Comité international de la Croix-Rouge," *Relations internationales*, 121 (5), 2005: 73–89.

Harvie, Charles, Kimura, Fukunari, Lee, Hyun-Hoon, *New East Asian Regionalism: Causes, Progress and Country Perspectives*, Northampton, Edward Elgar, 2005.

Hassner, Pierre, *La Terreur et l'Empire, vol. II, La Violence par la paix*, Paris, Seuil, 2003.

Hawkins, Darren, Jacoby, Wade, "How Agents Matter," in Darren Hawkins, David Lake, Daniel Nielson, Michael Tierney (eds.), *Delegation and Agency in International Organizations*, New York (NY), Cambridge University Press, 2006.

Heil, Alan, L., Jr., *Voice of America: A History*, New York (NY), Columbia University Press, 2003.
Hills, Alice, "Defence Diplomacy and Security Sector Reform," *Contemporary Security Policy*, 21 (1), 2000: 46–67.
Hochstetler, Kathryn, "Civil Society," in Andrew F. Cooper, Jorge Heine, Ramesh Thakur (eds.), *The Oxford Handbook of Modern Diplomacy*, Oxford, Oxford University Press, 2013, pp. 176–191.
Hocking, Brian, *Localizing Foreign Policy: Non-Central Governments and Multi-layered Diplomacy*, New York (NY), Palgrave Macmillan, 1993.
———, "Les intérêts internationaux des gouvernements régionaux: désuétude de l'interne et de l'externe?" *Études internationales*, 253, 1994: 409–420.
———, "Regionalism: An International Relations Perspective," in Michael Keating, John Loughlin (eds.), *The Political Economy of Regionalism*, London, Frank Cass, 1995.
———, *Foreign Ministries: Change and Adaptation*, New York (NY), Palgrave Macmillan, 1999.
———, "Gatekeepers and Boundary Spanners: Thinking About Foreign Ministries in the European Union," in Brian Hocking, David Spence (eds.), *Foreign Ministries in the European Union: Integrating Diplomats*, New York (NY), Palgrave Macmillan, 2005, pp. 1–17.
———, "The Ministry of Foreign Affairs and the National Diplomatic System," in Pauline Kerr, Geoffrey Wiseman, *Diplomacy in a Globalizing World: Theories and Practices*, New York (NY), Oxford University Press, 2012, pp. 123–140.
———, "Diplomacy and Foreign Policy," in Costas M. Constantinou, Pauline Kerr, Paul Sharp (eds.), *The Sage Handbook of Diplomacy*, London, Sage, 2016, pp. 67–78.
———, "The Ministry of Foreign Affairs and the National Diplomatic System," in Pauline Kerr, Geoffrey Wiseman, *Diplomacy in a Globalizing World: Theories and Practices*, 2nd edn., New York, Oxford University Press, 2018, pp. 129–150.
Hocking, Brian, Melissen, Jan, *Diplomacy in the Digital Age*, The Hague, Clingendael Institute, 2015.
Hocking, Brian, Melissen, Jan, Riordan, Shaun, Sharp, Paul, "Integrative Diplomacy for the 21st Century," *China International Strategy Review*, 2013: 53–88.
Hocking, Brian, Spence, David (eds.), *Foreign Ministries in the European Union: Integrating Diplomats*, New York, Palgrave Macmillan, 2002.
Hofmann, Stephanie C. "The Politics of Overlapping Organizations: Hostage Taking, Forum Shopping, and Brokering," *Journal of European Public Policy*, 26 (6), 2019: 883–905.
Hooghe, Liesbet, Marks, Gary, *Multi-level Governance and European Integration*, Lanham (MD), Rowman & Littlefield, 2001.
———, "Delegation and Pooling in International Organizations," *Review of International Organizations*, 10, 2014: 305–328.

House of Commons, *The Strategic Defence Review White Paper*, London, House of Commons, 1998.

Huijgh, Ellen, "Public Diplomacy," in Costas Constantinou, Pauline Kerr, Paul Sharp (eds.), *The SAGE Handbook of Diplomacy*, London, Sage, 2016.

Hunter, Felt, "How NBA Star Dennis Rodman Came to Stand Between the World and Nuclear War," *The Guardian*, 14 September 2017.

IISD, n.d., *Bulletins des négociations de la Terre*.

Inis, L. Claude, Jr., *Swords into Plowshares: The Problems and Progress of International Organization*, New York (NY), Random House, 1964.

Jackson, Ian, *The Economic Cold War: America, Britain, and East-West Trade (1948–1963)*, Palgrave, New York (NY), 2001.

Jacques, Julien, "L'Espagne en France. Les centres culturels espagnols dans l'Hexagone au XXe siècle," Paris, Université Paris-1 Panthéon-Sorbonne, Masters Dissertation in History, 2015.

Jeong, Ho-Won, *International Negotiation*, Cambridge, Cambridge University Press, 2016.

Jepsen, Henrik, "Nothing Is Agreed Until Everything Is Agreed," *Issue Linkage in the International Climate Change Negotiations*, Århus, Politica, 2013.

Jervis, Robert, *Perception and Misperception in International Politics*, Princeton (NJ), Princeton University Press, 2017.

Joana, Jean, *Les Armées contemporaines*, Paris, Presses de Sciences Po, 2012.

Johnson, Tana, "Looking Beyond States: Openings for International Bureaucrats to Enter the Institutional Design Process," *Review of International Organizations*, 8, 2013: 499–519.

Jönsson, Christer, Hall, Martin, "Communication: An Essential Aspect of Diplomacy," *International Perspectives*, 4 (2), 2003: 195–210.

Jüngerkes, Sven, *Diplomaten der Wirtschaft. Die Geschichte des Ost-Ausschusses der Deutschen Wirtschaft*, Osnabrück, Fibre, 2012.

Kabir, Arafat, "Twiplomacy and the Iran Nuclear Deal," *The Diplomat*, 11 December 2013.

Kandel, Maya, Quessard, Maud (eds.), *Les Stratégies du smart power américain*, Paris, Irsem, 2014.

Kanji, Laura, "Illustrations and Influence: Soft Diplomacy and Nation Branding Through Popular Culture," *Harvard International Review*, 18, 2016: 40–45.

Kantchev, Georgi, "Diplomats on Twitter: The Good, the Bad and the Ugly," *Wall Street Journal*, 24 February 2015.

Karns, Margaret P., Mingst, Karen A., "International Organizations and Diplomacy," in Andrew F. Cooper, Jorge Heine, Ramesh Thakur (eds.), *The Oxford Handbook of Modern Diplomacy*, Oxford, Oxford University Press, 2013, pp. 142–159.

Karvonen, Lauri, Sundelius, Bengt, *Internationalization and Foreign Policy Management*, Gower, Aldershot, 1987.

Keck, Frédéric, "Goffman, Durkheim et les rites de la vie quotidienne," *Archives de philosophie*, 75 (3), 2012: 471–492.
Keck, Margaret E., Sikkink, Kathryn, *Activists Beyond Borders: Advocacy Networks in International Politics*, Ithaca (NY), Cornell University Press, 1998.
Kellner, Douglas, "Celebrity Diplomacy, Spectacle and Barack Obama," *Journal of Celebrity Studies*, 1 (1), 2010: 121–123.
Kennedy, David, *A World of Struggle: How Power, Law, and Expertise Shape Global Political Economy*, Princeton (NJ), Princeton University Press, 2018.
Keohane, Robert, *After Hegemony: Cooperation and Discord in the World Political Economy*, Princeton (NJ), Princeton University Press, 1984.
———, *International Institutions and State Power*, Boulder (CO), Westview, 1989.
Kerr, Pauline, Wiseman, Geoffrey, "Introduction," in Pauline Kerr, Geoffrey Wiseman (eds.), *Diplomacy in a Globalizing World: Theories and Practices*, New York (NY), Oxford University Press, 2017, pp. 1–18.
Kerry, John, "Digital Diplomacy. Adapting Our Diplomatic Engagement," *DipNote*, 6 May 2013.
Kessler, Marie-Christine, *La Politique étrangère de la France. Acteurs et processus*, Paris, Presses de Sciences Po, 1999
———, *Les Ambassadeurs*, Paris, Presses de Sciences Po, 2012.
Kim, Rakhyun E., "The Emergent Network Structure of the Multilateral Environmental Agreement System," *Global Environmental Change*, 23 (5), 2013: 980–991.
Kingah, Stephen, Quiliconi, Cintia (eds.), *Global and Regional Leadership of BRICS Countries*, New York (NY), Springer, 2017.
Kirton, John, *G20 Governance for a Globalized World*, London, Routledge, 2015.
Klein, Asmara, Laporte, Camille, Saiget, Marie (ed.), *Les Bonnes Pratiques des organisations internationales*, Paris, Presses de Sciences Po, 2015.
Knudsen, Dino, *The Trilateral Commission and Global Governance: Informal Elite Diplomacy (1972–1982)*, London, Routledge, 2016.
Krishnan, Aparna, Kurtzberg, Terri, Naquin, Charles, "The Curse of the Smartphone: Electronic Multitasking in Negotiations," *Negotiation Journal*, 30 (2), 2014: 191–208.
Krotz, Ulrich, Schild, Joachim, *Shaping Europe: France, Germany and Embedded Bilateralism from the Elysee Treaty to Twenty-First Century Politics*, Oxford, Oxford University Press, 2012.
Kurbalija, Jovan, "The Impact of the Internet and ICT on Contemporary Diplomacy," in Kerr Pauline, Wiseman Geoffrey (eds.), *Diplomacy in a Globalizing World: Theories and Practices*, Oxford, Oxford University Press, 2012, pp. 141–159.
———, "The impact of the Internet on Diplomacy," in Pauline Kerr, Geoffrey Wiseman (eds.), *Diplomacy in a Globalizing World: Theories and Practice*, 2nd edn., New York, Oxford University Press, 2018, pp. 151–169.

Kuyper, Jonathan W., Backstrand, Karin, "Accountability and Representation: Non State Actors in UN Climate Diplomacy," *Global Environmental Politics*, 16 (2), 2016: 61–81.

Kuznetsov, Alexander, *Theory and Practice of Paradiplomacy: Subnational Governments in International Affairs*, London, Routledge, 2014.

Lachapelle, Guy, Maltais, Bruno, "Diversité culturelle et stratégie sub-étatiques: le cas du Québec," *Revue internationale de politique comparée*, 12 (2), 2005.

Langhorne, Richard, "The Regulation of Diplomatic Practice: The Beginnings to the Vienna Convention on Diplomatic Practice (1961)," in Christer Jönsson, Richard Langhorne (eds.), *Diplomacy, vol. II, History of Diplomacy*, London, Sage, 2004, pp. 315–333.

Lanxade, Jacques, Tenzer, Nicolas, *Organiser la politique européenne et internationale de la France*, Paris, La Documentation française, 2002.

Lasswell, Harold, *Propaganda Techniques in the World War*, New York (NY), Alfred A. Knopf, 1927.

Lebourg, Nicolas, "Les dimensions internationales du Front national," *Pouvoirs*, 57 (2), 2016: 105–113.

Lee, Donna, "The Growing Influence of Business in UK Diplomacy," *International Studies Perspectives*, 5, 2004: 50–54.

Lee, Donna, Hudson, David, "The Old and New Significance of Political Economy in Diplomacy," *Review of International Studies*, 30 (3), 2004: 343–360.

Leguey-Feilleux, Jean-Robert, *The Dynamics of Diplomacy*, Boulder (CO), Lynne Rienner, 2009.

Leira, Halvard, "A Conceptual History of Diplomacy," in Costas M. Constantinou, Pauline Kerr, Paul Sharp (eds.), *The Sage Handbook of Diplomacy*, London, Sage, 2016, pp. 28–38.

Lequesne, Christian, "EU Foreign Policy Through the Lens of Practice Theory: A Different Approach to the European External Action Service," *Cooperation and Conflict*, 50 (3), 2015: 351–367.

———, *Ethnographie du Quai d'Orsay. Les pratiques des diplomates français*, Paris, CNRS Éditions, 2017.

Lequesne, Christian, Paquin, Stéphane (eds.), "Federalism and International Negotiation," *International Negotiation* (Special Issue), 2 (22), 2017.

Littoz-Monnet, Annabelle (ed.), *The Politics of Expertise in International Organizations: How International Bureaucracies Produce and Mobilize Knowledge*, New York (NY), Routledge, 2017.

Littoz-Monnet, Annabelle. 2017. "International Bureaucrats as Shapers of Bioethical Standards: Expert Knowledge as a Bureaucratic Tool," *International Studies Quarterly* 61 (3): 584–595.

Lomenie, L. H. de, Brienne, Comte de, *Mémoires*, vol. I., Paris, 1919.

Lorenzini, Sara, *Due Germanie in Africa. La cooperazione allo sviluppo e la competizione per i mercati di materie prime e tecnologia*, Florence, Polistampa, 2003.

Loriol, Françoise, Piotet, Marc, Delfolie, David, *Splendeurs et misères du travail des diplomates*, Paris, Hermann, 2013.
Louis, Marieke, "Un parlement mondial du travail? Enquête sur un siècle de représentation tripartite à l'Organisation internationale du travail," *Revue française de science politique*, 66 (1), 2016: 27–48.
Lowenthal, Abraham F., Bertucci, Mariano E. (eds.), *Scholars, Policymakers, and International Affairs. Finding Common Cause*, Baltimore (MD), John Hopkins University Press, 2014.
Lucas, Didier (ed.), *Les Diplomates d'entreprise. Pouvoirs, réseaux, influence*, Paris, Choiseul, 2012.
Maillard, Denis, "1968–2008: le Biafra ou le sens de l'humanitaire," *Humanitaire*, 18, 2008, https://journals.openedition.org/humanitaire/182, accessed 24 February 2017.
Mandelbaum, Michael, *Mission Failure: America and the World in the Post Cold War Era*, Oxford, Oxford University Press, 2016.
Manor, Ilan, "The Social Network of Foreign Embassies in Israel," *Exploring Digital Diplomacy*, 30 July 2014.
——, "Are We There Yet: Have MFAs Realized the Potential of Digital Diplomacy?" *Brill Research Perspectives in Diplomacy and Foreign Policy*, 1 (2), 2016: 1–110.
Maulde la Clavière, M., *La Diplomatie au temps de Machiavel*, 3 vols., Paris, Ernest Leroux, 1892–1893.
Massart-Piérard, Françoise, "Introduction à l'analyse des collectivités décentralisées et ses répercussions," in *Du local à l'international: nouveaux acteurs, nouvelle diplomatie*, *Revue Internationale de Politique Comparée*, 12 (32), 2005: 123–128.
Matsuda, Yasuhiro, "An Essay on China's Military Diplomacy: Examination of Intentions in Foreign Strategy," *NIDS Security Reports*, 7, 2006.
Matsuura, Koïchiro, "L'enjeu culturel au cœur des relations internationales," *Politique étrangère*, 4, 2006: 1045–1057.
Maus, Didier, "Le cadre institutionnel de la diplomatie parlementaire," *Parlement[s]. Revue d'histoire politique*, 1 (17), 2012: 14–36.
Mauss, Marcel, *Essai sur le don. Forme et raison de l'échange dans les sociétés archaïques*, Paris, Presses universitaires de France, 2007.
Mchugh, James T., "Paradiplomacy, Protodiplomacy and the Foreign Policy Aspirations of Quebec and Other Canadian Provinces," *Canadian Foreign Policy Journal*, 21 (3), 2015: 238–256.
Melissen, Jan (ed.), *The New Public Diplomacy: Soft Power in International Relations*, New York (NY), Palgrave Macmillan, 2005.
——, "Public diplomacy," in Pauline Kerr, Geoffrey Wiseman (eds.), *Diplomacy in a Globalizing World: Theories and Practices*, 2nd edn., New York, Oxford University Press, 2018, pp. 199–218.

Melissen, Jan, Mar Fernández, Ana (eds.), *Consular Affairs and Diplomacy*, Leiden, Brill Nijhoff, 2011.

Mérand, Frédéric, Hofmann, Stephanie C., Irondelle, Bastien, "Governance and State Power: A Network Analysis of European Security," *Journal of Common Market Studies*, 49 (1), 2011: 121–147.

Michelmann, Hans (ed.), *Foreign Relations in Federal Countries*, Montreal, McGill University Press, 2009.

Michèle, Sabban. "Réchauffement climatique: les régions veulent avancer," *Le Monde*, December 29, 2009.

Michelmann, Hans J., Soldatos, Panayotis (eds.), *Federalism and International Relations: The Role of Subnational Units*, Oxford, Oxford University Press, 1990.

Minear, Larry, Smith, Hazel, "Introduction," in Larry Minear, Hazel Smith (ed.), *Humanitarian Diplomacy: Practitioners and Their Craft*, New York (NY), United Nations University Press, 2007, pp. 1–4.

Mingant, Nolwenn, "Hollywood et le Département d'État: une liaison dangereuse?" *Géo-économie*, 58 (3), 2011: 67–73.

Ministry of Defence, *The Strategic Defence Review: A New Chapter*, London, Ministry of Defence, 2002.

Mirrelees, Tanner, *Hearts and Mines: The US Empire's Culture Industry*, Vancouver, Toronto, UBC Press, 2016.

Mock, James R., Larson, Cedric, *Words That Won the War: The Story of the Committee on Public Information* (1917–1919), Princeton (NJ), Princeton University Press, 1939.

Moeglin, Jean-Marie, Péquignot, Stéphane, *Diplomatie et 'relations internationales' au Moyen Âge (IXe-XVe siècle)*, Paris, Presses universitaires de France, 2017.

Moran, W. L., *Les Lettres d'El Amarna*, Paris, Cerf, 1987.

Morand, James L., *Interview, Foreign Affairs Oral History Project Information Series*, Arlington (VA), Association for Diplomatic Studies and Training, 9 June 1994, ADST, 1998.

Morin, Jean-Frédéric, Orsini, Amandine, *Politique internationale de l'environnement*, Paris, Presses de Sciences Po, 2015.

Morgan, Roger, Bray, Caroline (eds.), *Partners and Rivals in Western Europe: Britain, France and Germany*, Aldershot, Gower Publishing Company, 1986.

Mourlon-Druol, Emmanuel, Romero, Federico (eds.), *International Summitry and Global Governance: The Rise of the G-7 and the European Council*, London, Routledge, 2014.

Muldoon, James P., Jr., "The Diplomacy of Business," *Diplomacy & Statecraft*, 16 (2), 2005: 341–359.

Muldoon, James P., Aviel, JoAnn F., Reitano, Richard, Sullivan, Earl (eds.), *The New Dynamics of Multilateralism: Diplomacy, International Organizations, and Global Governance*, Boulder (CO), Westview, 2010.

Nagelschmidt, Martin, "Les systèmes à niveaux multiples dans les régions transfrontalières en Europe. Le cas du Rhin supérieur et des nouvelles coopérations à la frontière est de la RFA," *Revue internationale de politique comparée*, 12 (2), 2005: 223–236.

Nelson, Michael, *War of the Black Heavens: The Battles of Western Broadcasting in the Cold War*, Syracuse (NY), Syracuse University Press, 1997.

Neumann, Iver B., *At Home with the Diplomats: Inside a European Foreign Ministry*, Ithaca (NY), Cornell University Press, 2012.

Neustadt, Richard, *Alliance Politics*, New York, Columbia University Press, 1970.

Newman, Edward, Thakur, Ramesh, Timan, John (eds.), *Multilateralism Under Challenge? Power, International Order and Structural Change*, Tokyo, United Nations University Press, 2006.

Nicolson, Harold, *Diplomacy*, London, Thornton Butterworth, 1950.

Nielson, Daniel, Tierney, Michael, "Delegation to International Organizations: Agency Theory and World Bank Environmental Reform," *International Organization*, 57, 2003: 241–276.

Nisbet, Erik C., Kamenchuk, Olga, "The Psychology of State-Sponsored Disinformation Campaigns and Implications for Public Diplomacy," *The Hague Journal of Diplomacy*, 14 (1–2), 2019: 65–82.

Norman Lear Center, USC, "The Cultural Diplomacy of KCON," https://learcenter.org/cultural-diplomacy-kcon, accessed 13 June 2018.

Nye, Joseph, "Soft Power," *Foreign Policy*, 80, 1990: 153–171.

———, *Soft Power: The Means to Success in World Politics*, New York (NY), Public Affairs, 2004.

———, *The Future of Power*, New York (NY), Public Affairs, 2011.

———, "Soft Power and Public Diplomacy Revisited," *Hague Journal of Diplomacy*, 14 (1–2), 2019: 7–20.

OCDE, *L'Examen par les pairs, un instrument de l'OCDE pour la coopération et le changement*, Paris, 2003.

———, "Peer Review: A Tool for Co-operation and Change," in *Development Co-operation Report 2002: Efforts and Policies of the Members of the Development Assistance Committee*, Éditions OCDE, Paris, 2003, https://doi.org/10.1787/dcr-2002-6-en.

———, *Perspectives de l'OCDE sur la politique de la réglementation*, Paris, 2015.

———, *OECD Regulatory Policy Outlook 2015*, Éditions OCDE, Paris, 2015, https://doi.org/10.1787/9789264238770-en.

Oriano, Michel, "'Play It Again, Sim': Sim Copans ambassadeur de la musique américaine en France," *Revue française d'études américaines (RFEA)*, Special Issue, 2001: 6–15.

ORSAM, "Symposium Japan-Turkey: Dialogue on Global Affairs," *Meeting Evaluation*, 8 August 2016.

Orsini, Amandine, *La Biodiversité sous influence? Les lobbies industriels face aux politiques internationales d'environnement*, Brussels, Éditions de l'université de Bruxelles, 2010.
Outrey, Amédée, "Histoire et principes de l'administration française des Affaires étrangères," *Revue française de science politique*, 3, 1953: 491–510.
Pamment, James, *New Public Diplomacy in the 21st Century: A Comparative Study of Policy and Practice*, New York, Routledge, 2012.
Paquin, Stéphane, "Paradiplomatie identitaire en Catalogne et les relations Barcelone-Madrid," *Études internationales*, XXXIII (1), 2002: 57–98.
———, *Paradiplomatie identitaire en Catalogne*, Laval, Presses de l'université de Laval, 2003.
———, *Paradiplomatie et relations internationales. Théorie des stratégies internationales des régions face la mondialisation*, Brussels, PIE/Peter Lang, 2004.
———, "Les actions extérieures des entités sub-étatiques: quelle signification pour la politique comparée et les relations internationales?" *Revue internationale de politique comparée*, 12 (2), 2005a: 129–142.
———, "La paradiplomatie identitaire: le Québec, la Flandre et la Catalogne en relations internationales," *Politique et sociétés*, 23 (3), 2005b: 176–194.
———, "Federalism and Compliance with International Agreements: Belgium and Canada Compared," *The Hague Journal of Diplomacy*, 5, 2010: 173–197.
———, "Federalism and the Governance of International Trade Negotiations in Canada. Comparing CUSFTA with CETA," *International Journal*, 68 (4), 2013: 545–552.
Paquin, Stéphane, Kravagna, Marine, Min, Reuchamps, "Paradiplomacy and International Treaty Making: Quebec and Wallonia Compared," in Min Reuchamps (ed.), *Minority Nations in Multinational Federations: A Comparative Study of Quebec and Wallonia*, London, Routledge, 2015, pp. 160–180.
Pells, Richard, *Not Like US: How Europeans Have Loved, Hated and Transformed American Culture Since World War II*, New York (NY), Basic Books, 1997.
Péquignot, Stéphane, "Figure et normes de comportement des ambassadeurs dans les documents de la pratique. Un essai d'approche comparative (Ca. 1250–Ca. 1440)," in Stefano Andretta, Stéphane Péquignot, Jean-Claude Waquet (eds.), *De l'ambassadeur. Les écrits relatifs à l'ambassadeur et à l'art de négocier du Moyen Âge au début du XIXe siècle*, Rome, École française de Rome, 2015, pp. 87–111.
Petiteville, Franck, Placidi-Frot, Delphine (eds.), *Négociations internationales*, Paris, Presses de Sciences Po, 2013.
Pfister, Roger, *Apartheid South Africa and African States: From Pariah to Middle Power (1961–1994)*, London, Tauris Academic Studies, 2005.
Piattoni, Simona, *The Theory of Multi-level Governance: Conceptual, Empirical and Normative Challenges*, New York (NY), Oxford University Press, 2010.
Pigman, Geoffrey Allen, *Contemporary Diplomacy: Representation and Communication in a Globalized World*, Cambridge, Polity Press, 2010.

———, "The Diplomacy of Global and Transnational Firms," in Andrew F. Cooper, Jorge Heine, Ramesh Thakur (eds.), *The Oxford Handbook of Modern Diplomacy*, Oxford, Oxford University Press, 2013, pp. 192–208.

Plantey Alain, *La Négociation internationale au XXIe siècle*, Paris, CNRS, 2002.

Pollack, Mark, *The Engines of European Integration: Delegation, Agency, and Agenda Setting in the EU*, New York (NY), Oxford University Press, 2003.

Post, Emily, *Etiquette: The Blue Book of Social Usage*, New York (NY), Funk & Wagnall, 1940.

Postel-Vinay, Caroline, *Le G20, laboratoire d'un monde émergent*, Paris, Presses de Sciences Po, 2011.

———, *The G20: A New Political Order*, New York, Palgrave Macmillan, 2014.

Pouliot, Vincent, *International Pecking Orders*, Cambridge, Cambridge University Press, 2016.

———, *L'Ordre hiérarchique international*, Paris, Presses de Sciences Po, 2017.

Pouliot, Vincent, Cornut, Jérémie, "Practice Theory and the Study of Diplomacy: A Research Agenda," *Cooperation and Conflict*, 50 (3), 2015: 297–315.

Public Diplomacy Magazine, *The Power of Non-state Actors*, Los Angeles, University of Southern California, 2014.

Putnam, Robert, "Diplomacy and Domestic Politics: The Logic of Two-Level Games," *International Organization*, 42, 1988: 427–460.

Queller, Donald E., *Dictionary of the Middle Ages*, New York (NY), Scribner, 1984.

Ramel, Frédéric, Prévost-Thomas, Cécile, *International Relations, Music and Diplomacy*, New York (NY), Palgrave Macmillan, 2018.

Rana, Kishan, *Asian Diplomacy: The Foreign Ministries of China, India, Japan, Singapore and Thailand*, Genève, DiploFoundation, 2007.

Rappaport, Roy, *Ritual and Religion in the Making of Humanity*, Cambridge, Cambridge University Press, 1999.

Raspail, Hélène, "Contrôle de validité des actes juridiques des organisations internationales," in Évelyne Lagrange, Jean-Marc Sorel (eds.), *Droit des organisations internationales*, Paris, LGDJ, 2013.

Rewizorski, Marek, *The European Union and the BRICS: Complex Relations in the Era of Global Governance*, New York (NY), Springer, 2016.

Richardson, Ian, Kakabadse, Andrew, Kakabadse, Nada, *Bilderberg People: Elite Power and Consensus in World Affairs*, London, Routledge, 2011.

Risse, Thomas, Sikkink, Kathryn, "The Socialization of International Human Rights Norms into Domestic Practices: Introduction," in Thomas Risse, Stephen C. Ropp, Kathryn Sikkink (eds.), *The Power of Human Rights: International Norms and Domestic Change*, Cambridge, Cambridge University Press, 1999, pp. 1–38.

Roche, François, *La Crise des institutions nationales d'échanges culturels en Europe*, Paris, L'Harmattan, 1998.

———, "La diplomatie culturelle dans les relations bilatérales. Un essai d'approche typologique," *Sens public*, revue web, Université de Montréal, 2006.

Roche, François, Piniau, Bernard, *Histoires de diplomatie culturelle des origines à 1995*, Paris, Ministère des Affaires étrangères/ADPF, 1995.

Roosen, William, "Early Modern Diplomatic Ceremonial: A System Approach," *The Journal of Modern History*, 52 (3), 1980: 452–476.

Rosenau, James, *Turbulence in World Politics: A Theory of Change and Continuity*, Princeton (NJ), Princeton University Press, 1990.

Rosenberg, Emily, *Spreading the American Dream: American Economic and Cultural Expansion (1890–1945)*, New York (NY), Hill & Wang, 1982.

———, *Financial Missionaries to the World: The Politics and Culture of Dollar Diplomacy (1900–1930)*, Durham, Duke University Press, 2003.

Rosoux, Valérie, "Négociation internationale," in Thierry Balzacq, Frédéric Ramel (eds.), *Traité de relations internationales*, Paris, Presses de Sciences Po, 2013, pp. 795–821.

Rosselli, Mariangela, "Le projet politique de la langue française. Le rôle de l'alliance française," *Politix*, 9 (36), 1996: 73–94.

Roux, Georges, *La Mésopotamie*, Paris, Seuil, 1995.

Rozental, Andrés, Buenrosto, Alicia, "Bilateral Diplomacy," in Andrew F. Cooper, Jorge Heine, Ramesh Thakur (eds.), *The Oxford Handbook of Modern Diplomacy*, Oxford, Oxford University Press, 2013, pp. 229–246.

Rüel, Huub, Wolters, Tim, "Business Diplomacy," in Costas Constantinou, Pauline Kerr, Paul Sharp (eds.), *The SAGE Handbook of Diplomacy*, London, Sage, 2016, pp. 564–576.

Ruggie, John G. (ed.), *Multilateralism Matters: The Theory and Praxis of an Institutional Form*, New York (NY), Columbia University Press, 1993.

Ryfman, Philippe, "L'action humanitaire non gouvernementale: une diplomatie alternative?" *Politique étrangère*, 3, 2010: 565–578.

Sandholtz, Wayne, Stone Svweet, Alec (eds.), *European Integration and Supranational Governance*, Oxford, Oxford University Press, 1998.

Saner, Raymond, Yiu, Lichia, "Business-Government-NGO Relations: Their Impact on Global Economic Governance," in Andrew F. Cooper, Brian Hocking, William Maley (eds.), *Global Governance and Diplomacy: Worlds Apart?* New York (NY), Palgrave Macmillan, 2008, pp. 85–103.

Satow, Ernest M., *A Guide to Diplomatic Practice*, London, Longmans, Green & Co, 1922.

Saulnier, Christine, "Le rôle des prêtres fétiaux et l'application du ius fetiale à Rome," *Revue historique du droit français et étranger*, 58 (2), 1980: 171–199.

Schelling, Thomas C., *Arms and Influence*, New Haven (CT), Yale University Press, 1966.

———, *Stratégie du conflit*, Paris, Presses universitaires de France, 1986.

Schiffrin, Deborah, "Handwork as Ceremony: The Case of the Handshake," *Semiotica*, 12 (3), 1998: 189–202.
Schmidt, Eric, Cohen, Jared, *The New Digital Age: Reshaping the Future of People, Nations and Business*, London, John Murray, 2013.
Schmitt, Olivier, "International Organization at War: NATO Practices in the Afghan Campaign," *Cooperation and Conflict*, 52 (4), 2017: 502–518.
Schmitter, Philippe C., "A Revised Theory of Regional Integration," *International Organization*, 24 (4), 1970: 836–868.
Schweizer, Peter, *Reagan's War: The Epic Story of His Forty Years Struggle and First Triumph over Communism*, New York (NY), Doubleday, 2002.
Seib, Philip, *Real-Time Diplomacy: Politics and Power in the Social Media Era*, New York (NY), Palgrave Macmillan, 2012.
Serres, Jean, *Manuel politique du protocole*, Paris, Éditions de la Bièvre, 1992.
Sharlach, T. M., "Diplomacy and the Rituals of Politics at the Ur III Court," *Journal of Cuneiform Politics*, 57, 2005: 17–29.
Sharp, Paul, *Diplomatic Theory of International Relations*, Cambridge, Cambridge University Press, 1999.
Sikkink, Kathryn, "The Power of Principled Ideas. Human Rights Policies in the United States and Western Europe," in Judith Goldstein, Robert O. Keohane (eds.), *Ideas and Foreign Policy: Beliefs, Institutions, and Political Change*, Ithaca (NY), Cornell University Press, 1993, pp. 139–170.
Slaughter, Anne-Marie, *A New World Order*, Princeton (NJ), Princeton University Press, 2004.
———, "America's Edge: Power in the Networked Century," *Foreign Affairs*, 88 (1), 2009: 94–113.
———, "How to Succeed in the Networked World: A Grand Strategy for the Digital Age," *Foreign Affairs*, 95 (6), 2016: 76–89.
Smith, Hazel, "Humanitarian Diplomacy: Theory and Practice," in Larry Minear, Hazel Smith (eds.), *Humanitarian Diplomacy: Practitioners and Their Craft*, Tokyo, New York, and Paris, United Nations University Press, 2007, pp. 36–62.
Smouts, Marie-Claude, Battistella, Dario, Petiteville, Franck, Vennesson, Pascal (ed.), *Dictionnaire des relations internationales*, Paris, Dalloz, 2003.
Snidal, Duncan, Thompson, Alexander, "International Commitments and Domestic Politics: Institutions and Actors at Two Levels," in *Locating the Proper Authorities*, Ann Arbor (MI), Daniel Drezner (ed.), University of Michigan Press, 2003, pp. 197–233.
Snyder, Alvin, *Warriors of Disinformation*, New York (NY), Arcade Publishing, 1995.
Soldatos, Panayotis, "An Explanatory Framework for the Study of Federated States as Foreign-Policy Actors," in Hans J. Michelmann, Panayotis Soldatos (eds.), *Federalism and International Relations: The Role of Subnational Units*, Oxford, Oxford Press, 1990, pp. 34–38.

Sorenson, David, *The Process and Politics of Defense Acquisition: A Reference Handbook*, New York (NY), Praeger, 2008.
Soutou, Georges-Henri, *L'Or et le Sang: Les buts de guerre économiques de la première guerre mondiale*, Paris, Fayard, 1989.
Sparks, Colin, "Global Integration, State Policy and the Media," in Terry Flew, Petros Iosifidis, Jeannette Steemers (eds.), *Global Media and National Policies: The Return of the State*, New York (NY), Palgrave Macmillan, 2016, pp. 49–74.
State Department, *Congressional Budget Justification for Foreign Operations*, Washington (DC), SD, 2010.
Stollberg-Rilinger, Barbara, "Zeremoniell, Ritual, Symbol. Neue Forschungen zur Symbolischen Kommunikation in Spätmittelalter und Früher Neuzeit ," *ZHF*, 27, 2000: 389–405.
Stollberg-Rilinger, Barbara, Althoff, Gerd, Goetzmann, Jutta, Puhle, Matthias (Hrsg.), *Spektakel der Macht. Rituale im Alten Europa (800–1800)*, Katalog und Essayband zur Ausstellung des Kulturhistorischen Museums, Magdeburg, Darmstadt, 2008.
Strange, Susan, *States and Markets*, London, Pinter Publishers, 1988.
———, "States, Firms and Diplomacy," *International Affairs*, 68 (1), 1992: 1–15.
Stuenkel, Oliver, *India-Brazil-South Africa Dialogue Forum (IBSA): The Rise of Global South*, London, Routledge, 2016.
Susskind, Lawrence E., Ali, Saleem H., *Environmental Diplomacy: Negotiating More Effective Global Agreements*, Oxford, Oxford University Press, 2014.
Tambiah, Stanley J., "A Performative Approach to Ritual," *Proceedings of the British Academy*, 65, 1979: 113–169.
Tavares, Rodrigo, *Paradiplomacy: Cities and States as Global Players*, Oxford, Oxford University Press, 2016.
Taylor, Philip M., *The Projection of Britain British Overseas Publicity and Propaganda (1919–1939)*, Cambridge, Cambridge University Press, 1981.
———, *Munitions of the Mind: War Propaganda from the Ancient World to the Nuclear Age*, Glasgow, Patrick Stephens, 1990.
Tenenbaum, Charles, "La médiation des organisations intergouvernementales: un maillon essentiel," in Guillaume Devin (ed.), *Faire la paix. La part des institutions internationales*, Paris, Presses de Sciences Po, 2009, pp. 101–131.
———, "Mediation by International Organizations," in Guillaume Devin (ed.), *Making Peace*, New York, Palgrave Macmillan, 2011, pp. 67–92.
Tenzer, Nicolas, *L'Expertise internationale au cœur de la diplomatie et de la coopération du XXIe siècle. Instruments pour une stratégie française de puissance et d'influence, rapport au Premier ministre, au ministre des Affaires étrangères et européennes, au ministre de l'Économie, de l'Industrie et de l'Emploi et au ministre du Budget, des Comptes publics et de la Fonction publique*, Paris, La Documentation française, 2008.
———, *Quand la France disparaît du monde*, Paris, Grasset, 2008.

―――, "Les marchés internationaux du droit: une clé pour notre stratégie extérieure," *Les Petites Affiches*, 238, 2010.
―――, "L'expertise internationale," in Thierry Balzacq, Frédéric Ramel (eds.), *Traité de relations internationales*, Paris, Presses de Sciences Po, 2013, pp. 1169–1182.
Thakur, Ramesh, "Multilateral Diplomacy and the United Nations: Global Governance. Venue or Actor?" in James P. Muldoon, Joann F. Aviel, Richard Reitano, Earl Sullivan (eds.), *The New Dynamics of Multilateralism: Diplomacy, International Organizations, and Global Governance*, Boulder (Co), Westview, 2010.
Therwath, Ingrid, "La diaspora indienne aux États-Unis comme acteur international," in Christophe Jaffrelot (ed.), *New Delhi et le monde*, Paris, Autrement, 2008.
Thiemeyer, Guido, *Internationalismus und Diplomatie. Währungspolitische Kooperation im europäischen Staatensystem (1865–1900)*, München, Oldenbourg, 2009.
Thobie, Jacques, "L'emprunt ottoman 4% (1901–1905): le triptyque finance-industrie-diplomatie," *Relations internationales*, 1, 1974: 71–85.
Thudcroz, Christian, *Petit traité du compromis. L'art des concessions*, Paris, Presses universitaires de France, 2015.
Tolba, Mostafa K. (ed.), *Global Environmental Diplomacy, Negotiating Environmental Agreements for the World (1973–1992)*, Cambridge, MIT Press, 1998.
Touval, Saadia, Zartman, I. William (eds.), *International Mediation in Theory and Practice*, Boulder, CO, Westview Press, 1985.
Trachtenberg, Marc, *Reparation in World Politics: France and European Economic Diplomacy (1916–1923)*, New York (NY), Columbia University Press, 1980.
Tuch, Hans, *Communicating with the World*, New York (NY), St. Martin's Press, 1990.
Twomey, Anne, "Commonwealth of Australia," in Hans Michelmann (ed.), *Foreign Relations in Federal Countries*, Montréal, McGill University Press, 2009.
"USIA: Films for Export Only," *Human Events*, 27 February 1965, p. 6.
Vaïsse, Maurice, *La Puissance ou l'influence? La France dans le monde depuis 1958*, Paris, Fayard, 2009.
van Ham, Peter, *Social Power in International Politics*, London, Routledge, 2010.
Van Langenhove, Luk, "The Transformation of Multilateralism: Mode 1.0 to Mode 2.0," *Global Policy*, 1 (3), 2010: 263–270.
Vassort-Rousset, Brigitte (ed.), *Building Sustainable International Couples in International Relations: A Strategy Towards Peaceful Cooperation*, London, Palgrave Macmillan, 2014.
Veuthey, Michel, "Humanitarian Diplomacy: Saving It When It Is Most Needed," in Alexandre Vautravers, Yivita Fox (ed.), *Humanitarian Space and the International Community: 16th Humanitarian Conference*, Geneva, Webster University, 2012, pp. 195–209.

Veyne, Paul, *L'Empire gréco-romain*, Paris, Seuil, 2005.
Viltard, Yves, "Diplomatie des villes: collectivités territoriales et relations internationales," *Politique étrangère*, 3, 2010: 593–604.
Von Eschen, Penny M., *Satchmo Blows Up the World. Jazz Ambassadors Play the Cold War*, London, Harvard University Press, 2004.
Walder, Francis, *Saint-Germain ou la négociation*, Paris, Gallimard, 1992.
Warlouzet, Laurent, "The Centralization of EU Competition Policy: Historical Institutionalist Dynamics from Cartel Monitoring to Merger Control (1956–1991)," *Journal of Common Market Studies*, 2016: 725–741.
Watson, Adam, *Diplomacy: The Dialogue Between States*, London, Eyre Methuen, 1984.
Weinfeld, Moshe, "Covenant Making in Anatolia and Mesopotamia," *Journal of the Ancient Near Eastern Society of Columbia University*, 22, 1993, pp. 135–139.
Wendling, Cécile, "L'approche globale dans la gestion civilo-militaire des crises: analyse critique et prospective du concept," *Cahiers de l'Irsem*, 6, 2010.
Wenkel, Christian, *Auf der Suche nach einem 'anderen Deutschland'. Das Verhältnis Frankreichs zur DDR im Spannungsfeld von Perzeption und Diplomatie*, Munich, De Gruyter Oldenbourg Verlag, 2014.
Wheeler, Nicholas J., *Trusting Enemies: Interpersonal Relationships in International Conflict*, Oxford, Oxford University Press, 2018.
Wight, Martin, *Power Politics*, London, Penguin Books, 1979.
Wike, Richard, Stokes, Bruce, Poushter, Jacob, Fetterolf, Janell, "US Image Suffers as Publics Around World Question Trump's Leadership, America Still Wins Praise for Its People, Culture and Civil Liberties," *Pew Research Center*, 2017, pp. 1–108.
Winham, Gilbert, "Negotiation as a Management Process," *World Politics*, 30 (1), 1977: 86–113.
Wiquefort, Abraham de, *L'Ambassadeur*, La Haye, Jean & Daniel Steucker, 1680–1681.
Wiseman, Geoffrey, "'Polylateralism': Diplomacy's Third Dimension," *Public Diplomacy Magazine*, 4, 2010: 24–39.
———, "Diplomatic Practices at the United Nations," *Cooperation and Conflict*, 50 (3), 2015: 316–333.
Woolcock, Stephen, Bayne, Nicholas (eds.), *The New Economic Diplomacy: Decision-Making and Negotiation in International Economic Relations*, Ashgate, Aldershot, 2007.
Wursthorn, Kévin, "S'adapter en milieu hostile: l'institutionnalisation de la diplomatie d'entreprise du groupe Total au Moyen-Orient des années 1950 aux années 1960," Presentation during the conference 'De nouvelles pratiques diplomatiques?' Paris, Paris-I Panthéon-Sorbonne, 14 October 2016.

———, "La Compagnie française des pétroles au Moyen-Orient: une diplomatie d'entreprise à l'avant-garde de la présence française dans les années 1950," *Relations internationales* 171 (3), 2017: 85–96.

Xie, Tao, "China's Soft Power Obsession," *The Diplomat*, 2015: 27–34.

Zartman, I. William, "Negotiation as a Joint Decision Making Process," *Journal of Conflict Resolution*, 21 (4), 1977: 619–638.

———, "La politique étrangère et le règlement des conflits," in Frédéric Charillon (ed.), *Politique étrangère. Nouveaux regards*, Paris, Presses de Sciences Po, 2002, pp. 275–300.

———, *Negotiation and Conflict Management: Essays in Theory and Practice*, London, Routledge, 2008.

———, "La multilatéralité internationale: essai de modélisation," *Négociations*, 17 (1), 2012: 37–50.

———, *Preventing Deadly Conflict*, Cambridge, Polity Press, 2015.

Zhang, Shuguang, *Beijing's Economic Statecraft during the Cold War (1949–1991)*, Baltimore (MD), Johns Hopkins University Press, 2014.

Zipper de Fabiani, Henry, "La 'diplomatie de défense,' composante essentielle de la diplomatie préventive. Vers une nouvelle symbiose entre diplomatie et défense," in Centre Thucydide (ed.), *Annuaire français des relations internationales*, Paris, Bruylant, 2002, pp. 614–629.

Zürn, Michael, Binder, Martin, Ecker-Ehrhardt, Matthias, "International Authority and Its Politicization," *International Theory: A Journal of International Politics, Law and Philosophy*, 4 (1), 2012: 69–106.

Index

A
Amarna archives, 4
Ambassador, 6–8, 12, 56, 80, 81, 92, 93, 115–117, 119, 126, 129–133, 136, 222, 223, 289, 290, 307, 313
Ancient Greece, 3–5, 102
Apartheid, 102
Arbitration, 5
Authoritarian regime, 228, 229

B
Benchmarking, 82, 148
Bilateral partnerships, 27
Bilderberg Circle, 70

C
Camp David, 103, 105
Celebrity diplomacy, 289, 290
Civil society, 23, 25, 26, 32, 87, 98, 189–192, 248, 249, 292, 311
Club of Rome, 70

Coalition, 27, 46, 63, 76, 77, 135
Cognitive openness, 201
Collective security, 37, 66, 212, 272, 281
Communication, 3, 10, 13, 14, 79–83, 85, 86, 93, 94, 99, 103, 107, 108, 112, 113, 134, 140, 141, 183, 186, 188, 198, 260, 281, 291, 293, 304, 312, 313
Comprehensive Economic and Trade Agreement (CETA), 20, 56, 173, 220
Confidence, 8, 205, 268–270, 274
Congress
  Berlin, 8
  Paris, 8, 233
  Vienna, 8, 36, 105, 115, 130
  Westphalia, 8, 19, 36
Consensus, 41, 45, 70, 86, 103, 151, 203, 245, 304
Consul, 22, 126, 214
Convictions, 199, 201, 202

Cooperation, 13, 20–24, 26, 29–32, 38, 56, 57, 64, 66, 67, 73, 74, 76, 77, 97, 106, 140, 145, 146, 148, 157–159, 163, 170, 172, 175, 178–180, 212, 216, 217, 227, 230, 234, 237, 246, 247, 268, 270, 271, 273, 274, 276, 277, 279, 287, 310
Credentials, 7, 8, 115, 116, 133

D

Diplomacy
  ancient Near East, 3
  bilateral, 19, 20, 32, 135, 228, 229, 263
  catalytic, 50
  classical, 3, 4
  coercive, 99, 184, 190, 215
  digital, 80, 81, 83–88, 91, 93, 94, 137, 289, 312
  etymology, 2, 11, 12
  modern, 6, 7, 13, 36, 91, 111, 270, 279, 308
  multilateral, 35–45, 47, 141, 161, 164, 187, 212, 213, 217, 219, 220, 235, 236
  parliamentary, 37, 175–178
  polylateral, 184
Diplomat, 9, 10, 13, 56, 80, 92, 93, 97, 108, 130, 131, 133, 136, 137, 151, 184, 313
Diplomatic corps, 11, 128, 130, 132, 161
Diplomatic network, 57, 90, 91, 229, 302
Diplomatic practices, 3, 8, 36, 39, 112, 115, 134, 141, 146, 156, 161, 162, 164, 168, 172, 174, 185, 187, 188, 257, 260–262, 265, 293, 311, 312
Disinformation, 80, 90, 93, 299, 304

Doctors Without Borders (Médécins sans frontières/MSF), 183, 259–261

E

Economic warfare, 211
Effectiveness/Efficiency, 46, 64, 111, 112, 127, 130, 137, 142, 148, 188, 197, 203, 242, 250, 268, 270, 272, 311
Emotion, 13, 97, 108, 205, 260, 262
European Union (EU), 20, 21, 23, 24, 28, 32, 40, 41, 45, 46, 50, 54, 56, 58, 59, 65, 68, 71, 83, 87, 88, 92, 127, 133–136, 138, 144, 145, 147, 148, 150, 151, 156, 158–160, 162, 173, 175, 178, 200, 217, 220, 224, 234, 235, 258, 268, 298

F

Florence, 126
Foreign policy, 2, 8, 9, 12, 13, 40, 50, 57, 59, 65, 84, 85, 88, 89, 91, 92, 125, 128, 129, 133–137, 156, 159, 169, 172, 174, 180, 183, 196, 199, 202, 206, 211, 227, 234, 236, 262–264, 269, 273, 276, 279–281, 283, 286, 297, 299, 310, 312
Francophonie, 41, 51, 52, 59, 75, 175, 176, 178, 231, 234, 236

H

Handshake, 102, 112, 117, 118, 205
Hollywood, 282–289, 291, 292

I

Infotainment, 280, 292

INDEX 343

International authority, 156, 163, 164
International Committee of the Red Cross (ICRC), 40, 188, 257–259, 261, 262, 264, 265
International Humanitarian Law (IHL), 255–259, 263, 264
International Labour Organization (ILO), 39, 40, 142

L
Leadership, 46, 68, 82, 89, 100, 198, 203
League of Nations (LN), 35, 37–40, 43, 140, 147, 216
Legal personality, 142–144, 258
Legitimacy, 72, 104, 121, 137, 142, 143, 145, 160, 189, 193
Lobbying, 24, 25, 190, 223, 248, 284, 298, 300–305

M
Military attaché, 23, 277
Ministry of Foreign Affairs (MFA), 22, 27, 43, 75, 80, 84, 85, 89–92, 127, 128, 130, 131, 133, 134, 137, 219–221, 230, 231, 276

N
Naming and shaming, 260, 261
Negotiation
 behavioral approach, 105
 cultural approach, 105
 definition, 12, 183, 254
 strategic approach, 105
Neo-functionalism, 156–159, 163
Nuncio, 6, 7

P
Peacekeeping, 38, 54, 146, 162, 273, 276

Peer pressure, 148
Perception, 9, 46, 86, 92, 102, 106, 108, 129, 142, 198, 201, 202, 204, 205, 274, 289
Procurator, 6, 7
Protocol, 2–4, 41, 80, 111, 112, 114–116, 119, 120, 161, 243–245, 247, 249
Protodiplomacy, 51, 53, 168, 169

Q
Quai d'Orsay, 76, 128, 130–132, 223, 230, 310

R
Representation, 7, 9, 10, 23, 30, 39, 40, 47, 52, 57, 85, 89–91, 93, 111, 121, 125, 127–130, 134–137, 142, 173, 175, 183–185, 187, 188, 193, 200, 222–224, 258, 308
Reputation, 13, 148, 204, 235, 246, 273, 304
Responsibility to protect (R2P), 256
Right to intervene, 207
Ritual, 4, 5, 112–121

S
Security Council, 27, 38, 44, 162, 256, 310
Situation, 6, 23, 31, 32, 44, 47, 51, 85–87, 99, 117–121, 126, 132, 136, 140, 142, 162, 173, 174, 185, 203, 206, 208, 253, 260, 262–264, 270, 271, 276, 277
Social media, 80, 81, 83–86, 88, 89, 91, 92, 94, 137, 304
Soft power, 76, 82, 228, 235, 269, 272, 273, 280, 291–293, 298, 302

Summit, 21, 66, 69, 71, 73, 74, 76, 79, 88, 136, 162, 190, 191, 219, 240–242, 248
  Paris, 69
  Rio, 191, 241, 242, 248
  Stockholm, 191, 240, 241

T

Talks, 28, 68–70, 86, 88, 89, 99, 103, 151, 162, 168, 227
Transatlantic Trade and Investment Partnership (TTIP), 20, 87, 88, 224
Treaty, 7, 26, 36–38, 47, 65, 69, 139, 144, 145, 147, 150, 159, 180, 186, 189, 215, 218, 223, 224, 243, 246, 261
Trilateral Commission, 70
Twitter, 80, 81, 86, 88, 89, 91, 92, 137, 198

U

United Nations (UN), 20, 27, 35, 37–47, 54, 57, 58, 63, 65, 68, 72, 74, 75, 88, 92, 127, 129, 135, 140, 141, 144, 146, 147, 149–151, 156, 162, 175, 179, 180, 185, 187, 191, 192, 200, 207, 218, 228, 234, 236, 239, 241–243, 245, 246, 254, 256–259, 262–264, 289, 298, 312

V

Veto, 38, 44, 46, 135, 143, 163
Visits, 21, 22, 25, 29, 57, 117–119, 175, 177, 187, 270, 290, 303

W

Wikileaks, 82, 134
World Trade Organization (WTO), 27, 39, 40, 44–46, 59, 148, 150, 175, 190, 217, 219, 235, 244, 245

Made in United States
North Haven, CT
15 August 2023